I0831774

Fictions of Conversion

Fictions of Conversion

Jews, Christians, and Cultures of Change in Early Modern England

Jeffrey S. Shoulson

PENN

UNIVERSITY OF PENNSYLVANIA PRESS

PHILADELPHIA

Published by
University of Pennsylvania Press
Philadelphia, Pennsylvania 19104-4112
www.upenn.edu/pennpress

Printed in the United States of America on acid-free paper

10 9 8 7 6 5 4 3 2 1

A Cataloging-in-Publication record is available at the Library of Congress
ISBN 978-0-8122-4482-3

For Sophia Elizabeth, Oliver Hart, and Emily Clara

נפשי קשורה בנפשם

This is the famous stone
That turneth all to gold.
—George Herbert, "The Elixir"

Contents

Fictions of Conversion

Introduction

> On a huge hill,
> Cragged, and steep, Truth stands, and he that will
> Reach her, about must, and about must go . . .
> —John Donne, "Satire III"

In 1534, at the direction of Henry VIII, who had been acclaimed "Defender of the Faith" by Pope Leo X a mere thirteen years earlier, England turned from being a Catholic nation to a Protestant nation; when Henry's son was crowned as Edward VI in 1547, a series of sweeping and far more radical church reforms were instituted, making the break with Rome even more pronounced and seemingly definitive; yet following the young king's death in 1553, Mary Tudor's reign brought with it the return of Catholicism as the official state religion; with Elizabeth's assumption of the throne in 1559, Protestantism again became the regnant religion. In the space of twenty-five years, then, England converted three times. If, for some of its contemporary Protestant observers and chroniclers, the trajectory of the English Reformation lent itself to a historiography that narrated these political and religious developments as providential changes all leading to a millenarian fulfillment of God's special favor to the "Elect Nation," the speed and fitfulness with which these changes transpired could also lead observers to worry over their permanence and authenticity. Even during the relative calm of the Elizabethan Settlement the national conversion to Protestantism was repeatedly challenged, not only by those who remained loyal to the Pope, but also by Puritans and other Protestants of the "hotter" sort, who insisted that the break with Rome remained incomplete. Elizabeth's successor, James I, undertook extensive efforts to sustain the peace of this religious settlement; the

English Bible that has taken his name, for example, was produced with the hopes of providing a scripture acceptable to a wide cross-section of the English population, from urban, bourgeois Presbyterians to rural Anglican aristocracy, and even to recusant Catholics and non-conformists. Yet James's reign was only in its second year when an English convert to Catholicism by the name of Guy Fawkes was discovered preparing to bomb the houses of Parliament; the Gunpowder Plot was quickly tied to a network of English Catholics, among them several Jesuits, setting off a wave of anti-Catholic paranoia and repressive legislation targeting recusancy and the persistent, often secret, Catholic presence in England. Clearly, conversion was not a finite, discreet process. Religious change could lead to salvation, but it could also breed deceit and treachery. Those on all sides of the religious conflicts of the period could be forgiven for harboring deep-seated suspicions about conversion's value, or even the capacity for human agents to effect and control its outcome.

This book takes the conversionary demands and competing claims for adherence made by different confessional identities in early modern England as the starting point for an investigation into the dynamics of change during the period and the anxieties produced by these religious, political, social, economic, and cultural changes. Current scholarship has revealed how ongoing and incomplete was the English Reformation. The Elizabethan Settlement sought to construct an ideologically and religiously coherent English identity, but these explicit and persistent efforts also attest to the resistance they continued to meet publicly and privately, in the urban centers and in the countryside, in the north and in the south. The boundaries between Catholicism and Protestantism, not to mention within and among newly emerging Protestant denominations, remained permeable and shifting; at one time or another throughout much of the sixteenth century most Englishmen and women—whose parents and grandparents very well may have attended a different church than they were attending—would have found it necessary to be somewhat circumspect, if not downright deceptive, about their own religious beliefs and practices. The "fictions of conversion" I examine in this study find their first expressions within the confessional transitions and shifts that happened with some frequency over the course of England's Long Reformation. So threatening to any sense of stability was this fraught history that its alarming implications often demanded to be projected outward onto an alien identity, whose potential for transformation offered both promise and peril but who could, in theory, be kept distinct from emerging formulations of

Englishness, especially by virtue of his or her physical absence from England during the period in question: the Jew.

Even as the English Reformation gave rise to the providentialist historiography of John Foxe and others, it also precipitated a distinctively English interest in—some might even called it an obsession with—the Jews who had been entirely exiled from England's midst nearly 300 years earlier. English millenarian and eschatological writings inevitably included speculations about the "Calling of the Jews" or "the Great Restauration," the anticipated mass conversion of the Jews to (a specifically English version of) Christianity as one of the final steps preceding Christ's Second Coming. The Whitehall Conference of 1655 convened by Oliver Cromwell to discuss the legal readmission of Jews to England cannot be understood outside this apocalyptic climate. Yet before the conversion of the Jews became a staple topic for English millenarians in the seventeenth century, Jews already found their way into the English imaginary within an elaborate and self-contradictory network of fictions of conversion. The late medieval and early modern English stage offered audiences encounters with Jewish moneylenders and merchants, powerbrokers and panderers who were forced or who (seemingly) chose to convert; but also with desirable Jewish women, potential wives and mothers to future Christian children, who converted by marrying Christian husbands. English sermons celebrated the baptisms of individual Jews; but they also inveighed against stubborn Jewish resistance to Christian salvation, often in the same sermon. Jews held out the tantalizing possibility of redemption through conversion, particularly powerful insofar as they had once been God's chosen people and could recover that status again, even as they also manifested the fearful effects of preterition, to use Calvin's term for those *not* elected to salvation. The Jewish trajectory of falling in and out of divine favor was seen as anticipating the more recent trajectory of English providential history in its peripatetic path of reformation. But depending on where that Jewish history resolved itself—with God or as God's enemies—such parallels could bode well or ill for English Christianity. Jewish conversion (collective or individual) offered the most dramatic form of divine reconciliation; but Jews also threatened to undermine the salvific power of conversion whenever they refused, reneged, or, worse, revealed themselves to have converted under false pretenses.

Indeed, it is the specter of *false* Jewish conversion, in particular, that haunts the English fictions of conversion I examine in this book. To speak of Jews in Tudor and Stuart England was, with almost no exception, to speak of Iberian Jews and their descendants, those who had fled the forced conversions, expulsions, and subsequent Inquisition that had obliterated the largest and most prosperous Jewish population of the Middle Ages. This history of Iberian Jewry stands directly behind these fictions of conversion, for the *limpieza di sangre*, or blood purity laws that were the legacy of the forced conversions of fourteenth-century Spain, gave legal justification for Old Christian antipathy toward *conversos*, enforcing a Jewish designation on those who had converted to Christianity in order to avoid expulsion, forfeit of property, or execution. English encounters with Jews—occasionally on English soil, more often in the Levant, and especially in the growing Jewish communities of the Low Countries—were nearly always with descendants of this recent history of forced conversion. English Protestants like Henry Ainsworth (whose work figures significantly in later chapters of this book) spent considerable portions of their lives in close proximity to, and learning from, the Jews of Amsterdam. It is no coincidence that Ainsworth, and other English scholars like Hugh Broughton, Matthew Slade, and John Paget, drew so heavily on Jewish scholarship in his own biblical commentaries. Nor is it surprising that these Puritan Hebraists wrote extensively on and worked for the conversion of the Jews to Christianity.[1] The Amsterdam Jewish community, concentrated primarily in the Vloomberg quarter of the city, was composed almost entirely of descendants from the Spanish and Portuguese Sephardic community that had fled either before or after undergoing conversion to Catholicism. Many of those who had converted to Christianity used their migration to Amsterdam as the occasion openly to recover their Jewish identities. Others remained Christians, even as they retained ties with this recently reconstituted Jewish community.[2] Conversion was *the* topic of the seventeenth-century Amsterdam Jewish community, the same community from which, only a few decades later, Menasseh ben Israel would call out to England for a change in its policy toward Jews living there.[3] The experiences of *conversos* and former *conversos* called particular attention to the persistence of a naturalized notion of Jewishness, one that could be construed positively and not just in the negative light it was cast as a function of the Iberian blood purity laws. *Conversos* who reclaimed their Jewishness often did so explicitly as a recovery of an identity embedded in the body and familial lineage. But even those *conversos* who remained (proudly) Christian made special claims about the value of their Jewish ancestry, asserting the importance of the seed of Israel to the vitality and future of Christianity.[4]

The promulgation of "philo-semitic" writing in mid-seventeenth-century

England reveals the intense ambivalence with which Jews and Jewish conversion were regarded during this time. On the one hand, advocates of Jewish toleration made their case for the legal readmission of Jews on the strength of the millenarian expectation of mass Jewish conversion: Jews should be welcomed to a tolerant, Protestant England because it would accelerate the process of their total elimination through their transformation into Christians. On the other hand, as we shall see below, what was more worrying to many English writers than the thought that Jews had not or would not convert was the possibility that they would indeed convert, for the successful conversion of the Jew would signal the disruption and destabilization of the organizing differences that gave definition to Christianity in opposition to Judaism. And yet, as I argue in the chapters that follow, the notoriously embattled nature of *converso* identity—its exemplification of the disputed permanence of conversion—could also contain a potentially advantageous, if also unsettling, property, the quality of changeability. In the figure of the *converso,* early modern Englishmen and women would have recognized an uncannily familiar religious chameleon, someone whose economic, social, and political circumstances required a religious conversion, conformity, or counterfeiting that challenged the consolidation of a coherent identity. The legacy of forced conversions practiced in previous centuries in Spain and Portugal found its way into the writings of English Protestants, particularly in their efforts to distinguish their religion from what they regarded as the corrupt and ineffective practices of the Catholic Church. Though English Protestants prided themselves on the self-evident truth of the Christianity they professed, one of the effects of the history of forced conversions they sought to disown and, especially, of the Judaism *marranos* were believed to continue to practice secretly, was to underscore anxieties about permanence and change, authenticity and pretense, in the accounts of conversion that proliferated during the period. John Donne captures the paradoxical permanence of change as a feature of human existence in one of the several sermons he preached as Dean of St. Paul's—years after his own conversion to Anglicanism—on the Sunday that annually marks the conversion of Paul: "The people will change into contrary opinions; And whereas an Angel it selfe cannot pass from East to West, from extreame to extreame without touching upon the way betweene, the people will pass from extreame to extreame, without any middle opinion. . . . All change their minds; High as well as low will change, But I am the Lord; I change not. I and onely I have that immunity, Immutability; . . . all can, all will, all do change, high and low."[5] Drawing the contrast between the characteristic volatility of human existence and the reassuring stability of divine immutability, Donne's conversion sermon succinctly encapsulates the paradox of conversion that lies at the heart of my analysis. While a Christian listener would have certainly desired a conversionary experience like the paradigmatic event that turned Saul the Pharisee into Paul the Apostle, he or she would have also no doubt worried that such a dramatic change, "from extreame to extreame," was not the final word. "High as well as low will change," Donne reminds his congregation. Those not yet saved might hope for the salvation offered by conversion, but the conversion preached especially in the Protestant churches required constant vigilance and self-examination, never offering the absolute certainty so many ostensible converts craved. By exposing the often implicit yoking of the Jewish convert to the master trope of conversion, I argue that these fictions of conversion attest to a fraught intermingling of anxieties about, and expectations for, change that permeates early modern English culture.

Written long before he took on the position of dean at St. Paul's, where he delivered his sermon on Paul's conversion, Donne's "Satire III" can serve to illustrate the fraught tension between the affirming and threatening features of the cultures of change they seek to construct, even as it also provides an example of the unanticipated recourse to the Jew as a means for thinking through the dynamics of transformation. "Of Religion," as it is titled in the manuscript, presents a speaker torn between "kind pity" and "brave scorn" as he meditates on the devotional demands of "our mistress fair religion." Donne wonders whether and how religion might achieve the same commitment that "virtue" had earned in the "first blinded age," the pre-Christian era when men were inspired to heroic acts in pursuit of "earth's honor" (9).[6] Writing at a transitional moment in his life, poised between the Catholicism of his youth and the Anglicanism of his later adulthood and clerical calling, the poet expresses dismay over the risks young men like himself are prepared to take for the sake of adventure and valor. He ticks off a list of hazards an intrepid soldier of fortune might encounter in such efforts; the sequence begins with a series of dangers associated with military activities, mercantile escapades, and geographic explorations:

> Dar'st thou aid mutinous Dutch, and dar'st thou lay
> Thee in ships' wooden sepulchers, a prey
> To leaders' rage, to storms, to shot, to dearth?
> Dar'st thou dive seas, and dungeons of the earth?

Has thou courageous fire to thaw the ice
Of frozen north discoveries?

(ll. 17–22)

Drawing upon the paradoxes and juxtapositions Donne uses so effectively in his other lyrics, the lines brilliantly undermine the very vitality they seem to admire, placing the daring sailors in ships that are already sepulchers, watery tombs; the men give over their courageous lives to the "dungeons of the earth." And just a few lines later the poet invokes the conventions of the love poem (where such paradoxes and inversions are his stock-in-trade), as he mocks the hyper-masculinity of the Petrarchan lover who must insist on the superiority of his beloved over all others: "and must every he / Which cries not, 'Goddess!' to thy mistress, draw, / Or eat thy poisonous words?" (ll. 26–28). But between these two kinds of excessive (and implicitly misplaced) valor, of the adventurer and of the lover, Donne interposes a very different cluster of examples:

and thrice
Colder than salamanders, like divine
Children in th'oven, fires of Spain, and the line,
Whose countries limbecks to our bodies be,
Canst thou for gain bear?

(ll. 22–26)

These are obscure lines, intervening between two far more common expressions of virility and conquest. For if the framing passages speak to a kind of masculine virtue defined by the conventional notions of military prowess or erotic insistence, these intervening examples come from an entirely distinct realm, the world of religious conflict and forced confessional choices. The heat of these lines is the heat of religious oppression as it tests the mettle of the faithful, whether they be Shadrach, Meshach, and Abed-nego, the companions of Daniel thrown into the fiery furnace by Nebuchadnezzar in Daniel 3, or the victims of the Spanish Inquisition suffering public immolation at an *auto da fé*. What's more, in describing countries like Spain, which epitomize religious oppression, as "limbecks to our bodies" (25), Donne deploys an alchemical image that calls upon its associations with religious conversion—a point that is of central concern below, in Chapter 4—while undermining those very associations, insofar as the transformations are specifically of bodies and not souls.

Although the first portion of Donne's poem (through l. 42) sets out to distinguish between an improper devotion to worldly matters, which will "wither away and pass" (l. 36), and a more suitable commitment to "true religion" (l. 43), the lines that refer to the suffering endured by those who are oppressed for their religious beliefs, placed where they are in the poem between military and erotic defiance, appear to conflate these worldly kinds of commitment with those of the religious realm, rather than keeping them distinct (and evaluating their relative merits). Is the "gain" in question to be achieved in this world or the next? Religious choice in this poem seems to be a way to think about other, apparently more mundane choices, even as those other choices ostensibly contrast with the options of ecclesiastical affiliation. Indeed, the very soul that ought to be the true object and subject of religious devotion becomes in this poem a means to experience physical pleasure in the world, as the poet laments how "thy fair goodly soul, which doth / Give this flesh power to taste joy, thou dost loathe" (ll. 41–42).[7] As is so often the case in Donne's poetry, from the erotic *Songs and Sonnets* to the devotional *Divine Poems*, the conventional language and imagery of these two seemingly disparate realms converge, overlap, define, and sometimes contradict each other. Holy Sonnet 18, for example, famously takes up a question similar to the shaping dilemma of "Satire III"—how to identify to the true church—drawing on the erotic language of Song of Songs as it asks, "Show me dear Christ, thy spouse . . . / Betray kind husband thy spouse to our sights, / And let mine amorous soul court thy mild dove . . ." (ll. 1, 11–12). The paradox of openness and fidelity upon which the sonnet is built depends upon the conflation of the erotic and the religious, the secular and the spiritual. More specifically, what should be perceived as a sign of fickleness and adulterous infidelity within one context (the erotic) becomes the sign of sincerity and faithfulness, indeed a means of confirmation, in another (the religious or ecclesiastical). Christ's spouse, the true church, reveals its identity by virtue of its attraction of new lovers, those who turn to it in an erotically charged act of conversion.

The call in "Satire III" to "seek true religion," which deploys this same potentially paradoxical convergence of the erotic and the religious, presumes an understanding of ecclesiastical commitment as a choice to be made from an array of possibilities. The poem not only raises the question of religious commitment in the abstract, it defines religion precisely as a choice to be made among a range of competing options. After considering with dissatisfaction five different alternatives—Mirreus's Catholic Rome, Crant's Protestant Geneva, Graius's Anglican England, Phrygius's rejection of all confessional affiliations, and Gracchus's embrace of all—the poet nevertheless insists, "Of force must one, and forced but one allow; / And the right" (ll. 70–71). The stakes are high, the compulsion to choose, and choose correctly, strong. The poem works toward a rejection of any one specific religious choice grounded in power and force, preferring instead a path that has a goal but no apparent end:

> On a huge hill,
> Cragged, and steep, Truth stands, and he that will
> Reach her, *about must, and about must go*;
> And what the hill's suddenness resists, win so.
> (ll. 79–82, emphasis added)

Truth cannot be attained through a direct path, a straight line; its "suddenness," that is, the steep incline and rapid ascent one must overcome to reach it, resists such a direct assault. The goal, "Truth," can only be achieved through indirection, specifically, through turning and turning again in a potentially infinite process where the turning itself becomes prioritized. The image is of a switchback trail, a physical path for reducing the "suddenness" of ascent into smaller, incremental climbs; but turning is also at the heart of the term Donne would have used for a more directly religious model of spiritual choice, conversion. The image, in fact, calls to mind one of the most celebrated humanist conversion narratives, Petrarch's letter to Dionisio da Borgo about his ascent of the highest mountain in Provence, Mount Ventoux. In that letter, Petrarch wrote of his spiritual transformation in relation to the difficult experience of making the very steep climb. There, Petrarch's efforts (and he makes more than one) to minimize the rapid nature of the ascent—its suddenness—by finding a less steep path turn out to be wasteful and unsuccessful: "I had failed to find an easier path, and had only increased the distance and difficulty of the ascent."[8] Petrarch learns from this experience, coupled with the fortuitous reading of select passages from Augustine's *Confessions* (specifically, Book 10, which recounts Augustine's own conversion), that he must take a far more direct path to virtue and God's love. "Thou must perforce either climb the steeper path, under the burden of tasks foolishly deferred, to its blessed culmination," Petrarch writes, "or lie down in the valley of thy sins."[9] Donne, however, uses the image of the severe ascent to the summit of Truth to derive a very different insight. His poem offers a knowing account of the confessional alternatives in early modern England, the competing claims they make for authority: "Is not this excuse for mere contraries / Equally strong; cannot both sides say so?" (ll. 98–99). And within this context of competing alternatives, "Satire III" embraces the transformative possibilities, the recursive turnings "about . . . and about," of conversion.[10] Donne's promotion of conversion is not a function of its power to transform conclusively. Petrarch may have felt the need to commiserate "the universal instability of human conduct."[11] But the changes and turns that Donne's poem validates offer a value in and of themselves, exclusive of where those turns appear to lead.

Read as a fiction of conversion, Donne's "Satire III" also points to the linchpin of this book's argument, that the figure of the Jew is the embodiment of both the promise and the peril of change. If the poem's concern is with the possibilities and efficacy of conversion, then its reference to the Spanish Inquisition and to all that an ecclesio-juridical procedure suggests about the potential inauthenticity of Jewish conversion threatens to call into question these religious transformations. The poem seems, momentarily at least, to invite an identification between the *converso* targets of Spanish religious oppression and the speaker's other figures of courage and defiance. Readers of Donne's poetry will remember another moment of ambivalent identification with Jews, indeed, an out-Jewing of the Jews, in Holy Sonnet 11. That poem begins with an astonishing identification between its speaker and Jesus at it calls upon the conventional associations with Jewish perfidy in their rejection of Christ—"Spit on my face ye Jews." But quickly, and just as astonishingly, the speaker's orientation turns away from this *imitatio Christi* to an over-identification with Christ's oppressors, as he "pass[es] the Jews' impiety" in his crucifying of Christ daily, a function of his own sinful quotidian life. The *converso* and the Jew are, for Donne, certainly hazardous figures of treachery. The very hazards they figure, however, present compelling opportunities for adaptation and development.

This book's early chapters focus on the convergence of English writings on religious conversion and the Jewish question, using it as a means to study other features of English culture. My argument in the later chapters draws out the implications of this convergence by proposing that English cultural expression is permeated by what I am calling fictions of conversion. Conversion is not only the means through which to understand the fitful development of English religious history. Indeed, I argue that conversion does not merely function as a figure for change; rather, these fictions of conversion serve as a nexus for the negotiation of various kinds of change, often in conflict with one another. Conversion becomes a means through which other technologies of transformation—translation, alchemy, and enthusiasm—are figured during the period under consideration, roughly 1575 to 1675. My analyses in the chapters that follow are greatly indebted to the important studies that have appeared in recent years reasserting the importance of religion to the understanding of early modern culture. In particular, I have drawn on the insights of critics like Jonathan Burton, Nabil Matar, Molly Murray, Michael Questier, and Daniel Vitkus, who have all written on features of religious conversion in early modern England.[12] The "Jewish Question" in early modern England has also received crucial attention in the past two or three decades; I have learned much from the important work of Janet Adelman, David Katz, Michael Ragussis, Jason Rosenblatt, and James Shapiro, among others.[13] As in Donne's "Satire III," where religion is both distinguished from and the discursive framework for other features of lived experience, conversion provides a dynamic language for a period of dynamic and unpredictable change that extends beyond the shifting fortunes of competing churches. Situated at the hinge point of change, the converted Jew repeatedly surfaces as a particularly apt figure for the fraught tension between old and new, continuity and rupture, that is at the center of early modern English cultures of change. Cypher for and catalyst of change, the *converso*/Jew functions as the paradigmatic fiction of conversion.

Chapter 1 examines some of the key features of English writings on religious conversion. After a brief overview of the early models of Christian conversion, beginning with Paul and Augustine, I turn to early Reformation discussions of the processes and effects of conversion. In the writings of Luther and Calvin, and particularly in the ways in which their early writings shaped English Protestant "morphologies of conversion," it is apparent that conversion is defined precisely by its incomplete, ongoing nature. The recursive, fitful progress of this "evangelical" formulation of conversion was consistent with—may even be partly attributed to—what I have already characterized as the peripatetic path of the English Church. Such ecclesiastical turns and the laws used to enforce them created the conditions under which questions of authenticity and counterfeiting became a central feature of English fictions of conversion. The second half of this chapter reads a range of writings about conversion and confessional difference from the period, by figures including John Foxe, Thomas Cooper, and Daniel Featley, for the ways in which such texts assimilate—and convert—a language of authentic and inauthentic religious transformation taken from the discourse of Judaism and marranism. By exposing this important conjunction between English ecclesiastical and evangelical conversion on the one hand and Jewish conversion on the other, I establish a key premise of the remaining chapters of the book, that is, that the figure of the Jew-as-convert/Jew-as-converter generates the other English fictions of conversion I take up, even those technologies of transformation that are not ostensibly about religious change.

As with every other feature of religious life, English Protestants of the sixteenth and seventeenth centuries looked to the Bible for precedents in their writings about conversion. While the New Testament may be said to describe explicit examples of conversion—Paul's, most notably—the Old Testament's precedents were not so immediately apparent. There were, nevertheless, a number of examples drawn from the Old Testament to which early modern English divines turned. In Chapter 2, I examine exegetical and sermonic literature on the four most commonly cited Old Testament converts, Jethro, Rahab, Ruth, and Naaman. Insofar as the relationship between the Old and New Testaments was, itself, characterized in the language of conversion, and inasmuch as this transformation was grounded, especially for early modern Protestants, in an exegetical hermeneutics that revised earlier notions of allegory, this chapter is especially concerned with the function of typology as a means for integrating historical and allegorical interpretations of Scripture. Given Rahab's and Ruth's (material, maternal) positions within Christ's genealogy (as recounted in Matthew and Luke), my analysis reveals how the "conversions" of these two Gentile women function far more ambivalently as displacements of Israel-of-the-flesh by Israel-of-the-spirit than do the conversions of their male Gentile counterparts, Jethro and Naaman. Whereas readings of Rahab and Ruth are especially concerned with delineating the boundaries between Jew and Gentile, accounts of Jethro and Naaman address themselves more frequently to political and juridical questions, implicitly defining English identity along national and institutional lines.

Having focused specifically on matters of religious conversion in these first two chapters, the next three chapters turn to other fictions of conversion, following a rough chronological order, to investigate the cultural anxieties and expectations associated with the rapid religious, economic, social, and political changes occurring in England.

Taking as its subject the work of translation as an especially prominent and influential technology of transformation in the period, Chapter 3 considers the nearly concurrent appearance of seminal texts that were converted from their original, ancient languages to the idiom and culture of early modern England, the King James Version of the Bible (1611) and Chapman's complete translation of Homer's *Iliad* (1611) and *Odyssey* (1614). My analysis opens with an examination of the complex transmission and evolution of the terms used to refer to "conversion," from their earliest iterations in the Hebrew Bible, through the Greek Septuagint, the Latin Vulgate, and several medieval and early modern English versions, up until the King James Bible. Beginning in Hebrew as a means for depicting recovery and return, the terms deployed in different languages gradually accumulated connotative associations, suggesting completion and innovation that are intimately tied to the shift implied in the transformation of the Hebrew Bible into the Old Testament and, more generally, of the particularized idea of Israelite identity and practice into the universalism of Pauline Christianity. In noting the changes of denotation and connotation that accompany the translation from one language to another, I argue that linguistic translation functions as a fiction of conversion. Following this preliminary meditation on the relationship between translation and religious change, I turn my attention to the status of names in translation, particularly when the names, like Isaac or Odysseus, have meanings of significance to the narratives but also serve to represent some kind of irreducible identity. To what extent do the King James Bible and Chapman's Homer carry over (*trans latio*) the task of translation to names, and what does it mean to translate a name? The very notion that translation is possible suggests the erasure of—or at the very least, the insignificance assigned to—the cultural, semiotic, and even epistemological differences that distinguish one language from another. Translations depend upon the prioritizing of some core meaning, a transcendental signified, that is not bound to the particularities of the language in which a text has been written. Names function preeminently to signal particularity and difference, to formulate an identity against generic homogeneity. Challenges pertaining to translation are thus particularly heightened and exaggerated at moments of naming.

If the analysis of translation as a fiction of conversion reveals how language both transforms and is transformed in the process, the same may be said about the technology of transformation to which I turn in the following chapter, alchemy. Chapter 4 examines the striking resurgence of interest in alchemy at nearly the same time as the emergence—and often in the work of the same proponents—of the new science. Alchemy is, of course, best known as a technique for transmuting base metal into gold, refining matter into quintessence (the fifth element, surpassing air, fire, water, and earth). But early modern alchemists repeatedly insisted upon the self-reflexive nature of their procedures. In producing the elixir, the philosopher's stone, through an esoteric process of transmutation, the alchemist was also producing an agent of further changes and, perhaps most important, effecting his own transformation, his own conversion. In light of alchemy's inherently transformative and potentially destabilizing qualities, then, I am particularly concerned in this chapter with how alchemy was understood as a "Jewish" science in the period and served to figure the disruptive effects of conversion. The burgeoning interest in alchemy (and the corresponding proliferation of alchemical skeptics) coincided with the flourishing of a variety of millennial and eschatological writings, many of which held as one of their primary expectations the conversion, en masse, of Jews. When alchemy was linked to Jews and Judaism during the early modern period, to the advantage and/or detriment of both, the transformational potentials of alchemy were often conflated with the proselytizing impulses that so often characterized the early modern English encounter with Jews. I use alchemy's fictions of conversion as a means to read the relationship between Shakespeare's *The Merchant of Venice* and Ben Jonson's *The Alchemist*, and conclude the chapter with an analysis of the alchemical imagery in Henry Vaughan's poetry in relation to mid-seventeenth-century millenarian expectations for Jewish conversion.

In my fifth and final chapter, I bring into the foreground some of the questions that have remained implicit throughout the earlier chapters. I have suggested that at the heart of these discourses of transformation is the destabilizing question of authenticity. When conversion is said to have transpired, how can one be certain that the transformation is complete, reliable, or stable? Has the transformation genuinely captured and changed the essence of the pre-conversion person, text, or object? And if so, to what extent can such a transformation properly be said to have worked upon a person, text, or object whose irreducible identity has been preserved? Is the *fiction* of conversion the constructed and contrived nature of the transformation or the fictive assertion of continuous identity, or even identity itself? Chapter 5 focuses on mid- and late seventeenth-century English writings that raise the matter of an interior, irreducible self more explicitly and problematically than any of the material in the preceding chapters. If the early modern discourses of conversion betray an anxious uncertainty about the authenticity of religious transformation, then the phenomenon of enthusiasm, direct divine inspiration, which was an extreme outgrowth of the reforming movements that frame my analysis of conversion, makes these anxieties explicit. Even the most vehement critics of religious enthusiasm found it difficult to dismiss these claims and the calls to religious change with which they were typically combined, for they understood that to do so would be to undermine the bedrock premise of a revealed religion like Christianity. Yet such claims also threatened to disrupt emerging notions of national coherence and identity because they pitted these fictions of individual conversion against the imagined communities that were taking shape amidst the tumult of the English Civil Wars, Interregnum, and Restoration. As a final literary test case, I read the lively mid-seventeenth-century debates about enthusiasm in juxtaposition with John Milton's four-book epic, *Paradise Regained*, which I examine in the context of Milton's fraught identification with groups like the Quakers, Ranters, and Fifth Monarchists (to name only the most notorious of many radical groups from the period). Milton's final poem, about a savior who must come to know what his very identity as such means, raises particular concerns about verifying the unverifiable. In one final take on the Jewish question, *Paradise Regained* may be said to depict the conversion of Jewish messianic expectations (a timely question, indeed, in the context of the Sabbatean movement that took Europe by storm in the late 1660s) into Miltonic Christianity's anxious reimaging of the nature of salvation.

Chapter 1

"The Jews Perverted and the Gentiles Converted": Confessions and *Conversos*

> The Wolfe is made a Sheepe euen then, when gaping, hee is at poynt to enter into the Fold. The Physitian of his soule (praysed be the power of his grace) heales him in the midst of his madnesse; and restores him in the very extremity of his Disease. No height of sinne can forbid the force of grace. Alwayes, the more the weight of sinne, the greater the worke of saluation. True Conuersion, is neuer too late: though late conuersion, proues scarcely true.
>
> —John Gaule, *Practique Theories* (1630)

The Christian discourse of conversion begins with Paul, whose turn from Pharisaic persecutor of Jesus and his followers to apostle to the Gentiles (especially as it is described in Acts 9) marks a dramatic, miraculous transformation. The question of Paul's conversion, however, has become a hotly contested one in recent years, part of a more extensive interrogation of the so-called parting of ways, the division (one of many, in fact) within the post-Temple Mediterranean Jewish community that ultimately produced the two distinct religions we now call Judaism and Christianity. Though I do not intend to describe this lively and important scholarly controversy in any detail, it is worth observing that this very pressing contemporary question is also at the heart of the writings about conversion in early modernity. Nearly every Christian writer who speaks about the calling of the Jews or about the conversion of an individual Jew also conjures this primal scene of separation, the initiating division that must be healed through conversion. Perhaps the most vivid instance of this correlation appears in the work of the English millenarian Joseph Mede, whose "Mystery of *S. Paul's* Conversion: *or*, The Type of the Calling of the Jews" sets out, in table form, ten aspects of Paul's conversion that are prophesied to find direct parallels in the imminent conversion of the Jews.[1] Paul's writings—and particularly his conversion on the road to Damascus—mark the transformation of Jew to Christian for early modern readers far more so than do the events narrated in the gospels. In modern scholarship, Paul's writings are also foundational, but their meanings for the question of conversion are far less clear. A. D. Nock's seminal work on conversion, "the old and the new," as his subtitle insists, renders Paul's turn to Jesus as "a complete change of face . . . the first conversion to Christianity of which we have knowledge."[2] Alan Segal breaks down the influence of Paul's conversion into stages, moving from Paul's ecstatic, visionary experience as described in his letters, to Luke's characterization in Acts of Paul's experience as typical of all Gentile conversions, to the later attempts, first in pastoral epistles like 1 Timothy and then in early post-biblical Christian writings, to make Paul in an explicit paradigm for the conversion experience.[3] More recently, Paula Fredriksen has argued for the "mandatory retirement" of the term "conversion" when speaking about Paul, who never thought of himself as anything but a Jew, even when he was preaching Christ's salvation to the Gentiles.[4] In many ways, this contemporary scholarly controversy captures the very tensions built into the early modern fictions of conversion under analysis in this book. Nock's characterization of Paul's conversion combines the language of continuity with radical change, as he describes Paul's "inner need to discover an interpretation and reconciliation of the old and the new in his religious life."[5] I take Nock's evocative phrase as a helpful expression of my provisional, working definition of conversion; the various formulations of conversion I shall be discussing participate in the rhetorical coordination of the impulse to reconcile old and new. Continuity and rupture figure side by side in the work of conversion; the language of change serves as a site of intense ambivalence. This chapter begins with an account of early Christian writings on conversion that will serve, in turn, as the context for a discussion of the particularly problematic discourse of conversion within the period of the English Reformation. The chapter concludes by making explicit the implicit ties these Reformation fictions of conversion had to the intensely anxious and ambivalent representations of Jewish conversion and marranism.

As we saw in Donne's sermon, some early modern readers looked to Paul's experience on the road to Damascus as an account of the extremities conversion could traverse, "from extreame to extreame, without any middle opinion." In his sermon on "Sauls cruelty. Pauls Conuersion," the Anglican clergyman John Gaule (1603/4–1687) gave vivid expression to these extremes:

> Saul is now on his iourney; the best iourney that euer hee tooke; the worst that euer hee vndertooke. It was wickedly purposed, happily disposed; ill attempted, well atchieued. Now is he neere to Damascus, neere to Euill puporsed; but (oh the Wisedome and Goodnesse of Diuine Prouidence!) nearer to Grace offered. The Wolfe is made a Sheepe euen then, when gaping, hee is at poynt to enter into the Fold. The Physitian of his soule (praysed be the power of his grace) heales him in the midst of his madnesse; and restores him in the very extremity of his Disease. No height of sinne can forbid the force of grace. Alwayes, the more the weight of sinne, the greater the worke of saluation. True Conuersion, is neuer too late: though late conuersion, proues scarcely true.[6]

Stressing the miraculous nature of Paul's conversion, Gaule concludes his observation with a pair of comments that display the apprehension many of his contemporaries would have felt about their own salvation. When true conversion occurs, it is always, by definition, on time; one can never be certain, however, of the authenticity of one's conversion, especially when it comes "late." In fact, so extreme, abrupt, and violent was Paul's conversion that readers found it very difficult to regard it as a model to be emulated. In a sermon on Paul's conversion that Donne preached four years prior to his 1628/29 sermon, he remarked that while the "Ecclesiastical Story abounds with examples of occasionall Convertits, and upon strange occasions . . . yet the Church celebrates no Conversion, but this. . . . Here was a true Transubstantiation, and a new Sacrament."[7] Paul's conversion was exceptional, not exemplary. As David Cressy has shown, the feast commemorating Paul's conversion had even been omitted from the official Elizabethan church calendar.[8] Donne's sermons on the event marked a departure from the established tradition at St. Paul's Cathedral. Indeed, the very exceptionality, the miraculous quality of Paul's conversion may also help to explain why, more often than not, its invocation as a paradigm (as in Mede's table) was linked to the miraculous calling of the Jews.

The timeliness of conversion was related to another feature of writings about conversion, especially within the context of the early Reformation. While Augustine, who, after Paul, served as the other key early model of

Christian conversion, included images of creation and renewal in his representations of the religious transformation he underwent, newness was a rather fraught matter for many of the early reformers.[9] Emerging from within the same cultural climate that gave rise to the humanistic return *ad fontes*, to the sources, proponents of the Reformation were wary of novelty; hence, arguments for reform were typically framed in terms of a return to the original expression of faith and practice of apostolic Christianity. Since innovation was deemed the wrong way to present the teachings of Protestantism, the notion of conversion as rupture, break, or even new creation posed a challenge for reformers who, as Judith Pollman has suggested, "presented [their] program to believers as one of learning old truths and of unlearning bad habits, not as one of changing personality."[10] Reformers had good reason to be wary of any suggestions of novelty. In defending his own conversion to Catholicism, Benjamin Carier described his process of studying the English church's break with Rome:

> I was sorie to heare of change and of a new Religion, seeing, me thought, in reason if true religion were Eternall, then new religion could not be true. But yet I hoped that the religion of England was not a chance or new religion, but a restitution of the olde, and that the change was in the Church of Rome, which in processe of time might, perhaps, grow to be superstitious and Idolatrous; and therefore that England had done well to leaue the Church of Rome, and to reforme it selfe, and for this purpose, I did at my leasure and best oportunitie, as I came to more iudgement read ouer the Chronicles of England, and obserued all the alterations of religion that I could find therein: but when I found there that the present religion of England was a plain change, and change vpon change, and that there was no cause of the change at all of the first but only that King HENRY the eight was desirous to change his old Bed-fello.[11]

Donne's Satire may have offered an affirming view of change; yet Carier's history lesson teaches a very different, more uneasy, understanding of change, one implicitly associated with human capriciousness and excess, particularly exemplified by sexual immorality (in this case, Henry's desire for a new wife and new heir).

Despite efforts by some modern historians to locate a precise moment, a turning point, in the life of Luther or Calvin that marked their respective breaks from the Catholic church and their conversions to "Protestantism," given the potential suspicions aroused by claims of novelty, it should not be surprising to us that the writings of these reformers are noteworthy for the *absence* of any such pivotal event or rupture. Luther's so-called tower experience, the revelatory moment he describes in his writings when he came to understand the centrality of faith to salvation, only looks like a conversion experience in retrospect for the reader who expects to find it somewhere—anywhere—in Luther's self-representations. In his *Lectures on Romans*, for example, Luther is far more intent upon representing conversion as an ongoing struggle rather than as a decisive, fixed event. A person may be converted in baptism only once, according to Luther, but he may be converted again and again in penitence. "If, therefore, we are always repenting," Luther notes, "we are always sinners, and precisely thereby we are righteous and being made righteous; we are partly sinners and partly righteous, i.e., nothing but penitents."[12] He is strongly critical of the view that a Christian's salvation can be secured permanently and with assurance during his lifetime. As Marilyn Harran has noted, Luther regarded change itself as a constant; and as such, conversion could never be a one-time-only affair.[13]

The influence of humanism's return to classical sources on Luther and his followers can be seen in an understanding of conversion along the philosophical lines first elaborated as early as *The Republic*, where Plato speaks of education as a "reorientation of a mind from a kind of twilight to true daylight."[14] Plato's idea of a philosophical *peristrophe*, turning, could also be found at the heart of one of the earliest Christian conversion accounts, predating Augustine's *Confessions* by more than 200 years, Justin Martyr's *Dialogue with Trypho*. In recovering these earlier classical influences, Luther and his humanist followers were also departing from an understanding of conversion that had come to dominate Christian writings since at least Bernard of Clairvaux, that of religious intensification by means of a commitment to monastic life.[15] For reformers like Luther, conversion was far more about an ongoing reorientation. Rather than locating their turns in instantaneous moments of epiphanic inspiration like Paul's Damascene experience, reformers were more likely to be drawn to, and model themselves after, the philosophically conditioned, incrementally achieved conversion of Augustine, who, after much self-conscious, intellectual, searching, picked up a book, read, and was changed.[16]

A similar understanding of conversion as incremental, recursive, and incomplete can be found in the writings of Calvin. Stressing the impossibility of any conversion without God's initiating role, Calvin notes, "with such bondage of sinne therefore as Will is deteined, it cannot once moove it selfe to goodnesse, much lesse applie itselfe. For such mooving is the beginning of turning to God, which in Scriptures is wholy imputed to the grace of God."[17] As he suggests in his account of his own religious development, however, Calvin does not regard this imputation of grace as instantaneous and definitive. In fact, Heiko Oberman has convincingly shown that Calvin's famous use of the word *subito* in his commentary on the Psalms, which has lead some of his readers to perceive his conversion as sudden, is better understood as unexpected (in the sense of unmerited): "for Calvin the primary connotation of conversion is not salvation but vocation, a call to service. This conversion comes *subito*, i.e., *praeter spem*, against all expectations, exactly because it could hardly have come to someone less suited to public office."[18] Calvin's *Institutes* speaks of the restorative work of conversion as happening "not in one moment or one day, or one yeare, but by continuall, yea sometimes slowe proceedings . . . this war hath no end but in death."[19] Given the enormous influence Calvin's writing exercised on English Protestantism throughout the sixteenth and seventeenth centuries, it is hardly surprising to find English writings on conversion replete with accounts of its ongoing, incomplete, impermanent nature. For example, the "morphology of conversion" that took shape within the writings of the influential Cambridge theologian and Puritan writer William Perkins (1558–1602) delineated a series of incremental steps—noteworthy for their non-linear, often retrogressive advance—through which one could hope and expect to proceed on the way toward salvation.[20] 2 Peter 1.10, a favorite verse for Perkins and his readers, called upon the faithful to "give diligence to make your calling and election sure: for if ye do these things, ye shall never fall." A supernatural supplanting of the mortal will by the granting of grace, conversion was not something to be achieved through human agency or action. And yet, according to Perkins, one could experience one's predestined salvation through the repeated scrutinizing of one's claim of faith and how that faith manifested itself in particular works.[21] Perkins is clear, however, that "saving faith" is distinguished by the persistence and return of doubt. As Charles Cohen astutely observes, "A person believes in Christ when he or she stops believing in oneself. The paradox of laboring for preparation is that to receive faith, one must fail to get it, and that in having failed, one succeeds."[22] The Puritan conversion experience takes place repeatedly and is defined by the elusive, endlessly receding nature of any assurances. When conversion seems to have concluded is, precisely, when it has failed. This awareness of conversion's ongoing quality was, understandably, occasion for anxiety and concern. Gaule, for example, speaks of "Conuersion inchoate," even as he insists that "Conuersion is none, if not compleat."[23] Conversion could hardly be considered "compleat" in sixteenth- and seventeenth-century English theological discourse.

Between Churches: Ecclesiastical Change

Historians presume (often implicitly) two different kinds of religious conversion in early modern English writing, which appear to describe two different kinds of experience, and which lend themselves to different kinds of language and representational strategies. On the one hand, conversion can refer to the achievement—or perhaps better, the reception—of salvation, an experience that occurs often without any specific or explicit change in denominational identity. Following Michael Questier's study of early modern English conversion, we might broadly refer to this kind of change as "evangelical" conversion.[24] Evangelical conversion dominated Puritan writings from the late sixteenth century and all through the seventeenth century. Thanks in large part to the writings of Perkins, an extensive theoretical and phenomenological apparatus was elaborated, serving as the basis for scores of conversion narratives that appeared in England, Scotland, and, especially, the North American colonies well into the eighteenth century. One of its hallmarks, and the feature that has occupied most modern scholars, was its inward turn, its focus on consciousness, subjectivity, and interiority; as such, the evangelical conversion narrative has been taken as the harbinger of the modern self (with all its neuroses and anxieties), especially as it has come to be narrated by its generic descendent, the autobiography.

But conversion also has a far more public aspect, especially when it refers to changes in religious or confessional affiliation, whether it be from Islam or Judaism to Christianity (or vice versa), from Catholicism to Protestantism (or vice versa), or even from one denomination of Protestantism to another (e.g., from Anglicanism to Congregationalism or Presbyterianism to Quakerism). Questier has called these conversions "ecclesiastical." Such conversions were often quite dramatic, literally serving as the subjects for numerous stage productions, ranging from the so-called Turk plays to Marlowe's and Shakespeare's infamous depictions of Jewish conversion to dramas of intra-Christian conversion by Dekker, Massinger, and Middleton.

Ecclesiastical conversion was also a reliably provocative theme for a sermon or treatise and lent itself well to the extensive religious polemics that kept the printing presses so busy during the period. Without minimizing some key differences between evangelical and ecclesiastical conversion, however, I suggest that they nevertheless share particular characteristics, the most significant of which is the destabilizing effect these changes can have on those who undergo the conversions and those who bear witness to them as readers or audiences. The theological understanding of evangelical conversion by reformers as incomplete was confirmed by—indeed, I would argue it was partially a consequence of—the fitful history of the English Reformation. Looking back at the recursive turnings from Catholic to Protestant to Catholic to Protestant, the English writers seeking to give shape to their own incremental, evangelical conversions had an obvious model—on a national scale—for the ongoing, incomplete nature of religious transformation. Conversely, as I noted earlier, Luther and Calvin were concerned with stressing the continuity between their teachings and ancient apostolic Christianity, their recovery of what had been—or should have been—central to its religious formulations all along. Even when conversion narratives emerged as a recognizable genre or form in seventeenth-century England and colonial America, they could be said to draw upon the discourse of continuity, as much as rupture, to combat the more phenomenologically apparent sense of discontinuity since Henry VIII's break with Rome.[25]

Catholic writers also recognized the dynamic and recursive nature of conversion. Carier, an English clergyman and chaplain to James I who converted to Catholicism in 1613 and who had been, as we have already seen, quite critical of change for its own sake, even seemed to take some solace in the repeated changes that had characterized recent English church history:

> It is a sure rule of Policie, that in every mutation of State, the Authors of the Change will for a while shew themselues honest, rather of spite then of conscience, that they may disgrace those, whom they have suppressed, but it doth neuer hold in the next generation. You shall scarce heare of a Puritan father, but his sonne proues either a Catholike or an Atheist. Mutinous souldiers, whilest the enemy is in the field, will be orderly, not for loue of their Generall, but for feare of the enemie: but if they be not held in the ancient disciplines of warres, they will vpon the least truce or cessation, quickly shew themselves.[26]

Implicit in Carier's cynical account of "every mutation of State" is some notion of a core identity that will—or can—only be kept hidden for so long before it reveals itself. The very "Authors of the Change" behave in a fashion that marks a split between their "conscience" and their "shew" of honesty. What's more, the people ruled by "Policie" may adopt religious postures in response to external pressures but those conversions are fleeting, lasting only as long as the external pressures persist. Englishmen seem to have embraced Protestantism—even Puritanism, in Carier's account—but scratch the surface and you will find Catholics and Atheists, a rather unexpected combination coming from the pen of a man defending his turn to Catholicism. The periodic, and occasionally notorious, conversions from Protestantism to Catholicism in the late sixteenth and early seventeenth centuries revealed the tenuousness and instability of the Elizabethan Religious Settlement and bore witness to what Questier has evocatively described as "man's general tendency to stagger in religion."[27] Indeed, the phenomenon of multiple, or serial, conversions, which has come under recent scholarly examination, further attests to the ebbs and flows of religious affiliation during this period.[28] There was, in fact, no systematic delineation of the doctrinal and practical differences between Anglican and Catholic religion until the 1590s, when Andrew Willet published his *Synopsi Papismi, That is, A General View of Papistrie* (London, 1592). That English Protestantism could have gone more than fifty years, from the initial break with Rome under Henry VIII, without spelling out its specific divergences from Catholicism underscores how ill defined religious identities could be during the period. The proliferation of conversion tracts and "motive literature" in the first quarter of the seventeenth century, in the wake of the publication and multiple reprintings of Willet's tract (and others like it), speaks directly to efforts at fixing the boundaries that were being crossed (and sometimes recrossed) by these conversions.

Recusancy, Casuistry, and Conversion

Conversion narratives and first-person explanations or justifications of ecclesiastical turns gave open expression to these boundary crossings. As spectacular as they sometimes were, however, far more common than such public examples of religious change (and the instabilities they revealed) were the many private expressions of religious dissent and nonconformity precipitated by the official religious policies of both the English and the Catholic churches. In 1566, seven years after the Acts of Supremacy and Uniformity, Pope Pius V formally forbade English Catholics from attending Church of England services. Until then, Catholics had found ways to attend services—and thereby obey the law mandating their presence—while still signaling in large and small ways their dissent. These "church papists," as they were called by wary Protestants, remained a feature of English religious life well into the seventeenth century.[29] From 1566 on, however, recusancy—the refusal to attend Church of England services—became far more common. It nevertheless took Elizabeth and the English clergy another fifteen years or so before they responded to the growth of recusancy with a series of laws making the penalties for failing to attend church services or for harboring Catholic priests much more severe. By the end of the sixteenth century, the pressures on English Catholics had become so strong that anyone wishing to practice Catholicism (which included refusing to attend Church of England services) did so very much at his or her own risk. Catholicism had become a country-house religion, the faith of the gentry and their dependents, especially in the southeast, who could afford secretly to maintain their own private priests outside of the persistent surveillance of government and church officials.[30] Enforced conformity in the form of church attendance was not merely a hoop through which a secret Catholic could jump and then expect to be left alone; as Questier has shown, "the formal procedure for conforming was no formality."[31] Catholic objections to church-papistry found many formulations, grounded in, among other things, the importance placed on witnessing authentic faith. Conformity, while certainly not identical with conversion, was not entirely distinct from it either, and many who did initially conform for the sake of self-preservation became more than "church-papists" over time.

Recusancy and conformity were not exclusively Catholic concerns, however, and as English Protestants, especially in urban centers like London, became increasingly radicalized and dissatisfied with the Church of England, Parliament turned its attention to Puritan non-conformists as well. In 1593, the extension and strengthening of what had been largely seen as anti-Catholic legislation was aimed at "Protestant sectaries." By the end of the sixteenth century, a "recusant" could be either a Catholic or a Puritan.[32] In a text written in defense of church-papistry and Catholic conformity, an anonymous Catholic priest commented on the amalgamation of these very different confessional identities: "But admit that Recusancy were improperly said an naturall signe, yet it would naturally signifie no more a Catholique then a Brownist (for he refuseth likewise to goe to Church) or any other

Sectary. Although a posteriori it might be thought by discourse to signifie some one displeased with the Protestant Church, but why, or wherefore, it would never signifie."[33] All that could be known with certainty about a recusant was his refusal to attend Church services. His motives for refusing conformity remained opaque, the subject of speculation. While Allison Shell may be correct to suggest that a convert "could not avoid being the site of interpretive clashes,"[34] much the same could be said of those who had not openly converted or even conformed but whose behavior situated them in the middle ground, the interstices between open confessional identities. The nonconforming parallels between Catholics and Puritans (or Brownists) can begin to explain the otherwise nonsensical but surprisingly common equation of the two often made by supporters of the Church of England. The shared strategies of presenting one public identity while preserving another, different, inner life made for very strange bedfellows indeed. These strategies also had the inevitable effect of casting doubt on all claims for religious change.

Addressing himself to the drama of the period, Lionel Trilling famously suggested that the Elizabethan era is precisely when the very notion of "sincerity, of the own self and the difficulty of knowing and showing it," became a matter of overt concern, noting how frequently such matters were featured in the flourishing world of the stage, itself a site of performing sincerity.[35] From the perspective of the Church of England establishment, this division between an inner and an outer life presented phenomenological and practical challenges as much as it presented epistemological and ontological ones. Richard Hooker, the great Anglican theorist of church government, took up these matters directly, arguing that outward conformity was all the church could reasonably expect: "For neither doth God thus bind us to dive into men's consciences, nor can their fraud and deceit hurt any man but themselves. To him they seem such as they are, but to us they must be taken for such as they seem. In the eye of God they are against Christ that are not truly and sincerely with him, in our eyes they must be received as with Christ that are not to outward show against him."[36] In what appears to be a sensibly pragmatic response to the impenetrability of individual conscience, Hooker essentially throws up his hands, expecting God to sort it all out. "The Church of God may therefore contain both them which indeed are not his yet must be reputed his by us that know not their inward thoughts," writes Hooker, even "them whose apparent wickedness testifieth even in the sight of the whole world that God abhorreth them."[37] Hooker resolves the epistemological instability of conversion produced by the potential disjunction between inner belief and outer behavior—what Shakespeare's Scottish king, Duncan, laments as "no art / To find the mind's construction in the face" (*Macbeth* I.iv.11–12)—by fixing his attention on conforming church attendance, ignoring, even, further "apparent wickedness" that could readily be understood to bear witness to God's disfavor. If the ambiguities surrounding conversion and the shifting borders between confessional identities defied—even as they invited—interpretation, one solution was to try to avoid the question entirely. On the one hand, such an official response sought to foster sincere religious identity. On the other hand, it rewarded—at least temporarily—insincere conformity.

Duncan's theatrical dismay at the radical disjunction between inner thoughts and outward behavior comes in the context of a recently defeated rebellion that was exclusively political in nature but, as is often noted, Shakespeare's play was written in the wake of a key crisis in the history of the English Reformation, the Gunpowder Plot of 1605. Reluctantly rousing himself to answer the knocking at the gates of Macbeth's castle just prior to the discovery of Duncan's treacherous assassination, the porter complains, "Faith, here's an equivocator, that could swear in both the scales against either scale; who committed treason enough for God's sake, yet could not equivocate to heaven" (II.iii.5–6). The reference to equivocation is a pointed allusion to the method favored by Catholics for evading accusations of political disloyalty and religious dissent. Shakespeare's contemporaries would not have needed director's notes to remind them that Jacobean England's most notorious equivocator, the Jesuit author of "The Treatise of Equivocation," Henry Garnet, had only recently been executed for his alleged involvement in the plot to destroy the House of Lords and kill James I. Equivocation and related strategies, like casuistry and mental reservation—evasions of incriminating questioning by Anglican officials—epitomized the interpretive instability that emerged as a function of confessional conflicts and the pressures to convert or conform.[38] In the aftermath of the Gunpowder Plot, a statute aimed at Catholic recusancy went out of its way to address the phenomena of equivocation and mental reservation. But even statutes such as these appear not to have addressed the issue to the full satisfaction of some English Protestants. More than thirty-five years later, at the start of a decade of newly violent religious conflicts among different Protestant groups, Daniel Featley expressed his frustration at the resilience of Catholic equivocation: "Let there be an Oath advisedly penned, in tearmes most expresse and significant, with all the cautions that the wit of man can devise against all manner of evasions, and backed with never so many direfully imprecations and anathema maranathaes upon the soule of him that shall by any slight, cunning, falshood or periurie either violate or invalidate and evacuate this Oath: yet these men can with a wet finger either loosen it by a forged and forced interpretation, or untie the knot by a mentall reservation, or cut it asunder by a Papall dispensation."[39] The possibility of casuistry calls into question the reliability of language itself. Featley worries that arguments made by some Catholics—including the anonymous priest to whom his animadversions presented a response—in favor of occasional church conformity would eliminate "a partition Wall betweene loyal Protestants and disloyall Papists: Now the Ephraimites have learned to speake Shiboleth as plaine as the Gileadites, whereas before they could but lispe Siboleth." Seeking some outward, visible (or audible) sign to distinguish Papist from Protestant, Featley hopes, apparently in vain, to fix religious differences in an oath the taking of which would require a Catholic to deny his (Roman) faith, thereby clearing the way for his adoption of the true (Anglican) faith. The permeability of ecclesiastical boundaries that was an essential feature of the saving power of conversion—one had to be able to cross it to convert, after all—was also the source of its destabilizing reversibility and epistemological indeterminacy. And Catholic advocates of conformity knew this very well. Featley's anonymous priest writes quite explicitly, "if I seeme to Protestants to be a Protestant; what am I worse for that? . . . For me to take benefit of their ignorance, and to hide myselfe in persecution, untill either the glory of God, or good of my neighbour shall urge me to discover myselfe: I cannot yet finde my selfe any law forbidden."[40] Taking full advantage of such uncertainty—the "benefit of their ignorance"—Catholics, as well as dissenting Protestants, exploited the instability of the English religious settlement and the wavering history of the reformation's advance to carve out a space for confessional difference by refusing "an indiscreet discovery of a mans Religion without necessitie or obligation."[41] It was often directly to their advantage to promulgate some fiction of conversion precisely to invoke the volatility of religious transformations and rapid cultural shifts.

The Specter of Crypto-Judaism

The passage cited above from Richard Hooker's *Laws of Ecclesiastical Polity* reveals a keen awareness of the disjunction between outward behavior and inner belief, a rupture that emerges in a particularly powerful way within the context of early modern fictions of conversion. Hooker argues that given this discontinuity, the only proper recourse for the Church of England is to allow the continued attendance and participation of even those who might be suspected of harboring heretical views. In articulating his strikingly open understanding of the "Church of God," what we might call a "narrowly sectarian toleration,"[42] Hooker takes a long historical view of the presence of schism and religious deviance among God's people: "Idolatry severed of old the Israelites, iniquity those scribes and Pharisees from God, who notwithstanding were a part of the seed of Abraham, a part of that very seed which God did himself acknowledge to be his Church. The Church of God may therefore contain . . . them which indeed are not his yet must be reputed his by us that know not their inward thoughts."[43] The Israelites, the Pharisees, i.e., the Jews, were the original fictions of conversion, figures whose turns—away from or toward "true" religion—cohered within a discourse of religious change that resolved the theological and epistemological instabilities produced by such transformations through the delineation of explicit boundaries. It was against Jewish "iniquity" that true Christian religion took on its defined shape. As noted above, one way in which early modern writers addressed anxieties about permanence and change in a rapidly transforming world was by asserting continuity rather than rupture at the heart of what they described in the process of this change. Yet even as the Reformation sought to assert its continuity with apostolic Christianity, it was also heir to apostolic Christianity's own highly fraught relationship with the Jewish tradition(s) from which it needed to distinguish itself. This originary break was understood alternatively as an innovation—the canon of Scriptures was reformulated to include and be completed by a *New* Testament—or as the authentic continuity (and fulfillment) of the assurance of redemption promised in the *Old* Testament.[44] That is, Christianity's very origins manifested a tension between old and new, between continuity and change, between *re*turn and *con*version (turning *back* and turning *toward*). In its gloss on Galatians, Paul's intense and impatient meditation on the continuities and differences between Israel-of-the-flesh and Israel-of-the-spirit, the Geneva Bible offers an early Protestant version of the tension between innovation and permanence. "The Galatians, of Painims began to be Christians," observes the gloss, "but by false apostles were turned backewarde to begine a newe the Iewish ceremonies, and so instede of going forward toward Christ, they ran backewarde from him" (note on 4.9). The vertiginous combination of "began to be Christians" and "begine a newe the Iewish ceremonies" or "going forward toward Christ" and "ran backewarde from him" depict a series of turns not unlike the "about . . . and about" we saw in Donne's third Satire. The Geneva commentators construe Paul as criticizing the Galatians for being both too innovative and too traditional.

Jewish conversion (not to mention its failure) has been a constitutive element of Christian fictions of conversion from the writings of some of the earliest Church Fathers. Examples can be found throughout early modern English commentaries and sermons of the inter-animating connection between the salvation of the Gentiles and the damnation of the Jews. Daniel Price's exuberant description of the transference of God's favor from Israel of the flesh (Jews) to Israel of the spirit (Gentiles) is representative:

> And here first behold the greatest Change, mutation, alteration, metamorphosis that euer was: foes received as friends, aliants as citizens, enemies as servant, the reiected as elected, the sonnes of the bondwoman made free, strangers to the promise made heires. The Gentiles who had no couenant in hope, no hope in God, no God in the worlde, are now conuerted, accepted, approued. On the other side behold with terror and trembling, the right Oliue tree made a wilde branch, the Citizens made aliants, the heires made strangers, Iacob supplanter, supplanted, Esau reiected, received, Israell, made Ismaell, Ismael made Israell, and the Israelites to whom appertained the adoption, the glory, and the covenant, and the giving of law, and the service of God, and the promise, are now a forward generation. The Iewes peruerted, and the Gentiles conuerted.[45]

Delighting in the language of change ("mutation, alternation, metamorphosis"), Price depicts the calling of the Gentiles precisely in the language of conversion. For the Gentiles to have been converted *to* Christ, the Jews had to turn *from* Christ. The reversal of fortunes only works in this closed economy because there appears to be an unstated law of conservation of salvation. Christian redemption is predicated on Jewish preterition. The Gentiles were indeed converted, but only because, it would seem, the Jews were perverted.

Chapter 11 of Paul's letter to the Romans, which speaks of the recovery of salvation for Israel following "the fullness of the Gentiles" (verse 25), appears to foresee an enlarging of the promise to include both Jews and Gentiles. Drawing on Paul's figure of the olive tree in Romans 11, Thomas Cooper anticipates the salvation of the descendants of Japheth and Shem: "So that Iapheth must be perswaded and enlarged, aswell as Shem. The Gentiles must bee conuerted, aswell as the Iewes. . . . Hee accomplisheth it in particulars, as pledges of a more plentifull Harvest: and he permitteth obstinacie to come vpon the Iew, that the wilde Oliue might be engrafted."[46] Gentile salvation, for Cooper, can only be achieved when Jews are rejected. Yet once this wild branch has been grafted onto the tree, the natural branches will be returned to their origin as well. A worrying implication of the closed economy of salvation, however, is that even the future possibility of Jewish conversion to Christianity, the Jewish recovery of its favored status, may pose a threat to the Christians who currently enjoy their role as God's new elect. Even when early modern writers anticipate, call for, or celebrate Jewish conversion (when it happens individually from time to time, for example), the salvation this conversion promises brings with it anxieties about its implications for the endurance of Christian election. The perdurability and authenticity of Jewish conversion is repeatedly undermined even as it is acclaimed. In a sermon brilliantly analyzed by Janet Adelman, for example, the Protestant martyrologist John Foxe uses the occasion of the conversion of a Spanish Jew, Yehuda (who was baptized with the name Nathaniel), to address the future salvation of the Jewish people. Turning to the same passages from Romans that Christian readers before and after him would invoke, Foxe notes,

> testimonie of the Apostle [Paul, in Romans] is sufficient argument to declare, that the Iewes shalbe restored againe, if I be not deceived. But when that returne of the Iewes shalbe, the diuines are not fully agreed upon. When the fulnes of the Gentiles shall come (sayeth S. Paul.) . . . peraduenture we will interprete this fulnes in this wise: that the Iewes shal continue so long in blindenes, as the Gentiles did in vnbeliefe, whiles the Iewes remayned in beliefe: and that the fulnes of the Gentiles shall seeme to be accomplished, when as the Gentiles may prescribe as long continuance in the possession of Gods Church without the Iewes, as the Iewes did first enioy their synagogue without the Gentiles.[47]

The implied corollary of this dynamic mirroring between Jews and Gentiles in the cycle of salvation and damnation is that once the Jews return to "belief," the Gentiles shall return to their "blindenes." In order to stave off the threat of this loss, Foxe constructs the Jewish convert as unavoidably and eternally tainted by his Jewish heritage. As Adelman notes, even before the language of race and ethnicity has begun to cohere around its modern usage,

Foxe speaks explicitly in terms of the natural inheritance of the Jews as "that vnbeliefe, which being more noisome then any persistent botch, may rightly & properly be called the Jewish Infidelitie, & seemeth after a certaine maner their inheritable disease, who are after a certaine sort, from their mothers women, naturally carried through peruerse frowardnes, into all malitious hatred, & contempt of Christ, & his Christians."[48] Unbelief is a congenitally Jewish disease, passed from mother to child; it is a fixed, *unchanging* feature of Jewish nature. Conversion can therefore have only limited success in overriding such natural propensities. Indeed, Jewish conversion becomes, within this rubric, inevitably and by definition, false and unstable.

Foxe takes his cue from Paul's image of the limbs of the olive tree and, in a fascinatingly ironic inversion of Paul's allegorical hermeneutics, his characteristic detaching of the spirit from the letter, Foxe reliteralizes the figure, apparently untroubled by the reversal: "Againe the very first yssues of our Christian faith sprang out of that stocke, from whence we Gentiles must needs confesse to haue receiued the very entry and fundation thereof. It appeareth therefore that this was not a general rejection, neither that the whole race was drawen altogether into the same gulfe of perdition, but a portion onely, and the same Paul tearmeth them to haue bene cut of."[49] The Jew is both the original site of Christian faith and the embodiment of its loss. He makes salvation available to the Gentile by serving as its founding figure, even as that salvation transfers to the Gentile only when it leaves the Jew. Yehuda's explicit (former) identity as a Spanish Jew—his confession, which was originally written in Spanish and translated into English, is appended to Foxe's sermon in the 1578 publication—is not merely coincidental to the significant emergence of a naturalized, proto-racial definition of Jewishness in Foxe's sermon. The history of Iberian Jewry stands directly behind this English text. As David Graizbord has shown, one of the lasting effects of the historical sequence of forced conversions, blood purity laws, expulsions, and the subsequent Inquisition on the Iberian peninsula, was the convergence of theories of Jewish racial corruption and religious deviance.[50] This convergence had a local habitation and a name in early modern Europe: the *marrano*.

Despite efforts to identify its etymology, no convincing argument has been offered for the origins of the use of the term *marrano* to designate (not fully) converted Jews. Norman Roth has discovered one of the earliest mentions of the term in the records of the *Cortes* (parliament) of Soria, convened by Juan I of Castile in 1380, ten years before the most extensive Spanish efforts to force Jews to convert en masse.[51] But it remains uncertain whether the word's relation to the Spanish term for swine is what contributed to its use in this context or was rather an effect of its use as a derogatory epithet. Whatever its origins, it was a term known in England at least as early as 1576, when Arthur Hall used it in his letter, describing an encounter between a Spanish soldier and Charles V, in which the soldier rudely called the Emperor "a *Marano*, the most odious name wc that nation, & as many more, as eyther Ruffian or Rogue can deuise."[52] John Florio's English-Italian dictionary (1611) offered the following definition: "Marâno, a nick-name for Spaniards, that is, one who descended of Iewes or Infidels and whose Parents were neuer christened, but for to saue their goods will say they are Christians. Also as Marâna."[53] Responding to the notorious case of John Traske, whose preaching attracted an alarming number of followers, Lancelot Andrewes feared specifically the contaminating, converting influence of Traske's "Judaizing" practices (including Saturday Sabbath observance and dietary laws), calling him "a very christened Jew, a Maran, the worst sort of Jews that is."[54] And Francis Bacon included the term in his 1625 *Apopthegmes*, explaining why, in Spain, proper public reverence is not always shown to the holy Sacrament: "in Spaine, there be so many Iewes and Maranos."[55] As these examples attest, the term was associated in early modern England parlance with Ibero-Judaic irreligion and, especially, with counterfeit behavior, deception, and secrecy.[56]

Modern scholarship remains somewhat divided over the extent to which Jews who converted to Christianity from this period deliberately (and secretly) retained certain features of their previous religious identity. On the one hand, in his study of the Inquisitorial records from the sixteenth century, Norman Roth is adamant that just about all the charges brought against *conversos* were fabricated and that there is hardly any evidence of real crypto-Judaism. Indeed, Roth suggests, Jews often cooperated with or used the Inquisition to avenge themselves on the *converso* community, with which they understandably had very tense relations; there was no love lost there.[57] On the other hand, David Gitlitz has concluded from his own analysis of documents from the period that "crypto-Judaism and a strong Jewish identity were very real phenomena among many new Christians."[58] Certainly, the evidence of the late sixteenth-, early seventeenth-century Dutch Jewish community, which was composed entirely of first- and second-generation Jewish immigrants from the Iberian peninsula, would seem to support Gitlitz's contention. And though Traske himself had recanted his Judaizing doctrines, his influence persisted, especially among English radicals living in Amsterdam, including Hamlet Jackson and Christopher Sands, who frequently made direct contact with Dutch Jews.[59] David Katz has further shown that the "so-called secret community of Marrano Jews in Elizabethan London was . . . hardly secret at all."[60] The experience of *conversos* and those who came to reclaim their Jewishness (in Amsterdam or London) served as evidence of the persistence of Jewish identity for the English with whom they came into contact, whether it was understood in proto-racial terms or along exclusively theological lines.

Crypto-Judaism, Crypto-Catholicism, and the Fiction of Conversion

Though the specific term *marrano* was used infrequently in English writings, the examples that do exist from the period demonstrate an awareness of the phenomenon the term was said to describe; they are evidence of a larger concern with inauthentic Jewish conversion and also of the associations such conversions had with Spain. Intense English interest in, and hostility toward, Spain and Portugal (before and after the defeat of the Armada in 1588) coincided with the growth of the Jewish and *converso* communities in the Low Countries as they fled from those same regions. David Graizbord has noted, "The view that Portuguese immigrants and their descendants were ipso facto New Christians, and that all conversos of Lusitanian origin were secret Jews, arose in Spain in response to the Portuguese migrations of the late sixteenth and early seventeenth centuries."[61] By the early seventeenth century, "Portuguese" or "Portuguese nation" had become firmly identified with Jew or crypto-Jew not only in Spain but in England as well. John Florio's dictionary informed its English readers that the term "Spaniard" could also signify "a jew," and, as Eric Griffin has shown, for many in England "the Castilian language came to function simultaneously as a sign of Hispanicity *and* an index of Jewishness."[62] This identification of Iberian Catholicism with Jewishness can also help to explain the frequent portrayal, in Protestant attacks on the papacy, of *English* Catholics as Jews. The Geneva Bible's gloss on Galatians 4.10, for example, aligns Jewish and Catholic concerns with ceremony. Paul may have been concerned with those who were turning to the laws and traditions of Judaism rather than the grace and salvation offered by Christ. But for the Geneva Bible readers, Paul's concern includes features of the Catholic calendar as well: "Ye obserue dayes, as Sabbaths, newe moones, &c; ye obserue moneths as the first and seuēth moneth: ye obserue times; as Easter, witsontide, the feast of Tabernacles: ye obserue yeres as the Iubile, or yere of forgiuenes, which beggerlie ceremonies are most pernicious to them which haue receiued ye swete libertie of the Gospel, and thrusts itsel backe into superstitious slauerie." Foxe, whose *Book of Martyrs* is preeminently consumed by its anti-Catholic polemic, makes the analogy explicit in his sermon on the conversion of Yehuda/Nethaniel, where he notes how Jews "wallow[] continually in a most filthy puddle of pestilent error, not much unlike to the Romish Synagogue in this our age, whose senses seeme to be tippled with the same dolldreanche."[63] As I have argued elsewhere, accusations of Judaizing were not necessarily limited to one confessional affiliation or another in early modern England; Catholics frequently described their Protestant opponents as Pharisees even as they were being accused of excessive ceremonial Judaizing in their devotion to traditions and fixed forms of worship. But the combination of anti-Spanish, anti-Catholic, and anti-Jewish discourse during this period deserves particular attention with respect to the complicating and unsettling dynamics of conversion.[64] One especially suggestive example of this convergence appears in Featley's polemic against the Jesuits who, he claims, demanded recusancy of English Catholics for no reason other than self-enrichment. By insisting that English Catholics transport their children overseas for their education, Jesuits were guaranteeing for themselves a regular stream of paying students. "In this respect," writes Featley, "these Iesuites may rightly be called Suits . . . not only in respect of their swinish and Epicurian lives in their Styes beyond the Seas, but because their societie herein resembles that Sow in Martiall which farrowed in the Theater by a wound there received: so this Order by the wound received from the State (I mean the penalties inflicted upon Romish Catholiques for Recusancie) hath growne fruitfull and exceedingly multiplied."[65] Though Featley stops short of calling the Jesuits *marranos*, the resemblance between the two epithets, Suits (from the Latin *suidae*, swine) and *marranos* (Spanish for swine), is tantalizing enough. The plights of Jewish *conversos* and persecuted Catholics paralleled each other in significant fashion, lending themselves to similar strategies of survival and, in turn, similar kinds of condemnation.[66]

The *marrano* embodied simultaneously the corrupt religious practices and traditions from which English Protestantism sought to distinguish itself *and* the preeminent example of the costs and abuses entailed in the violent imposition of religious conformity and forced conversion.[67] English writings about conversion are particularly intent upon distinguishing the proper use of persuasion from the improper use of coercion. In his conversion sermon, Foxe speaks of the contaminating idolatry in the Catholic church, "out of which puddle has issued wonderful stench, so amongst al other, nothing more noisome then those pestilent Botches of imageworship, breadworship, wineworship, crosseworship, signes & pourtraictes of visible creatures." The real cost of such corruption, for Foxe, is in the alienation of the Jewish people: "the view whereof cause the true and sincere profession of the Christians to be loathsome to the Iewes, to their great hinderance and preiudice. . . . what maruel was it . . . if [the Jews] being offended with this open idolatrie, did so long refraine from vs, and from the discipline of our faith."[68] In one of several treatises he wrote about conversion, deploying many of the features of Perkins's morphology of conversion to discover the "Truth of and Effectual Conversion," Thomas Cooper discusses the ways in which a government can "cool" the "first love" of a new convert's passion, conviction, and commitment to Christ, including "when it insulteth and lords it ouer the conscience, by inquisition into the secrets of the heart, and violent forcing the same, contrairie to the tendernes, and true information thereof."[69] Cooper's use of the term "inquisition" is not accidental, invoking, as it does, precisely the history of Iberian persecutions of Jewish converts as a cautionary tale. It is in Cooper's writings that we find some of the most explicit conjunctions of what Questier had called the "evangelical" and "ecclesiastical" models of early modern English conversion. In his account of the "Gathering of the Gentiles, and the Finall Conuersional of the Jewes," published five years after his meditation on the "converts first love," Cooper inveighs against all but divine means for achieving conversion: "Thus is God the Author of our conuersion. But by what meanes doth he accomplish the same? Doth he vse miracles, to amaze, or tortures to compel? Doth hee vse Enthusiasmes, to inspire, or Dreames, to reveal a worke vnto us? Surely no: The holie Ghost (saith) God perswade Iapheth. That is, God incline the heart, & allure the minde of the Gentiles, by convincing their consciences, with the power of truth, & framing their will."[70] Cooper not only dismisses the efficacy of torture in the work of conversion, he expresses equal wariness of miracles and inspirations, "Enthusiasmes," in the successful achievement of religious changes. As I shall argue in my final chapter, religious change elicited by religious enthusiasm served as a limit case for the fictions of conversion circulating during the period, insofar as claims of divine inspiration threatened to call into question the very authenticity of the revealed religion. Cooper appears to have sensed the potential dilemma posed by insisting, on the one hand, on an exclusively divine impetus for all turnings to God and, on the other hand, the inefficacy of miracles, amazement, and inspiration. He reiterates his rejection of torture and physical compulsion, "And therefore, as this condemneth all Antichristian Tyrannie, whereby all hope of sound conuersion is utterly cut off, whilest by extremitie of torture the bodily life is depriued," but follows this rejection with a seemingly contradictory call for civil authorities *not* to tolerate the very Catholicism that had been the exemplar of such unjust religious authoritarianism: "so also the negligence of the Christian Magistrate is iustly reproued, in leaving the papist his libertie, or winking at him, shewing extreme crueltie to his soule, while he pretends clemencie to his body. And if the refractorie must bee compelled from a false worship to the meanes of a true: Oh then! farre be it from the heart of godly Magistrate, to tolerate a false religion."[71] Cooper stops short of describing exactly what he would regard as an acceptable way of compelling "from a false worship to the means of a true," one that does not exemplify "Antichristian Tyrannie." And when he considers the history of England's treatment of Jews, he speaks out of two sides of his mouth, noting how Scriptures "iustly condemneth our base and odious account of that Holy Nation, and also reprooveth our cruell dealing toward them: so it teacheth vs, to pray heartily for their Conuersion, and to vse all holy meanes for the effectuating thereof."[72]

The tension between "cruell dealing" and "holy meanes" informs both early modern English expectations for Jewish conversion (perhaps the most dramatic version of Questier's ecclesiastical conversion) and early modern English expectations for conversions within the Church (Questier's evangelical conversion). Lancelot Andrewes, for example, takes up this theme in his 1619 Ashe Wednesday sermon, distinguishing between conversion by some external power and "when without wrench or screw we turn of ourselves. And that man who being under no arrest, no bridle in his jaws, shall in the days of his peace resolve of a time to turn in and take it, that many hath great cause to rejoice and to rejoice before God. . . . And so may we turn, and such may all our conversions be: 1. Voluntary, without compulsion; 2. To God, without declining; 3. With the heart, not in speculation; with the whole heart entire, no purpose of recidivation!"[73] Praying for a conversion that is permanent and not forced, Andrewes describes the nature of the dilemma early modern fictions sought to solve—or at least to express. The rapid and repeated religious shifts, which brought with them efforts at enforced conformity that carried, in turn, their own problematic associations with a religious past from which English Protestantism repeatedly sought to distinguish itself, gave rise to a culture defined by and anxious about change.

The additional factor of a significant number of Englishmen who "turned

Turk," becoming Muslims (by choice or by compulsion) during the course of their contact with the Maghreb, Levant, or the Ottoman Empire, deepened English anxieties about conversion and change.[74] Even when they were not central players in this dramatic instance of religious change—one that posed a range of other threats given the considerable military and mercantile might of the Ottoman Empire and the Barbary state—Jews functioned as cyphers for Christian concerns about conversion. Marlowe's *The Jew of Malta* brings the Jew, Barabas, together with the Moor, Ithamore, forging a partnership of political and economic destabilization. Robert Daborne's *A Christian Turned Turk* represents the spectacular career of the real-life Christian pirate, John Ward, who had scandalized the world by "turning Turk"; but lurking in the background of Daborne's staging of these events is the character Benwash, a Jew who had converted to Islam out of his desire to protect his own interests. These and numerous other "Turk Plays" were particularly concerned with the process of apostasy and return. Archbishop Laud's 1637 promulgation of "A Form of Penance and Reconciliation of a Renegado or Apostate from the Christian Religion to Turkism" attests to official efforts to bring these transformations under doctrinal control, as do the numerous sermons from the early seventeenth century marking these *re*turns of men who had *turned* to Islam. Edward Kellet uses such an occasion to speak of "such as are among vs, though not of vs, such as are to choose Religion; Ambo-dexters, Nullifidians, such Amphibia, as can liue, both on Land and Water, or such as haue stayned their soules with some blacke sinnes: these are the Chamelions which will change colour with euery ayre, and their beliefe, for matters of small moment."[75] The very absence of specific reference to the particular offense of having converted *to Islam* (as opposed, say, to Catholicism) in Kellet's colorful description of ambidextrous, amphibious converts reflects the larger concern with the frequency of religious change in general, as does William Gouge's sermon prompted by a similar occasion, which speaks of mandated recantations and confessions that "time after time [have] been done in all reformed Churches: And that not only by such as have returned from Paganisme, Turcisme, and Iudaisme; but also from Anabaptism; and Popery."[76] Apostasy and return, in Gouge's account, are a common—if regrettable—feature of seventeenth-century English life. Still, if one is to lament the change of a convert who has "turned Turk," one ought to celebrate the change of a convert (re)joining the Church.

One of the most powerful tools English divines had for giving shape and definition to these profoundly volatile phenomena was the rooting of conversion in biblical sources. Paul's conversion may have served as the initiating moment for Christian history but, as we have seen, the depiction of that transformation as innovative and discontinuous with the past carried with it particularly problematic theological corollaries with respect to the status of those who enjoyed a privileged relationship with the divine before the Gentiles, the Jews. To address these challenges, early modern writers looked for paradigms of religious transformation in the *Old* Testament, constructing fictions of conversion out of those biblical narratives to establish a reassuring continuity grounded in identity and sameness, even as they described difference and transformation. It is to these biblical models that I now turn.

Chapter 2

"Thy People Shall Be My People": Typology, Gender, and Biblical Converts

God's charge to Abram in Genesis 12.1, "Get thee out of thy country, and from thy kindred, and from they father's house, unto a land that I will show thee," captures the inextricable link between the formation of a new identity and the necessary separation from earlier attachments such a new identity demands; in answering this divine call, Abram enters into a privileged, covenantal relationship with God. He differentiates himself from the surrounding world, turning away from his own family and people to establish a new community. Abram is also the first biblical character to acquire a new name as a function of this changed relationship with God. As the text elaborates on the covenant between God and Abram several chapters later, God tells Abram, "Neither shall thy name any more be called Abram, but thy name shall be Abraham: for a father of many nations have I made thee" (Gen. 17.5).[1] This name change—yet another way in which identity comes into being through difference—marks a further moment of transformation, one that came to stand for a turn to the God of Israel and, subsequently, to the God of Christians. Janet Adelman has observed that for the early modern reader the name Abraham encoded "the contested genealogy that expresses Christianity's vexed relation to Judaism . . . [by recording] the moment of Jewish displacement," the moment at which Abram, *avram*, ceased to be the fleshly father of the Israelites and became, instead, Abraham, *avraham*, the spiritual father to the Gentiles.[2] Christian biblical commentaries read the change of Abraham's name as the formal confirmation of a kind of proto-conversion begun at the moment God called on Abram to leave his land and family. The gloss to Genesis 17.5 in the Geneva Bible (1560) observes that while Abram may have been father according to the flesh, Abraham was father "of a farre greater multitude by faith."[3] The Catholic Douay-Rheims Bible (1609) offers a similar understanding: "For albeit Abraham was natural father of foure nations, the Ismaelites, Madianites, Idumeans, and the Israelites, yet he was spiritual father of manie more, to wit, of al nations that beleue in Christ from his owne time to the end of the world" (65). Elaborating even further on the implications of this first biblical conversion, the English Separatist, Henry Ainsworth, provides the following explication of the name change: "*a multitude*:] that is, *of many nations*, as Paul expoundeth it *Rom*. 4. 16–17, where the Apostle sheweth a twofold seed, that which is of the Law, and that which of the Faith of Abraham, who is the Father of us all. So by the *multitude of nations*, is meant besides his natural posteritie, all Christian beleevers in the world, *Gal*. 3. 28. 29. Who should inherit from him, (as children receive inheritance from their fathers,) the justice that is by faith, & blessedness accompanying the same, through the covenant of grace, propagated by Abrams doctrine and example: see Rom. 4 and Gal. 3."[4] Citing key passages from Paul's letters to the Roman and to the Galatians, Ainsworth makes explicit the conversion of Abraham from the genealogical father of Israel of the flesh, "his natural posteritie," to the typological father of "all Christian beleevers," Israel of the spirit. There is nothing especially unusual or innovative about Ainsworth's annotation. It is, as Adelman has noted, consistent with a long-standing reading of Abraham beginning at least as early as Augustine. What is noteworthy in Ainsworth's comment, however, is the source he offers for such a reading. His annotation continues, "To this the Hebrew canons doe accord: *A stranger* (they say) *bringeth first fruits &c. for it was sayd to Abraham, a father of a multitude of nations, have I given thee* to be, (*Gen*. 17. 5.) *Behold he is Father of the world, which shalbe gathered under the wings of the majestie of God: Maimony in Misn. Treat. Of Firstfruits, chap. 4 S. 3*." As evidence of Abraham's status as father of all *Christian* believers, Ainsworth explicitly cites *Jewish* rabbinical authorities, specifically the deliberations of Maimonides in his legal code, the Mishneh Torah. I shall return to this rabbinic interpretation, and how Ainsworth might have come to know it, below. For the moment, however, I want to take note of this striking use of Jewish sources in the Christian discourse of conversion, a use that might be said to convert the Jewish reading through its integration, even as it argues for the Christian *telos* of that reading. The early modern English discourse of conversion seems inevitably to depend upon an underlying transformation of Jewishness, even when Jews are not the explicit subject of these fictions of conversion.

Abram's conversion to Abraham (and its attendant implications for Jewish or Christian notions regarding the status of converts) assumes even further significance when we recall that Abram does not answer God's call to depart the land of his birth alone. The text in Genesis continues, "And Abram took Sarai his wife, and Lot his brother's son, and all their substance they had gathered, and the souls that they had gotten in Haran, and they went forth to go into the land of Canaan" (Gen. 12.5). The phrase "the souls that they had gotten in Haran" captured the imagination of many early modern readers. Though the Geneva Bible's gloss understands it simply to mean "as well seruants as cattel," Ainsworth, who was quite familiar with earlier Jewish interpretations, cites the Aramaic targumim in his annotation: "*had made,*] that is, *had gotten*, to weet into their possession, as the Greek manifesteth. But this may be meant, not onely of getting them to their service (as I. Sam. 8, 16.) but also winning them to the faith of God: as the Chaldee paraphrast sayth, *hath subdued unto the law:* which is very probable by that example of his howshold soldjers, Gen. 14, 14, and his commendation for teaching his house, Gen: 18.19. and their receiving the wound of circumcision, Gen. 17, 23. So Thargum Ierusalemy also calleth these, *soules of proselytes*, (or *converts*)."[5] Not only was Abraham the first convert, according to this reading, he was also the first proselytizer. As we saw in Chapter 1, early modern conversion was never understood as a self-contained process. Comments like Ainsworth's reveal yet another facet of conversion's open-endedness: its fullest significance emerges within its capacity to reproduce itself, to lead to further conversions, even as this self-reproducing quality can also undermine its stability and reliability. For Abraham's conversion to mean anything, he also needed to be credited with having converted the souls who accompanied him on his journey. Ainsworth singles out "the wound of circumcision," the mark of the flesh Abraham was charged to inflict on himself, his children, and all the male members of his household in 17.23, as evidence of this conversion, suggesting again the complex dynamic between carnal and spiritual readings—and what Paul would make into the paradigmatic distinction between Judaism and Christianity—inevitably raised by the figure of the first patriarch. That only the male "souls" whom Abraham "had made" could receive this "wound" is not incidental to my analysis in this chapter.

Abraham's role as convert and converter served for other early modern readers as an occasion to meditate on the boundaries that separated the saved and the unsaved and, in particular, on other early examples of those who succeeded in crossing that boundary. Sixteen years after Ainsworth first published his annotations on Genesis, the English theologian and schoolmaster Thomas Hayne invoked the example of Abraham in offering the following observations concerning the soteriological meaning of the change that transpired after the death of Christ:

> At which time the *partition wall was broken downe*, and liberty was granted *to goe into the way of the Gentiles*. Before which time that way *did not so barre out the Gentiles*, but that God left them a *way* to come into the *Iewes Church*, and divers particular persons did returne, by Gods great mercy, to the true faith, drawne to it by such instruments and meanes as it pleased God to use. As namely the *soules which Abraham got and converted at Charan, Eliezer of Damascus his Steward, all or a great part of his 318 souldiers: a great multitude of sundry sorts of people that went out of Egypt with the Israelites:* also *Iethro* a Midianite, *Rahab* a Chananite, *Ruth* a Moabite, *Naaman* a Syrian . . .[6]

Before Christ, the only access to salvation available to anyone, Jew or Gentile, was through the "*Jewes Church*." Those souls whom Abraham brought with him from Haran, therefore, were following the only path they could to obtain God's mercy by converting, which was to attach themselves to the Jewish body (and to mark their own bodies accordingly). But these unnamed souls are not the only examples of precocious Gentiles that Hayne provides, concluding his list with four specific names, Jethro, Rahab, Ruth, and Naaman. In this chapter I will consider how these "converts" from the Hebrew Bible figured within the early modern English discourse of conversion. Despite the fairly extensive exegetical tradition to which I have already begun to allude, the Bible offers no explicit example of a formal conversion, a transformation, of or shift in religious identification marked by particular rituals and specific procedures. Circumcision and immersion in biblical narratives may function as signs of covenantal acceptance and spiritual purification, but their codification into Jewish or Christian conversion rituals happens well after the biblical canon is complete. As Hayne's comment indicates, despite the absence of any formal accounts of conversion, however, Jewish and Christian readers located within the biblical text several paradigmatic converts. This chapter reads those biblical exempla and the exegetical traditions that developed around them to give greater depth to—and discover some of the terms of—the fictions of conversion with which I am concerned. Understood as particularly vivid instances of transition and models for the passage from one (unsaved and unfavored) state to another (saved and favored), these biblical "converts" offer both potentially affirmative and unsettlingly problematic test cases for the delineation of an English Christian polity and its capacity to assimilate the outsider. I shall argue that the differences between male (Jethro and Naaman) and female (Rahab and Ruth) biblical figures prompted different hermeneutical strategies that, in turn, reveal the extent to which the persistent English concern with Jews and Jewishness as both honored antecedent and reviled other is also bound up with irresolvable gendered contradictions.

Jethro's Rejoicing

The patriarchal narratives in Genesis recount instances of divine calling, tests of faith, covenantal promises, and exogamous marriages that imply a shift of familial identity and affiliation. Because the first book of the Pentateuch is concerned with God's evolving relationship with a single human actor and his/her immediate family, however, those instances in Genesis that have been subsequently construed as proto-conversions, whether it be the calling of Abram and his name change to Abraham, or the marriage of Asenath, an Egyptian, to Joseph,[7] can be distinguished from the examples to which I now turn. Indeed, the difference between the rather isolated and isolating call of Abraham and the paradigmatic moment of national distinction, the Exodus from Egypt, may be said to constitute one of the key divisions between how early Jewish and early Christian readers constructed their fictions of conversion. For the Christian tradition, Paul's conversion in the New Testament was preeminent; but in seeking out precedents in the Old Testament, Christian readers more often than not turned to the calling of Abram and his name change to Abraham. As Paul himself insisted repeatedly, it was Abraham's faith "that was counted unto him for righteousness" (Rom. 4.3, cf. Gal. 3.6–9). In becoming the father of many nations, of the Gentiles, Abraham's "conversion" served to dissolve national or ethnic distinctions. For the rabbinic tradition, the Israelites' Exodus and ensuing Sinai Theophany (with the giving of the Law that it entailed) served as the prototype for conversion. In converting to Judaism, one was joining the people of Israel and was thereby inheriting the legacy of Sinai.[8]

This is not to say that Christian readers took no interest in those so-called converts who emerge in the Old Testament after this moment of national definition, as we saw above in Hayne's comment. Following the story of the Exodus, it becomes possible for the first time to speak of an entire people, the Israelites. It is striking, therefore, that immediately after the events of Exodus 1–17—which constitute the descendants of Abraham, Isaac, and Jacob into a nation—we learn of the figure of Moses' father-in-law, whose rejoicing at the news of God's redemption of the children of Israel has come to be interpreted by some readers as a formal attestation of faith and an example of conversion. The context of Jethro's bearing witness to the supremacy of the God of Israel is crucial to a fuller understanding of how he might have functioned within the early modern discourse of conversion, and so it is worth a brief discussion.

Exodus 18 is not the reader's earliest biblical encounter with Moses' father-in-law. When he first flees to Midian after his exchange with the two quarreling Hebrews in Exodus 2, Moses meets the seven daughters of the priest of Midian, identified in 2.18 as Reuel, at a well. It is a scene that strongly recollects two earlier well-betrothal scenes in Genesis, when Abraham's servant encounters Rebecca (Gen. 24.10–27) and when Jacob comes upon Rachel (Gen. 29.1–14); were this latest iteration of the type scene to follow its precursors more fully, we might expect these Midianite women—one of whom is destined to become Moses' wife—to be related to him in some recognizable fashion (Rebecca is, after all, Abraham's grand-niece and Rachel is Jacob's first cousin). As Midianites, however, the relation is far more distant (they are descended from the son of Abraham and Keturah, the wife he took following the death of Sarah), a distance made apparent inasmuch as it does not follow the pattern established in the earlier two well scenes. A shared yet distant family origin has been displaced by the emergence of peoples and nations, the Israelites and the Midianites. Indeed, not being in possession of complete knowledge about his own familial origins (he has just fled from Pharaoh's house, where he was raised), Moses can hardly be expected to recognize the distant kinship he shares with the Midianites. The reader's knowledge of Moses' origins stands in stark contrast to Moses' own sense of rootlessness, reinforced by the seven daughters identifying him as an outsider, an Egyptian (Ex. 2.19), even, when they report their initial encounter to their father.[9] Moses' interactions with Reuel are quite brief and his marriage to Reuel's daughter Zipporah happens rather unceremoniously (again, unlike the elaborate exchanges and negotiations that precede Isaac's and Jacob's marriages). Indeed, so apparently insignificant is Reuel at this early stage in the narrative that the text makes no effort to preserve the same name, or to explain the otherwise inexplicable shift from Reuel (as he is called in 2.18) to Jether/Jethro (as he is called in 4.18) when Moses informs his father-in-law of his desire to return to Egypt to inquire of the welfare of his brethren.

So the reader would be excused if she or he did not expect to hear from Reuel/Jether/Jethro again, and it is precisely the unexpected reappearance of Moses' father-in-law in Exodus 18 that gives particular force to his far more fleshed-out interaction with Moses. This surprise is compounded, I think, when we learn not only of Jethro's renewed role but also that Moses had not entirely cut his ties with his father-in-law and the world of Midian. On the contrary, Moses had sent his wife and their two sons *back to Midian* at some unspecified point during the events of the exodus; when Jethro comes to join the newly liberated Israelites in their desert camp, he brings Zipporah, Gershom, and Eliezer with him. Jethro's world is thus both distinguished from Moses' Israelite community—the text reminds us at 18.3, itself a seemingly excrescent repetition of 2.22, that Gershom's name derives from Moses' sense of alienation among the Midianites[10]—and still connected to it by virtue of his daughter's and grandchildren's continued residence with him. In contrast to the story of Ruth, to which I turn my attention below, Moses' decision to send his wife and children back to Midian marks an ongoing affiliation, or at least an as-yet-ill-defined boundary, between Israelite and alien. The equivocal relationship between Jethro, the Midianite priest (Heb. *cohen*), and the children of Israel contributes to the rich ambiguity informing his attestation to the greatness of Israel's God: "And Jethro rejoiced for all the goodness which the Lord had done to Israel, whom he had delivered out of the hand of the Egyptians. And Jethro said, 'Blessed be the Lord, who hath delivered you out of the hand of the Egyptians, and out of the hand of Pharaoh, who hath delivered the people from under the hand of the Egyptians. Now I know that the Lord is greater than all gods: for in the thing wherein they dealt proudly he was above them' " (Ex. 18.9–11). When Jethro expresses joy at Israel's deliverance, it is explicitly the deliverance of a people not his own. What's more, his celebration of the Lord's greatness is comparative—"the Lord is greater than all gods"—not exclusive.[11] He concludes his celebration of God's greatness with a sacrifice and ritual meal, but his status as outsider persists. Indeed, this very capacity to look at Moses and his dealings with the Israelites as an outsider, especially one who recognizes the functional value of *divine* hierarchy (and not monotheistic exclusivity), gives rise to Jethro's proposal of a system of *judicial* hierarchy in 18.19–23. Jethro clearly does not become fully integrated into the Israelite community. He may acknowledge God's greatness, but in verse 27 he returns to his own land.[12]

Curiously, however, Moses' father-in-law reappears on two more occasions in the Bible, as if to suggest that the text cannot quite decide upon his position within the people of Israel. Just as the Israelites are preparing to decamp and resume their peripatetic journey to the land promised to them by God, we read, yet once more, that Moses seeks the assistance of his father-in-law: "And Moses said unto Hobab, the son of Raguel the Midianite, Moses' father-in-law, 'We are journeying unto the place of which the Lord said, "I will give it you": come thou with us, and we will do thee good: for the Lord hath spoken good concerning Israel'" (Num. 10.29). The syntax of the King James Version, which I have quoted here, implies that Hobab is Raguel's son (the translation somewhat inexplicably changes its spelling of the name from Reuel in Exodus to Raguel in Numbers, even though the Hebrew is unchanged), but in the Hebrew it is somewhat clearer that Hobab is (here) the name of Moses' father-in-law *and* also Reuel/Raguel's son. But in whatever version she or he encounters the text, the reader may be forgiven for a little confusion. Hadn't Moses' father-in-law returned to his own land back in Ex. 18.27? And wasn't his father-in-law's name Jethro?[13] The difficulties continue to mount, as we read of Hobab's desire, again, to return to his own land and kindred and of Moses' explicit reason for wanting Hobab's ongoing presence in the camp: "'Leave us not, I pray thee, forasmuch as though knowest how we are to encamp in the wilderness, and thou mayest be to us instead of eyes'" (Num. 10.31). Only a chapter earlier, in Num. 9.15–23, the text had provided an elaborate account of the process of journeying and camping carefully observed by the Israelites, a process dictated by the descent and ascent of the cloud of God's presence, signaling, presumably, God's approval. And a scant three chapters later God will command Moses to send the twelve spies to search the land of Canaan in a pre-invasion reconnaissance mission. Why, therefore, should Moses require Hobab's assistance? Hasn't the text provided ample examples of divine guidance?

And finally, what is Hobab's response to Moses' request that he remain with the camp? The text is notably silent on the matter; Moses promises his father-in-law, "What goodness the Lord shall do unto us, the same will we do unto thee" (10.32) and the next thing we read is of the Israelites' departure from the mount of the Lord. With Hobab? Without Hobab? It is a question that remains unaddressed until, perhaps, one final reference to Moses' father-in-law in the book of Judges. There, amidst a thicket of details concerning political and military alliances and conflicts between the Israelites and the surrounding nations in the land of Canaan, we read of Heber the Kenite, who had separated himself from the rest of his people by forging an alliance with Jabin, the king of Hazor (and Israel's enemy). The Kenites, it emerges, are "of the children of Hobab the father-in-law of Moses" (Judges 4.11), implying that, though they are a separate people, there had been a peaceful relationship between the Kenites and the Israelites, one that Heber disrupted by entering into a friendship with Jabin. From these details we might conclude that, whether or not Hobab had acceded to his son-in-law's request that he remain with the Israelites to serve as a native informant during their journey to Canaan, he soon separated himself again from Moses and the people to establish his own familial line, the Kenites. And if we read just beyond the story of Deborah and Barak in which these details of Heber the Kenite and his ancestry are to be found, we further see that the next nation to conquer the Israelites in that relentless cycle of conquest and redemption characteristic of the book of Judges is none other than Midian, the same Midian with which Moses' father-in-law (Reuel? Jethro? Hobab?) had been identified.

So what are we to make of this elaborate and confusing network of associations and narratives concerning the figure of Moses' father-in-law? They certainly do not present a coherent account of a figure who begins with one ethnic/national/religious identity and turns completely and unalterably to another. Yet they do appear to be concerned with such questions of identity and affiliation. Jethro's celebration of the power of Israel's God wields a rhetorical efficacy that is clearly a function of his status as a non-Israelite. Hobab's potential role as a guide during the desert travels of the Israelites would be meaningless if he were not a native informant, someone with knowledge not otherwise available to Moses and the Israelites. The text seems unwilling to admit Jethro fully into the community, to assimilate him and thereby eliminate his otherness, his difference from that community. His value and credibility inhere specifically within his alien identity.

Jethro's ambiguous status gave rise to strikingly divergent interpretations in the post-biblical period. Most early rabbinic sources depicted Jethro as a model convert, someone whose whole-hearted celebration of God's power exemplified the best kind of proselyte.[14] Jewish Hellenistic writers, however, were far less sanguine about Jethro's *bona fides*. Philo's Jethro is noteworthy for his superficiality and fickle nature. Josephus celebrates Jethro's wisdom and his contributions to Jewish jurisprudence but he completely omits any suggestion that Jethro ever converted to Judaism.[15] The early church fathers took scant notice of Jethro. Origen used his story as example of the presence of valuable wisdom among the pagans. Augustine puzzled over Jethro's status and concluded that Jethro never converted.[16] It is clear that Jethro's general absence from most Patristic writings is due, in part, to his complete absence from the New Testament. Still, Moses' father-in-law did draw the attention of some early modern English readers.

The Geneva Bible's gloss on Jethro succinctly distills the two opposing perspectives I have described in the biblical account. Clearly troubled by the idea that Moses would agree to marry the daughter of an idolater, and an officiant at idolatrous rituals at that, the writers of the gloss offer two brief comments. First, on the question of the meaning of the phrase *cohen midyan*, usually translated as a "priest of Midian," the gloss proposes an alternative interpretation: "Or, prince." Second, the gloss reads Jethro's blessing of the Lord as evidence "that he worshiped the true God, and therefore Moses refused not to marry his daughter." These two comments seek to minimize Jethro's distance from the community to which he is attaching himself: he is not a pagan priest, he is a prince who already worships Israel's God, at least in some rudimentary form. In this respect, he is entirely suitable to serve as Moses' father-in-law. Yet the gloss balances its domestication of Jethro with the following comment several verses later: "Godlie counsel oght euer to be observd, thogh it come of our inferiors: for to such God often times giueth wisdom to humble them that are exalted." Jethro is Moses' inferior, according to this gloss, insofar as he is not an Israelite and by virtue of his alien status. Moses' willingness to take advice from his father-in-law can only serve as the kind of moral instruction proposed by this comment if Jethro remains outside (and beneath) the community of the faithful. The gift he bestows on Church is the gift of his inferior nature. Significantly, I think, neither of these representations of Jethro suggests anything about conversion. Jethro is either a God-worshipper before he encounters Moses or he is a Midianite and therefore ethnically subordinate to Moses and the Israelites. Subsequent comments on Jethro's status pursue this intermediary identity—neither fully alien nor fully of the people of God—with notable consistency.

The sixteenth-century Puritan minister, Richard Greenham, for example, uses Jethro's story as a means to advocate for a kind of syncretic accommodation of a wide range of Christian beliefs. Beginning with the premise that Moses would never have chosen to live among real idolaters in Midian, and that therefore Jethro could not have been a pagan worshipper of idols, Greenham goes on to draw two lessons: "first, that if we haue the chiefe and principall points of religion with vs although there may be some wants and defects, yet that we make much of Gods great blessing therein, and labour carefully & diligently to vse them, shewing our selues thankful to that which is wanting vnto vs. Secondly, that the Lord will alwayes haue some to keepe his truth, to the glorie of his own name and the condemnation of the wicked."[17] Preaching and writing during a period characterized by the Elizabethan religious settlement, Greenham looks to Jethro's interactions with Moses as exemplary for what they teach about the need to acknowledge religious differences even as these differences ought to be eliminated. Conversion does not enter into Greenham's reading of Jethro, who is already to be considered *within* the community, however broadly construed that community might be. Greenham goes on to extend Jethro's story as a model for how "we may learne to trie our religion," enumerating the different features of Jethro's actions that confirm his avowals of belief: "*Iethroes* religion may be tried by these notes. 1. That he reioyced more for the deliuerance of Gods people, than for the promotion of his sonne. 2. Because he was carefull to confirme his faith, by the experience of them which had receiued greater graces. 3. Because his ioy did breake out into an open profession of sacrifice. 4. His diuine speech and good counsaile which he gaue to *Moses*, doth testifie that he was a pure worshipper of God: at the least he held the chiefest, and was not a nouice in religion."[18] In this account, Jethro exemplifies a kind of limit case for what might be acceptable in matters of faith. Greenham reads Jethro's story for its capacity to delineate boundaries *from within* a religious and political culture necessarily anxious about the demands the Acts of Supremacy and Uniformity had placed on the English people. Writing amid the confessional tensions of the second half of the sixteenth century, Greenham looks to Jethro for an example of how to identify common ground among apparently divergent doctrinal views.

Though Greenham sidesteps the matter of Jethro's conversion, other English discussions of Moses' father-in-law do take it up more explicitly. Citing one of his favorite philological and exegetical authorities, the Spanish commentator Alonso Tostado (1400–1455), Andrew Willet represents Hobab's desire to return to his people in Numbers as determinative: "Neither yet was *Iethro* a perfect worshipper of God, and so circumcised, as the people of Israel were: for if he had beene circumcised, hee had beene bound to keepe the whole law, as the Apostle reasoneth, *Gal.* 5.2. as all the festivities and other ordinances of Israel: and then he being incorporated by circumcision into the people of God, and so become a proselyte, would not have desired to returne to his people, as he doth, *Numb.* 10."[19] For Willet, Jethro's tentative affiliations with the people of Israel contributed to the construction of boundaries between religious communities determined by ritual and law. The absence of any mention of circumcision in the accounts of Jethro's interactions with Moses and the Israelites is key, for Willet. Jethro did not convert, for such a conversion would have meant a specifically Jewish conversion. Other readers, especially in the 1640s and 1650s, insist more firmly on Jethro's identity as a proselyte. The great English Hebraist John Lightfoot describes Jethro as "the first Proselyte to the Jewish Church," making this claim in the context of his discussion of the wise men whom Herod sent to seek out the Christ child in Matthew 2. For Lightfoot, Jethro's conversion serves to anticipate the conversion of these wise men, for they are both "*Arabian* . . . and of the seed of *Abraham*."[20] Jethro's status as a convert matters to Lightfoot specifically because it anticipates a second transformation, the culmination of the first, in the New Testament's announcement of Christ's birth. Other mid-seventeenth-century commentators, like Alexander Ross and Henry Hammond, also regard Jethro as a convert; in fact, Hammond further cites Jethro's conversion for proof of the Jewish practice of baptism as part of the conversion ritual, pointing to two sections of the Talmud, Tractate Gittin and Tractate K'rithoth.[21] When these later readers argue for Jethro's proselyte identity, his definitive turn to Israel's God, the matter does not rest there but becomes, instead, an adumbration of a further turn from Israel of the flesh to Israel of the spirit. If Jethro is to be understood as a convert, then he must also anticipate the conversion of the old covenant to the new, circumcision of the flesh to circumcision of the heart.

Throughout the early modern period, however, Jethro's name most frequently appears within discussions of legal institutions, systems of court hierarchies, and other judicial processes. Within this particular context, there are reasons for preserving Jethro's alien, Gentile status since, as a non-Israelite, but one who preserves within him the seed of Abraham (having descended from the Midianites and, more important, carrying with him the rudiments of the true faith), he can stand for the value of, and biblical precedent for, Gentile influence on Christian jurisprudential thought. He embodies the ancient divine truths dispersed throughout the peoples of the world—the *prisca sapientia*—now reconsolidated and refined in the Christian state. Whether, as a convert, Jethro adumbrates the dematerializing of circumcision or, as a non-convert, he plays the role of preserving general legal principles, his early modern legacy is one of abstraction, of a shift from the body (and its potential corruption) to the spirit. Much the same may be said of the other male biblical "convert," Naaman, to whom I now turn.

Naaman's Anti-Recusancy

Naaman's story is far more limited in scope than that of Jethro: a commander in the army of the king of Aram, or Syria, Naaman suffers from an apparently incurable case of leprosy. Upon the advice of one of his wife's maidservants, a captive from the land of Israel, and with the permission of his Aramean king, Naaman seeks the help of the Israelite prophet, Elisha. That the Israelite maidservant is a captive among the Syrians immediately reminds the reader of the ongoing state of war that exists between Israel and the king of Aram. These geo-political tensions serve as an essential frame for what ensues. Rather than go directly to Elisha, Naaman first approaches the king of Israel, who immediately suspects his request as a ploy: "Am I God, to kill and to make alive, that this man doth send unto me to recover a man of his leprosy? Wherefore consider, I pray you, and see how he seeketh a quarrel against me" (2 Kings 5.7). Elisha learns of this visit, however, and before Naaman can return home the prophet invites him for an audience. Naaman is dismayed by the unceremonious and (in his view) disrespectful reception he is given—Elisha does not even greet him personally, let alone lay hands on him to heal him—and he is even more miffed by Elisha's prescription, which is to bathe seven times in the Jordan River: "Are not Abana and Phrapar, rivers of Damascus, better than all the waters of Israel?" Naaman asks. "May I not wash in them, and be clean?" (5.12). Insisting on the superiority of Syrian waters, Naaman presents himself as the paradigmatic chauvinist-nationalist, a believer in the supremacy of his own people and his own land, jealous of his dignity and honor. Nevertheless, he is convinced by servants that he has little to lose in attempting Elisha's solution and, just as the reader expects, the moment Naaman completes the seventh bathing in the Jordan he emerges completely cured, "and his flesh came again like unto the flesh of a little child" (5.14). This vivid image of rebirth is completed when Naaman returns to Elisha and proclaims his new faith in the God of Israel: "Behold, now I know that there is no God in all the earth, but in Israel . . . for thy servant will henceforth offer neither burnt offering nor sacrifice unto other gods, but unto the Lord" (5.15, 17). Naaman, it would seem, has been born again into the community of believers in the God of Israel, leaving behind his earlier forms of worship.

But not quite. For Naaman quickly goes on to propose a caveat to his seemingly unqualified embrace of Israel's God: "When my master goeth into the house of Rimmon to worship there, and he leaneth on my hand, and I bow myself in the house of Rimmon: when I do bow down myself in the house of Rimmon, the Lord pardon thy servant in this thing" (5.18). That is, Naaman expects to remain in the service of the king of Aram—Israel's political and military antagonist!—and his service will require Naaman to continue to participate in the worship of Aram's gods, even if only as a show of loyalty to the king. More surprising than Naaman's request is that Elisha appears to accede to it—at least he does not immediately deny it with the sense of outrage we might have expected from an Israelite prophet who has otherwise been inveighing against Israel's idolatrous failings.

Did Naaman convert? Modern critics have called attention to the repetition of the Hebrew stem *sh'v'* in the story as a means of reinforcing the underlying theme of repentance and redemption. "As [Naaman's] flesh 'turned around' (וישב)," writes Robert Cohen, citing 2 Kings 5.14–15, "now Naaman the man 'turned around' (וישב) to face his healer."[22] There may be, in other words, a targeted reference to the concept of *return* in the Hebrew Bible that becomes, in Christian readings, a fiction of conversion. In the relatively few references to Naaman in rabbinic literature, he is usually praised for his celebration of God's power (less qualified than Jethro's relativistic assertion of God's might), but he is hardly cited as a model convert the way that Jethro sometimes is. Naaman obviously did not join the people of Israel. Not only did he return to his own people, he resumed his function as an officer in the very army that could attack Israel in the future. Nor did his pledge of loyalty to Israel's God come without mitigating conditions. He seems to have continued to function within the ceremonial context of Aram's worship even while insisting that he only believes in the God of Israel, which may account for the scant attention the rabbis paid to his story. Gerhard Von Rad has suggested that the two requests Naaman makes of Elisha—prior to inquiring about the permissibility of his continued attendance on his king during religious rituals, Naaman also asks to bring back to Syria two donkey-loads of soil from Canaan—represent the two extremes of a new convert's experience. On the one hand, Von Rad argues, Naaman seeks the insulation of the soil of the Holy Land, and by extension the God who presides over that land, to protect him from the onslaught of heathen influences he is likely to face. On the other hand, Naaman wonders whether his shift in belief really constitutes the significant change or turn in his life it first appears to be. Must I leave my people and my former life once I commit myself to Israel's God? Von Rad delights in Elisha's non-response: "Elisha dismisses the man. Indeed, one has the impression that he thrusts him out into the uncertainties of his future life without providing for him any moral or religiously detailed guidance at all. He leaves him completely to his new faith, or better, to God's hand which has sought and found him."[23] It is clear, I think, that Von Rad's characterization of Naaman's story depends heavily on a modern Protestant notion of conversion as the act of the individual, a choice whose implications are only really relevant in the relationship between the believer and his newly found God. Naaman serves, for Von Rad, as a prototype for Paul.

The narrative in 2 Kings is not so definitive in its depiction of what Naaman has done and what it means for his future as a proclaimer of God's power. It is true that his post-proclamation behavior becomes exemplary in contrast to the mercenary and deceptive actions of the Israelite Gehazi who, ignoring Elisha's explicit refusal of payment, seeks to enrich himself by preying on Naaman's newly expressed good will. But the denouement of this brief story and the transference of the leprosy from Naaman to Gehazi would appear to suggest that the narrative's primary concern is with the failings of Israelites like Gehazi and not the enlargement of God's people with "converts" like Naaman. Unlike Jethro, Naaman does not resurface again in the Hebrew Bible, nor, for that matter, do we read of any family that descends from him. He becomes a *marrano avant la lettre*, noteworthy for his disappearance rather than his continuing legacy.[24] The only subsequent biblical reference to his story occurs in the Gospel of Luke, where Naaman's example is cited as an instance of Jesus' wistful musing that no prophet is accepted in his own country: "Many lepers were in Israel in the time of Eliseus the prophet: and none of them was cleansed, saving Naaman the Syrian" (Luke 4.27). In this New Testament context, it would seem, Naaman has indeed come to stand far more explicitly for the figure of the alien who converts, or at least who is saved. And it makes sense that, of all the four gospels, this reference would appear only in Luke, the gospel most clearly addressed to a community of Gentile readers seeking a way to locate themselves in Jesus' "Jewish" story. You are like Naaman, Jesus appears to be saying to his Gentile audience, and like Naaman, you will be saved even if the Jews to whom I have first appeared are not.

Early modern references to Naaman's conversion are even less frequent than to Jethro's, attesting to the difficulty of imagining an ambiguous conversion in a positive light. The Geneva Bible's gloss sounds the recurrent theme of the faithful among the infidels and, further, "that the infidels esteem those who do good to their country." In "A Christening Sermon," a homily on 2 Kings 5, Thomas Fuller describes the Syrian general in terms reminiscent of the Geneva Bible's characterization of Jethro: "*Naaman*, though hee was a Prince, yet hee was but a Pagan; and in this respect, the lowest Hebrew was higher than hee; *Elisha* therefore would teach him to learne himself; that hee was not proper to receive so great favours, as being but a Goat, and no lost sheepe of the Fold of Israel."[25] The concern in both these texts is to use Naaman's story to reinforce national divisions and genealogical distinctions. A goat, not one of Israel's flock of sheep, Naaman remains outside the fold, a different species, even while declaring his faith to the God of Israel.

Some early modern readers, however, saw in Naaman a precedent for the fraught religious predicament facing English non-conformists. A version of the analogy I suggested above between Naaman's story and the "*Marrano* Condition" found its way into the serious—and occasionally life-threatening—controversy among English Catholics regarding the question of church papistry, the permissibility of attending Protestant church services. Gregory Martin includes an unusually extensive annotation to the Catholic Douay translation of 2 Kings 5 (called 4 Kings in the Catholic canon) in which he addresses this question directly, insisting that the biblical story differs from the contemporary situation in time, place, and person. Martin vehemently objects to those Catholics who cite Naaman's example as an "excuse" to allow them to "goe sometimes to Protestantes common prayers, or sermons," that is, to act as church-papists. In Naaman's time, unlike early seventeenth-century England, the Gospel had not yet been promulgated "neither al Articles of faith were so expressly taught, nor the external profession thereof so strictly commaned." In Syria, Naaman's attendance at the temple of Rimmon could not be viewed as a scandal by its inhabitants, since no other Syrians had professed the true religion; "but in a christian countrie, where al beare the name of Christians, especially where men are at controuersie about the true Christian religion, al that frequent, or repaire to the same assemblies, for publique seruice of God, are reputed to be of the same religion, or els dissemblers." And finally, according to Martin, Naaman's refusal to attend his king at the temple of Rimmon, and to bow in during the service, would have been taken as a sign of disloyalty to the king rather than a refraining from religion. In England, on the other hand, "those who refuse" to participate in Protestant services "can not be iudged disloyal, because it is sufficiently knowne, that Catholiques refuse of mere conscience" and not out of disloyalty to the crown. Martin concludes, "Personal presence at heretical seruice in England

[is] a distinctive signe of conformity to heresies."[26] Even though he is regarded as an early proselyte, therefore, Naaman cannot serve in any paradigmatic or exemplary fashion precisely because the boundaries his biblical attestation of fidelity may have helped to construct are under threat of dissolution amidst the confessional conflicts in early modern England.

But the Douay Bible was not the only English Catholic voice to speak to the validity of recusancy and the value of Naaman's example. Naaman's name appears repeatedly in the internal Catholic disputes over recusancy and conformity, with those advocating some form of church-papistry citing his example affirmatively and those opposing any kind of conformity that denied the authentic witness of Catholic truth, differentiating Naaman's case from that of the English Catholic.[27] Some thirty years after the publication of the Douay Old Testament, an anonymous priest published the treatise, "A Safeguard from Shipwracke to a Prudent Catholike," advising fellow Catholics that they were permitted to attend Church of England services. As we saw in Chapter 1, English Catholics and their critics were enmeshed in a complex set of arguments concerning authentic religious expression, interiority and outward practice, counterfeiting and non-conformity, all of which resonated profoundly with the experiences of Jewish converts, forced and otherwise, of the previous several centuries. In "A Safeguard from Shipwracke," however, the anonymous author looks to the story of Naaman to defend his position that Catholics are permitted to attend Protestant services to safeguard their lives and livelihoods, and prevent "the danger of death, losse of fortunes, ruine of posteritie and the like."[28] "For we contend that to goe to a Protestant Church, is by no law forbidden, but a thing indifferent, and by a good intention may be made really good without any dissembling. And they bring us an example of a thing, which in doing, many sinnes are committed: so that for the reasons which I have given, I conceive that the authoritie of the said renowned Doctors concludeth nothing against our assertion; unlesse the Protestants were an assembly of fallen heretiques, where there were danger of sinne by subversion or the like, which can never be proved."[29] What matters, for this writer, is less the physical location and disposition of the Catholic's body at church than his disembodied, abstracted "good intention." For both Naaman and the church papist, physical presence at doctrinally unacceptable worship is a "thing indifferent," insignificant because it is just the work of the body, not the heart or the mind. To invoke Naaman's precedent as evidence that Catholics ought to attend Protestant churches, however, could also be perceived as *minimizing* of religious difference, the blurring of boundaries between Israel and Syria, on the one hand, and Catholics and Protestants, on the other. As I have indicated, this Catholic text is no longer extant in its original version; we have it because it was reproduced by Daniel Featley, a Protestant divine, who published marginal animadversions, responses, to the Catholic priest, under the title *Vertumnus Romanus*. Featley's annotations to the priest's discussion of the example of Naaman are noteworthy, since on the practical question at issue, he and the priest are in agreement: they both insist that Catholics should attend Protestant church services. Featley, however, cannot allow the implication of the priest's argument, or of the claims made by earlier Catholic writers, to pass without comment. Concerned that a reader might entertain the possibility of an equivalence between the idolatry of the Temple of Rimmon and the worship in a Protestant Church, even if only to dismiss such an equivalence, Featley offers six different ways to understand the exchange between Naaman and Elisha, which either render Naaman's statement differently—it is a fault of the translation to see it as a request about the future; rather, Naaman is describing his earlier, pre-conversion, practices—or read Elisha's response as a dismissal of Naaman's request. Where the priest uses Naaman's example to minimize the Catholic's violation of core principles of belief when he goes to a Protestant church, Featley uses Naaman's story to reassert a bold boundary between his community of the faithful and those on the outside.

What alarms the priest more than doctrinal differences is the specter of pretense and equivocation, which he does not locate in Naaman's story, or Catholic recusants, but rather in a vaguely defined group practicing "pretended piety." He goes on to argue:

> But you will say: they [i.e., Catholics] deny their faith in this act [of attending a Protestant Church]. I deny that. They deny onely recusancie with an ill conscience, and not religion. Yet I grant that such Schismaticks professe no faith at all. And if there be any other opinion of men concerning them, it is malicious and pharisaical, generated by the craft and deceit of others, under the *species* of pretended piety, making people beleeve, that there is sinne and scandall in the act, when there is none; and if any Protestant thinketh otherwise of this; they have it from the erroneous customary opinion of some Catholiques revealing the same.[30]

In other words, any Protestant or Catholic who attends a church different from the one to which he adheres is not violating religious principles; those who would claim otherwise have no religious principles to violate. They are, rather, behaving "malicious[ly] and pharisaical." The intrusion of the age-old anti-Jewish canard in the priest's effort to reduce the creedal differences between Catholics and Protestants is no accident. Boundaries, it would seem, cannot be eliminated in one context without their reassertion in another. The invocation of Jewish alterity and mendacity in this context may further account for the absence of any explicit language of conversion in this reading of Naaman's story.

For all its provocative use of the figure of Naaman, however, the Catholic priest's discussion of the biblical story and Featley's marginal animadversions do not take up more than a few pages. Like Jethro, Naaman does not figure very prominently at all in early modern discourses of conversion. The case is altogether different in the next two examples I shall consider, Rahab and Ruth. That both these biblical figures are female, that they raise far more explicitly the specter of Jewish conversion, and that their interpreters are significantly more inclined to invoke typological readings of their stories, connect their stories and distinguish them from their male counterparts. In his lectures on Ruth, the Swiss reformer Ludwig Lavater implies difference between male and female converts, even as he speaks collectively of Jethro, Naaman, Rahab, and Ruth as Gentiles who enjoyed salvation in Christ: "God hath a care of the GENTILES, and also . . . hath hys chosen amongest them, as IETHRO, NAAMAN the SIRIAN . . . and the NINEVITES, &c, Not that we say that they were saued without Christ. Also he would haue RAHAB and RVTH ioyned to the seed of ABRAHAM, that the MESSIAS might be born of them in his appointed tyme."[31] Separating male biblical "converts" from female biblical "converts," Lavater focuses on the availability of salvation through Christ's intervention in the case of men like Jethro and Naaman, and adds almost as an afterthough a comment on the cross-pollination of Jew and Gentile in the cases of Rahab and Ruth, who "ioyned the seed of ABRAHAM." Whereas these male converts have been chosen by God for salvation, these female figures function exclusively as the physical means by which the salvation of Christ becomes available. The soteriological demands of Christ's incarnation are met in the bodies of the female convert.

Rahab: The Seed of Faith and the Cursed Stock

Camped on the eastern side of the Jordan River in Shittim, the Israelites prepare to enter the land of Canaan promised to them by God. As the second chapter of the book of Joshua recounts, Joshua sends two spies to explore the region of Jericho and presumably identify its military strengths and weaknesses. Their first stop on this mission is at the home of Rahab, a harlot (זונה, in Hebrew) living inside the city. Rahab goes to great lengths to hide these Israelite spies from the king of Jericho, who had gotten wind of their presence in his city. First, she stows them on her roof and covers them in flax; then she tells the king's men, who have come looking for them, that the Israelites have already left; and finally, she advises them to hide up in the hills for three days until the king's search for them ends and they can return safely to their camp. In exchange for her help—and the great risk she undertook in assisting them—Rahab has the men promise that when the Israelites succeed in conquering the city, they will save her and her family from destruction. She prefaces this request with her own statement about God's irresistible might. Rahab's righteous behavior contrasts with her status as a Canaanite (and potential enemy), but even more so with her problematic and threatening sexuality; indeed, the seemingly innocuous detail that Joshua sent the spies from Shittim takes on greater significance given its association with the corrupting sexuality as experienced by the Israelites in Numbers 25 (a point relevant to the story of Ruth, as well). The spies' choice of Rahab's home as an initial outpost on their reconnaissance mission seems clearly to be a function of her status as a harlot. As a harlot, she would have been situated in an easily accessible location and would likely have had access to information through gossip that other, more respectable residents of the city might not know. Rahab's transgressive sexuality is an essential element of her story.

The role Rahab's assistance plays in the conquest of Jericho, however, remains an open question. Perhaps one of the best known stories in the Bible, Joshua's capture and destruction of Jericho by circling it while sounding the horns seems to bear no relation to what the spies may or may not have learned during their time under the protection of Rahab. Still, Joshua keeps the spies' promise to Rahab, reminding his armies to spare her and her household in 6.17. And indeed, once the conquest is complete, the narrative repeats that Rahab and her family escaped destruction and, further, that "she dwelleth in Israel even unto this day" (6.25), suggesting that her initial avowal of belief in Israel's God was preliminary to a fuller integration into the people of Israel. Though this is the last time Rahab is mentioned in the Hebrew Bible, she does also figure in the New Testament. According to the lineage of Jesus offered at the beginning of the Gospel of Matthew, Rahab married Salmon and gave birth to Boaz.[32] Rahab, a woman who begins her story as part of a nation with whom the Israelites are specifically in conflict (in Deuteronomy 7.2–4, God warns the Israelites not to marry women from the seven nations occupying Canaan), not only gains admission into the Israelite community but comes to play a central role in the Davidic line. She is further cited among the exemplars of faith in Hebrews 12.31 and, perhaps in some tension with this Hebrews reading, the letter of James (famously dismissed by Luther as an "epistle of straw") celebrates Rahab for having been "justified by works, when she received the messengers, and had sent them out another way" (James 2.25).

Despite all these apparent celebrations of Rahab's goodness and her identification with the heritage of faith and/or works that preceded Christ's birth, there remains a lingering sense of the text's discomfort with her complete assimilation. Though Joshua orders that she and her family be saved, they do not immediately join the people: "And the young men that were spies went in, and brought out Rahab, and her father, and her mother, and her brethren, and all that she had; and they brought out all her kindred, *and left them without the camp of Israel*" (Josh. 6.23, emphasis added). If Rahab is portrayed as a convert to Israel's God, if her status as a Canaanite harlot is really meant to emphasize how dramatic her turning to God is, why does the text linger on this detail of her exclusion, even if it is only temporary? The assurance two verses later that she and her family continue to live among the Israelites to this day, in its very insistence, reveals a persistent anxiety, even xenophobia.[33] Even at this moment when the text insists that she and her family "dwelleth in Israel even unto this day," the reason it gives is not Rahab's faith in God, but rather "because she hid the messengers, which Joshua sent to spy out Jericho" (6.25). Rahab's union with the people of Israel is not without its own qualifications.

As with Jethro and Naaman, the exegetical traditions that developed around the figure of Rahab reflect some of these complexities. Josephus's first-century rewriting of Rahab's story reduced her role in the conquest of Jericho (playing up, instead, the work of the spies) and, more central to my concerns, minimized her expressions of belief in Israel's God. Rabbinic literature, by contrast, magnified Rahab's pre-conversion sinfulness and correspondingly celebrated her statement concerning God's power, comparing it favorably to Jethro's and Naaman's parallel statements (the midrash regarded Rahab's assertion as more absolute, less qualified). Early church fathers, such as Clement of Rome and Justin Martyr, appear to have drawn on these rabbinic traditions, but they supplemented them with typological interpretations of details, most notably the red cord Rahab used to identify her house to the invading Israelites (2.18), which came to signify Christ's blood and the means to salvation.[34] Augustine, however, was troubled by Rahab's deception of the king's men who came seeking the spies and sought ways to mitigate the importance, efficacy, and especially the necessity of her lying in his sermon *Contra Mendacio*.[35] The picture of Rahab that emerges from classical and medieval commentary appears ambivalent, inclined to a sympathetic reading but not without considerable qualifications.

For early modern interpreters of Rahab's story, these varying understandings of her significance came into more explicit contact with one another. Rahab was important as a mother, a carnal figure in the pre-history leading up to Christ. Through her marriage to Salmon and the child she bore to him, she contributed her Gentile blood to the body of Christ. As a genealogical ancestress to the Davidic line, Rahab also signaled the calling of the Gentiles. Thomas Bentley's comment is representative: "For after this, shee being a Gentile or Heathen, dwelt in Israel, and there was married to Salmon Prince of the tribe of Juda, and bare unto him a sonne called Booz, who after tooke to wife Ruth, the Moabitish woman another Gentile, of whom came Obed, Jesse, David, and so lineally Christ, and all to save both Jewes and Gentiles." Connecting Rahab to Ruth, Bentley not only reads their stories as versions of one another, he makes explicit the genealogical relationship they had. Yet Bentley also reads Rahab as exemplary of "the great mercie of God, that in so great and common a destruction, he would vouchsafe to draw such a miserable sinner as this Rahab the harlot was, voyd of all good works, onely by faith, to repent, and confesse his name, as shee did to both hers and others saluation for her sake."[36] Following the lead of the Letter to the Hebrews, Rahab becomes for Bentley a model of faith. She remains so seventy years later in William Gouge's particularly extensive account of Rahab, in which he marvels how Hebrews "giveth instance of a notorious sinner, which was *Rahab*, to provoke the worst to repent and believe. This is a strong enducement thereunto: for it the Faith of eminent persons, if the faith of weak women, if the faith of multitudes work not upon us, let us be ashamed to come short of one that was an *Harlot*."[37] In this account, the literal/historical (Rahab as lineal ancestor to Christ), the allegorical/typological (Rahab as foreshadowing the calling of the Gentiles), and the moral/tropological (Rahab as model for all repentant and redeemed sinners) converge in an especially pronounced fashion. In these convergences, particularly because the stakes are so high with respect to the ancestry of Christ and the displacement of the Jews (Israel of the flesh) by the Gentiles (Israel of the spirit), the tensions and conflicts between different modes of reading emerge.[38]

Though the weight of Gouge's commentary on Rahab reads her conversion as anticipating—and clearing the way for—the salvation of the Gentiles, Gouge also interprets Rahab's story as prefiguring the pre-millennial Jewish conversion. This expectation is no minor matter for Gouge who, among other things, contributed a signed epistle to and helped publish Henry Finch's *The Worlds Great Restauration. Or the Calling of the Ievves* (1621), an influential text in the burgeoning millennial excitement concerning the anticipated conversion of the Jews to Christianity.[39] Gouge returns to the theme of Jewish rejection and conversion in a sermon published in the midst of the English Civil Wars, where he undertakes a meticulous study of Paul's claims concerning the calling of the Jews in his letter to the Romans.[40] At the very peak of the debates about readmitting Jews to England in the early 1650s, Gouge invokes the example of Rahab, combining typology and historical induction explicitly to invert the status of Gentile and Jew. "The instance of Rahab giveth evidence that God had Gentiles among his people, and accounted members of the true Church," argues Gouge, and thus, despite the Jews having collectively rejected—and been rejected by—Christ, there remains the future expectation of the calling of the Jews (back) to favor. "Hereby the Lord sheweth himself to be no respecter of persons," Gouge writes. "The like he doth now concerning the recalling of the rejected Jews. (*Rom.* 11. 25, 26.) There ever have been since their rejection some Jews professing the Christian faith, *Rom.* 11. 1. &c. The promise which God made for calling the Gentiles, moved the Jews to entertain such Gentiles as came in to them, and to pray for others. The like ground have we to do the like duty on the behalf of Jews."[41]

Gouge uses Rahab's story of conversion to upend the relationship between Jew and Gentile. If, prior to Christ's coming, Jews enjoyed a privileged relationship with God to which only some Gentiles, like Rahab, were given access (in anticipation of the general calling of the Gentiles), with the advent of Christ, Gentiles have now assumed that privileged position and Rahab's story can serve to describe the few Jews who have not rejected Christ (so as to anticipate the more general calling of the Jews). Like many other so-called philo-Semites of the mid-seventeenth century, Gouge seems to be advocating a more tolerant and humane attitude toward his contemporary Jews. Yet it is clear from this and other statements like it that the tolerance of the Jew as outsider depends entirely on the Jew's willingness to forego his otherness through conversion. The theological supersession of Judaism by Christianity has the further effect of erasing the alterity of the Jew, not by admitting him into the community of believers, as conversion is presumed to function, but rather by interpreting him out of existence. The paradox of this reasoning arises in the contradiction between the central insistence on Rahab's lineal, genealogical role in the birth of Christ (even as she "was of the cursed Stock of the *Canaanites*") and the subsequent erasure of that genealogy's value. The paradox finds one of its most succinct expressions in Gouge's phrase, "the seed of Faith."[42] Describing Rahab's fate as a proselyte, Gouge observes, "she and hers dwelt for ever among the *Israelites*: so as true Converts, though strangers, after good proof, are to be accounted as those who are born in the Church."[43] Even as Gouge celebrates her full acceptance among God's people through her expression of faith, he cannot escape the language of nativity, of being *born* into the Church.

As Gouge's phrase, "after good proof," implies, Rahab's story also becomes for him an occasion to consider the inevitable tensions that could arise between one's religious loyalties and one's political or national loyalties. Having noted that Rahab "preferred Gods Church before her own Country," Gouge reads Rahab's story morally (as well as typologically) in order to show "wherein ones Country is to be preferred, and wherein the Church." In cases that he characterizes as "Civill affaires," "In differences betwixt his own Country and another of the true Religion, about their Rites of Titles in secular matters, and priviledges," and "In secret differences betwixt his Country, and the other of the true Religion, where the cause is not openly known, by the common subjects," Gouge concludes, an individual is "bound to prefer his own Country before the other." Conversely, a person must favor his allegiance to his faith in the following instances: "When there is speciall warrant, either by inward divine instinct (which Rahab had) or by express command," "When ones Country is by God devoted to destruction," "When some members of ones Country are to be punished for intolerable impiety," "When ones Country seeks the ruin of the Church meerly for Religion sake," and "When there is such deadly fewd betwixt ones Country and the Church, as they cannot both stand together." Citing Jesus' pronouncement in Luke (14.26) that a man must be prepared to despise his own father and mother, Gouge concludes, "We are therefore in the foresaid cases to pull out the bowells of natural affection, and in the cause of God to prefer him before all.[44] Writing in the midst of the intense political and religious conflicts of the English Civil Wars, Gouge's discussion of these matters would have been far more than an intellectual exercise, having immediate practical implications for his audience, whatever their confessional loyalties might have been. As Gouge's language suggests, these accounts of conversion elicit a profound conflict between modes of identity that depend on nation, community, and ethos—"the bowels of natural affection"—and religious conviction, a conflict that does not always favor the universalizing impulse of Pauline Christianity wherein there is "neither Jew nor Greek . . . bond nor free . . . male nor female" (Gal. 3.28). This is a conflict that becomes even more pronounced in the far more extensive discussions of Ruth the Moabite.

Ruth the Moabite

Though the book that bears her name covers a mere four chapters, the story of Ruth extends its biblical reach by virtue of implicit and explicit references to a range of scriptural passages. The plight of Ruth the Moabite during the time of the judges and her redemption by—and marriage to—Boaz, a prominent member of the tribe of Judah, is structurally linked to two earlier biblical tales that depict the seductions of male heads of household by women who find themselves in apparently hopeless and powerless situations: the account of the daughters of Lot and their father that follows the destruction of Sodom and Gemorrah (Gen. 19.30–38) and the story of Tamar's deception of her father-in-law, Judah, who is unwilling to marry his younger son to Tamar after the death of his two older sons (Gen. 38).

The link is not only a thematic one, but also a genealogical one. The product of the union of Lot with one of his daughters is Moab, from whom Ruth descends. The product of the union of Judah and Tamar is Peretz, from whom Boaz descends. Childless, widowed, and transplanted within the people of Israel, Ruth repeats the actions of her biblical predecessors, submitting herself and her body to the will of Boaz, to obtain justice in the form of the levirate marriage to which her mother-in-law, Naomi, believes she is entitled. Ruth's story may be said to redeem those of Lot's daughters and of Tamar, though, for Ruth's sexually provocative, nighttime visit to Boaz results in his immediate assumption of responsibility, providing him with the opportunity to enact the צדקה, the righteousness, that could only be extracted from Judah by means of a painful and humiliating plot. Unlike Lot's daughters, Ruth does not have to ply Lot's narrative counterpart, Boaz, with wine to convince him to fulfill his duty to her. Unlike Tamar, Ruth immediately earns the respect of Judah's descendent; she does not have to go through the shame of public confrontation and denunciation; she is, instead, willingly espoused by Boaz. Ruth's offspring is not like Peretz, the son of Judah and Tamar (whose name means "breach"), but is the subdued Obed (whose name suggests servitude and duty). Having effected this redemption, the union of Ruth and Boaz produces the line that directly leads to David, God's anointed king and, for Christian readers, the progenitor of the human line that will lead to the birth of Jesus.

Ruth's story connects not only to these two patriarchal narratives from the book of Genesis. Her status as a Moabite woman also links her to the sordid tale of Balak and Balaam in Numbers 22–25, which culminates in the direct biblical connection between Moabite women and sexual licentiousness: "And Israel abode in Shittim, and the people began to commit harlotry with the daughters of Moab." Indeed, in Deuteronomy 23.4–8, where the Israelites are commanded, "An Ammonite or a Moabite shall not enter into the assembly of the Lord; even to the tenth generation shall none of them enter into the assembly of the Lord for ever," one of the primary reasons given for the permanent exclusion of the Moabites from the Israelite community is their role in the Balak and Balaam story and their corruption of the people. That Ruth descends from these very same Moabites (who were descendants of the incestuous encounter between Lot and his daughter), and that she achieves her entrance into the Israelite community through the very actions that had previously been regarded as so menacing, first through her marriage to Naomi's son and then through her midnight visit to Boaz, cannot but be read as a pointed revision—perhaps even an abrogation—of the earlier biblical restriction against any contact between Moabites and Israelites. Indeed, it might even be said that Ruth's alien identity—her extreme difference from Boaz and his people—staves off the contaminating threat of incest that haunts both the story of Lot's daughters and the story of Tamar and Judah.

In breaking down these clearly delineated boundaries between communities, the story of Ruth has been read by both ancient and modern readers alike as a universalizing lesson, a narrative that refuses to respect the divisions between nations and peoples, favoring instead the religious bonds between people who share a common faith. The frequent occurrence of the Hebrew stem *sh' v'* in the Ruth story (it appears more than ten times in the first chapter alone), the term that would come to stand for conversion in later translations,[45] seems to anticipate the application of a conversionary framework to the story. Classical rabbinic commentaries constructed Ruth to be among the first converts, deriving many of the laws associated with the conversion process from her story.[46] The early church fathers regarded Ruth as exemplary for her embrace of the true faith, a view that found later expression in many of the sermons and biblical commentaries of the early modern period, Protestant and Catholic, Anglican and Puritan, Presbyterian and Non-Conformist. Ruth's famous words to Naomi at the conclusion of chapter 1, "Whither thou goest, I will go; and where thou lodgest, I will lodge; thy people shall be my people, and thy God my God," seem, momentarily at least, to gesture to a community undivided by differences of national or ethnic origin, let alone doctrinal disputes.

Such universalizing readings, however, account for only one side of Ruth's story. As I observed in the examples of Jethro, Naaman, and Rahab, a foreigner's status as such, especially when that foreignness is characterized directly as antagonistic to Israel, makes his or her choice to join the Israelites particularly meaningful. Bonnie Honig has demonstrated how Ruth's commitment to Israel and its God becomes more profound and meaningful in direct proportion to the extremity of her otherness and the depth of enmity between Moab and Israel. The most powerful testimony to Israel's worth is the testimony provided by the most unlikely person, she who comes from the most hostile culture. Were it possible to cleanse Ruth of her foreign identity, the price of such cleansing would be the very gift of validation she has to offer.[47] This is an aspect of Ruth's story—the possibility of transforming the most base to the most pure—that had special appeal to many early modern readers, and I return to it below. As Ruth's celebrated pronouncement to Naomi makes clear, nations, gods, and lands are necessarily linked; as was the case with Rahab, the shift of allegiances that defines her so-called conversion happens amidst acts of war and conquest, clashes between peoples over land—the period of the judges is nothing but a succession of geo-political conflicts. The "conversions" of Rahab and Ruth, if they can be called that at all, are hardly functions of the "universal" nature of the Israelite religion. Rather, they are precisely matters of national or ethnic distinctiveness. Rahab's profession of faith comes with a parallel declaration of enmity toward her nation of origin. She is fully aware of the battle to come that will lead to the destruction of Jericho and specifically requests that Joshua preserve her and her immediate family. Ruth embraces the Israelite God along with the Israelite nation and the Israelite land. Her decision to return to Judah with her mother-in-law does not appear to be a function of any prophetic characterization of Israel as a light unto the nations or even in anticipation that the nations will one day recognize the God of Israel as the one God. It is a function, instead, of her localized, personal commitment to Naomi. This commitment then turns into a dedication to Naomi's nation and God.

The importance of these national divisions comes into special relief if we contrast the "conversions" of Rahab and Ruth with those of Jethro and Naaman (whose very name, it will be recalled, means "faithful"). Jethro, as we saw, never completely integrated into the Israelite community, maintaining a separate, if quite ambiguous, existence on its margins. And Naaman's profession of faith in 2 Kings 5.15 is nothing but a ritual confession, one that comes to serve as a model for the testimonies of faith sprinkled throughout the Gospel narratives and the Acts of the Apostle, but not for any expectation of the dissolution of national boundaries. Jethro's and Naaman's turns to the Israelite God do not entail the crossing of national and ethnic difference. Rahab's and Ruth's transitions give these crossings special prominence.

Nowhere is the persistent tension between foreignness and integration more evident than in the final chapter of Ruth. Ruth's desire to find a place for herself in the Israelite religion is only fully achieved by her entering an Israelite family through the highly regulated mode of the levirate marriage. Her "conversion" is not completed in chapter 1 by her passionate speech to Naomi; rather, it is consummated when she is redeemed through the social, civil, legal, and marital institutions distinctively endemic to Israelite religion. Boaz's dispassionate articulation of the law of levirate marriage in 4.10 marks the formal entrance of Ruth the Moabite into the community of Israel. The ideological function these laws serve in foregrounding the particularity of Ruth's entrance into the community is made even more striking when we recognize that neither the institution of the levirate marriage nor the command to redeem the land of a dead kinsman as they are described in the Pentateuch technically apply to the specific situation in the book of Ruth. First, a levirate marriage is commanded only on the brother of a deceased husband who has left his wife childless and only when that brother lives in the same household: "If brethren dwell together, and one of them die, and have no child, the wife of the dead shall not marry without unto a stranger: her husband's brother shall go in unto her, and take her to him to wife, and perform the duty of a husband's brother unto her" (Deut. 25.5). Neither the unnamed kinsman nor Boaz is Machlon's brother, and neither of them lives in the same household as Ruth and Naomi. Indeed, the very strong language that posits the institution of the levirate marriage as a resistance to the intrusion of otherness, the "stranger" (איש זר in Hebrew), would seem to raise the question of whether Ruth is eligible for a levirate marriage.[48] Second, in Ruth 4.5, Boaz makes an explicit legal connection between the inheritance of Elimelech's fields and the levirate obligation to Ruth, arguing that if the more immediate kinsman wishes to redeem the lands, he must also marry Ruth. This is a connection that is not found in the Pentateuch's articulation of the inheritance laws and the laws of levirate marriage.[49]

The apparent contradiction between the prohibition against a Moabite entering the community of Israel and the story of Ruth (and especially her placement in David's ancestry) gave rise to one of the most extreme instances of the rabbinic reversal of biblical law. The Talmud imagines Doeg the Edomite, a supporter of Saul, making an extra-textual challenge to David's anointing by citing the biblical prohibition against Moabites: "Before you ask [David] whether he is fit for kingship ort not, ask him whether he is fit to marry into the congregation or not." The irony of Doeg's Edomite origins would surely not have been lost on the rabbis as they put this objection into his mouth. But the rabbis also imagine an immediate response, one they put into the mouth of Saul's general, Abner: "[When the Torah prohibits an] Ammonite, it does not [prohibit] an Ammonitess, [when it prohibits a] Moabite, it does not [prohibit] a Moabitess" [עמוני ולא עמונית מואבי ולא מואבית].[50] The rabbis appear to have sensed the insufficiency—even the counter-intuitiveness—of this response, for they allow Doeg a further challenge, one that expresses the apparent absurdity of this distinction. And Doeg's challenge finds no answer. David's supporters are dumbfounded and the very legitimacy of his claim to the kingship of Israel looks to be in jeopardy until another of David's supporters draws his sword on Doeg and threatens, "Whoever does not accept this ruling [הלכה] shall be impaled by the sword. Thus have I received it from the law court of Samuel of Ramah: [the prohibition is against] an Ammonite and not an Ammonitess, against a Moabite and not a Moabitess." The sword settles the matter, inasmuch as it defends a revision that now appears to have divine sanction (as it was transmitted prophetically to Samuel). But this extraordinary aggadic supplement betrays the anxiety about Ruth's role that informs the biblical narrative, too.

Hardly a universally applicable process of transformation, then, Ruth's "conversion" demands one specific exception after another. The book of Ruth had to revise extremely specific marital and property laws so as to provide some structural way to bring the stranger into the fold. Her own act of volition, as moving as it is, seems not to have been sufficient. When she does or says anything, Ruth is, throughout the book, "Ruth the Moabite." And once Boaz redeems Ruth by marrying her, she virtually disappears from the book. The narrative ends not by celebrating the acceptance of Ruth, but the homecoming and reintegration of Naomi, for whom Ruth is said to have borne a son. Ruth becomes a reproductive machine, a body that bears a child; rather than enjoying the blessings of Rachel and Leah, to whom she is explicitly compared by the town elders in 4.11, she becomes more like Bilhah and Zilpah, the handmaids used by these matriarchs as surrogate mothers to produce the sons they felt obliged to bear in their desperate competition with one another. The very comparison lays bare its inadequacy. Ruth, our quintessential convert, is elided, overlooked, diminished. Rahab's story, though not as fleshed out, projects a similar set of concerns and it is significant that she, too, disappears from the Hebrew Bible after the fall of Jericho, only to reappear when she is placed in the Matthean genealogy of Jesus. The convert from outside—the national and ethnic other—is never fully acknowledged as a member of the community.

The "conversion" of Ruth can be said to pull in two different directions, on the one hand offering a vision of a universal, catholic community, undivided by national or ethnic differences, on the other hand reinscribing the very national, ethnic, and religious particularities it seemingly erases. These were features of Ruth to which ancient and medieval readers were sensitive. Early Christian commentaries on the book of Ruth included discussions of particular historical details (chronological placement, geographic peculiarities, etc.); moral and pragmatic lessons to be derived (the importance of faith and loyalty); and allegorical readings that depict Ruth as a type of the church (adumbrating the salvation of the Gentiles).[51] Each kind of reading tended to emphasize a different feature of Ruth's story, pointing to its universality or its particularity. Yet the medieval four-fold exegetical method managed mostly to sustain and coordinate these multiple readings in ways that kept them distinct, thereby minimizing the potential tensions (and even contradictions) among them. This is not to say that medieval Christian commentary was free of conflicting interpretations; nevertheless, one does not find a commentary that combines in the same discussion a detailed explication of the historical and genealogical importance of Ruth's story vis-à-vis the birth of Christ with an allegorical reading of Ruth as the Gentile Church (let alone as an anticipation of the recovery of the Jew's synagogue). This range of readings, when it appears in a single commentary, is presented sequentially, in clearly distinct discussions hygienically kept apart to avoid any hermeneutical contamination.[52] Such careful exegetical organization is homologous to what Kathleen Biddick has described as the medieval fabrication of "contemporary Jews as the first ethnographic 'primitives,' since . . . medieval mapping practices denied coevalness to Jews. . . . There is a persistent and systematic tendency to place Jews in a time other than the supersessionary present of Christendom." That is, just as the literal, typological, moral, and anagogical readings of a text remain distinct, even as they overlay or supersede one another, so too medieval Christianity posits a sequential succession to its relationship with Judaism.[53] A purity of interpretive discourse is aligned with a purity of religious identity.

Though clearly a product of these medieval hermeneutics, the rise of early modern humanist approaches to biblical study and the integration of these new methodologies into Reformation reading practices (which also commonly entailed the rejection of the four-fold method)[54] coincided with a shift in the construction of Christianity's relationship to Judaism. While the impulse to cast Jews as antique relics never entirely disappeared, this view increasingly came into conflict with developing notions of Jewish contemporaneity. It may no longer be possible to accept the stark demarcation that used to divide medieval from renaissance, pre-modern from early modern in older historiography, but to deny a process of changes and shifts—however complex, interrupted, contradictory, or even recursive they might have been—is tantamount to eliding historical difference, and homologous to a notably Christian, universal ahistoricism to which the Jew posed a particularized challenge. Jews served as more than simply timeless hermeneutic ciphers or textual custodians. They were also sources of living knowledge; as I argued above, in Chapter 1, some English Protestants like Henry Ainsworth spent significant portions of their lives in close proximity to, and learning from, the Jews of Amsterdam. Ainsworth, and other English scholars such as Hugh Broughton, Matthew Slade, and John Paget, drew heavily on Jewish scholarship in their own biblical commentaries, nowhere more so than in their writings on Jewish conversion. The possibility and expectation of Jewish conversion expressed by early modern English Protestants gave Jews a contemporary reality and immediacy that they had not had since their expulsion from England in 1290. The sermons and commentaries on Ruth and her conversion manifest an anxious tension between the universalizing impulse that erases ethnic and national differences and the particularizing drive to preserve and evaluate these differences. As a mode of reading biblical texts, typology reflected a parallel convergence of the temporal flattening built into its supersessionary model and the acknowledgment of the integrity of historical events in their particularities. Unlike medieval allegory (or typology, as the two were mostly indistinguishable for much of the early history of biblical interpretation), which mined the Old Testament for symbolic representations—mimesis—of Christian truth, early modern typology affirmed the historical reality of the event that was also said to adumbrate (and be fulfilled by) its antitype. Just as early modern encounters with Jews recovered their contemporaneity even as they sought to convert them, so too typology recovered the Old Testament's historicity while at the same time working to transform—and fulfill—it in the Christian truth it anticipated.[55] These typological tensions were especially pronounced in renderings of a female convert like Ruth, whose body so intimately and unavoidably rooted Christian soteriology within a discourse of nation and people, participating in what Kim Hall has called a "narrative of alien culture."[56] Ruth's status as a sexually available woman—and her potentially aggressive sexuality in her approach of Boaz—played a critical role in her conversion and, as such, could not simply be ignored. Typology's fraught synthesis of the literal and the figurative did not always or necessarily result in contradictions, but in the case of Ruth (and Rahab, as well), the female body becomes the site of just such a contradiction.

Typology, Coverture, and Conversion

The Geneva Bible's headnote to the book of Ruth served as the touchstone for most subsequent English Protestant readings. It prefaces the text with an explanation of the book's eponymous character:

> This book is instituted after the name of Ruth: which is the principall person spoken of in this treatise. Wherein also figuratively is set forth the state of the Church which is subject to manifold afflictions, and yet at length God giveth good and ioyfull issue: teaching vs to abide with pacience till God deliuer vs out of troubles. Herein also is described howe Iesus Christ, who according to the flesh ought to come from Dauid, proceeded of Ruth, of whom the Lorde Iesus did vouchsaue to come, notwithstanding shee was a Moabite of base condition, and a stranger from the people of God: declaring unto vs thereby that the Gentiles should be sanctified by him, and ioyned with his people, and that there should be but one sheepefolde, and one shepeheard. And it seemeth that this historie appertaineth to the time of the Iudges.

Conflating the supersession of typology and the stubborn particularities of history, the headnote reads Ruth both as a figure for the Church and as a material and maternal ancestor of Christ. Note how the gloss grapples with the paradox of the human ancestry of Jesus, who is also, of course, the Son of God: "Jesus Christ, who according to the flesh *ought* to come from David" (emphasis added). Yet even this historicizing component occasions a further typology in which Ruth's status as a Moabite prefigures the inclusion of the Gentiles in the salvation made possible through Christ. Typology's hermeneutical effect here, and more generally in the conversion of the Hebrew Bible to the Old Testament, is to elide material Israelite/Jewish history. Even as it acknowledges how typology might be unsettled by the counternarrative of history, Edward Topsell's observation toward the end of his 1596 commentary on Ruth is a succinct account of how this hermeneutical method works: "the summe, drift, and scope of the Scripture, dependeth vpon Christ . . . because all the godlike that are named therein, were eyther his Fathers according to the flesh, or else the singular types prefiguring his person."[57] Even when Reformation readers seem to be reading the Hebrew Scriptures for historical information, these readings regard the material world, past and present, as a mere shadow of the Christian truths they anticipate. Nearly a century after the Geneva Bible's first publication, Thomas Fuller echoes the headnote's language. Fuller comments that "the conversion of Ruth the Moabitesse . . . typifie[s] the calling of the Gentiles, that as he took of the blood of a Gentile into his body, so he should shed the blood out of his body for the Gentiles, that there might be one Shepheard, and one Sheepfold."[58] By extending the Geneva Bible's summary to speak directly about the process of conversion, Fuller succinctly encapsulates the paradox of Christian soteriology: Christ's incarnation demands the mixing of the material essence—the blood—of Jew and Gentile; yet when he sheds that blood on the cross, thereby effecting universal salvation for all, those corporal differences, indeed bodies in general, collapse into the universal, undifferentiated Sheepfold. When a figure like Ruth conforms to both possibilities in Topsell's "eyther . . . or . . ." description, that is, when Ruth is seen as an ancestor "according to the flesh" and as a "singular type . . . prefiguring [Christ's] person," the alignment of the typological and the historical is both more satisfying and more unsettling.

Ruth serves as a type for the conversion of the Gentiles in many early modern commentaries. The twenty-eight German sermons of Swiss reformer Ludwig Lavater, which were translated by the great heresiologist Ephraim

Pagitt (at the ripe age of eleven!) and published in English in 1586, assert that "in that Rvth denied her countrie religion, and embraced the Israelites religion, the vocation of the Gentiles is prefigured, who leauing their superstitions, turned to the God of Israel."[59] Topsell's lectures on the book of Ruth follow the lead of the Geneva Bible: "Againe, in this history, there is deliuered vnto vs, the hope which the fathers had concerning the calling of the Gentiles, for this mariage of Ruth into the kindred of Christ, who was a Gentile, & by nature none of the people of God, did plainely foretell that the Gentiles shoulde be called in Christ, for as hee tooke parte of his humane nature of them, so he shewed vs that hee would giue the same for them, that there might be no difference in his bodye, between Iewes & gentiles, but that the power of his death, the graces of the spirite, and the knowledge of redemption might redounde to all."[60] Christ's body, understood as a material phenomenon, becomes typologically disembodied in the undifferentiated synthesis of Jew and Gentile. The promise of the Book of Ruth in these accounts thus becomes universally applicable in the same way that Ruth's expression of faith serves to erase the national and ethnic boundaries that divide Israel from Moab. Ruth resolves the troubling tensions between homogeneity and heterogeneity in these visions of a universal, Christian salvation grounded in the promise to Israel now available to all. On the one hand, her story redeems the story of Lot's daughters, which thematizes the problem of homogeneity and endogamy in terms of incest, by functioning as the paradigmatic exogamous wife. The Geneva Bible's gloss on Genesis 19.37 observes that the Moabites, "as they were borne in moste horrible incest, so were they and their posteritie vile and wicked." Their posterity, that is, until Ruth. On the other hand, Ruth's integration into the Jewish body maintained a necessary integrity for the purposes of transmitting the promise of salvation. Noting the anomalous presence of Ruth (along with Tamar, Bathsheba, and Rahab) in a lineage that otherwise listed only men, the Geneva gloss argues, "Albeit the Iewes nomber their kinred by the malekind: yet this linage of Marie is comprehended vnder the same, because she was married to a man of her owne stocke & tribe." That Tamar, Rahab, and Ruth (and possibly even Bathsheba) precisely did not marry men of their "owne stocke & tribe" makes this comment especially remarkable for its reassertion of a national/ethnic integrity by virtue of its typological elision of these historical counter-examples.

In his commentary *Ruth's Recompense* (1628), Richard Bernard places special stress on the power of Ruth's faith to break down the boundaries between nations:

> Religion and grace maketh such as be of seuerall nations, to loue one another; to loue forrainers being religious, better then friends, kindred and old acquaintances not religious. Ruth is in loue with Naomi a Iew, and esteemeth not of Orpha her countrey woman; for indeed, Religion maketh a more sure coniunction, in a more blessed kindred then nature, hauing God for our Father, the Church for out Mother, the Saints for our Brethren, the Spirit of God for the bond of our vnion, which maketh vs to desire to liue and die together. . . . The same Spirit that vniteth the heart of one godly person to another, vnitheth the same to all the rest, as being together members of Christs mysticall body.[61]

Bernard argues that religion replaces nature by offering a new bloodline, a new family. In this typological model that informs the conversionary process, faith supersedes nature and ethnic origin, folding the believer into the mystical body of Christ and the Church. Topsell's account of Ruth's integration into "the kindred of Christ" and Bernard's celebration of the "loue of forrainers being religious" recollect *The Merchant of Venice* (first performed in the same year that Topsell's sermons were published), where Jessica describes her pending elopement with Lorenzo:

> Alack, what heinous sin is it in me
> To be ashamed to be my father's child!
> But though I am a daughter to his blood,
> I am not to his manners. O Lorenzo,
> If thou keep promise, I shall end this strife,
> Become a Christian and thy loving wife.
> (II.iii.15–20)

The early modern discourse of Christian conversion depends upon the language of mystical incorporation and disembodiment, in which the idea of universal salvation seems to refuse ethnicity as a category of identity. Given the central importance of property and inheritance to both Ruth's and Jessica's stories, it is helpful to invoke the legal principle of couverture, the common law doctrine whereby a woman's legal and property rights were subsumed first by her father and then, upon marriage, by her husband. Portia explicitly invokes this doctrine when she hands over all that she owns to Bassanio upon his successful choice of the leaden casket. Ruth and Jessica become *femmes couvertes* with respect to their religious and ethnic identities, and not simply with respect to their financial and legal standing. This couverture, the erasure of their individual, embodied subjectivities, is achieved simultaneously by their marriage to their husbands, and by their conversion to Christ. Their status as women enmeshed in a range of economic as well as religious exchanges is not secondary to the fictions of conversion into which they are written, but rather an elemental component of them.[62] Fuller makes this convergence of religious conversion and the erasure of femininity an explicit conclusion of his discussion of Ruth, contrasting "women so strangely disguised with phantastick fashions" whose transgressive sexuality and wearing of "Man-like Clothes and shorne Haire" proves them "to be very Monsters," with "worthy Ruth taking upon her, not the Clothes, but the Courage; not the Haire, but the Heart; not the Attire, but the Resolution of a Man, yea, and more then of a Man."[63] It is difficult not to think of this contrast in relation to the common practices of early modern theater and especially to the cross-dressing Jessica undertakes to facilitate her escape from her father's house (she explicitly remarks on the embarrassment she feels in appearing before Lorenzo dressed in boy's clothes in language that parallels her embarrassment at being her Jewish father's daughter). Mary Janell Metzger has argued that for Jessica, becoming one with the body of Christ requires not only her marriage to a Christian but also the conversion of her body in distinctly racial and gendered terms.[64] Fuller's contrast of "women so strangely disguised" with Ruth's becoming "more than a man" shows that this conversion of the female alien body (Moabite, in Ruth's case, Jewish, in Jessica's) is really an erasure of that body through its complete transcendence. The paradox of such erasure, of course, is that it is itself an effect of the historical, economic, and social realities of early modernity.[65] Bernard observes that shared beliefs "maketh vs to desire to liue and die together," that is, to constitute a specific national, political entity. Even within the supersessionary and universalizing model, Bernard takes notice of the persistence of Ruth's identity as a Moabite in the narrative: "Yet note how the holy Ghost, in naming *Ruth*, omitteth not to shew againe her Countrey, and that shee was a Moabitesse, and not an Israelitesse by birth, and but daughter in law to *Naomi*, yet she came with her to Bethlehem, and that in safety."[66] The transcendence or supersession of difference within Christ's mystical body remains incomplete—indeed it cannot be completed by the very logic of Christ's salvation—because Ruth's Moabite origins are crucial to the salvific promise to which she gives her name and body.

Particularizing, Property, and Mutability

For all their universalizing power, therefore, there remains in these fictions of conversion an anti-typological impulse, one that brings the materiality of lived history into relief. If Bernard takes delight in how Ruth's story shows that "religion and grace maketh such as be of seuerall nations, to loue one another," they nevertheless remain of several nations. These national particularities surface repeatedly in the commentaries and sermons on Ruth. The tension between history and typology finds early expression in Lavater's translated sermons, where he insists, "But here is a bad errour whiche wee shoulde confute in many wordes. Some doe make Boaz a figure of the Messias and Ruth of the Church the spouse of the Messias. I doe not denie but that hee with his spouse is diuersly figured in the scriptures, but I had rather follow the simple and literall meaning of the place &c. They which doe delight in allegories let them seek them elsewhere."[67] Lavater explicitly argues for the resistance to an abstract, ahistorical understanding of the details of Ruth's story. One reason for sending readers elsewhere to find pleasure in allegories is the persistent awareness of the extensive ceremonial, marital, and property laws that make up much of the final chapter of Ruth. While I have not found any early modern commentaries that take note of the book's extraordinary application of the Pentateuch's regulations concerning levirate marriage and inheritance to which I alluded earlier, neither have I found any commentators from the period who seek to allegorize these laws, nor, as is often the case in many Protestant discussions of Jewish ceremonial law, do they dismiss the detailed accounts of these procedures as archaic, irrelevant, or superseded by the advent of Christianity's new dispensation.[68] Topsell and Bernard, for example, offer prolonged discussions of the levirate ceremony and the redemption of Elimelech's land, adducing extensive lessons concerning the contemporary English laws of real estate purchase, inheritance, the need for the witnessing of certain commercial, marital, and real estate transactions, and more. Topsell writes, "The vse of this doctrine is to teach and instruct vs, first what dutie we owe to the Magistrates, who haue greater care and charge ouer vs for the peace and of our Countrie, and publike welfare, then Parents for our maintenance, and priuate obedience . . . whereby wee may iustly complaine of the slacknesse of our vnhappy age, wherein men murmur and grudge at any charge which ariseth for our Prince, but especially that there are so few, which in all their liues haue prayed for Prince or Magistrate."[69] Just as in the biblical account these laws function to assert an ethnic specificity, so too in the early modern commentaries these laws occasion extensive discussions of property laws that are largely constitutive of national definitions. Indeed, as Topsell's final observation suggests, Ruth's story also occasioned polemics about contemporary politics and religious divisions.

The permanence of real property constituted an antidote or counterweight to another, unsettling feature of the book of Ruth. Early modern English readers took special interest in the moment that separated Ruth from her sister-in-law Orpah. Both were faced with the same choice, and Naomi explicitly urged them both not to follow her, yet one elected to return to her home in Moab while the other joined Naomi. This was a scene that prompted extensive discussion in sermons and commentaries, revealing anxieties about mutability and potentially fakery in the conversion process. Topsell remarks on Orpah's tears and brief hesitation before leaving Naomi: "Euen so hypocrites may forsake the worlde and their friendes, ioyne themselues to God and his people, trauaile and profite in Religion towardes the heauenly Ierusalem, bee readie to weepe with them that weepe, and lament with them that lament: and in any good action, set his foote as farre forth as the best: yet, some occasion giuen, eyther for profite or pleasure, feare or daunger, sodainely turneth sayle, and commeth to the worlde againe."[70]

Topsell's commentary suggests that worldly exigencies—"profite or pleasure, feare or daunger"—threaten to turn the convert back to the world. Yet even as these worldly forces could undermine the proselyte's decision, the means by which Ruth became fully a part of the Israelite community was precisely through the enforcement of detailed procedures for property, marriage, and inheritance. Concerns about inauthentic conversions were not hypothetical, as comments by Topsell reveal. He notes that Naomi's preliminary urging of her daughters-in-law to return to Moab admonishes believers "to be careful whom they receive into their company, and how gentlye they must entreate them when they finde their fidelity: the ravens will not feede their owne birds or young ones so long as they bee naked till their feathers come out, and they knowe them to be their owne, which jealousy of foules must teach us, that if wee see not the evident tokens of godlynes, we must not receive, yea our owne kinsmen into the secrete of our hearts to communicate unto them the sweet felowship we haue with Christ, for many daily creepe into the church to espie our liberty."[71] The image of the raven that holds off tending to her young until she is sure of its identity gets to the heart of the inherent tensions in these meditations on conversion. While they celebrate an overcoming of the boundaries of family and kind, they depend upon the very language of family and kind for their definitions. Richard Bernard echoes Topsell's admonitions, reminding his readers of the dire consequences for those who do not exercise caution in these "deceitful days" and "fraudulent times."[72]

"Deceitful dayes" and "fraudulent times" were not the only factors that led early modern English readers to express caution about conversions, however. Protestants frequently measured their own *bona fides* against Catholicism, and when it came to questions of policy and practice with regard to conversion, the Catholic Church provided vivid examples of the path not to take. The Protestant commentaries used Ruth's story as an occasion to remark specifically on the perils of forced conversions, with which they directly charged the Church of Rome. Lavater observes that "they doe not well who will driue others to Christian religion by deuises or vayne policies. For if afterwardes they vnderstand the matter to be otherwise then they heard, they will prosecute true religion with deadly hatred: we must deale with them with such arguments as are drawn out of the word of God."[73] Fuller's attack is even more vivid: "Go then ye bloody Jesuites, boast of those many millions of *Americanes* whom you have converted, who were not converted by the sword of the mouth, gained by hearing the Gospell, but compelled by the mouth of the Sword, forced by feeling your cruelty, witnesse those 70000 which without any catechising in the points of Religion, were at once driven to the Font like so many Horses to a watring Trough."[74] The forced conversion of native Americans was preceded, of course, by the forced conversions of Jews, and Lavater makes this association explicit, pointing out that such practices continue during his own time: "There are some at this day who doe study to bring the Iewes to their religion &, cast them into greater dangers, teaching them against the lawe prescribed to them of God to worship Idols and beleeue in a Messias made of bread, &c."[75] The specter of the Iberian forced conversions and the Inquisition it eventually produced haunted English fictions of conversion.[76]

Reading Ruth as a cautionary tale about forcing conversion to Christianity onto contemporary Jews, however, entailed making explicit the inversion at the heart of typological readings of the Old Testament book, that is, Moabite is to Israelite in Ruth as Jew is to Christian in early modern England.[77] Both Lavater and Fuller do just that. Lavater defends Elimelech's decision to migrate to Moab during the famine, insisting that his move to a foreign land did not necessarily mean a loss of religious identity: "Truely it appeareth that the IEVVES kept their religion vnder the ETHNICKE kinges, as they doe this daye vnder the Christians. There was not so great crueltie of those kinges against the IEVVES, as there is now at this daye of some Kinges and Princes (which will haue themselues to be called Christians) against the professors of pure doctrine."[78] And Fuller uses this inversion to pray for the contemporary calling of the Jews: "This was the privilege of the Jews, that they were styled Gods people, but now *Ammi* is made *Lo-Ammi*, and *Ruchama*, *Lo-Ruchama*; and we the Gentiles are placed in their roome. . . . O that he would be pleased to cast his eye of pitty upon the poor Jews, which for 1500 years and upwards have wandred without Law, without Lord, without Land, and as once they were, so once againe to make them his people."[79] These typological displacements and supersessions in the exegetical conversion of Ruth the Moabite into Ruth the Jew-of-the-flesh parallel in most respects what Christian readings of the patriarchal narratives did to the Abraham-Isaac-Ishmael story or the Isaac-Jacob-Esau story. The physical ancestor of Israel-of-the-flesh typologically converts into the spiritual ancestor of Israel-of-the-spirit. Isaac and Jacob become the fathers of the Church, while Ishmael and Esau become fathers of the Synagogue. Inheritance and blessing come to be determined by spiritual rather than genealogical lineage. The difference in Ruth's case, though, is that these displacements and supersessions depend explicitly on a preceding genealogical intermingling of Jew and Gentile, of Boaz and Ruth, in the line that produces Christ.

Even as the work of typology converts the material distinctions of national and ethnic differences into a universalized, undifferentiated mystical body of Christ, commentators of Ruth find important occasion to meditate precisely on matters of the body, the details of national identity as figured in racial and ethnic difference, as in the following passage from Bernard: "Note here, first, that *daughters of a bad race, may prooue good wives, and good children in law sometime*: as these daughters of Idolaters did; when God restraineth nature, and giueth grace withall. For many times there are tractable and gentle natures, where Religion is not grafted, these by good instruction, and Gods blessing, may proue excellent wiues. Children therefore are not euer to bee censured according to their parents; though it is dangerous to graft in a bad stocke: for an hundred to one, but a *Michal* will make a *Dauid* know that shee is *Sauls* daughter."[80] Steeped in the language of body and race, Bernard's comment may speak to the possibility of bridging an ethnic or national divide through the process of grafting, that is, conversion through marriage, but it is not especially optimistic about the likelihood of bringing about the necessary changes to an individual's carnal, familial predisposition. Grafting in from bad stock is always dangerous business. A suspicion about the efficacy of this process of ethnic grafting appears in Thomas Fuller's imagined dialogue between Naomi and her two sons just before they take wives from among the Moabites. Marriages to Moabite women have heretofore been forbidden, Machlon and Chilion argue, "with such strange women as are of a stubborn, obstinate and refractory nature, such as are likely to seduce their Husbands, whereas you see the mild, towardly, and tractable disposition of these women we meane to make our wives; we hope to plant these wild branches in Gods Vineyard, to bring these straggling sheep to his fold, to make them Proselytes to our Religion."[81] The sons see their desire to marry Moabite women in domesticating and conversionary terms. Fuller sides with Naomi, though, expressing doubts about the *a priori* justification of the incorporation of these "wild branches in Gods Vineyard." The only defense for the actions of Machlon and Chilion can arise after the fact from divine intervention: "Here may we see the power and providence of God, who made good use of these Mens defaults, as hereby to bring Ruth first to be a retainer to the family of Faith, and afterwards a joyfull Mother in Israel. This is that good *Chymick* that can distill good out of evill, light out of darknesse, order out of confusion, and make the crooked actions of men tend to his own glory in a straight line, and his Childrens good."[82] Even though their actions had positive results, they are still described as "defaults" and "crooked." As I shall discuss in Chapter 4, in figuring God's correction of this improper marriage as an alchemical process, Fuller calls upon a common trope for the process of conversion in early modernity. The mystification that clouds the alchemical process offers important analogies to the divergent constructions of Ruth's transformation in her biblical story. Alchemy is at once very specifically about material transformation *and* the quintessential refinement of bodies into a purity that effectively de-materializes them.

Fuller's own ambivalence about the fully transformational powers of conversion suggested in the Ruth story can be found in one of his closing remarks. In an extended celebration of Boaz's willingness to acknowledge his kinship to Naomi, who occupies a very different—and much lower—social class than he, Fuller writes: "All mankind is knit together in the same Father in the Creation, as at the Deluge; I know not who lay higher in Adams loynes, or who tooke the Wall in Eves Belly. I speake not this to pave the way to an Anabaptisticall paritie, but onely to humble and abate the conceits of proud men, who look so scornfull and contemptuous over their poore kindred."[83] If approaches to biblical "converts" cannot necessarily be categorized along confessional divides, that is, if the universalizing impulse located in the readings of these conversions narratives is manifest in an interpretation shared by doctrinal antagonists, this ecumenicism has its limits for readers like Fuller, who refuses what he dismissively calls "Anabaptisicall paritie." The breaking down of boundaries—by conversion or any other means—has its limits in early modernity, and these are limits that have crucial implications for the construction and negotiation of ethnicity throughout the early modern period.

Chapter 3

"The Meaning, Not the Name I Call": Converting the Bible and Homer

The Augustinian paradigm for conversion, inspired by the call of *tolle lege*, "Take up and read," proposes an important connection between textual encounter and religious transformation, a connection that may already be suggested by—or perhaps read back into—Jesus' explanation for his use of parables.[1] Mark (revised in Matthew and strikingly absent in Luke) reports Jesus' response to his disciples' confusion over the Sower Parable: "Unto you it is given to know the mystery of the kingdom of God: but unto them that are without, all these things are done in parables: that seeing they may see, and not perceive, and hearing they may hear, and not understand, lest at any time they should be converted, and their sins should be forgiven them" (Mark 4.11–12). Jesus distinguishes between the phenomenological experiences of sight and sound, on the one hand, and the epistemological experiences of perception and comprehension, on the other, distinctions that, I suggest, align with the gap that exists for readers of (or listeners to) a text in a language not their own. That is, the interpretation of the Sower Parable that follows in verses 13–20 serves the same function that the act of translation serves for those who encounter a strange tongue; both render an opaque utterance comprehensible. Indeed, that Jesus offers his explanation for the use of parables in this way signals that the dynamics of religious conversion are deeply entangled with the complexities of translation. Speaking in Greek, the Jesus of Mark (and Matthew) cites a passage from the Hebrew prophet Isaiah to elucidate his (Jesus') use of apparently opaque parables: "And he said, Go, and tell this people, Hear ye indeed, but understand not; and see ye indeed, but perceive not. Make the heart of this people fat, and make their ears heavy, and shut their eyes, lest they see with their eyes and hear with their ears, and understand with their heart, and convert, and be healed" (Is. 6.9–10). I have quoted the 1611 King James translations of both Mark (whose original is Greek) and Isaiah (whose original is Hebrew) to underscore Mark's explicit citation of the verse from Isaiah and the homogenization of the two texts by means of the Septuagint's rendering of Isaiah. As a means for understanding this chapter's concern with the function of translation as a fiction of conversion, I want to begin with a closer consideration of the passage from Isaiah and its subsequent transmission and transformation.

According to the King James Version, both Isaiah and Mark explicitly speak of conversion as the effect of successful perception and comprehension. In choosing the same word in both instances, the King James translators were following the precedent established in the Greek version of Mark, which describes this effect with the term επιστρεψωσιν so as to match the Septuagint's choice of that same term for the verse in Isaiah, where the original Hebrew word is שב. Long before any early modern English translations, the Vulgate had already rendered the passages in Isaiah and Mark with the same Latin term, *converatur*, and so it is hardly surprising to find the King James Version following suit. Earlier English translations, however, did not always use the same word in each instance. Miles Coverdale's 1535 Old Testament (which was done mostly out of the Latin Vulgate and, to a lesser extent, Luther's German version) translated the Isaiah passage with the term "conuert," but the 1525 Tyndale New Testament (translated directly from the Greek) with which it was combined had used "tourne" for the passage in Mark. Taking its cue from the Coverdale Bible, the 1560 Geneva translation rendered Isaiah's verse with "conuert" but transformed the passage in its Markan context into "turne." These early modern translations appear not to have placed as much of a premium on the homogenization of the Old and New Testaments, which is striking given the consistency in the Vulgate and also in the 1395 Wycliff Middle English translations (where "conuertid" appears in both Isaiah and Mark, parallel to the Vulgate from which it was translated). Even in the apparently slight difference between "convert" and "turn," and in the differing approaches taken by these medieval and early modern translations, we can begin to see a central tension between the homogenizing erasure of difference and the persistent heterogeneity and otherness that is at the very heart of fictions of conversion.

The notion that translation is possible suggests the erasure of—or at the very least, the insignificance assigned to—the cultural, semiotic, and even epistemological differences that distinguish one language from another.

Translations depend upon the prioritizing of some core meaning, a transcendental signified, that is not bound to the particularities of the language in which a text has been written.[2] In its erasure of these particularities, translation elides linguistic and rhetorical heterogeneity. This homogenizing effect is nowhere more apparent than in translations of the Bible. As the etymology of the word acknowledges, the Bible—*τα βιβλια*, the books—is a collection, an anthology of different texts written at different times by different authors. Even the devout view of the Bible as having been composed under the influence of the Holy Spirit does not preclude the recognition of the heterogeneous origins of the individual books. Readers of these different books in their original languages can perceive this heterogeneity and plurivocality, whether it is in the differences between the Hebrew of Genesis and the Hebrew of Isaiah or the Greek of Mark and the Greek of John. How much more so do these differences present themselves when the reader shifts from the Hebrew (and Aramaic) of the Old Testament to the Greek of the New Testament! When all these diverse texts are translated by the same person (or group of people) as part of a deliberate effort to adapt a consistency of style, the effect is necessarily to homogenize those differences in favor of a consistency of voice, tone, syntax, and diction.[3]

Consistency of language and style were matters of explicit attention for both the King James translators and their critics. In their preface, the translators acknowledge that "wee have not tyed our selves to an uniformitie of phrasing, or to an identitie of words, as some peradventure would wish that we had done." Yet the translators were not seeking to capture the stylistic idiosyncrasies of individual biblical writers as much as they were intent upon freeing themselves from the bondage of "words or syllables" to "savour more of curiositie." The irascible Hugh Broughton, as early as 1597, had asserted this consistency as a key desideratum of any translation of the Bible: "Constant memorye to translate the same often repeated in the same sort is most needefull."[4] Broughton's insisted on this uniformity in order to preserve the intertextual webs of connections woven between different books in Scripture. Indeed, Broughton was so dissatisfied with the results of the committee assembled by King James—onto which he had sought appointment vociferously and in vain—that he famously declared, "It is so ill done. Tell his Maiest. that I had rather be rent in pieces with wilde horses, then any such translation by my consent be urged upon poore Churches."[5] At the very origins of Protestant English Bible translations, however, the matter had been addressed rather differently. In the preface to his New Testament translation, which, it will be recalled, used the term "turne" in the passage from Mark, William Tyndale claimed an equivalence among the Hebrew, Greek, Latin, and English terms:

> Concerning this word repentance (as they vsed) penaunce/ the Hebrewe hath in the olde Testament generally (Sob) turne to be conuerted. For which the translacion that we take for Saint Jeromes hath most parte (conuerti) to turne or be conuerted/ & some tyme yet (agere penitentium). And the Greke in the new testament hath perpetually (Metanoeo) to turn in ye heart and mynde/ and to come to the right knowledge & to a mannes ryght wyt agayne. . . . And the very sense & signification bothe of the Hebrue & also of the Greke worde is/ to be conuerted and to turne to God with all the hart/ to knowe his wyll/ and to lyue according to his laws/ and to be cured of oure corrupt nature with the oyle of his spirite/ and wyne of obedience to his doctryne.[6]

In arguing for the essential correspondence of the Hebrew, Greek, Latin, and English, Tyndale invokes linguistic likeness for the purpose of criticizing the intervening corruption of the Catholic Church, whose use of the term "penance" carries with it the sacramental associations to which he and other Protestants objected so strongly. Rome had interrupted what would have otherwise been the continuity between the earliest apostolic Church and English Christianity and one of its primary tools for such corruption was linguistic difference.

The differences to which Tyndale refers, however, deserve further attention. The Hebrew שב in Isaiah is probably best rendered as *return* or *repent.*[7] Isaiah speaks to an audience that had once enjoyed a privileged relationship with God, lost that relationship, and was now being challenged to recover it through their own acts of atonement. The seemingly slight shift in nuance from the Hebrew שב (*re*turn) to the Greek επιστρεψωσιν (turn *to*) can begin to suggest the difference between reading Isaiah as part of the Hebrew Bible and reading the New Testament's fulfillments of Old Testament prophecies by placing them within its new framework.[8] As Aloys Dirksen and J. W. Heikkinen have shown, the term more commonly used in the Septuagint, and subsequently in the New Testament, to convey the Hebrew's sense of שב, return/repent, was, as Tyndale notes, μετανοειν.[9] It is the word at the heart of John the Baptist's call for repentance in Matthew 3.2 and it appears repeatedly in Jesus' own calls for repentance (e.g., Mark 1.15, Matt. 4.17, Luke 3.8, among others). The Septuagint's use of *επιστρεψωσιν* for the passage in Isaiah, and its subsequent interpolation into the gospel, begins the process of converting the Hebrew prophet's theme of repentance into the Christian—especially early modern Protestant English—conceptualization of conversion. Isaiah's homogenous Israelite audience is being called to *re*sume an earlier covenantal relationship with God. Mark's heterogeneous audience of Jews and Gentiles is summoned to a changing understanding of its relationship to the divine, *to* whom they must turn. The Greek term, *επιστρεψωσιν*, which conveys something of the same sense of "turning" as the Hebrew's שב, shifts the direction of that turn; the same might be said of the Latin *converatur*, which comes from the root *versare*, to turn, though by the time of Jerome's use of the word in the late fourth century CE *converatur* certainly did have the connotation of religious transformation. The earliest Latin readers of the Vulgate would have read of a call that very likely did entail an entirely new identification with the God of the Bible. The early modern English *be converted* fixes the meaning more firmly, depicting the effect against which the opacity of the message (of prophecy, in Isaiah, of parable, in Mark) is meant to guard as that religious transformation from one (unsaved) state to another (saved) state. What is more, the use of the passive form (which was adapted from the Latin passive but is not a feature of the Greek or Hebrew term) tacitly reinforces a Calvinist view of conversion, implying that such a transformation cannot be willed or initiated by the convert and must, instead, be the result of unmerited grace acting upon the convert. In his 1628/29 sermon on the conversion of Paul, John Donne makes precisely this point as he notes concerning the men of Malta in Acts 28, "it is not *they changed*, but *They were changed*, passively."[10] The Jesus of the gospels in the King James Version, which speaks of "conversion," brings the good news of something heretofore unknown and unexperienced, new wine in new bottles. Those who follow Jesus do so to a new destination and under a new dispensation prompted by God's will, not their own. As the final link in this chain of translations, then, early seventeenth-century readers of the English Bible would have understood this explanation of parables—and the communities of insiders and outsiders they constitute—as the instantiation of clearly delineated boundaries that can only be crossed by the process of conversion.[11] The shift from שב to *εσπιστρεψωσιν* to *converatur* to "convert" succinctly illustrates how translation enacts a process of transformation at the level of language that correlates with the complexities of conversion. It is to translation as a technology of transformation that I now turn.

The early modern period gave rise to an enormous increase in works of translation, much of it specifically motivated by efforts to proselytize, to transform individuals or whole communities with the power of words—and the Word—made newly available in a familiar idiom or vernacular. Luther's German translation of the Bible was one of the first and most influential in what would become an ever-expanding collection of sacred translations, not limited to Protestant Christianity. Under the auspices of the whole range of Christian confessional denominations, the Bible was translated into every European vernacular, as well as many Asian, African, and New World languages (the first Hebrew translation of the New Testament, by Elias Hutter, was also executed in this period).[12] What's more, Calvin's *Institutes of the Christian Religion*, Bellarmino's new Catholic catechism, and numerous other theological works found expression—and often different significance—in English, Dutch, French, Spanish, German, and Italian, not to mention the many European dialects not accorded the same status of language.[13]

Under the influence of humanism, the writings of classical antiquity also found new readers—and new meanings—in the proliferation of translations into vernacular languages. Michael Ryan has argued that the European confrontation with cultures and people whom they encountered during this period of exploration and early colonization was shaped by a textual encounter with the past.[14] According to Ryan, alterity was experienced as a temporal as well as a geographic disjunction; but since Christian humanism was already encountering and sometimes converting the pagan world of antiquity, New World pagans were quickly assimilated into the same transhistorical category and thereby made more recognizable and providentially convertible. In both encounters, translation played a crucial role.[15] Perhaps the most vivid English example of this convergence of the pagan past of classical antiquity with the pagan present of the New World is George Sandys's 1626 translation of Ovid's *Metamorphoses*, which he produced during his years serving as an administrator in the colony of Virginia. Dedicating his translation to Charles I, Sandys describes the conditions under which the translation was begun (during the reign of James I) and completed:

> Your Gracious acceptance of the first fruites of my Travels, when You were our Hope, as now our Happinesse; hath activated both Will and

> Power to the finishing of this Peece: being limn'd by that unperfect light which was snatcht from the howers of night and repose. For the day was not mine, but dedicated to the service of your Great Father, and you selfe: which, had it proved as fortunate as faithfull, in me, and others more worthy; we had hoped, ere many yeares had turned about, to have presented You with a rich and wel-peopled Kingdome; from whence now, with my selfe, I onely bring this Composure: . . . It needeth more than a single denization, being a double Stranger. Sprung from the stocke of the ancient Romanes; but bred in the New-world, of the rudenesse whereof it cannot but participate; especially having Wares and Tumults to bring it to light in stead of the Muses.[16]

A text "sprung from the stocke of the ancient Romanes, but bred in the New-world," Sandys's Englished *Metamorphoses* deploys the classical text in the service of colonial domestication even as its author expresses anxieties about a creeping corruption made possible by this act of cultural miscegenation, deploying the unmistakably naturalizing language of "stocke" and breeding. A primary difference between the European encounter with the classical pagan past and the contemporary pagan natives was the necessity, in the latter case, of enlisting the efforts of some of those natives as linguistic and cultural informants. These native informants served the role that, in the case of classical antiquity, had been served by a persistent historical continuity—suggested in notions like the *prisca sapientia* and *philosophia perennis*—to make the past accessible and familiar, however much that continuity obscured or otherwise transformed the history to which it gave access. European explorers, merchants, and colonists depended upon relationships with the natives of Asia, Africa, and the New World to learn the language and culture of their target audience. Even given the great disparities of power, this dependence necessarily made the process of cultural influence far more reciprocal and, in the eyes of some, potentially contaminating.

As I have already suggested, translation functions as a process of conversion, whereby a text is transformed from its original state and turned into another text which, however well it may capture many aspects of the original, necessarily takes on new and different meanings, meanings recognizable and significant to the culture and audience of the target language but which are not native to the world of the original language. Translation works to domesticate the foreignness of an alien text, but in the process, it also necessarily alters the culture of the target language. The change thus occurs both to the text under translation and to the language and culture into which that text is being translated. Richard Marsden has described a series of striking instances of just such alterations in his discussion of some of the very earliest translations of biblical texts into English, noting how certain Hebrew idioms—e.g., "falling face" and permutations thereof, or "lifting up one's eyes"—were transposed nearly word-for-word and subsequently naturalized in the Anglo-Saxon period. In examples like these, writes Marsden, "we may be able to see our language being created—and created in the image of Scripture."[17] As early as the eighteenth century, Joseph Addison had remarked on the effects of biblical translation on the English language, observing: "The Hebrew idioms run into the English tongue with a particular grace and beauty. Our language has received innumerable elegancies and improvements, from the infusion of Hebraism, which are derived to it out of the poetical passages in Holy Writ. They give a force and energy to our expression."[18] Even before Addison, early modern translators were alert to these alternatively contaminating or enriching effect of translations. George Chapman, in the preface to one of his earliest efforts at translating Homer, defends his use of non-native words in the following way: "For my varietie of new wordes, I have none Inckepot I am sure you know, but such as give passport with such authoritie, so significant and not ill founding, that if my countrey language were an userer, or a man of this age speaking it, hee would thanke mee for enriching him. . . . All tongues have inricht themselves from their originall (onely the Hebrew & Greeke which are spoken amongst us) with good neighbourly borrowing, and as with infusion of fresh ayre, and nourishment of newe blood in their still growing bodies, & why not ours?"[19] Chapman is responding to the influential and programmatic statements of one of England's first Greek scholars, John Cheke, who argued for a purity to the English language, unmixed with other tongues, "wherein if we take not heed bi tijm, ever borrowing and never paying, she shall be fain to keep her house as bankrupt."[20] The shared language of borrowing and usury in Cheke's pronouncement and Chapman's defense deserves further comment. Shylock, the Jewish usurer whose conversion was notoriously problematic and potentially incomplete, had appeared on the London stage only a year before Chapman's first Homer translations. It should come as no surprise, therefore, that early modern translators often correlated the effects of translation on the English language, explicitly or implicitly, with anxieties about these alternatively enriching and contaminating possibilities of religious conversion, the hope that new converts would enliven the body of Christ, coupled with the fear that by inviting new converts into the community of the faithful, that community made itself vulnerable to heresy, corruption, and impurity. As with so many fictions of conversion, the figure of the Jew embodies these anxieties, making unanticipated entrance in the unlikeliest of places.

Such anxieties were evident, for example, in the intense ambivalence with which early modern Christian Hebraists contended with claims of Jewish proprietary knowledge about the Hebrew Scriptures, claims made not only by Jews, but also by numerous Christian scholars. As the complex history of Christian Hebraism demonstrates, the function of the Jew in the study and transmission of knowledge of Hebrew differs from either the study of native languages in the New World or the "dead" languages of classical antiquity.[21] Jews were never wholly absent from the world of European Christianity—even when they were not, as in the case of England, physically present—with the advent of humanism and the Reformation, Jews and Judaism took on a decidedly new role in European religious and ethnic self-definition. I have already noted how the instability of Christian and Jewish identities in the early modern period makes it difficult to postulate broad generalizations about Christian attitudes toward Jews or Jewish attitudes toward Christians.[22] Identity is undoubtedly shaped by perceptions of otherness, but otherness is also a moving target. The Jewish-Christian encounter over a shared and contested textual heritage, especially in the context of new efforts to achieve more accurate or authentic translations, provides a particularly fraught instance of mutually constitutive formulations of identity and otherness, both at the level of the individual and the community. As English Christianity in its various confessional formulations sought to define and redefine its boundaries, the Jew proved to be a powerful—and powerfully ambivalent—formation of difference and continuity. Yet the differences the Jew embodied were often aligned with or contrasted to the differences and continuities located in the past of classical antiquity. In what follows, I offer a more specific discussion of this complex encounter with otherness through an examination of the translations of two texts that, more than most, raised the question of continuity and discontinuity between Judaism and classical paganism, on the one hand, and early modern England, on the other: the Hebrew Bible and the epics of Homer.

Nomen, Non-Omen

I begin this juxtaposition of the early modern Bible and the early modern Homer with a brief consideration of what is surely among the most influential modern critical comparisons of these two foundational texts: Erich Auerbach's opening chapter of his seminal study *Mimesis*. Auerbach's discussion has established the terms of difference—and self-identity—in subsequent discussions of the style of the Bible and Homer (their respective "representations of reality") even as many of the details of his argument have come under critical scrutiny by classicists, biblical scholars, and literary historians. Since translation grapples with the tension between identity and difference, and since Auerbach's assertion of a basic mimetic distinction between biblical and Homeric narrative is rooted in a deeper assumption of the non-equivalence of the Hebraic and the Hellenic that is also at the very center of European Christianity's resistance to claims for its Jewish origins, a closer look at the specific examples Auerbach cites in his comparison has value for my concern with fictions of conversion.[23] Auerbach's contrast of Genesis and the *Odyssey* draws on a long history of pairing classical and biblical literature. Early modern humanism's return *ad fontes*, to the sources, gave rise to more and more of these juxtapositions. Though I can find no explicit comparison of the binding of Isaac and Odysseus's scar in medieval or early modern discussions of these two texts, there are numerous examples of specific pairings of biblical and classical episodes for the purposes of mutual illumination. Comparisons between God's call to Abraham to sacrifice Isaac and Agamemnon's sacrifice of his daughter Iphegenia were fairly commonplace and often syncretistic, eliding the differences between Scripture and the ancient pagan myths. In his 1594 poem, "The Lamentation of Troy," John Ogle retells the moving story of Priam's recovery of the body of his son, Hector, from the Greek camp, as depicted in the final book of the *Iliad*, and describes the bitter tears Priam shed with the following lines: "Thus did the olde-man in his mellowed yeares / Bewaile the wind-fall of his fruit vnripe / . . . Nothing he said, but O my sonne, my sonne, / His breath stil stopping ere he halfe done." This image of a father bemoaning the premature death of his beloved son generates a series of biblical associations. First, Ogle depicts Priam's sorrow as exceeding King David's mourning for the death of his son, Absalom. Then, somewhat unexpectedly, the poem offers a counterexample:

The godly Patriarch *Abraham* did greeve,
In sacrifice to offer uppe his sonne:
Unto *I am* and but he did beleeve,
His flesh and bloud would such a murther shun.
    If flesh and bloud to loose a sonne be loth,
    Then needs must *Priam* who was meerely both.[24]

The lines assume a superiority to the biblical story; Priam was "merely" flesh and blood, unlike Abraham who, presumably, felt less grief when he was called to sacrifice his son because he had the advantage of belief. Yet Ogle invokes Abraham's religious superiority so as to invite deeper sympathy for Priam. Ogle asserts the priority and greater value of the scriptural tradition, but in the end he seems more interested in eliding the differences and merging the classical with the biblical.

Biblical commentaries and sermons also offer instances in which scriptural passages are juxtaposed with classical parallels. In a sermon preached at Whitehall in 1598, Cambridge professor of divinity Thomas Playfere attemped to elucidate the episode of doubting Thomas, as told in the twentieth chapter of the Gospel of John, by invoking Homer: "When Ulysses had beene long from home, no man almost at his returne knewe him, yet Euriclea his nurse espying by chance the marke of a wound in his foote, which he got by hunting the wild boare, by and by made him known to his friends. In like manner Thomas, beholding the wounds not of Christs feete onely, but also of his whole body, beleeveth verily, though the wilde boare out of the wood stroke fore at him that he might fall, yet that he hath nowe recovered himselfe, and is risen and returned home againe."[25] As in Ogle's poem, Playfere compares classical and biblical examples—Eurylcea's recognition of Odysseus's scar (which he inaccurately suggests leads to her making him known to others) with Thomas's acknowledgment of Christ's identity in the face of the evidence of the wounds of the crucifixion—so as to underscore both the similarities and the differences between the two episodes. The rhetorical effect, however, is to blur the distinctions—"the wilde boare out of the wood stroke fore at him that he might fall"—so that the language of the classical episode spills into and revises the biblical story. In one case (Ogle's poem), the biblical story is used to enrich the meaning of the classical episode. In the other case (Playfere's sermon), a classical episode is invoked to shed light on a biblical passage. Though these juxtapositions may explicitly seek to differentiate between the biblical and the classical examples, their rhetorical and exegetical effects depend precisely on a blurring of those distinctions, a translatability of conditions and details that portends the erasure of particularities.

The syncretistic impulse that stands behind so many of these comparisons and contrasts of biblical and classical lore threatens to violate the distinctiveness and particularity of each textual tradition. Auerbach, by contrast, is deeply committed to demonstrating each text's difference from the other. It is striking, therefore, that the two episodes Auerbach used to delineate these differences between narrative approaches in the Bible and Homer share a key detail to which Auerbach gives no attention, a detail that sits at the very heart of the question of identity and particularity. Homer's account of the premature recognition of Odysseus by his childhood nurse, Euryclea, as she bathes his feet and sees the scar he acquired in his youth while hunting a boar, also includes a preliminary tale that reports how Odysseus received his name. As an infant, the yet-to-be-named hero had been brought to visit his maternal grandfather, Autolycos, who was charged with the task of naming his grandson. Here is a more or less literal rendering of the moment: "My daughter's husband and my daughter, give him the name I shall tell you. Inasmuch as I have come here as one that has willed pain to (*οδυσσαμενος*) many, both men and women, over the fruitful earth, therefore let the name by which the child is named be Odysseus (*τωδ'Οδυσευς ονομ εστωεπωνυμον*)" (19.406–409).[26] Readers of the Greek will not be surprised by the overdetermined nature of Odysseus's name, as there are several key moments earlier in the epic that proleptically play on this etymology, using one form or another of the Greek *οδυσσομαι*.[27] The origin of Odysseus's name during this episode serves also to explicate those earlier wordplays, revealing the extent to which his story has always already been about a hero who has caused distress, been angry, provoked hatred, and suffered pain, all of which are partial meanings of the root *οδυσσασθαι*.[28] The recovery of the name's origin merges with the recollection of the scar's origin, as both serve to mark Odysseus with pain and suffering, forging a particularized identity. Yet the epic also cannily undermines a more stable reading of the name as an adumbration of Odysseus's troubled life—resisting the expected convention of *nomen-omen*—by introducing this range of nuanced meanings of the name's etymology *before* it offers its explicit account of the giving of that name.

Auerbach's biblical example, the story of the binding of Isaac in the book of Genesis, is also characterized by acts of naming, of both people and places. The chapter just prior to Genesis 22 reports the long-awaited birth of Isaac to his elderly parents. Genesis 21.3 states, "And Abraham called the name of his son that was born to him, whom Sarah bore to him, Isaac, יצחק." Readers of the Hebrew recognize immediately that the name has its apparent origins in two earlier episodes in which Abraham and Sarah separately responded to the improbable news that they would together produce a child. Abraham's response appeared first: ויצחק ויפל אברהם על־ פניו, "and Abraham fell on his face and laughed" (17.17). A chapter later, when she heard the news, Sarah responded in a similar fashion, ותצחק שרה בקרבה, "and Sarah laughed to herself" (18.12). Few biblical names are subjected to as much explicit wordplay as Isaac's. In addition to these two distinct episodes (which were often read to Abraham's credit and Sarah's detriment by rabbinic, patristic, and early modern exegetes), we read of Sarah's anxiety about her son growing up in the same house as Ishmael, the son of her handmaid: "And Sarah saw the son of Hagar the Egyptian, whom she had borne to Abraham, mocking [מצחק]" (21.9). And following the story of the binding, the text plays on Isaac's name one more time, describing the intimacy he enjoyed with his wife, Rebecca, whom he had tried to pass off as his sister in order to protect himself, "and behold Isaac was playing, מצחק, with his wife, Rebecca" (26.8). The joy, disbelief, mockery, and pleasure encapsulated in the one root, צ ח ק, rest just beneath the surface of the notoriously laconic account of God's call to Abraham to relinquish the son for whom he had waited for so long. As in the *Odyssey*, the naming of Isaac very nearly undermines any etiological reading. The laughter that precedes Isaac's birth may be construed as a sign of pleasure or incredulity. The laughter that follows his naming signifies mockery and abuse, but also tenderness and intimacy. In its various, often conflicting, iterations his name does not serve as a key to his identity, but rather as an interrogation of any such notion of fixed identity.[29]

Translation and Difference

Since neither the Bible nor the literature of Greek antiquity was accessible to most readers in their original languages, the early modern convergence of biblical and classical writings was both responsible for, and dependent upon, a dynamic proliferation of translations. It is no mere coincidence, then, that the most successful and influential translation of the Bible in English, the King James (or Authorized) Version, and the first (and for some time, only) full English translation of the *Iliad* and the *Odyssey*, by Chapman, appeared at virtually the same time. Chapman's translation efforts began with his *Achilles Shield* and *Seaven Books of the Iliades*, both in 1598, but culminated in his complete *Iliads* in 1611 and *Odysses* in 1614. King James I convened the Hampton Conference that began the translation process in 1604. The first edition of the King James Version was published in 1611.[30]

Some of the similarities and differences between these two seminal translation efforts deserve further comment. James's appointment of six separate committees responsible for different portions of the Old and New

Testament, under the direction and supervision of Lancelot Andrewes, recollects the precedent of the legendary story told about the first great translation of the Hebrew Bible, the Septuagint. Miles Smith's preface to the King James translation draws the parallel explicitly and repeatedly. King Ptolemy selected seventy-two Jewish scholars to work individually on complete translations of the Hebrew Bible. According to Philo's version of the legend, that the seventy-two translations produced by the seventy-two Greek-speaking Jews were identical to one another served as compelling proof that the Septuagint Bible was the product of divine inspiration and fully authentic.[31] Yet despite the analogous involvement of multiple participants in the translation of the King James Version, it is not these translators who lay claim to authority by virtue of inspiration, but rather George Chapman, who repeatedly draws connections between the divine *furor* that produced Homer's poetic corpus and his own visitations by the spirit of Homer as he completed his translation.[32] As a deliberate effort to quell religious dissent and to appease those "hot" Protestants dissatisfied with the Bishops Bible, the King James Version needed to ground its authority in a combination of philological scholarship and respect for tradition. Claims to divine inspiration by such a heterogeneous collection of scholars, representing different strains of Protestant thought and political sympathies, would not contribute to the success of a translation aimed at unifying a dangerously splintered English nation, especially when the original Protestant break directly challenged Catholicism's claims of divine inspiration for its authoritative version, the Vulgate.[33] Doctrinal demands produced a homogenizing, consensus-seeking approach. Chapman, on the other hand, sought to situate his own endeavor within the conventional mythos of the inspired poet, in part as a response to the critics of his translation efforts.

Both translations participated in a larger national discourse, one that regarded translation as serving the interests of a specifically English *polis*. As early as the reign of King Alfred the Great in the ninth century, translation was seen as a means of rescuing the English language, creating a sense of unity, and laying the foundations for English prose.[34] In prefatory comments to his translation of Erasmus's *Paraphrase of the New Testament*—a translation of a translation—Nicholas Udall argues, "A translatour travaileth not to hys own private commoditie, but to the behoufe & publique use of his countrey."[35] The King James translators and Chapman make similar assertions in their prefatory materials, assertions they couple with direct claims about the particularity of the English nation grounded in the distinctiveness of the English language. In this respect, they are following the precedent of Tyndale, who had insisted that the Hebrew of the Old Testament could be far more accurately rendered into English than into either Latin or any other European vernaculars: "the properties of the Hebrew tongue agreeth a thousand times more with the English than with the Latin. The manner of speaking is both one; so that in a thousand places thou needest not but to translate it into the English, word for word; when thou must seel a compass in Latin, and yet shall have much work to translate it well-favouredly, so that it have the same grace and sweetness, sense and pure understanding with it in the Latin and as it hath in the Hebrew. A thousand parts better may it be translated into the English, than into the Latin."[36] By suggesting this natural affinity between Hebrew and English, Tyndale distinguished himself from his predecessor, Martin Luther, who had insisted that his translation of the Old Testament into German was authentic precisely because it had successfully eliminated any traces of the original and was "rid of the Hebraisms so that no one can say that Moses was a Hebrew."[37] In such an extravagant claim we can readily see how fully intertwined are the two matters of conversion and translation. Luther's conversion of Moses into an early sixteenth-century German Protestant represents one side of the transformative possibilities of translation. The other side can be identified in the extent to which Chapman and the King James translators draw on the appeal to English distinctiveness in the context of their respective explanations of the presence of words not, apparently, native to the English language. These were the words that John Cheke had dismissed as "Inkpot words" (a characterization to which, as we have already seen, Chapman felt obliged to respond).[38] If the English language possessed distinctive qualities, those qualities could potentially be corrupted by the indiscriminate infiltration of foreign terms. In charting their *via media* between the extremes of Puritanism (as epitomized in the Geneva Bible) and Catholicism (as embodied in the Douay-Rheims translation), the King James translators assert:

> We have on the one side avoided the scrupulosity of the Puritans, who leave the old Ecclesiastical words, and betake them to other, as when they put *Washing* for *Baptism*, and *Congregation* instead of *Church*: as also on the other side we have shunned the obscurity of the Papists, in their *Azimes, Tunike, Rational, Holocausts, Praepuce, Pasche*, and a number of such like, whereof their late Translation is full, and that of purpose to darken the sense, that since they must needs translate the Bible, yet by the language thereof, it may be kept from being

> understood. But we desire that the Scripture may speak like itself, as in the language of Canaan, that it may be understood even of the very vulgar.

The rhetoric here is telling. The Preface seeks to render this act of translation as one that permits the Bible to "speak like itself, as in the language of Canaan," not, significantly, the language of the Jews, or of the people Israel, or even Hebrew. The term "of Canaan" situates the language in ancient and even pagan contexts. Yet the translators also insist that they have sought a language that can be understood "even of the very vulgar." Identity ("Scripture may speak like itself") and difference ("language of Canaan"), that which distinguishes the ancient text and that which makes it accessible to the early modern reader, uncomfortably inhabit the same sentence. Broughton's objections to the King James Version's lack of uniformity of terms used, which I cited above, might be assigned to the realm of pedantry, or they might be seen as a genuine effort to preserve a certain linguistic integrity, even in translation.

Matters of consistency and diversity of terminology take on further complications when it comes to names. I have already called attention to the range of meanings in the names of Odysseus and Isaac recognizable to the reader of classical Greek or Biblical Hebrew. But how should one convey these multiple meanings or suggest their different nuances in a translation? Indeed, challenges pertaining to translation in general are heightened and exaggerated at moments of naming. To what extent do the King James Bible and Chapman's *Odysses* carry over (*trans latio*) the task of translation to names, and what does it mean to translate a name? Names, of course, have a special relationship to identity, working against any such homogeneity. In one of the earliest efforts to formalize and defend something approximating standard English usage, Richard Mulcaster drew just such a connection between names and identities by citing the biblical precedent of Adam giving names to the beasts (Gen. 2.19) according to their natures: "what a cunning thing it is to give right names, and how necessarie it is, to know their forces, which be allredie given, bycause the word being knowen, which implyeth the propertie the thing is half known, whose propertie is emplyed."[39] Numerous guidebooks and supplementary charts appeared over the course of the sixteenth and seventeenth centuries to provide definitions of names and their languages of origin.[40] But a comprehensive understanding of the meaning of the name still leaves the translator in a quandary: What to do when English offers no equivalent for the Greek or the Hebrew that adequately captures both the name as a signifier of identity and the name as that which can be interpreted (Odysseus or יצחק)? In his essay on names, which was translated into English by John Florio in 1606, Michel de Montaigne commends a fellow countryman's recent French version of a classical oration for having "still kept the full ancient Latin names, without disguising or changing them, to give them a new French cadence. At first they seemed somewhat harsh unto the Reader, but now . . . custom hath removed all strangeness from us. I have often wished that those who write histories in Latin, would leave us our names whole, and such as they are: For, altering *Vandemont*, to *Vallemontanus*, and metamorphosing them, by suting them to the Græcian or Latin tongue, we know not what to make of them, and are often at a non-plus."[41] Montaigne insists upon retaining the particularity of the name, even if—or perhaps precisely because—it alienates the reader. Significantly, it is this persistence of the name's foreign quality that will eventually have the effect of familiarizing it: "Custom hath removed all strangeness." Translating names, or giving them the linguistic form of the target language, paradoxically makes them more strange: "We know not what to make of them." As we turn to naming episodes in Homer and the Bible, the paradoxical tensions between alienation and familiarization, particularization and universalization, will appear in the approaches adopted by Chapman and the King James translators.

Odysseus and Identity

Chapman's heroic couplets transform the naming episode in *Odyssey* 19 in the following terms:

> Daughter and Son-in-Law, sayd he, let then
> The name that I shall give him stand with men,
> Since I arriv'd here at the houre of paine
> In which mine owne kinde entrails did sustaine
> Moane for my daughters yet unended throes,
> And when so many mens and womens woes,
> In joynt compassion met of humane birth,
> Brought forth t'attend the many feeding earth.
> Let Odysseus be his name, as one
> Exposd to just constraint of all men's mone.
>
> (19.561–570)

It is a passage noteworthy for its universalizing gestures. Even at the moment of choosing a particular name, Autolycus points toward the collective of "many mens and womens woes" and "all men's mone." Furthermore, in a suggestive effort to reproduce some qualities of the Greek wordplay in his translation, Chapman deploys assonance, rhyme, and repetition to pair the lines "In which mine owne kinde entrails did sustaine" and "Moane for my daughter's yet unended throes" with the rhyme-word in the following line, "woes," and the phrase that concludes the passage, "Just constraint of all men's mone." But the full weight of the Greek's nominal etymology is clearly lost in translation and Chapman resorts to a marginal gloss, which quotes Johann Scapula, one of his two primary sources for such matters (the other was the Latin translation of Homer by Jean de Sponde). Chapman's annotation reads, "Autolycus gives his Grand child Ulysses his name, from whence the *Odysses* is derived, Οδυσσευς deriv'd of οδυξομαι, *ex* οδυνη, *factum*: signifying *dolorem proprie corporis, nam ira ex dolore oritur.*"[42] Noting further the origin of Ulysses in the Greek name, Odysseus, the gloss reveals precisely in its explanation just how wide a gap separates the Greek original and the English into which Chapman has translated it.

This is the only place in either the *Iliad* or the *Odyssey* in which Homer directly gives the origins of a character's name. As critics have long observed, the Greek is filled with plays on names—not just Odysseus's—and just about every name in the epic can be read philologically. Yet Odysseus is the only character whose name and its origins become matters of explicit attention. The uniqueness of this naming narrative is a function of the very fact that Odysseus's identity, in all its complexity and irreducibility, is of central importance throughout the poem. Indeed, the nature, persistence, and recognition of Odysseus's identity may be said to be the epic's primary theme. Odysseus himself uses the rich interanimation of name and identity specifically—and famously—as an effective weapon in his notorious escape from the Cyclops Polyphemus in Book 9. There, Odysseus gives his name as *Ουτις*, Nobody, an extraordinary, if temporary, denial of identity; commenting on this moment, Carolyn Higbie observes that Odysseus is "the only human ever to lie about his identity" in Homer's epics.[43] He nevertheless seems constitutionally incapable of leaving himself unnamed for long and, to his ultimate detriment, he does eventually identify himself to Polyphemus, giving the Cyclops precisely the nominal power to call down a curse from his father Poseidon, the very curse that produced all of Odysseus's wanderings. Here is Chapman's version of the lines in which Odysseus reasserts his name and identity to Polyphemus:

> Cyclop! If any aske thee who imposed
> Th'unsightly blemish that thine eye enclosed,
> Say that Ulysses (old Laertes sonne,
> Whose seate is Ithaca, and who hath wonne
> Surname of Citie-racer) bor'd it out.
>
> (9.673–677)

Chapman's marginal gloss on these lines focuses the reader's attention on the question of identity and naming: "Ulysses continued insolence, no more to repeate what he said to the Cyclop than to let his hearers know his Epithetes, and estimation in the world." As Robert Kawashima has noted, the presence of recognizable and repeated narrative formulae, like the epithet, produce an "art of the familiar."[44] Chapman's attention to Odysseus's use of these epithets suggests that he construes this moment as especially metafictional and self-conscious, precisely so as to pit the familiarity produced against the deliberate self-alienation and denial of identity from which Odysseus now emerges. In Homer's account, the meaning and the name are both central to the hero's identity. In an epic that repeatedly disguises its protagonist to prevent recognition, the name Odysseus carries with it special significance. Chapman gives full attention to such nominal significance in his translation and gloss.

Yet Chapman faces a particular challenge when he comes to the naming story in Book 19. The supplementary gloss he provides seeks to preserve the meaning alongside the name even as the translation necessarily severs the tie between the two. As if to call attention to the distinctiveness of this moment, this is the *only time* in the entire poem when Chapman refers to his epic hero as *Odysseus*. In every other instance, he defers to the well-established and far more familiar Latin tradition of calling him *Ulysses*. Chapman must embed his own renaming within the naming story, acknowledging, if only temporarily, the impossibility of a full translation and presenting his readers with a momentarily estranged, foreign character, a subject whose difference and singularity are preserved in the name that also signifies the constitutive features of his identity. If the Latin name Ulysses has been domesticated by centuries of European usage, Odysseus preserves an otherness, rendering his conversion incomplete.[45] The passage and its accompanying note mark the impossibility of complete translation, the residual foreignness of language, even as they work to erase that difference by assimilating any strangeness.[46] Nor does this tension between familiarity and estrangement dissipate in the wake of these earliest efforts to convert Homer into English. Some two and a half centuries later, Matthew Arnold would remark on subsequent renderings: "The real question is this—whether our living apprehension of the Greek world is more checked by meeting in an English book about the Greeks, names not spelt letter for letter as in the original Greek, or by meeting names which make us rub our eyes and call out 'How exceedingly odd!'"[47] Chapman seems intent upon eliciting from his readers at this moment of naming just such a reaction: Odysseus? How odd!

A closer examination of Chapman's handling of this entire scene reveals how this struggle to assimilate and digest that which defies transformation manifests itself at the level of grammar, as well. Here is a more or less literal translation of the passage that effects the transition from the narrative present (Euryclea's washing of Odysseus's feet) to the past (Odysseus's naming and the origin of the scar): "And the old woman took the shining cauldron from which she was about to wash his feet, and poured in cold water in plenty, and then added the hot. But Odysseus sat down at the hearth, and instantly turned himself toward the darkness, for he at once had a foreboding at heart that, as she took hold of him, she might notice his scar and the truth be made manifest. So she drew near and began to wash her lord; at once she recognized the scar."[48] By combining Euryclea's act of washing with the story of the scar, the original text flattens out any sense of *temporal* depth, producing what Auerbach had characterized as the poem's representation of "phenomena in a fully externalized form, visible and palpable in all their parts."[49] The washing, the naming, and the boar hunt happen in a paratactic sequence that gives equal prominence to each event, consistent with Aristotle's characterization of the Homeric mode as one of *πολυμυθος*, of many stories.[50] Chapman describes the initial stage of Euryclea's recognition in this way:

> Thus tooke she up a Caldron brightly scour'd
> To clense his feete in, and into it pour'd
> Store of cold wave, which on the fire she set,
> And therein bath'd (being temperately heat)
> Her Soveraign's feet—who turned him from the light,
> Since sodainly he doubted her conceit
> (So rightly touching at his state before),
> A scar now seeing on his foot that bore

An old note to discerne him, might descry
The absolute truth, which (witnest her eye)
Was straite approved.

(19.531–541)

Merging Ulysses' anxiety about being identified with Euryclea's incipient recognition, Chapman makes it difficult to determine who is "now seeing" the scar on his foot. The complex syntactical subordinations and parenthetical remarks in Chapman's periodic sentence blur the boundaries of identity and agency, collapsing the recognition into Ulysses' efforts to resist just such an identification. Instead of a temporal flattening, Chapman's account repeatedly shifts its subjective perspective. Commenting on these syntactical infelicities, George deForest Lord characterizes the disorganized effect as haphazard and inorganic.[51] I take the appearance of such a labyrinthine sentence at this pivotal moment to be a sign of the translator's particular struggle to formulate a coherent and consolidated identity for his hero, one that is both irreducible and recognizable. The original episode uses direct discourse (signaled by the vocative case, *Αὐτόλυκ'*) when it recollects how Euryclea had called upon Autolycus to name Odysseus: as the poem casts the reader back into the stories of Odysseus's naming by Autolycus and his subsequent scarring by the boar, the text shifts its entire attention to those events, leaving behind, if only momentarily, the occasion for these stories in favor of their direct narration. Chapman, however, combines indirect discourse with direct discourse, situating the series of secondary tales in a far more complex relation, temporally and narratively, to the primary story of the discovery of Ulysses' identity. Extending the naming speech further than the Greek original, Chapman places particular emphasis on the relationship between name and home:

When here at home he is arriv'd at state
Of man's first youth, he shall initiate
His practisd feete in travaile made abrode,
And to Parnassus, where mine owne abode
And chiefe meanes lye, addresse his way, where I
Will give him from my opened treasury
What shall returne him well, and fit the Fame
Of one that had the honor of his name.

(ll. 571–578)

The original may, indeed, suggest a parallel between the return to his home that Autolycus anticipates and the return home with which the *Odyssey* concerns itself more generally, but Chapman foregrounds that parallel, particularly in his special emphasis in the rhyming couplets, ***abrode-abode*** and *Fame-name*, connecting this parallel directly to the suggestion that Ulysses' name—and the identity it designates—will not be fully realized until the homecoming is complete.[52]

There is an important relationship between this special resistance of names to translation and what readers have long recognized as the allegorical quality of Chapman's version of Homer. The distance is rather short between translating a name into its meaning and using that translated meaning as the interpretive key to the character whom that name designates. Chapman spells out his allegorical perspective—one he inherits from the Neoplatonic reading of Homer the theologian—in his dedicatory epistle:[53]

> Nor is this all-comprising *Poesie*, phantastique, or meere fictive; but the most material, and doctrinall illations of *Truth*; both for all manly information of Manners in the yong; all prescription of Justice, and even Christian pietie, in the most grave and high-governd. To illustrate both which, in both kinds, with all height of expression, the Poet creates both a Bodie and a Soule in them. Wherein, if the Bodie (being the letter, or historie) seemes fictive, and beyond Possibilitie to bring into Act: the sence then and Allegorie (which is the Soule) is to be sought: which intends a more eminent expressure of *Vertue*, for her lovelinesse; and of *Vice* for her uglinesse, in their sever all effects; going beyond the life, then any Art within life, can possibly delineate. [A4^{v}]

Like Spenser before him, Chapman fashions a gentleman out of Ulysses, constructing a story that charts the gradual emergence of specific virtues in the face of challenges whose circumstances can be read as reflective of the struggles faced by Chapman's fit audience. Allegoresis has the effect of domesticating the strange, of converting the foreign to the familiar. That is, by construing a text as *speaking otherwise*, an allegorical reading works to recover a universalized, transcendent meaning. The early modern interest in names often reflected this allegorical impulse. In his dedicatory poem to Edward Lyford, author of a mid-century book on name etymologies, Edward Probee celebrates Lyford's project as a resistance to mutability and a recovery of stability: "For what can be more pleasing to a man, / Then th'*Allegory* of his *name* to scan? / To antient purity thou dost restore / Our *names*, as they first breath'd in time of yore."[54] Yet Chapman is also eager to preserve a particularity to his text, an individuality that, earlier in this same epistle, he pits against the world of politics. In his very fine discussion of Chapman's *Iliad*, Robert Miola remarks on the translation's "privatization of death," its reconstitution of the more formulaic, ritualized, and communal representations of death and mourning found in the poem's original text.[55] A similar tension between the communal and individual informs Chapman's rendering of the *Odyssey*. Remarking on the first word in the *Odyssey*—Ανδρα, Man—Chapman argues that in the figure of Ulysses he finds "the Mind's inward, constant and unconquered Empire, unbroken, unaltered with any most insolent and tyrannous infliction." Two warring forces face off in Chapman's *Odysses*. Moralizing generalities tend to oversimplify identity and compromise distinctiveness. Such a loss of distinctiveness represents a threat to an emergent formulation of subjectivity as both individual and defined by its relation to the state, an English state whose language is different than and more readily appropriate than other languages (according to Chapman) to the transformation of Homer's Greek. So Chapman adopts an approach to translating names—and the subjects they designate—that conforms to the Latin tradition to which he is heir (Ulysses), but which, when the meaning of the name itself is given direct attention, also lays claim to a distinctiveness (Odysseus). The problem is that at precisely that moment, the name, the character whom it signifies, and the language in which it is uttered present themselves as irreducibly other. In his *Poetics*, Aristotle set forth a theory of language that defines figurative usage as a kind of linguistic self-alienation: "By a . . . proper word I mean one which is in general use among a people; by a strange word, one which is in use in another country. Plainly, therefore, the same word may be at once strange and current. . . . Metaphor is the application of an alien name by transference." A name that also serves as a figure or allegory reveals how identity and its alienation are two sides of the same coin.[56]

"Thine Onely Sonne Isaac"

As in Homer, names have meanings in the Hebrew Bible. Unlike Homer, though, the Bible is filled with naming and renaming stories that expose and exploit those meanings. The text introduces most characters of significance with accounts of how they received their names. As we have seen in Chapter

2, some characters, such as Abraham, even receive new names at pivotal moments in their lives, episodes that early modern readers often construed as conversionary moments. And if this be less true of female characters, in a text notoriously sparse in women's voices, the most revealing moments of female subjectivity, beginning with Eve's birthing of Cain, happen when mothers or surrogate mothers name their children. Though his name is the subject of extensive wordplays, the actual naming of Isaac is one of the more oblique naming stories in the book of Genesis. Unlike the naming of Isaac's own twin sons, Jacob and Esau, or Jacob's thirteen children, the passage that reports Isaac's birth does not explicitly link his name to the laughter with which Abraham and Sarah had earlier greeted the news of her imminent pregnancy. The etymology may be clear, but the reader must draw the connection. Yet Isaac's name and identity *are* given central attention in the initial command by God to Abraham concerning the sacrifice. In what is nearly a parody of the cumulative, inexorable pacing of biblical parataxis, God instruct Abraham, קח־נא את־בנך את־יחידך אשר־אהבת את־ יצחק, "Take, please, your son, your only one, whom you loved, Isaac." Agonizingly drawing out the process of identification—after all, Abraham has another son, Ishmael, from whom Isaac must be distinguished—the verse runs through a series of increasingly specific descriptors before arriving at the irreducible name, Isaac. The effect of this parataxis was not lost on early modern readers. In an extraordinary sermon on this biblical episode, George Downame provided his own attempt at translation, followed by an understanding that echoes numerous earlier rabbinic and patristic commentaries: "Take thy sonne, thine only sonne, whom thou lovest, even Isaac. Alas, what need all these words? had it not bin sufficient to breake his heart, to have said, take thy sonne, and offer him, but he must be put in minde that he was his onely sonne whom he loved, even Isaac his joy? But the Lord having given him strength to beare, laieth loade upon him, and by every word which is added, he addeth to the weight."[57] Downame's translation and comment make effective homiletic use of the Hebrew syntax. The King James Version, however, modifies the strict parataxis of the original, framing the name with the descriptors, grammatically isolating Isaac as distinct from the adjectival phrases: "Take now thy sonne, thine onely sonne Isaac, whom thou lovest."[58] This re-ordering of the verse shifts the emphasis of the call away from the culminating and specifying name of the object of (potential sacrifice) and onto the love of a father for his son (and, by implication, the pain that will come from having to sacrifice that son). The translation's new syntax thereby redirects our attention away from the specificity of a call that refines the identity of Abraham's son and instead makes it more conducive to serving as a moral example to the reader by bringing our attention back to Abraham, the paradigm of faith identified by Paul in Galatians 3.6ff., and the biblical figure potentially to be followed by those who share Abraham's faith in God.

Despite this shift toward a more paradigmatic understanding of the trial of Abraham, one noteworthy change the early modern Protestant translations (including the King James) make to the tradition of the Vulgate (and repeated in the Catholic Douay-Rheims) is to avoid the explicit typology in the phrase that was rendered in Latin as *unigenitum*, only begotten son. Instead of overtly anticipating the use of this term in the New Testament, for example in John 1.14 or 3.16, and thereby directly asserting the typological relationship between the binding of Isaac and the Passion of Christ, the King James Version and most of its Protestant predecessors opt for a far more literal rendering of the Hebrew יחידך, your only one. Deborah Shuger has argued that Renaissance biblical scholarship managed difference differently than medieval scholasticism, which habitually looked for repetitive patterns, typologies, and exempla.[59] These typologies functioned as a particular species of allegory—indeed, they were often described explicitly as biblical allegories—and are thus related to Chapman's allegorical approach to Homer. The typological reading of the binding story was a central feature of Christian interpretation from the very beginning, as can be seen in Galatians or Hebrews. Though Shuger is correct to suggestion a shift in early modern reading practices, as I argued in Chapter 2, typology remained a central homiletic tool, one that depended upon the belief in a reading that transcended or completed the letter, even as it preserved some significance that was inextricably bound to the particularities of the literal.[60] In his extensive comments on the book of Genesis, Gervase Babington reads the twenty-second chapter as both a display of Abraham's faith and as offering, "a lively figure of Jesus Christ, bearing his owne cross towards the place of execution, even as yong Isaac dooth here the word to burne himselfe withal."[61] Five years before the completion of the King James Version, Henoch Clapham wrote of the "parable of Isaac" in Genesis 22, deploying yet a third term, related to type and allegory, to announce a transcendent, universalizing significance for the events the chapter narrates.[62] The term parable also recollects the association between Jesus' explanation of his mode of teaching his disciples and translation as a fiction of conversion with which I began this chapter. In his *Hexapla in Genesis*, following rather extensive comments on the different formation of

Isaac's name preceding Genesis 22, Andrew Willett refers to the typological reading of the binding story as a commonplace.[63]

Though no member of the King James translating committees would have denied the typological importance of the binding of Isaac and its anticipation of God's sacrifice of his only begotten son, these Protestant readers were also impelled by a need to preserve the historicity of the events in the Old Testament, a historicity inherently linked to the particularity of named characters. The earliest editions of the King James Bible included more than thirty pages of genealogical tables charting the historical line from Adam to Christ. The explanation the editors offer for such extensive genealogies delineates the relationship between individual and national identity: "The Spirit of God in the sacred Historie, hath laid down such helps, as are the light and life of all Nations originals. In them the circumstances of *Person*, *Time*, and *Place*, are the chiefe; else doe we wander without a guide: and of these the *Person* is principall." Typology, a powerful method of abstraction and universalization, cannot be permitted to overwhelm history and particularity. Without the specifics of person, the reader will wander through Scriptures "without a guide." The headnote to Genesis 22 in the Geneva Bible had informed its readers of the meaning of these events: "The faith of Abraham is proved in offring his sonne Izhak. Izhak is a figure of Christ." Omitting moralizing and typologizing headnotes of this sort, the King James translators surrounded their version of the Bible with a different kind of textual apparatus, one that asserts a persistent particularity and irreducibility.

The status of biblical names proved to be especially contentious in the competing early modern efforts to translate Scriptures. The 1560 Geneva Bible provided its readers with a "Brief Table of the Interpretation of the Propre Names which are chiefly founde in the old Testament." The editors' explanation for this table bears citing at length:

> Whereas the wickedness of the time, and the blindnes of the former age hathe bene suche that all things altogether have bene abused and corrupted, so that the very right names of diverse of holie men named in the Scriptures have bene forgotten, and now seme strange unto us, and the names of infants that shulde ever have some godlie advertisements in them, and shulde be memorials and markes of children of God received into his housholde, hathe bene hereby also changed and made the signes and badges of idolatrie and heathenish impietie, we have now set forth this table of the names that be most

> used in the olde Testament with their interpretations, as the Ebrewe importeth, partly to call backe the godlie from that abuse, when they shal know the true names of the godlie fathers, & what they signifie, that their children now named after them may have testimonies by their very names, that they are within that faithful familie that in all their doings had ever God before their eyes, and that they are bounde by these their names to serue God from their infancie & have occasion to praise him for his workes wroght in them & their fathers: but chiefly to restore the names to their integritie, whereby many places of the Scriptures and secret mysteries of the holie Gost shal better be understand. We have medled rarely with the Greke names, because their interpretation is uncertaine, & many of them are corrupted from their original, as we may also se these Ebrewe names set in the margent of the table, which have bene corrupted by the Grecians. Now for the other Ebrewe names that are not here interprate, let not the diligent reader be careful: for he shal finde them in places moste convenient amongst the annotations: at least so many as may seme to make for any edification, and understanding of the Scriptures.[64]

Names serve multiple functions, according to this account, and the Geneva translators regarded it as their task to restore all these functions. The first portion of this passage speaks of names in terms that situate them within the realm of allegory and typology. As "godlie advertisements," "memorials and markes of children of God," and "testimonies," names confer identities to the persons to whom they have been given as a function of their having meanings that precede and transcend the individual subject. Those identities are secondary, however, to God's "householde," into which they are received. Not unlike the Althusserian idea of interpellation, the Geneva translators' recovery of the original names (and their meanings) enmeshes—"they are bounde by these names"—the subject "within that faithful familie" and prioritizes the discursive framework in which the names circulate over the subjects constituted by these names. Yet the translators also insist upon the restoration of these biblical names "to their integritie," linking that integrity to ineffable, esoteric "mysteries of the holie Gost." That is, even as the table of names this passage introduces provides interpretations, the editors nevertheless insist that these Hebrew names offer something irreducible, inherent in the particularities of language and reference, that cannot be distilled from them through a process of linguistic, allegorical, or typological interpretation. The second half of the editors' explanation takes up the theme of discursive integrity—and its corruption—that I have identified as a central concern of all early modern translation efforts. That is, the moment different linguistic traditions converge, there also emerges a potential threat to distinctiveness and to the possibility of names being self-identical with the subjects they designate.

When English Catholics undertook their own translation of the Bible and did so "out of the authentical Latin," rather than from the Hebrew Old Testament and Greek New Testament, the question of names arose again.[65] In a striking claim to linguistic priority and authenticity, the Rheims translators attacked their Protestant counterparts for

> their intolerable liberty and license to change the accustomed callings of God, angels, men, places & things vsed by the Apostles and all antiquitie, in Greeke, Latin and all other languages of Christian Nations, into new names, sometimes falsely, and alwaies ridiculously and for ostentation taken of the Hebreues: to frame and fine the phrase of holy Scriptures after the forme of prophane writers, sticking not, for the same to supply, adde, alter or diminish as freely as if they translated Livie, Virgil, or Terence. Having no religious respect to keepe either the majestie or sincere simplicity of that venerable style of Christes spirit.[66]

In their estimation, the names of antiquity—and therefore of greatest authenticity—were those to be found in "Greeke, Latin and all other languages of Christian Nations." (Re)naming a biblical character in Hebrew was a sign of novelty, falsity, and ridiculous ostentation. In what may look from our vantage point to be a stunning self-contradiction, the Rheims translators construe the Hebraizing of Greek and Latin names to be a profaning of the sacred language of Scripture and equating it with the writings of pagan classical literature.

Given the lively sixteenth-century debate prompted by the translation of biblical names, it comes as no surprise that when James I and Lancelot Andrewes convened the committees to begin the process of making "a good [translation] better, or out of many good ones, one principal good one," among the explicit considerations raised was the matter of naming. The second of the fifteen "Rules to be observed in Translation," Archbishop Richard Bancroft's letter of instructions, calls for "the names of the Profyts and the holie Wryters, with the other Names in the text to be retained, as near as may be, according as they are vulgarly used." The translators were no doubt aware of the meanings inherent in every Hebrew name. Indeed, Babington argues that the Adamic language was Hebrew, "for so say the proper names of men and women, which remayne as yet and are Hebrew, being imposed then and not altered by Moses."[67] The practice of giving children content-laden English names like Eschew-evil or Learn-wisdom or Increase was a phenomenon widespread enough during this time for Ben Jonson mercilessly to satire in his plays.[68] Yet Bancroft's instructions insist on deferring to the names "vulgarly used." I think he means two different things by this phrase. First, the names should not be translated into their English meanings: Abraham and not Great Father, Joseph and not Increase, Samuel and not God Hears. Second, the translators are called upon to use the names that had been circulating for centuries as products of the Vulgate's vast influence.[69] Isaac is the name the Vulgate uses for the second patriarch (itself derived from the Septuagint's ισαακ). The Geneva translators had tried to distance themselves from this papist tradition—for which the Rheims Preface had taken them to task as being ridiculously ostentatious. Their second patriarch goes by the name Izhak, a far closer approximation of the Hebrew as it might have sounded to a sixteenth-century Christian Hebraist; the Geneva's table of names explicitly identifies the name Isaak as one of several that have been "corrupted by the Grecians." Even the 1568 Bishops Bible modified the name, calling him Isahac. In returning to the name "vulgarly used," Isaac, the King James translators are reassimilating a figure who threatened to become alien and exotic with an unfamiliar name. Much the way Chapman's Ulysses functioned vis-à-vis the Greek name Odysseus, the King James translator's preferred name for the second patriarch effectively sustains his conversion from a Jewish, Hebraic figure (יצחק) to a Christian, English one (Isaac).

Only a few years after the publication of the King James Version, Francis Bacon, in his *Novum Organum*, would wring his hands over the challenges posed by language "vulgarly used" to the acquisition of precise knowledge grounded in distinction and individuation: "Now words, being commonly framed and applied according to the capacity of the vulgar (*ex captu vulgi induntur*), follow those lines of division which are most obvious to the vulgar understanding (*vulgari intellectui*). And whenever an understanding of greater acuteness or a more diligent observation would alter those lines to suit the true division of nature, words stand in the way and resist change."[70] Looking at the matter of linguistic imprecision from the other side, Bacon nevertheless shares with the King James translators the view that vulgar usage confers and sustains familiarity, eliding difference and domesticating identity. In both the

King James Bible (Isaac) and in Chapman's Homer (Ulysses), Latin, the prototype for the language of the *vulgus*, serves as a mediating, acculturating idiom.

The apostle Paul's conversion pivots on a name change, from Saul to Paul (*Σαυλος* to *Παυλος*), that is also a shift from Hebrew to Greek. Naomi Seidman has argued that the radical transformation of the self, the rebirth of a new person at the moment of conversion, is at odds with an understanding of translation as the transference "of meaning 'whole' from one language to another, unaltered by the change in language."[71] My examination of the King James and Chapman translations suggests that the questions of identity and alterity posed by the particularly acute challenge of translating names produced incomplete conversions. When the King James translators do not translate the name and do not include any marginal glosses to convey the paronomastic quality of the name, the meaning is lost. A supplementary note to Isaac's naming would not necessarily have been out of order. The sixth rule in Bancroft's letter proclaimed, "Noe marginal notes att all to be affixed, but only for ye explanation of ye Hebrew or Greeke Words, which cannot without some circumlocution soe briefly and fitly be expressed in ye Text." Miles Smith's preface to the King James makes explicit the need for occasional marginal glosses, "doth not a margine do well to admonishe the Reader to seeke further, and not to conclude or dogmatize vpon this or that peremptorily? . . . diversitie of signification and sense in the margine, where the text is not so cleare, must needes doe good, yea is necessary, as we are perswaded." Though there are examples of such admonishments to the reader when names are given, for example when Leah and Rachel name Jacob's twelve sons and one daughter, in most of the key naming and renaming narratives in Genesis, of Cain, of Abraham and Sarah, of Isaac, of Jacob, the King James translators remain remarkably silent—to the great frustration of their readers who lack any Hebrew knowledge. How, for example, is a reader meant to make sense of the critical renaming of Jacob in the King James Version: "Thy name shall be called no more Jacob, but Israel: for as a prince hast thou power with God and with men, and hast prevailed." No note in the margin explains that ישראל conveys the sense of striving with God. The name remains opaque, strange, without sense. The gesture of making it familiar—Israel and not ישראל—like calling Odysseus Ulysses, obscures the significance of the name. Naming, and the identity it signifies, cannot admit "diversitie of signification." The conversion of the text, like the translation of the name, remains incomplete, pulled between the demands of irreducible identity and linguistic transparency.

Chapter 4

Alchemies of Conversion: Shakespeare, Jonson, Vaughan, and the Science of Jewish Transmutation

In February 2007 a memo was circulated by the offices of Georgia state legislator Ben Bridges, calling for the elimination of the teaching of evolution in public schools on the grounds that it was derived from "Rabbinic writings" and other Jewish texts. While it may come as a surprise to some that "tax-supported evolution science" is really a Jewish plot, and that "evolutionism" (*not* creationism) violates the separation of church and state, all it takes is a perusal of representative Bridges's source, www.fixedearth.com, to learn something of the depth and breadth of this pernicious conspiracy. According to the website's author, Marshall Hall, "Contra-scientific, Christ-hating Pharisee Kabbalist Occultists (using *theoretical non-science and phony physics*) have deceived the whole world into believing that 15 billion years of Big Bang Evolutionism has produced all that exists. Anyone can know that evolution is a lie by just studying the facts. But now anyone can also know that evolution is a double-damned lie. It has never been 'secular' science as the world has been led to believe. Rather, it has been a long labor of a Cabal of Pharisee Religionists to destroy the Bible's credibility from Creation to Jesus to Heaven."[1]

A plot this insidious can only have been secretly planned and executed by Jewish conspirators over thousands of years. As incontrovertible proof, Hall's obsessively cross-referenced and annotated website pulls out all the stops to confirm the Jewish identity of that notorious "Kabbalist physicist Albert Einstein" and so many other modern day Pharisees who occupy endowed chairs of physics and biology at universities around the country.

We may laugh at the absurdity of such an account, but I cite it here as a contemporary and admittedly extreme instance in the complex and controversial relationship between science and religion, a late avatar of my topic in this chapter, the inter-animation of discourses of alchemy (as both a scientific and a spiritual technology) and Jewishness in the early modern period. Insofar as alchemy served as a science of transmutation, it offers a rich context in which to explore questions of permanence and change, authenticity and fraudulence—and the anxieties and expectations these questions prompted—at the heart of both material and personal conversion. The striking early modern resurgence of interest in alchemy, almost at the same time as the emergence of the New Science (and often in the work of the progenitors of this new approach to natural philosophy), coincided with the flourishing of a variety of millennial and eschatological writings, many of which posited as one of their primary expectations the conversion, en masse, of Jews who had heretofore adhered stubbornly to their mistaken ways. When alchemy was linked to Jews and Judaism during the early modern period, to the advantage and/or detriment of both, the transformational potentials of alchemy were often conflated with the proselytizing impulses that characterized the early modern English encounter with Jews. The controversy animating much recent scholarship over the relative importance of esoteric, or spiritual, kinds of alchemy versus exoteric, or material, alchemical technologies is a direct corollary to the issues that inform the fraught legacy of alchemy's Jewish provenance in the early modern period.[2]

One of the first sustained modern attempts to address the ostensibly Jewish provenance of alchemical lore was Raphael Patai's *The Jewish Alchemists*. A collection of primary sources that have, at one time or another, been identified as Jewish in origin, Patai's book also includes the remarkable claim that the prestige attributed to Jewish alchemy was so great that non-Jewish alchemical writers were occasionally posthumously converted to Judaism, to give them more substantial authority and authenticity.[3] What is especially striking about this apparent judaizing of alchemy is that it seems to invert the fantasy of Jewish conversion to Christianity that was so often a concomitant of Christian esoteric and millenarian texts. The present chapter represents, in part, an investigation of Patai's claim, its background, and its further implications. I suggest that allusions to the supposed Jewish origins of alchemy, for better or for worse, are frequently embedded in eschatological discourses that anxiously raise the possibility of Jewish conversion while rendering such religious change potentially problematic in light of emerging notions of Protestant English identity. My account of alchemy's fraught Jewish provenance focuses on two distinct periods in early modern English culture, from 1592 to 1624 and from 1649 to 1660. A discussion of the first period serves, in turn, as the context for a reading of Ben Jonson's 1610 satire *The Alchemist* in relation to some of its dramatic precursors. The focus of the second period provides the basis for an enriched understanding of the oft-noted presence of alchemical imagery in the poetry of Henry Vaughan.

I want to stress that I am less interested here in the actual and verifiable Jewish *origins* of alchemical lore than I am in the divergent ways in which alchemical writers identified this esoteric knowledge with Jewish wisdom or, conversely, denied Jewish provenance or authenticity to "true" alchemy. In his important exploratory essay on the relationship between alchemy and Kabbalah, Gershom Scholem wrote rather dismissively of what he called the "market crier" explanation for alchemical texts labeled as kabbalistic. By this he meant the way in which Kabbalah might have been used superficially—sometimes just on the title page—as bait to lure curious but ill-informed readers to buy texts imbued with an aura of antiquity and the occult.[4] We ought not be too quick to write off that explanation simply because there may have been nothing authentic about the claims of Jewish or Kabbalistic origins for any given alchemical text. It is no mere coincidence, I think, that Scholem has characterized this tactic as a kind of bait and switch in ways that directly parallel the con games played by Subtle, Face, and Dol, the "venture tripartite" in Jonson's play. Furthermore, as Brian Copenhaver has observed, while the study of natural magic and alchemy, precursors to modern science, increasingly engaged in the empirical confirmation of their theoretical occultism, "a third source of confirmation for belief in natural magic . . . was *doxographic*, and it represented not so much a succession of ideas as a succession of names, attached, often vaguely, to ideas."[5] That is, the authority of the occult was vested in its pedigree, its transmission from one respected adept to another. It is on this characteristically vague, multivalent doxography of alchemy that I focus my discussion.

A Great Concealing

Assertions of links between Jewish learning and alchemy can be traced well back into the medieval period, though there is almost no evidence that alchemy actually originated or even underwent significant development within ancient Hebraic or rabbinic thought.[6] When medieval or early modern

Christian writers suggested Jewish origins for alchemical wisdom, these origins served mostly to confirm the esoteric nature of alchemy. As Scholem and others have noted, the extraordinarily influential works of the fifteenth-century Florentine humanists, Pico Della Mirandola, Marsilio Ficino, and others, contributed significantly to the rising prestige of Jewish mystical writings. The extensive intellectual exchanges between Pico and Ficino and Jewish scholars like Elia del Medigo and Johanan Alemanno, who initiated them into the world of Jewish Kabbalah as part of their syncretistic quest for the perennial philosophy, have been well documented. Though it was not especially focused on alchemy, the inclusion of Kabbalah within the rubric of the Hermeticism *cum* neo-platonism of Pico and Ficino, and especially the Christian interpretation of Jewish mystical traditions, would lay some of the groundwork for the more overt association of Kabbalah with alchemy.[7]

But the esotericism of Jewish wisdom could be a double-edged sword. It might authenticate such knowledge by virtue of its presumed antiquity, yet it might also raise suspicions about its deceptive, corrupting, even toxic, dangers. For example, a tract attributed to one of England's earliest and most celebrated alchemists, the Franciscan friar Roger Bacon, grapples with a primary challenge to the validity of alchemy, its inaccessibility or opacity to the uninitiated reader. Enumerating a series of reasons for these difficulties, Bacon laments how "things are obscured by the admixtion of letters of diuerse kinds, . . . with Hebrew, Greeke & Latin letters, all in a row. . . . They hide their secrets, writing them in other letters then are vsed in their owne counrty, to wit, when they take letters that are in vse in forreine nations, and feigne them according to their own pleasures."[8] Bacon suggests here that alchemical writing is characteristically difficult because of its linguistic hybridity. The arduous steps required to decipher a language corrupted by the "admixtion of letters of diuerse kinds" resemble the processes of refinement and distillation central to alchemical work. What is more, these difficulties bear important structural and ideological affinities to emergent discourses of national and even ethnic purity, especially at the heart of much of the writings about Jews and their potential conversion to Christianity.[9] On the one hand, as Jonathan Gil Harris has shown, "Jewish infiltration of the Christian body politic had been repeatedly coded in pathological terms . . . since the medieval period."[10] That is, Jews were often identified with corruption and impurity. In and of themselves they were corrupt; and, more important, their disruptive and poisonous presence in the Christian body politic would inevitably have corrupting effects on that body. On the other hand, Jews posed a threat to Christian identity, and particularly to the central Christian claim of soteriological supersession, that specifically stemmed from the resiliency of their Jewish lineage, the resistance to dilution and "admixtion" that made it so difficult for many European Christians to imagine the fully successful conversion of Jews to Christianity. This paradox is, as I have suggested in Chapter 1, the unspoken converse to the ideology of the laws of *limpieza de sangre*, or blood purity, the legacy of mass conversions in Spain and Portugal. While these laws may have been enacted to ensure the purity of the lines of Old Christians, that purity was threatened precisely by a Christian belief in the persistence of Jewish blood despite its dilution through marriages with Christians.

Bacon's discussion of the linguistic admixtions of alchemical writings grapples with these same tensions; what begins as some general observations concerning the challenging presence of Hebrew and Greek writing quickly become particular concerns with the language of the Jews. He goes on to compare the trials of deciphering the cryptic qualities of alchemical writings to the difficulties of readings texts in Hebrew and other Semitic languages that lack vocalization: "some haue hidden their secretes by their maners of writing, as namely by consonants only: so that no man can reade them, without he knowe the signification of the words: and this is vsual among the Iewes, Chaldeans, Syrians, and Arabians, . . . and therefore there is a great concealing with them, but especially with the Iewes."[11] The ambiguity of the pronominal referent in that final phrase, "a great concealing with them," draws our attention to the slippage between the abstractions of a technical discussion of linguistic idiosyncrasies and anxieties about the status of Jewish bodies, even when they may have undergone the process of religious conversion. As Bacon goes on to suggest, a language without vocalization, such as Hebrew, comes to figure the spiritless body that served as the foil or counterpoint for the transcending spiritual salvation Christianity offered. In vocalizing the lifeless consonants of the Hebrew writing, the Christian adept recovers and restores the wisdom that has been concealed within it. The Jew who converts to Christianity undergoes a parallel restoration in the recovery of his "true" life in the body of Christ. As we shall see below, during what some scholars have called the "vitalist moment" of the mid-seventeenth century, the Jewish provenance of ontological claims about the unity of matter and spirit was called directly into question. Though Bacon raises no such doubts, he does appear to invoke the threat of crypto-Judaism, a "great concealing" of the Jew's true nature in the garb of a practicing Christian.[12] The occult nature of Jewish identity cohered with and confirmed the connection between Jews and the hidden meanings of alchemical writings.

I have been treating Roger Bacon's authorship of this alchemical text as though it were a definitive, but in all likelihood the text was written some time in the sixteenth century, some three hundred years after Bacon lived. Pseudepigrapha are, of course, notoriously prevalent in esoteric writings, the *corpus hermeticum* being only the most famous example, but it is worth pausing for a moment to consider the dubious provenance of this particular text. "An Excellent Discourse of the Admirable Force and Efficacie of Art and Nature" was first published in English and ascribed to Bacon in 1597 in the collection entitled *The Mirror of Alchimy*, one of the earliest English alchemical volumes. This anthology of alchemical texts was a translation, with notable additions ("Bacon's" text being one of them), of a French text, *Le Miroir d'Alquimie*, published in 1557, which was in turn a translation, with its own earlier additions, of a Latin text, *De Alchimia*, published in Nuremburg in 1541.[13] As we saw above, in Chapter 3, translation's function as a technology of transformation has important relevance to any discussion of fictions of conversion during the early modern period. When a text is serially translated in this fashion—with new material added to it—we may well ask to what extent its content is either distilled or diluted by the process. My purpose here, however, is to consider the timing of this English edition.

The publication of "An Excellent Discourse" as part of the English alchemical anthology occurred within five years of the earliest performance of Christopher Marlowe's *The Jew of Malta*. In this play, the eponymous character, Barabas, repeatedly brags about all the menacing activities with which Jews had become associated and that anticipate Bacon's—or rather, pseudo-Bacon's—rhetoric concerning the Jewish origins of alchemical texts. In a speech that takes Marlovian delight in magnifying the villainy of which it boasts, Barabas begins with one of the more notorious libels about Jewish corruption, well poisoning: "As for myself, I walk abroad a-nights / And kill sick people groaning under walls; / Sometimes I go about and poison wells." Accusations of well poisoning and its frequent concomitant, the spreading of the plague, were often supported by assertions of Jewish expertise in the malevolent counterpart to alchemical knowledge, the crafting of toxins. As physicians, in particular, Jews were believed to possess semi-magical powers either to cure or to harm the sick.[14] Indeed, Jews living in various degrees of secrecy and openness in England in the early modern period who left any traces in the historical record were mostly physicians and merchants, both areas of endeavor with intimate, inextricable ties to alchemy.[15] Marlowe's Barabas had, at one time or another, participated in both activities. After describing his poisoning activities he thinks back further, to his earlier years when he trained in medicine, gleefully describing how he used his expertise as a physician to murder Christians:

> Being young, I studied physic, and began
> To practice first upon the Italian;
> There I enriched the priest with burials,
> And always kept the sexton's arms in ure
> With digging graves and ringing dead men's knells.

Marlowe's Jew of Malta goes further still, associating himself with acts of usury, extortion, and other forms of financial and mercantile deception, but also embodying the particular fear of the Jew as a corrupting presence in the body politic, one whose allegiances could never be trusted: "And in the wars 'twixt France and German, / Under pretence of helping Charles the Fifth, / [I] Slew friend and enemy with my strategems."[16] As has often been noted, these Jewish libels acquired a local habitation and a name just two years after the first performance of *The Jew of Malta*, and three years before the publication of pseudo-Bacon's meditations of Jewish alchemical knowledge, when the Portuguese *converso*, Roderigo Lopez, was tried and executed for having plotted to poison Queen Elizabeth, an accusation made especially believable by virtue of his role as a physician to the queen. Lopez's supposed last words on the scaffold before he was beheaded are infamous for the very same reason pseudo-Bacon expressed anxiety about the ambiguities of Hebrew writing. As William Camden reported it, Lopez "affirm[ed] that he had loved the Queen as he loved Jesus Christ, which from a man of the Jewish profession was heard not without laughter."[17] The exquisitely equivocating implications of these final words cannot but remind us of pseudo-Bacon's similarly ambiguous statement, "there is a great concealing with them, but especially with the Iewes."[18]

Our Librarians

Given the fraught stakes of alchemical doxography, it comes as no surprise that "Bacon's" text is not the only early modern discourse on alchemy whose compositional lineage is in doubt. Another important early modern text of alchemy offers a particularly rich example of the peripatetic journeys ascribed to esoteric knowledge and, indeed, the intellectual cache such a wandering pedigree might lend to the wisdom it offered. The origins of this text, the "Exposition of Hieroglyphicall Figures," remain uncertain. First published in French in 1612 by the editor and translator Pierre Arnaud de la Chevallerie as *Le Livre des figures hiéroglyphiques*, then translated into English in 1624 by an unknown Englishman who took the pen name Eirenæus Orandus, the text is ascribed to a fourteenth-century Parisian scribe and clerk by the name of Nicholas Flamel. Though materials within this text have been traced to medieval alchemical manuals, the narrative that introduces this text and describes how the knowledge came into Flamel's hands seems to be a later interpolation by Arnaud and further supplemented by the English translator.[19] Like pseudo-Bacon's "Excellent Discourse," therefore, the account attributed to Flamel to which I now turn is most likely a product of this later period.

Flamel's story makes more explicit than even pseudo-Bacon's text the complexities of a belief in the Jewish, kabbalistic provenance of alchemical knowledge. "Flamel" describes how he came upon a book with its title page inscribed "in great Capitall letters of gold, Abraham The Jew, Prince, Priest, Levite, Astrologer, And Philosopher, To The Nation Of The Jewes, By The Wrath Of God Dispersed Among The Gaules, Sendeth Health"; Flamel goes on to speculate that the book "had beene stolne or taken from the miserable *Jewes*; or found hid in some part of the ancient place of their abode."[20] These golden letters—and the story that accompanies them—suggestively capture the predicament of Jewish alchemy. Imprinted materially on the page, the letters promise the gold sought by all alchemists, attesting to the authenticity of the secrets the book contains. The mythic source of this knowledge, Abraham the Jew, a prince, a priest, a levite, an astrologer, and a natural philosopher, had reached the pinnacle of worldly, religious, and scholarly achievement. The wisdom Abraham preserved in his book is validated by virtue of its ancient origins among the Jews who once enjoyed God's exclusive favor, as Flamel continues, "although it was well and intelligibly figured and painted, yet no man could ever have beene able to understand it, without being well skilled in their *Cabala*, which goeth by tradition, and without having well studied their bookes." As in pseudo-Bacon's text, an understanding of alchemy's secrets depends upon a legacy of transmitted knowledge. What is more, Flamel's narrative appears to conform to the Augustinian doctrine of Jewish witness so thoroughly analyzed by Jeremy

Cohen.[21] Augustine explained the lingering existence of Jews living among Christian believers as a necessity precisely because they preserved the scriptural tradition sacred to Christianity. Jews were, in Augustine's memorable phrase, *custodes librorum nostrorum*, "guardians of our books," and *librarii nostri*, "our librarians."[22] Flamel's anecdote describing the origins of his book of Jewish alchemy serves as a literal example of such a custodial function. The title page of the book Flamel finds even conveniently includes the critical corollary to the Augustinian idea of Jewish witness in its reminder that the Jewish people were "by the wrath of God dispersed" among the nations.[23] Just as important as the Jewish origin of the book is that its subsequent peregrinations testify to Jewish opprobrium.

The complex dynamics of ethnic and religious identities may be seen in the title page of Abraham the Jew's book. Whether Flamel meant for his reader to think of this Abraham the Jew as the biblical patriarch or only his later namesake, the name Abraham would have necessarily evoked, for the early modern reader, the very origins of religious conversion insofar as it recollected the biblical name change from Abram to Abraham precisely at the moment of the establishment of the covenantal relationship between God and the first patriarch. The biblical patriarch needed to begin his life as Abram—and to father a specific nation of Jews—for his converted identity of Abraham to have the requisite significance. The slippage in Flamel's speculations about the means by which the book left the possession of Abraham the Jew and eventually came into Flamel's hands attests to this fraught ancestry. The book might have been stolen or taken from the "miserable" Jews, he speculates, or it might simply have been found and recovered from some part of the "ancient place of their abode," exactly as it was meant to be transmitted from the Jews to the Gentiles, from Abram to Abraham.[24]

Yet Flamel's accidental—or perhaps implicitly providential—acquisition of this Jewish book does not end the story of his coming into possession of the alchemical knowledge contained within it. He describes at length his frustration at his inability to understand the words and figures contained within the text. "In the end having lost all hope of ever understanding those *figures*," Flamel writes, "for my last refuge, I made a vow to God, and St. *James* of *Gallicia*, to demand the interpretation of them, at some *Jewish Priest*, in some *Synagogue* of *Spaine*: . . . and so much I did, that I arrived at *Montjoy*, and afterwards at *Saint James*, where with great devotion I accomplished my vow. This done, in *Leon* at my returne I met with a Merchant of *Boloyn*, which made me knowne to a *Physician*, a *Jew*, by Nation, and as then a *Christian*, dwelling in *Leon* aforesaid, who was very skilfull in sublime Sciences, called Master *Canches*."[25] This *converso* physician was "rauished with great astonishment and ioy" upon being shown the book and demanded to know how Flamel had come into possession of it. Over the course of the next several weeks, while they traveled together to Orleans, Master Canches began the process of deciphering for Flamel "the greatest part of [the] figures, where euen vnto the very points and prickes, he found great *misteries*." Though Canches died very soon after they had arrived in Orleans, he had succeeded in revealing the wealth of secrets in the book and, in gratitude for his assistance, Flamel "caused him to be buried in the *Church* of the *holy Crosse* at *Orleans*, where hee yet resteth; God haue his soule, for hee dyed a good *Christian*."[26] Augustine's doctrine of Jewish witness undergoes an important revision in this story. For while the book begins as a Jewish object whose value has been preserved exclusively for the use of its Christian reader, the Christian reader can only recover that value through the assistance of a Jewish interpreter. And yet, the authority by which his interpretations can be verified, i.e., that he is of the "Jewish Nation," cannot remain intact for fear that it may preclude the supersessionary abrogation of Judaism by Christianity. Master Canches was not just of the Jewish Nation, he became a Christian—the paradigmatic Spanish *converso* physician, no less—whose conversion was confirmed by his burial in the church of the Holy Cross.

The Sum of Something

Flamel's account of his encounter with Master Canches and the authority he vests in this Jewish teacher who allows him to learn or, perhaps, recover the wisdom that should, by rights, have been transmitted to the Christian world was a familiar story in the seventeenth century. In 1596, the English scholar Hugh Broughton began an exchange of letters with a Turkish Jew, Avraham Reuven. Broughton was one of the earliest Englishmen to attain a real proficiency in Hebrew and Aramaic. Like many second-generation Christian Hebraists, he studied these Semitic languages under the instruction of a fellow Christian, Antoine Chevalier, rather than any Jewish tutor. Indeed, for much of his early education, Broughton is likely to have had minimal contact with contemporary Jewish communities; any contacts he did have with living Jews would have likely been during his time on the Continent, especially in Amsterdam. Perhaps because Reuven was one of the few "real"

Jews with whom he had more than superficial contact, Broughton frequently cited this relationship to validate his claims to authority and special knowledge. Indeed, Broughton's many opponents—he had, by this time, succeeded in alienating himself from powerful figures in the English Church—accused him of completely inventing the figure of Avraham Reuven so as to give him—Broughton—some authority and credibility.[27] Despite these accusations concerning the inauthentic nature of the letters exchanged between Broughton and Reuven (written entirely in Hebrew), it is clear that this was a real correspondence. Reuven was no imaginary or purely textual Jew. It is equally clear, however, that while the correspondence between Broughton and Reuven did take place, Broughton profoundly misconstrued Reuven's letters. Broughton took the excessively complimentary tone of the letters he received to mean that Reuven wanted him to come to preach conversion to the Jews of Constantinople. Reuven was neither in the position to extend such an invitation—he did not have any rabbinical authority, having achieved whatever prominence he enjoyed as a minor poet—nor was he interested in Broughton's conversionary goals.[28] His letters to Broughton were not an invitation to sermonize, but part and parcel of a much more extensive commercial network of connections established between Turkish Jews and English merchants, diplomats, and divines. Reuven was one of many Jewish middlemen who played a crucial role in the rapidly expanding trade relationships between England and the Levant. Yet Broughton's millenarian enthusiasm for the prospect of Jewish conversion appears to have skewed his reading of this exchange. Among Broughton's best-known publications was his *Concent of Scripture* (it went through at least four printings), a meticulous and painstakingly researched treatise on prophetic literature that was meant to resolve once and for all the disparities between Jewish and Christian eschatological thought, thereby clearing away any remaining impediments to the collective conversion of Jews to Protestant Christianity.

Broughton and his eschatological writings were familiar enough to English audiences to have served as the basis for one of Ben Jonson's most withering attacks in his play *The Alchemist*. About midway through the satire, the comically self-indulgent Epicure Mammon makes the grave mistake of describing his ambitions of wealth in the apocalyptic terms of a Fifth Monarchy to Dol Common, who, he has been led to believe, is a wealthy heiress. Dol takes this oblique eschatological reference as her cue, counterfeiting an extended rant that invokes "Talmud skill," "Rabbi David Kimchi," "Onkelos," and "Aben Ezra." Face had earlier cautioned Mammon not to incite Dol in this direction:

She is a most rare scholar,
And is gone mad with studying Broughton's works.
If you but name a word touching the Hebrew,
She falls into her fit, and will discourse
So learnedly of genealogies,
As you would run mad, too, to hear her, sir.
(II.iii.237–242)[29]

I cite the Broughton-Reuven interchange and its interesting parallels with Flamel's story about his encounter with Master Canches as the bases for my working hypothesis of a deeper connection between Jonson's play and two earlier dramatic representations of Jewish commercial activity on the English stage, Marlowe's *The Jew of Malta* and Shakespeare's *The Merchant of Venice*. Though himself no imaginary Jew, Reuven served the same mercantile role his dramatic counterparts, Barabas and Shylock, had served on the English stage. While Broughton did not hesitate to enlist commercial interests in his efforts to expand his proselytizing amongst the Jews, Reuven and his fellow Ottoman Jews seem to have exploited these hopes as well, using them to leverage their own positions as intermediaries in the rapidly expanding, notoriously unpredictable trade markets. It has long been recognized that Jonson's satire of alchemical conmen is engaged in a complex critique of the emerging mercantile, capitalist economies of the early modern world.[30] All the gulls who fall prey to the "venture tripartite"—itself a clear reference to this new economy—serve as caricatures of the material schemes that were multiplying, seemingly out of control, with the development of new markets and economic instruments that promised the creation of wealth *ex nihilo*, or at least *ex nequam materia*, out of worthless material.[31] This specious promise was, of course, also at the heart of the medieval and early modern anxiety about another financial instrument, usury.[32] And so it is by this connection that I am led back several years earlier to the play that combines an anxious examination of nascent economic transformations with an equally anxious account of the dynamics of conversion, *The Merchant of Venice*.[33] Whether it refers to the transmutation of lead into gold, matter into quintessence, or Jew into Christian, conversion is an inherently destabilizing process.

Shakespeare's play appears to offer its conversions under the fiction of sincerity and permanence, yet, particularly in light of its coordination of monetary and personal conversions, the play renders these transformations as unstable or potentially inauthentic.

Probably written the same year Broughton received his first letter from Reuven (1596), Shakespeare's examination of the dangerous alchemy of usury directly links conversion to interest bearing and reproduction. When Bassanio successfully chooses the correct (leaden) casket and thereby wins the right to marry Portia (itself an alchemical conversion, since his choice of lead will be transmuted to the gold Portia possesses in great quantities), she commits herself to Bassanio in the following terms:

> You see me, Lord Bassanio, where I stand,
> Such as I am. Though for myself alone
> I would not be ambitious in my wish
> To wish myself much better, yet for you
> I would be trebled twenty times myself,
> A thousand times more fair, then thousand times more rich,
> That only to stand high in your account,
> I might in virtues, beauties, livings, friends,
> Exceed account.
>
> (*The Merchant of Venice*, III.ii.149–157)[34]

Portia combines the language of personal merit—itself a fraught idea for an English culture infused with Calvinist notions of unmerited grace and figured here in terms of abstract qualities like virtue and beauty—with the language of material wealth. In an anomalous alexandrine that metrically embodies her impulse toward excess in the additional foot, Portia's wish to be "a thousand times more fair" leads directly to her desire to be a thousand times more rich, the increase of both apparently constitutive of her being "trebled twenty times" herself. She *seems* to deflect any self-interest: "Though for myself alone / I would not be ambitious." Yet this very deflection serves to underscore the link between monetary gain and abstract value. Indeed, Bassanio makes no effort to hide his motives for seeking Portia's hand from Antonio, reassuring his friend earlier in the play that a marriage to this rich heiress will help him to pay off all his debts.

Portia goes on to represent herself as undergoing a personal conversion that combines material enrichment and immaterial, subjective transmutation:

But the full sum of me
Is sum of something—which, to term in gross,
Is an unlessoned girl, unschooled, unpracticed;
Happy in this, she is not yet so old
But she may learn; happier than this,
She is not bred so dull but she can learn;
Happiest of all, is that her gentle spirit
Commits itself to yours to be directed,
As from her lord, her governor, her king.
Myself, and what is mine, to you and yours
Is now *converted.*
(III.ii.157–167, emphasis added)

As we discover in her ingenious intervention in the court scene of Act IV, Portia is anything but "unlessoned . . . , unschooled, unpracticed." I shall turn in a few moments to the function of counterfeiting within the discourses of transformation. For now, however, I note that Portia's conversion of herself and what is hers is preliminary to her subsequent and necessary intervention in the dispute over the bond between Shylock and Antonio. While her wealth does not come in time for Bassanio to pay off the loan, her betrothal to Bassanio, and the conversion of her more abstract (and undersold) "virtues" to her new husband's disposal, do save his friend from the Jew's knife.

Jessica's marriage to Lorenzo is, of course, the play's other transmutation. Like Portia's conversion, it brings with it not only a newly Christianized wife, but also a lot of cash, as Shylock reportedly laments—"My daughter! O my ducats! O my daughter! / Fled with a Christian! O my Christian ducats!" (II.viii.15–16). Each of these conversions, because it involves a woman whose status undergoes a change in the context of marriage, lays bare the inseparability of material and spiritual transformation. As I noted above in my discussion of the book of Ruth, the function of *coverture* as a legal means of constructing the material, economic transformation of an unmarried woman to a married wife inevitably informed understandings of a woman's religious conversion in the context of marriage.[35]

But what of Shylock? His is the play's final, most memorable conversion and it is the one that lingers most uncomfortably, as the Jew-turn'd-Christian sulks off the stage: "I pray you give me leave to go from hence. / I am not well. Send the deed after me, / And I will sign it" (IV.i.394–96). That's the last we hear from Shylock, who must be converted from his menacing, homicidal ways.[36] If Shakespeare's play doesn't quite know what to do with the Jew, it works very hard to lighten his presence by eliminating him at the end of Act IV so that our final visions are of the other two, apparently more satisfying, conversions; the play closes with the idyllic visions of Lorenzo and Jessica, Gratiano and Nerissa, and Bassanio and Portia at the country estate of Belmont. Yet, as numerous critics have observed, the discomfiting ring trick Portia and Nerissa play on their new husbands, and its resolution through the self-sacrifice—yet once more—by Antonio, do not allow the audience to forget the troubling confusion of wealth and human flesh that almost cost Antonio's life and that forced Shylock, instead, to trade his life for half his wealth by becoming a Christian. While *The Merchant of Venice* is not explicitly alchemical, it draws on many of alchemy's tropes, establishing the connection between (apparently immaterial, mystified) money-multiplying and religious conversion. This is the subtext of the early exchange between Antonio and Shylock as they set the terms of their "merry bond." Moneylenders become connected to the discourse of alchemy through the alchemist's reputation as a counterfeiter and "coin-washer." Religious conversion parallels the process of alchemical transmutation. And Jews, as we have seen, were regarded as the problematical sources of alchemical knowledge. It is in Jonson's play about alchemical con artists that these points fully converge.

Fetching the Age of Gold

In reading *The Merchant of Venice* as a precursor to Jonson's play, I am arguing that *The Alchemist* takes up Shakespeare's fictions of conversion, multiplies and coordinates them even further, and in so doing probes the instability of these transformations. While Jonson's play includes no Jews in its dramatis personae, I suggest, as an imaginative exercise in its own right and in light of my account of alchemy's supposed Jewish provenance, that the Jew who had been ostensibly converted at the end of Shakespeare's play returns to haunt Jonson's stage in the guise of the alchemist. Combining the functions of the converter and the subject of conversion, the alchemist figures the contaminating instability of these fictions of conversion. My proposal of the transformation of Shakespeare's Shylock into Jonson's alchemist can be justified on the basis of several suggestive confluences. It is entirely likely that Jonson would have been aware of the association of Jews with alchemy and other esoteric knowledge. Jason Rosenblatt and Winfried Schleiner have shown that he was a beneficiary of the increased interest in the Judaic and Hebraic tradition that characterized this period in England, having corresponded with another great English Hebraist of the period, John Selden, in particular about a variety of esoteric and arcane matters.[37] As proof of the validity of the alchemist's power, Mammon invokes the *prisca sapientia*: "I'll show you a book where Moses and his sister / And Solomon have written of the art; / Aye, and a treatise penned by Adam" (*The Alchemist*, II.i.81–83).[38] This intellectual and religious search for a perennial philosophy was conversionary in its very constitution, transforming all ancient wisdom, regardless of its apparent provenance, to Christian truth.

But the nexus of Jew and alchemist and its relevance to Jonson's play extend further still. Alchemists were notorious for their offensive smells as a result of their intimate work with various compounds, especially sulfur. When she tries to settle an early dispute between Subtle and Face, Dol Common complains, " 'Sdeath, you abominable pair of stinkards, / Leave off your barking, and grow one again" (I.i.117–18). Thomas Browne's *Pseudodoxia Epidemica* reports a false belief that had reached epidemic proportions in early modern Europe, "That Jews stinck naturally, that is, that in their race and nations there is an evil savour" (Bk. IV, chap. X). Strong odors were also associated with the plague (certain kinds of smells were thought to cause the plague, others were thought to cure it).[39] And there was, of course, a very powerful connection, relished maliciously by Marlowe's Jew of Malta, between Jews and the plague. As Cheryl Lynn Ross has shown, Subtle epitomizes the social confusion characteristic of plague-ridden London, the milieu in which Jonson's play was first performed. "From the perspective of the dominant culture," she writes, "the only purpose of a marginal figure like Subtle is to act as a boundary between things and people belonging to the system and those who don't."[40] We have already come to know this liminality from Shakespeare's play, where, in the court scene, Portia seeks to clarify the same distinction, asking, "Which is the merchant here? And which the Jew?" (IV.i.173). This was a feature of the Jew in Shakespeare's precursor text, *The Jew of Malta*, as well, where Barabas's unabashedly Machiavellian behavior served to lay bare the same cynically self-interested attitudes of the Maltese Christians, from friars to princes. Though never identified as Jews, Subtle and his co-conspirators serve virtually the identical cultural function as the Jew, combining the same threatening, contaminating characteristics.

When the wary Surly accuses the alchemists of cheating through obfuscation and obscurity, Subtle defends precisely the esoteric quality of alchemical knowledge, in language quite reminiscent of pseudo-Bacon's observations about the admixtion of foreign languages and unvocalized letters in alchemical writings:

> And all these, named,
> Intending but one thing: which art our writers
> Used to obscure their art. . . .
> Was not all the knowledge
> Of the Egyptians writ in mystic symbols?
> Speak not the Scriptures oft in parables?
> Are not the choicest fables of the poets
> That were the fountains and first springs of wisdom,
> Wrapped in perplexèd allegories?
> (II.iii.198–200, 202–207)

In addition to recollecting my discussion in Chapter 3 of the scriptural connection between parables and conversion, Subtle's argument links directly to the anxieties over identity and difference specifically elicited by the study of Jews and Judaism in the early modern period. As we saw in the alchemical texts attributed to Bacon and Flamel, Jews were regarded as the guardians of a text written in a language to which only a very few Christian could lay claim and who, in their resistance to the conversionary impulses of the Christian communities in which they lived, were often represented as having resorted to obfuscation, cant, "mystic symbols."

Furthermore, the initial exchange between Subtle and Ananias at the beginning of Act II, scene v appears to conflate the status of alchemical lore and the sanctity of esoteric language. When Ananias identifies himself as "a faithful brother," Subtle deliberately misconstrues this to mean that Ananias is also an alchemist—a *different* kind of faithful brother—rather than a radical (sectarian) Protestant.[41] Behind these two competing notions of privileged status was, of course, the superseded claim of Jewish election. It is significant, then, that the characters discover the differences between alchemists and Puritans in the terrain of language, where Subtle approvingly cites a motley assortment of "panarchic knowledge" in Greek and Latin and Ananias replies, "All's heathen but the Hebrew." The joke here is that while Ananias would not have understood the Hebrew had he heard it (even if he might have recognized it by means of the trickle-down effect of Christian Hebraism), he was far more likely to know the High Dutch (given the flight of his radical Protestant brethren to the Low Countries) that Mammon had earlier claimed as the Adamic *ursprach*.

The internecine conflict within the cabal of conmen with which the play opens—and which returns at the end, when Face, Subtle, and Dol comically double- and triple-cross each other—has intriguing parallels with a noteworthy internal dispute within the small community of Portuguese *converso* merchants living in England. A particular business quarrel ended especially badly when one party denounced another party as Judaizers, at which point the Lord Chamberlain, the Earl of Suffolk, stepped in and issued an expulsion order for all Portuguese merchants living in London.[42] The year was 1609, a year before the first performances of *The Alchemist*. It is difficult to imagine a better way to capture English anxieties about the contaminations of commercial and mercantile greed than to render parallel internal conflicts on the stage. Such competition was not, of course, exclusive to the Portuguese *converso* community, and, as Deborah Harkness has shown, the influx of "strange" purveyors of alchemy and medicine was deeply resented by the English, "because alien natural science practitioners drew clients away from citizens in the tight London market, and because their very unfamiliarity made them stylish to urban consumers." Even more suggestively, she describes several cases in which disgruntled English sellers of medical remedies claimed that some English-born natural science practitioners were counterfeiting their language and dressing in exotic clothes in order to pretend to be foreigners and thereby improve their business.[43] Scholem's market-crier explanation for claims of Jewish provenance for alchemical knowledge was not limited, it seems, to printed materials. Abel Drugger's desperate search for a competitive edge in this cut-throat market, his turn to the alchemist for some magical assistance (I.iii.6–16), reflects the contaminating effects of these fictions of conversions.

At this point, a reasonable question may arise: If Jonson had been thinking about Jewish converts when he wrote his play, why did he not make the Jewish-alchemy nexus more explicit, perhaps even making one of his conmen a Jew or a *converso*? Here I think we need to remember an important detail of Jonson's own biography: Jonson was, himself, a convert from the Protestantism into which he was born to the Catholicism to which he turned during one of his several stints in prison.[44] While I am reluctant to invoke the playwright's biography as the key to all mythologies, I do think that Jonson might have been particularly sensitive to the question of religious conversion and accusations of secret religious difference or resistance, especially as a Catholic recusant in an English culture that had undergone in the previous sixty or seventy years a series of abrupt and disruptive religious changes, Catholic to Protestant to Catholic to Protestant. Peter Stallybrass and Allon White have noted that Jonson was quite prone to accuse others of what he made a career doing himself, attacking his contemporary dramatists as pilferers and cozeners even as his plays worked in a very similar fashion.[45] It is not difficult to see that Jonson took a real delight in the deceptive practices of his alchemical conmen and, perhaps moreso, in the chaos they created.[46] The play, after all, does not end with a moralizing come-uppance for all the members of the "venture tripartite." Subtle and Dol do have to flee from the authorities without most of the wealth they had helped to accumulate, but they escape otherwise unscathed. More importantly, Face, who resumes his prior identity as Jeremy, servant to Lovewit, owner of the London house where all the shenanigans of the play transpired, is *rewarded* for his ingenuity and his (perhaps inadvertant) enriching of his master. As critics have noted, the play's end recollects the Parable of the Talents (Matt. 25: 14–30), with Jeremy assuming the role of the good and faithful servant and the selfish gulls like Surley, Mammon, Ananais, and others being cast out weeping and gnashing their teeth.[47] As destabilizing as these fictions of conversion might have been, and as threatening as they might have appeared to the social order, they also held an unmistakable appeal, especially strong for a Catholic recusant convert in Jacobean England like Ben Jonson.

This ambivalent rendering of religious conversion finds intriguing expression in Jonson's choice of names for his two Anabaptist brethren. Tribulation Wholesome is, of course, a characteristically Jonsonian name, a caricature of the Puritan impulse to translate biblical names into their overdetermined English meanings, and in this case one that gestures specifically toward the millenarian impulses the play satires. Ananias is an even richer choice, as it recollects the biblical figure of Ananias from Acts 9, the very person to whom Saul of Tarsus is led after his blinding on the road to Damascus, *the* paradigm of the Christian conversionary experience. It will be recalled that when Ananias first receives the vision of Jesus directing him to find Saul and lay his hands on him, Ananias expresses serious concerns: "Lord, I have heard by many of this man, how much evil he hath done to thy saints at Jerusalem: and here he hath authority from the chief priests to bind all that call in thy name" (Acts 9.13–14). Ananias gives explicit voice to suspicions about the authenticity of Saul's turn to Jesus, perceiving him as a threat to the new Christian community—and, for the early modern audience, a very specifically Jewish threat, at that. Jesus reassures Ananias, "Go thy way: for he is a chosen vessel unto me, to bear my name before the Gentiles, and kings, and the children of Israel" (9.15). Jesus adumbrates, in this reassurance, that recognizably Pauline universalism to which Saul of Tarsus would give such forceful expression in his epistles, "There is neither Jew nor Greek, there is neither bond nor free, there is neither male nor female: for ye are all one in Christ Jesus. And if ye be Christ's, then are ye Abraham's seed, and heirs according to the promise" (Gal. 3.28–29). The episode in Acts encapsulates both the anxieties and the hopes embedded within the discourse of conversion, a discourse that highlighted differences so that they might, eventually and providentially, be fully elided. For Jonson to use the name Ananias, so closely linked with this originary moment of Christian conversion, to designate a Puritan figure on whom the play clearly casts a witheringly critical eye, speaks to the fraught status of conversion in all its facets.[48]

My argument is not simply about an array of interesting correspondences between Jews and alchemy on the English stage; nor does it stand or fall on the relevance of Jonson's own experience of conversion to Catholicism. Rather, this discursive convergence helps us to see how Jewish conversion, the ambition and even millenarian expectation of the Jewish turn to Christianity, could also elicit a striking anxiety about cultural contamination that was directly a function of the motility and mutability upon which the idea of conversion depended. In language that seems to parallel Portia's combination of personal and monetary conversion, Subtle's first account of transformation conflates the personal and the alchemical, as he describes his role in the makeover of his partner, Face:

> Thou vermin, have I ta'en thee out of dung,
> So poor, so wretched, when no living thing
> Would keep thee company but a spider or worse?
> Raised thee from brooms and dust and watering pots?
> Sublimed thee and exalted thee and fixed thee
> I' the third region, called our state of grace?
> Wrought thee to spirit, to quintessence, with pains
> Would twice have won me the philosopher's work?
> Put thee in words and fashion? Made thee fit
> For more than ordinary fellowships?
>
> (I.i.64–73)

The alchemical vocabulary of sublimation, spirit, and quintessence underscores the immaterial, subjective aspect of transmutation. Alchemical literature repeatedly stressed that the transmutation of lead to gold was a particular aspect of a much more systemic transformation, one meant to convert *the practitioner* of alchemy into that fifth element, the *quintessence*. What is most striking about this initial speech is that it is *not* offered as part of a scheme to dupe anyone. In this first scene Subtle and Face know exactly how inauthentic their claims for alchemical transmutation are, yet Subtle resorts to that same language of conversion to formulate his attack on Face's supposed ingratitude. While the play's obviously satirical stance implies that its instances of conversion are uniformly inauthentic, superficial, and deceptive, this first version of transmutation seems to have gulled even the con artists themselves. Intoxicated by this language of transformation, Subtle reveals the destabilizing effects of his own fictions of conversion. Indeed, one might well argue that transformation *does* occur in the play, in the form of the disguises and cozenings and the wealth they accrue.[49]

Recollecting Portia's desire to be "A thousand times more fair, then thousand times more rich," Subtle describes alchemical projection so as to render conversion as a self-procreating process, assuring Mammon that the money he has given them will reproduce "As, if at first, one ounce convert a hundred, / After his second loose, he'll turn a thousand" (II.iii.108–109). Whereas in Shakespeare's play, the rapacious aspects of commercial life could be projected onto the Jew and apparently excised by his conversion and disappearance, Jonson's play depicts an entire society contaminated by this material self-interest. Subtle simultaneously embodies that greed and infects his surroundings with it. Subtle, Face, and Dol join in their "venture tripartite" (I.i.135) for the purpose of self-enrichment. The play makes no effort to hide this purpose, even for a moment, introducing the audience to its three principal characters, and their strategems, in isolation from any gulls. Of course, in order for their schemes to work, they must hide their avarice, *converting* their motives to more honorable pursuits—aiding others, scientific and philosophical progress, even the fulfillment of millenarian expectations for the end of days. Yet, their schemes equally depend upon the authentic self-interest of their victims. Mammon's ambitions are purely, unabashedly self-indulgent. Kestrel and Dame Pliant seek to improve their class standing. Even Tribulation Wholesome and Ananias, who wear the Anabaptist garb of religious enthusiasm, make no effort to disguise their need for money and power. And it is, of course, directly relevant to this line of analysis that the solution Subtle proposes for their money needs is the counterfeiting of coins. These counterfeit coins, like spurious religious conversions, are deceptive, undetectable, disruptive. An imprint covers over something undesirable that nevertheless remains in tact. In Shakespeare's play, Shylock's conversion raises the specter of this kind of counterfeit conversion—if only to supress it. That earlier play seeks to contain the disruptive presence of the Jew by converting him, but there is an excess that comes back to haunt the English stage in the person of Subtle, the alchemist. As the play's imaginary Jew, Subtle converts and is converted. As in *The Merchant of Venice* and the "true" story of Broughton and Reuven, Jonson's play juxtaposes commercial, exploitative ambitions and the language of spiritual transformation. With the Jew's ostensible conversion, the boundaries that served to organize desirable and undesirable traits breaks down. Figured in the alchemist's transformation of everything, even himself, conversion's refining properties are undermined by the inherent instability they reveal.

Mosaical Wisdom

If the English concern with alchemy in the late sixteenth and early seventeenth centuries was haunted by the ghostly presence of a crypto-Jewish legacy, the publication of an even wider range of alchemical texts roughly a half century later demands to be read in the context of a distinctive shift in the English discourse about Jews. Elizabethan and Jacobean Jews were primarily stage representations or shadowy figures whose identities were never fully confirmed. Writings about their expected conversion were largely theoretical and speculative. As I have shown in my reading of Jonson's play, the anxieties they manifested were somewhat diffuse and untethered. During the Civil Wars, Interregnum, and Restoration, however, debate about the possible readmission of actual, open Jews to England made their reality as individuals and as a community a far more immediate and potentially concrete concern. Such a shift can be detected in mid-seventeenth-century pronouncements on alchemy's Jewish origins, as well. While earlier intimations of the possible Jewish provenance of alchemy were largely oblique aspects of the transmission of this specialized wisdom, adjuncts of the fifteenth-century Hermetic revival and its syncretistic embrace of Kabbalah, the specter of Jewish authority became a more overt element of both alchemy's acceptance and its rejection amidst the explosion of enthusiasm in England in mid-century.

In his extended investigation into the miraculous transformation of

"Sauls Cruelty" in "Pauls Conuersion," John Gaule draws explicitly on the language of alchemy to describe the prototypical transformation of Jew to Christian: "The Tare, is made Wheate: the childe of wrath, a vessel of Election: the prodigie of Nature, a Miracle of Grace. Euen a Wolfe, is transformed to a Sheepe: O strange *Metamorphosis!* beside, aboue, beyond all heathen Dreames. I will always prayse the power of that Alchymist, that can refine such pure ghold, & precious, from so rough & base a mettall."[50] Gaule's 1630 tract is one of many, particularly in the mid-seventeenth century, that draw provocative parallels between the proselytizing impulses embedded in the "philo-semitism" of numerous millenarians and enthusiasts and the conversionary ambitions in the work of alchemy. J. T. Young has written that just as "all metals aspired to become, indeed were destined to become, gold[,] Jews . . . were likewise destined to mature into Christians"[51] One of the most important English alchemists of the period, Thomas Vaughan, made the repeated observation that "natural magic" (as alchemy was sometimes called) had its origins with Adam and its transmission most directly via the Jewish sages and the Kabbalah. Aware that such a claim might threaten the supersessionary narrative at the heart of Christian accounts of Jewish learning, Vaughan is careful to qualify his story of origins:

> I must therefore build my *Discourse* on the *Traditions* of those *Men,* to whom the *Word,* both *Written* and *Mysticall* was intrusted, and these were the *Jewes* in Generall, but more particularly their *Cabalists.* It is not my Intention to rest on these *Rabbins* as *Fundamentals,* but I will iustifie their Assertions out of *Scripture,* and intertain my Reader with *Proofes,* both *Divine* and *Humane.* Finally, I will passe out of *Judaea* into *AEgypt* and *Graece,* where againe I shall meet with these *Mysteries,* and prove that this *Science* did stream (as the *Chimists* say, their *Salt-Fountain* doth) out of *Jewrie,* and *watered* the whole *Earth.*[52]

Addressing explicitly the relationship between theoretical, empirical, and doxographic bases for alchemical knowledge, Vaughan claims to reinforce the Jewish pedigree of alchemy with verifiable proofs. Like many of his contemporaries, Vaughan is eager to embrace Jewish learning as long as it can be made to conform to his Christian perspective, one that expects Jews to pass through their final stage of evolution and fulfill their potential through conversion. Indeed, the means by which this esoteric knowledge was transmitted from its Jewish origins to contemporary English adepts became a consistent theme in mid-seventeenth-century English alchemical writings. As we saw in the examples of pseudo-Bacon's text and the framing narrative added to Flamel's writings, material that may have had earlier origins took on different significance when it was made available in new English translations, anthologies, or digests. One of the most influential continental alchemists on mid-seventeenth century English natural magic was a figure who lived a century earlier, Theophrastus Philippus Aureolus Bombastus von Hohenheim or, as he came to be known, Paracelsus.

The larger history of Paracelsianism and its reception in Europe is less my concern here than the two-staged impact Paracelsus's writing had on English esotericism.[53] In the 1580s and 1590s, his work helped to revolutionize medicine, essentially overturning or displacing the Galenic orthodoxy of humoral theories in favor of an iatrochemical understanding of the exogenous origins of disease. Though these new approaches clearly had their origins in Paracelsus's work, they were in the main not openly attributed to him because his name was attached to critiques that depicted him as religiously heterodox to the fragile Elizabethan Compromise.[54] When his name did appear affirmatively and explicitly in this early phase, his defenders sought to identify him with key figures in the early Reformation, thereby suggesting that, just as the reformers had restored Christianity to its earliest apostolic roots, so too Paracelsus had recovered a purer, more authentic natural philosophy. In 1585, for example, Richard Bostocke wrote of Paracelsus, "He was not the author and inuentour of this arte as the followers of the Ethnickes phisicke doe imagine, as by the former writers may appeare, no more then *Wicklife, Luther, Oecolāpadius, Swinglius, Caluin, &c.* were the Author and inuentors of the Gospell and religion in Christes Church, when they restored it to his puritie, according to Gods word, and disclosed, opened and expelled the Clowdes of the Romish religion, which long time had shadowed and darkened the trueth of the worde of God."[55] Resisting the charge of innovation that, as we saw in Chapter 1, could be used to undermine the theological claims of the early reformers, Bostocke enlisted the alchemical language of purification to describe the parallel achievement of Luther, et al., and Paracelsus. Defended as alchemy's Luther, Paracelsus continued to exercise an important influence on medical writing throughout the first part of the seventeenth century. Like the progress of the Reformation more generally in England, the more volatile and revolutionary implications of Paracelsus's thought did not find full expression until the 1640s and 1650s.

Largely as a result of Paracelsus's belated influence, however, the alchemical work that came to dominate England by the mid-seventeenth century posited matter's animated quality. This understanding of the physical world, identified variously as monism, animist materialism, or vitalism,[56] was characteristically at odds with normative Christian metaphysics. Notable for its grounding in a Hebraic ontology, vitalism differs fundamentally from Christianity's dualist separation of matter and spirit by insisting on the indivisibility of body and soul and the infusion of all material substance with the power of self-determination.[57] By the 1650s a significant rift amongst alchemical adepts had developed between the proponents of a dualist mysticism associated with the German theologian Jakob Böhme and the monistic vitalism derived from Jan Baptist van Helmont.[58] It was from van Helmont that English alchemists drew most heavily and especially through van Helmont that the work of Paracelsus came to be known and embraced in English circles.[59] In the annotations to his 1652 collection of alchemical texts, the decidedly Paracelsian *Theatrum Chemicum Britannicum*, the single most influential assembly of alchemical writings in the English language, Elias Ashmole observes,

> Hence it is that the *Power* and *Vertue* is not in *Plants, Stones, Mineralls,* &c. (though we sensibly perceive the *Effects* from them) but tis that *Universall* and *All-piercing Spirit*, that *One operative Vertue* and *immortall Seede* of *worldly things*, that *God* in the beginning infused into *Chaos*, which is every where *Active* and still flowes through the *world* in all kindes of things by *Universall extension*, and manifests it selfe by the aforesaid *Productions*. Which *Spirit* a true *Artist* knows how-so to handle (though its *activity* be as it were *dul'd* and streightly *bound up*, in the close *Prison* of *Grosse* and *Earthie bodies*), as to take it from *Corporiety*, free it from *Captivity*, and let it *loose* that it may freely *worke* as it doeth in the *Ætheriall Bodies*.[60]

Ashmole's language in this passage betrays some of the tensions that arise in the convergence of this vitalist ontology with a Christian metaphysics. "*Earthie bodies*" hold the spirit in captivity, but it is the artist's (i.e., alchemist's) task to free that "*Immortall seede* of worldly things" precisely so that it may manifest its full virtue in "*Ætheriall Bodies*." In a work made available in English in 1657, Paracelsus explicitly linked vitalism like the kind described above in Ashmole's observations with rabbinic thought:

> The Rabbins hold every natural beginning to be either matter, or cause of the matter, *viz.* the four Elements. But here beginnings must be well

> understood; for there are beginnings of Preparations, and beginnings of Composition, and beginnings of Operation: for the Artist was commanded to devise work in Gold; that is, from the object to the possibility: for if the matter be glorious, the form must be glorious: and though the spiritual Nature be more operative, yet bodily Nature must predominate eternally: *so that to make the corporal spiritual, and the spiritual corporal, is the whole scope of the intention.*[61]

Here, Paracelsus's identification of Jewish sources for the centrality of vitalism to the alchemical project suggests a respect for Jewish authority that reflects what Copenhaver has called the doxographic.[62]

Other English alchemists indebted to Paracelsus also invoked the doxographic lineage of natural magic, rooting it in a Hebraic heritage. Robert Fludd, one of the most important alchemical writers to come from England in the first half of the seventeenth century, had difficulty finding a receptive audience in his native country and was forced to find printers and a much wider readership on the Continent. One of his last works, *Mosaicall Philosophy*, was published posthumously in England in 1659, however, in a climate far more receptive to his heavily Paracelsian writings. In it he makes explicit the claims for Hebraic alchemical authority:

> The wisest amongst those Pagan Naturalists, did steal and derive their main grounds or principles, from the true and sacred Philosopher *Moses*, whose Philosophy was originally delineated by the finger of God, forasmuch as the fiery characters thereof, were stamped out or engraven in the dark Hyle, by the eternall Wisdom, or divine Word. . . . Although the foresaid pagan philosophers, did usurp the Mosaicall principles unto themselves, and, the better to maske their theft, did assigne unto them new Titles; yet because they were not able to dive into the centrall understanding of them, nor conceive or apprehend rightly, the mystery of the everlasting Word, they erected upon their principles or foundations but a vain and worldly wisdom, carved out, not from the essentiall Rock of truth, nor relying on Christ, the onely corner-stone, but framed after a human invention, and shaped out according unto the elements of this world.[63]

Fludd presents here an account of the corruption of alchemy's authorizing doxography. This account of the displacement or misapprehension of the origins of alchemical wisdom—and its corollary loss of efficacy—found its way also into the writings of Thomas Vaughan. In one of his most important treatises, whose title, *Magia Adamica*, itself communicates the primordial source of the wisdom it purports to offer its reader, Vaughan explicitly delineates the doxographic peregrinations of the perennial philosophy at the core of all alchemical lore. He writes,

> To proceed then, I say, that during the *Pilgrimage* of the *Patriarchs*, this *Knowledge* was delivered by tradition from the *Father* to his *Child*, and indeed it could be no otherwise, for what was *Israel* in those Dayes, but a *privat Familie?* Notwithstanding when God appointed them their Possession, and that this *private house* was multiplied to a *Nation*, then these *secrets* remained with the *Elders* of the *Tribes*, as they did formerly with the *Father* of the *Familie*. These *Elders*, no doubt, were the Moysaicall *Septuagint*, who made up the *Sanhedrim*, God having Selected some from the rest, to be the *stewards*, and *Dispensers* of his *Mysteries*. Now that *Moses* was acquainted with all the *abstruse Operations*, and *Principles* of *Nature*, is a Truth I suppose which no man will resist. That the *Sanhedrim* also participated of the same Instruction and Knowledge with him is plain out of *Scripture*, where wee read, That *God took of the spirit that was in Moses, and gave it to the Seventy.*[64]

This initially familial and tribal transmission of "the *abstruse Operations*, and *Principles of Nature*" subsequently becomes, in Vaughan's telling, the possession of the Jews, their "*spiritual Birthright*." Yet in a passage that curiously combines the primary, privileged status—the chosenness—of the Jews with respect to this wisdom with its seemingly unproblematic displacement, Vaughan goes on to write, "This *Mysterie* was their *Inheritance*, and they *possest* it *intirely*, being the *Annointed Nation*, vpon whom *God* had powred forth his *spirit*. By *Tradition* of the *Jewes*, the *Ægyptians* came to be *instructed*, From the *Ægyptians* these secrets descended to the *Graecians*, and from the *Graecians* (as we all know) the *Romanes* received their *Learning*, and amongst other *common Arts*, this *Magicall mysterious one*."[65] Noteworthy for its modification of Fludd's earlier condemnation of pagan philosophers for having usurped the "the Mosaicall principles unto themselves . . . the better to maske their theft," Vaughan's account reads the process whereby the perennial philosophy was transmitted from Hebrew to Gentile writers as continuous, uninterrupted, and necessary.

Indeed, there appears to be an impulse amongst some of the mid-century alchemists like Thomas Vaughan to look past religious divides for the purposes of preserving wisdom regarded as valuable and authentic. This syncretism could even serve to mitigate the persistent English Protestant hostility toward Catholicism. In the following passage, Elias Ashmole quotes a contemporaneous writer who bemoans the destruction of medieval alchemical manuscripts preserved by monks for the sole reason that they bore the Red Letter of the Catholic Church: "A Juditious Author speaking of the Dissolution of our Monasteries, saith thus: Many Manuscripts, guilty of no other superstition then Red letters in the Front, were condemned to the Fire; and here a principall Key of Antiquity was lost to the great prejudice of Posterity. Indeed (such was Learnings misfortune, as that great Devastation of our English Libraries, that) where a Red letter or a Mathematicall Diagram appeared, they were sufficient to intitle the Booke to be Popish or Diabolicall."[66] Though by no means advocating an unqualified embrace of England's Catholic past, the "Juditious Author" whom Ashmole cites is clearly eager to avoid future unnecessary losses of valuable materials simply by virtue of their mistaken identification with papistry. The baby of *prisca sapientia* must not be thrown out with the bathwater of confessional hostilities.

Within this syncretistic context, Judaism's role in alchemical lore, including its animist legacy, was something to be celebrated as long as it was understood to prepare the way for its refinement and sublation into Christian soteriology. Vaughan remarks, "The *Primitive Professors* of this *Art,* had a *literal Cabala.* as it appeares by that wonderfull, and most ancient *Inscription* in the *Rock* in *Mount Horeb.* It conteines a *Prophecie* of the *Virgin Mother,* and her Son *Christ Jesus.* ingraven in *Hieroglyphic* fram'd by *Combination* of the *Hebrew letters,* but by whom God onely knows, it may be by *Moses* or *Elijah.*"[67] Resembling the conversion of Hebraic wisdom into Christian insight we saw in the account of Flamel and Master Canches, Vaughan's tableau begins with the Kabbalah of Moses or Elijah but concludes in the prophecy of the Virgin Mother and her son, Jesus Christ. The authoritative Hebraic wisdom of Moses or Elijah, encrypted as it is, frames the prophecy of Christian salvation.

"False Chymick Art"

Such syncretism had its limits, however, and in the convergence of the discourses of alchemy and Jews these limits found expression in terms related to language we have already encountered. The following passage, taken from Vaughan's treatise on Adamic magic, contrasts with the observations concerning linguistic purity and the vocalization of language found in the pseudo-Bacon text I discussed above: "To Conclude, I would have the Reader observe, that the false Grammaticall *Cabala* consists onely in *Rotations* of the *Alphabet,* and a *Metathesis* of *Letters* in the *Text,* by which means the *Scripture* hath suffered many *Racks,* and *Excoriations.* As for the *true Cabala,* it useth the *Letter* onely for *Artifice,* whereby to *obscure,* and *hide* her *Physicall Secrets,* as the *Egyptians* heretofore did use their *Hieroglyphics*" (*Magia Adamica,* 53–54). Unlike the symbols Master Canches helped Nicholas Flamel decode, in Vaughan's account here the language of the Jews no longer contains within it even the possibility of inherent esoteric value, however much there might also be the threat of a "great concealing." Instead, the letters function, at best, exclusively as artifice, while the "false Grammaticall *Cabala*" actually tortures and deforms scriptural wisdom. In one of his many extensive annotations to the alchemical texts he brought together in his influential collection, Ashmole offers a parallel condemnation of the improper fetishizing of Hebrew, comparing the superficial knowledge of astrology with the empty use of the language of the Jews: "He that understands no more of Astrologie (nor will make further use of it) then to quack with a few Tearmes in an Horary Question; is no more worthy to be esteemed an Astrologian than Hee who hath onely learnt Hebrew may be accounted a Cabalisticall Rabbi. Tis true, he may be so fraught with words, as to amuse the unlearned, with Canting noyse thereof, but what is that if compared to the full and intire knowledge of the Language."[68] Ashmole sounds like he is taking a page right out of Jonson's satirical attack on alchemical conmen, yet, unlike Jonson, Ashmole does so specifically to defend alchemy. We can begin to see a shift, in passages like these, from a wariness about the potential deception or contamination threatened by the Jewish provenance and transmission of alchemical lore to a more complete separation of Jewish—and therefore false—esotericism from true, authentic natural magic.

This separation is apparent in the writings of Paracelsus, too. If Paracelsus was instrumental in the reorientation of alchemy toward religious and philosophical knowledge, as Antoine Faîvre and others have noted, there is an important difference between Renaissance Italian Neo-platonism and German post-Lutheran esotericism.[69] Ostensibly, this difference was grounded in Paracelsus's objection to the reverence and authority accorded the "pagan" philosophers; the other side of this development, however, was a noteworthy de-Judaizing of biblically grounded mysticism. Paracelsus offers numerous overtly hostile remarks concerning the role Jewish thought might have played in the refinement of this emerging natural philosophy. On the matter of medical knowledge, a crucial element of his alchemy, Paracelsus remarks,

> As regards medicine the Jews of old boasted greatly, and they still do, and they are not ashamed of the falsehood . . . ; they claim that they are the oldest and first physicians. And indeed they are the foremost among all the other nations—the foremost rascals, that is . . . [God] also put a curse on those who protect the Jews and who mix with their affairs, and yet they vindicate for themselves all praise of medicine, they have not inherited it from their forefathers but have stolen it from others, from strangers by robbery as it were. . . . Medicine has been given to the Gentiles, and therefore we revere and praise the Gentiles as the most ancient physicians.[70]

Paracelsus's alternately affirmative identification of Jewish thought at the root of alchemy and hostile rejection of Jewish authority in matters of iatrochemistry, or medical alchemy, resemble the path Luther, Paracelsus's exact contemporary, followed from his initial excitement about Jewish-Christian dialogue to his venomously antisemitic accounts of Jewish corruption. Whether or not such parallels are more than mere coincidence, it is certainly the case that Paracelsus gives voice to a suspicion of Jewish corruption of ancient wisdom not unlike his reforming counterpart. In another text, Paracelsus warns of "those arts that are studyed and contrived by men themselves, . . . such as the Jews . . . have published, and . . . are (to speak properly thereof) much rather void of Spirit, are false and Sophisticate Alchimy."[71] What makes Jewish alchemy false is the absence of "Spirit," precisely its betrayal of the vitalism for which Jewish thought had been credited.

In his effort to explain the characteristic difficulties of alchemical texts, Ashmole, as we have just seen, is wary of attributing esotericism's obscurities to the peculiarities of the Hebrew language. His explication of lingering mysteries in the transmission of alchemical wisdom embeds a different kind of oblique reference to the (im)possibilities of Jewish conversion. In his introductory epistle, Ashmole writes, "Past *Ages* have like *Rivers* conveied downe to us, (upon the floate,) the more *light*, and *Sophisticall* pieces of *Learning*; but what were *Profound* and *Misterious*, the weight and solidity thereof, sunke to the Bottome; Whence every one who attempts to dive, cannot easily fetch them up: So, that what our *Saviour* said to his *Disciples*, may (I hope without offence) be spoken to the Elected *Sons of Art; Unto you it is given to know the Mysteries of the Kingdome of God; but to others in Parables, that seeing they might not see, and hearing they might not understand*."[72] As will be recalled from the beginning of Chapter 3, the passage cited here from the gospels, itself a quotation from the book of Isaiah, has a final phrase that has been notably omitted in Ashmole's text, *v'shav v'rafa loh*, μηποτε επιστρεψωσι και αφεθη αυτοιʃ τα αμαρτηματα, "lest any time they should be converted, and their sins should be forgiven them" (Isa. 6.10, Mark 4.12). I suggest that there may be a reason beyond mere brevity for Ashmole's truncation of the passage, an unspoken impulse to elide the text's more immediate and common use within the discourse of religious conversion. Alchemy's transformative power, its work of conversion, must be deployed only with the greatest care and circumspection to protect against counterfeiting, false changes. The obscurity of alchemy's system of symbols becomes a means through which to separate its false, corrupting manifestations (coded increasingly as Jewish) from its genuinely salvific, conversionary expressions, which, as the omission of any explicit reference to conversion in the Isaiah passage suggests, becomes verifiable tautologically, that is, only to those who have already been converted.

Paracelsus speaks directly to the instability and impermanence inherent in false alchemy, which he has already identified as Jewish in origin: "For albeit those kind of masters do therein prate of many a crooked way, and do vainly promise meer golden Mountains (which notwithstanding are haply far enough off from them) yet, that false Chymick art bestows nothing at all constant, but is only wont to spend much charges and costs, and procure rash labours, and doth (finally) oftentimes waste away the body and life it self."[73] The "false Chymick art" increasingly identified with Jews in this period was emblematic not only of the vain promises of "meer golden Mountains." Such empty promises—ambitious but inevitably false—also came to be associated with the highly fraught discourse of Jewish readmission and the expectations for mass conversion such calls for their return typically presumed. Raising the bogey of authenticity, Paracelsus's condemnation of Jewish alchemy as false and inconstant is related to the anxieties elicited by these expectations, which reached a fever pitch amidst the millenarian fervor of mid-seventeenth-century England. A further tantalizing convergence of the discourses of Jewish readmission (and its implied possibility of Jewish conversion) and Jewish alchemy appears in Menasseh ben Israel's open plea to Cromwell and Parliament for his fellow Jews. As part of his account of the favored status Jews have enjoyed in other cities and courts, Menasseh cites the example of a Jewish alchemist whose reputation extended throughout Europe:

> Who can enumerate the number of ours who are renowned by fame and learning? . . . And almost all the Princes of Italy honoured with all kind of honour Abraham of Colorni; as appears by a letter written to him by Tommaso Garzoni in his work *La Piazza Universale*. . . . So at this day we see many desirous to learn the Hebrew tongue of our men. Hence may be seen that God has not left us; for if one persecutes us, another receives us civilly and courteously; and if this prince treats us ill, another treats us well; if one banishes us out of his country, another invites us by a thousand privileges.[74]

The specific reference here is to Abramo Colorni (1544–1599), a highly respected Jewish alchemist and engineer, whose purported skills in *chrysopoeia*, the art of gold-making, made him a much sought after guest in several European courts.[75] Menasseh's brief but evocative citation of Colorni's example—as an instance of the serial hospitality offered to Jews throughout the world—is meant to serve as evidence of the resiliency of Jewish providential value ("God has not left us"), a fascinating contradiction to the argument embedded in the title page of Abraham the Jew's book (discovered by Flamel) that Jewish dispersion amongst the nations was a sign of God's wrath. Menasseh proposes this providential persistence as reason for Jewish readmission to England, implying a kind of transformational potential as compelling argument.

As has often been noted, bound up with the intensely ambivalent and potentially far more immediate English encounters with Jewishness of the mid-seventeenth century—the kind Menasseh was advocating—were also the very meaning, validity, and permanence of an English nation undergoing extraordinary and volatile religious, political, social, and cultural changes.[76] If the preceding pages have given the impression that alchemy's Jewish provenance remained an explicit theme in all mid-century English writings on natural magic, I must now revise that impression. For what is most noteworthy about Ashmole's *Theatrum Chemicum Britannicum*, the key mid-century anthology of English alchemical texts, is the *absence* of any significant Jewish doxography either in the texts he has collected or in Ashmole's extensive annotations. Jewish authority—either to be validated or to be questioned—does not come up in any way that is comparable to earlier English alchemical texts or those translated into English, like Bacon's or Flamel's. The elision of Jewish authority is directly correlated, I suggest, to the specifically nationalist project of Ashmole's book, its repeated and insistent claim to a distinctively English lineage for alchemical knowledge. Ashmole remarks in his introduction, "If we do but ingeniously Consider, we shall judge it more of Reason, that we looke back upon, then neglect such pieces of Learning, as are Natives of our owne Countrey, and by this Inquisition, finde no Nation hath written more, or better, although at present (as well through our owne Supineness, as the Decrees of Fate,) few of their Workes can be found."[77] The problem, according to Ashmole, is not that England has not contributed significantly to the corpus of alchemical learning. It is, rather, that these English contributions have been lost, forgotten, or overlooked in favor of non-native texts. Sounding much like John Cheke arguing against the importing of "Ink horn" terms, Ashmole seeks to recover England's alchemical purity, as well as its priority. His claims for English privilege are nearly identical to claims made in the same period about England's seemingly belated church reforms in relation to its legacy of early reforming efforts. In one of his anti-prelatical tracts, for example, John Milton observes that God "hath yet ever had this Iland under the speciall indulgent eye of his providence; and pittying us the first of all other Nations, after he had decreed to purifie and renew his Church that lay wallowing in Idolatrous pollutions, set first to us a healing messenger to touch softly our sores, and carry a gentle hand over our wounds: he knockt once and twice and came againe, opening our drousie eye-lids leasurely by that glimmering light which *Wicklef*, and his followers dispers't."[78] England comes first in these accounts, both as the progenitor of church reform and the locus of alchemical wisdom. This is a privileged status directly corresponding to the claims of "elect nation" that shifted the idea of chosenness from the Jews to the English. And, as John Foxe implied in his sermon on Jewish conversion,[79] the other side of the coin of English election was Jewish preterition. As in the more general discussion of the place of Jews in England, an alternative voiced by many—William Prynne providing the most verbose example—was a resounding "no place." The displacement of Jewish election onto the English cohered, for some with an argument for the absence of Jews and Jewishness—either in doxographic authority or bodily presence.

Not all writers concerned with natural magic and anxious about the possible arrival of Jews to English shores were eager to dismiss alchemy's ostensible Jewish origins. Another alternative to the elision of alchemy's erstwhile "Jewishness" could be found in those hostile to the very idea of esotericism in all its forms and formulations. Critics of alchemy, who typically included it within the rubric of radical religious enthusiasm, sometimes highlighted the identification of this pseudo-science with Judaism. In my final chapter I argue for a characteristic identification of enthusiasm with false Jewish messianism by those critical of the proliferating radical religious sectaries of mid-century England (Levellers, Ranters, Muggletonians, Quakers, Fifth Monarchists, Familists, and others). If these so-called enthusiasts were inclined to regard alchemy as a vivid, material example of the promise of conversion by which means they bestowed authority and authenticity onto Jewish wisdom, conversely, those who were skeptical of alchemy very often expressed suspicion of the possibility of any immediate and total conversion of Jews to Christianity. Judaism's associations with alchemy worked for these critics, as well. If alchemy owed its origins to Jewish wisdom, all the more reason, in their view, to condemn this pseudo-science in its entirety.[80]

"Thou Only Fall'st to Be Refined Again"

By way of bringing this chapter to a close, I now turn to some of the poetry written during this period, particularly that of Thomas Vaughan's twin brother, Henry, whose work has long been recognized as containing traces, explicit and implicit, of alchemical influence and imagery.[81] Rather than propose new sources for such alchemical material, I want to suggest that these alchemical images ought to be read in relation to another theme Vaughan addresses in several of his poems, the Jews, their historical recalcitrance, and their anticipated conversion. As my argument thus far should suggest, I regard these two themes as related and mutually constitutive. The historical context I have presented here—the ambivalent rendering of alchemy's ostensible Jewish provenance coupled with the controversy over the Readmission question—provides us with a new way of seeing the proliferation of alchemical imagery in the mid-seventeenth century. The emergence of a different kind of alchemy—the "spiritualization" of alchemy—would appear to track emerging anxieties about Jewish conversion in the context of their potential readmission to England.

There is shift in the valence of alchemical references in early modern English literature. As Stanton Linden has noted in his exhaustive survey of alchemy in English literature from Chaucer to the Restoration, alchemy was nearly uniformly the subject of—or means for writing—satire from the late Middle Ages through Jonson's play.[82] Indeed, it may well be said that Jonson's play marked the culminating moment of that trend in alchemical literary history. Just as its satirical possibilities had seemed to run their course, however, alchemy began to find new and more philosophical or religious expression. The 1633 publications of John Donne's *Poems* and George Herbert's *The Temple* denote the beginnings of this reorientation.[83] The next stage in this development, from the mostly generic ways in which Donne and Herbert deploy their alchemical figures to the far more detailed, knowing use of such ideas in Vaughan's poetry, correlates with further shifts in the discourses of alchemy and Jewishness in the period.[84] Like Donne and Jonson, Vaughan underwent his own religious conversion, which he describes in the preface to the 1655 edition (second) of *Silex Scintillans*. This conversion process is quite explicitly a function of, and has implications for, the poetry of Vaughan's contemporary England. Vaughan laments how corrupting the "idle words" of "wits," i.e., non-sacred poets, can be to their readers, how they have a lasting impact well beyond the lives of the writers. "Divers persons of eminent piety and learning (I meddle not with the seditious and *schismatical*) have, long before my time, taken notice of this *malady*; for the complaint against *vicious verse*, even by peaceful and obedient *spirits*, is of some antiquity in this kingdom" (139).[85] He then goes on to lament the new availability of "foreign vanities," lewd and lascivious romances originally written in French and Italian now being translated into English. Fortunately, however, Vaughan identifies the emergence of a countervailing poetic movement. "The first, that with any effectual success attempted a *diversion* of this foul and overflowing *stream*, was the blessed man, Mr. *George Herbert*, whose holy *life* and *verse* gained many pious *converts*, (of whom I am the least) and gave the first check to a most flourishing and admired *wit* of his time" (142). In a path that closely matches the structure of the conventional conversion narrative I discussed above in Chapter 1, modeled on the paradigms of Paul and especially Augustine, Vaughan undergoes his transformation as a function of reading, in this case the poetry of Herbert. As such, the poetry comes to resemble the elixir or philosopher's stone at the center of the alchemist's pursuit: it is both the end product of a process of transmutation and endowed with the power, in turn, to produce further transmutations. Herbert's poetry has transformed the "quaint words, and trim inventions" of profane lyrics into "a sweetness ready penned" (as he describes in his miniature *ars poetica*, "Jordan [II]"); this transformation paves the way for a conversion of alchemical figures for more affirmative use than was characteristic of their earlier deployment in the satirical mode. Other mid-century writers also regarded poetry as both in need of transformation and capable of effecting subsequent conversion. Writing within a year of Vaughan's account of the salutary (and salvational) effect of Herbert's poetry on him, Abraham Cowley worried over the deleterious effects of most contemporary poetry and saw his role, in part, to recover its sacred purposes. "It is time to *Baptize* it in the *Jordan*," writes Cowley, "for it will never become clean by bathing it in the *Waters* of *Damascus*. There wants, methinks, but the Conversion of *That* and the *Jews*, for the accomplishing of the *Kingdom* of *Christ*."[86] As with so many other depictions of change I have addressed in this book, the language of transformations seems inexorably to move back to the original fiction of conversion, the Jew.[87]

If Henry Vaughan sought to continue the process of poetry's conversion begun by Herbert and advocated by Cowley, he also gave considerable thought to the conversion of the Jews. Indeed, as Nabil Matar has noted, Vaughan's work on both parts of *Silex Scintillans* coincided precisely with the most intense concern with Jews in seventeenth-century England, between 1649 and 1655. Unlike many of his fellow Anglicans, however, Vaughan eagerly anticipated the imminent conversion of the Jews, expecting them to join with the Royalist cause to defeat the Parliamentary forces.[88] In poems like "The British Church" and "The Shepherds," from the first part of *Silex Scinitllans* (1650), Vaughan offers a surprisingly affirmative depiction of the Jews, whom he constructs as prototypes for the true Christian. Indeed, so positive was the latter poem's rendering of the ancient Israelites that a portion of it found its way into a letter addressed to Menasseh Ben Israel that combined an invitation to the Jews to resettle in England and to convert to Christianity.[89] As Matar has suggested, Vaughan's estimation of the Jews and their conversionary potential continued to evolve in the wake of the defeat of Royalist forces and the establishment of the Protectorate. By the time the second part of *Silex Scintillans* was published in 1655, Vaughan's depictions of Jews had become more critical. Still, in his poem, "The Jews," he gives voice to the recognizable expectation of Jewish restoration, making vivid use of Paul's image of the olive branches from his letter to the Romans: "O then that I / Might live, and see the olive bear / Her proper branches! Which now lie / Scattered each where. . . ." The poem's final stanzas render these eschatological expectations in relation to English election:

You were the eldest child, and when
Your stony hearts despised love,
The youngest, even the Gentiles then
Were cheered, your jealousy to move.

Thus, Righteous Father! Dost thou deal
With brutish men; Thy gifts go round
By turns, and timely, and so heal
The lost son by the newly found.

The redemption of the Gentiles—and more particularly of the English—functions very much like the philosopher's stone (and "baptized" poetry). Itself the result of conversion, Gentile salvation has the further effect of bringing about the conversion of the Jews, God's erstwhile "chosen stock." Reversing the contaminating intrusion of corruption that was at the heart of anxious representations of "Jewish" alchemy in the Elizabethan and Jacobean periods, Vaughan's alchemical process spreads its soteriological influence from Gentile to Jew. Even the language of turning, "Thy gifts go round / By turns," evokes the cultures of change animated by these fictions of conversion.

The convergence of alchemical figures with the discourse of Jewish conversion can be seen in a number of Vaughan's poem. "Religion," from the first part of *Silex Scintillans*, longs nostalgically for a now lost immediacy in human-divine relations, describing a series of biblical examples followed by the lament, "We have no conference in these days" (ll. 1–20). Stalwart of the Anglican church though he is, Vaughan is surprisingly dissatisfied with the standard Christian reading of this historical shift as a transition from the old covenant, or "truce" and "treaty," as he calls it, to the new dispensation through Christ, the "mediator," and under the aegis of the Church (ll. 21–28). The poem then describes the long and tortured path Religion must follow, a path that is a kind of negative image of the doxographic course of esoteric transmission described by Henry's twin brother Thomas and others. If natural magic follows a stream that sometimes takes it underground to preserve its integrity and stave off corruption, Henry writes that "Religion is a spring / That from some secret, golden mine / Derives birth, and thence doth bring / Cordials in every drop, and wine" (ll. 29–32). Over time, however, this spring has passed through "earth's dark veins," picking up poisons and contaminants, so that it is now "puddle, or mere slime / And 'stead of physic, a disease" (ll. 43–44). Unlike the Elizabethan and Jacobean association of contamination with Jewish influence, Vaughan suggests that the Hebraic heritage stands for the purity of religion that has since been corrupted by the "green heads" who say "That now all miracles must cease" (ll. 25–26). Invoking a transformative vocabulary that Vaughan so frequently draws upon, the poem concludes with a plea to God to "Heal then these waters. . . . And turn once more our *Water* into *Wine*" (ll. 49, 52). A lost authenticity must be recovered.

"Resurrection and Immortality," which also appeared in the first part of *Silex Scintillans*, begins with an epigraph taken from Hebrews 10.20. That verse, the chapter from which it was drawn, and the whole letter to the Hebrews, for that matter, are concerned centrally with the transition from the old law to the new gospel, from the insufficient means of salvation proposed by sacrifices and legal structures in the Jewish Scriptures to the fulfillment of those promises of redemption through the blood of Christ. Of all the passages from Hebrews, Vaughan has sought to highlight a verse that preserves the necessary path to Christian salvation through the Jewish body. Verse 20 establishes the focus of the poem: "By that new, and living way, which he hath prepared for us, through the veil, which is his flesh." The poem's dialogue between body and soul is noteworthy for its recovery of the flesh rather than the need to transcend it entirely. This is a poem imbued with the vitalism I have identified with Hebraic thought. The silk worm's metamorphosis, a standard alchemical trope, occasions the body's meditation on its fate at death. The conversion this metamorphosis represents seems initially to suggest a falling away of the dust, the body, at the moment of resurrection. In lines that directly echo—and then convert—Donne's poem "The Broken Heart," the soul's reply, however, reminds the body that God's providential covenant ensures "no thing can to Nothing fall, but still / Incorporates by skill, / And then returns, and from the womb of things / Such treasure brings, / As *Phoenix*-like renew'th / Both life, and youth."[90] The unusually intransitive use of the verb "incorporates" calls special attention to the resilience of the body even as "the womb of things" and "*Phoenix*-like" situate the poem firmly within a network of alchemical language. Stanton Linden has provided an account of possible sources for the extensive alchemical imagery in this poem, identifying the *Corpus Hermeticum* and Vaughan's own translation of Anselm's treatise, *Man in Glory*, as the two most important analogues.[91] We lose a full appreciation of the significance of these sources, however, if we fail to acknowledge them as part of a vitalist heterodoxy that draws on a distinctively Hebraic ontology. This Hebraic monism serves, in turn, as the fundament for a poem that concludes in an explicitly eschatological register, "One everlasting *Sabbath* there shall run / Without *succession*, and without a *sun*," followed by another biblical citation, this time the final verse from *the* paradigmatic Old Testament apocalyptic text, Daniel: "But go thou thy way until the end be, for thou shalt rest, and stand up in thy lot, at the end of the days" (12.13). Citations of Daniel inevitably carried with them associations with messianic expectations that included Jewish conversion.[92] Vaughan's interweaving of the language of alchemical transformation, personal salvation, and Hebraic monism, framed by the two scriptural passages that evoke the once and future salvation of carnal Israel, i.e., the Jews, marks the poem as a fiction of conversion. The burden of this conversion is to recover the Jewish body even as it renders it Christian.

Current academic trends in the history of chymistry, spearheaded by historians like William Newman and Lawrence Principe, have sought to distinguish the "hard-headed," mechanistic, distinctively non-spiritual work of alchemy up until the thirteenth century (largely a product of the translation and dissemination of Arabic texts in the middle ages) from the "mystical overlay" alchemy began to acquire in the fifteenth century, and which became especially prevalent in England in the mid-seventeenth century, when the quest for the philosopher's stone started to figure the process of the soul's refinement. Characterizing the sacred texts and spiritual terminology in early modern alchemical writings as "a relatively unproblematic use of images, concepts, and terms drawn from the religious culture of the time, rather than evidence that alchemical practices were concerned primarily or essentially with the spiritual enlightenment or development of the practitioner," Principe and Newman go on to argue that "the view which sees alchemy as an essentially spiritual activity, and which maintains that the degree or character of alchemy's religious or theological content renders it distinct from other branches of contemporaneous natural philosophy (and particularly from 'chemistry') is an ahistorical formulation which postdates the early modern period and was fully developed on in the context of nineteenth-century occultism."[93] As I have shown in this chapter, the soteriological component, the pursuit of salvation Newman and Principe read as only figurative, is inextricably linked with a pronounced vitalism.[94] That this vitalism was a central feature of Hebraic, rabbinic, and kabbalistic thought is no small irony: the work of alchemy converts to Christianity precisely at the same moment that it becomes more Jewish.

And so we return to our friends at fixedearth.com. What strikes me in reading the antisemitic screeds of Marshall Hall alongside the scholarly work of critics like Newman and Principe is that, as different as they are (and I certainly do not mean to imply any hostility to Jews in the writings of these respected historians), they both manifest an anxiety about the purity of discourse. For Hall, it is the purity of an extreme, fundamentalist Christianity grounded in what he would no doubt defend as biblical literalism. For Newman, Principe, and other contemporary historians of alchemy, it is the purity of a body of work whose credibility as precursor to "real" science can only be preserved if the hazy, anti-empirical esotericism of so-called spiritual alchemy is filtered out and delegitimized. It hardly seems accidental that, in both cases, what must be eliminated in one final alchemical process of sublimation are the heterodoxical dregs associated with the corrupting figure of the Jew.

Chapter 5

Conversion and Enthusiasm: Radical Religion and the Poetics of *Paradise Regained*

The fictions of conversion I have addressed in the preceding chapters render their transformations as changes from one more or less visible state/status to another, whether it be the "conversion" of Rahab and Ruth from heathen to Hebrew, biblical text and Homeric epic from ancient language to modern vernacular, or base metal to gold and quintessence. In each of these case studies, I have suggested that at the heart of these discourses of transformation is the potentially destabilizing question of authenticity. When conversion is said to have transpired, how can one be certain that the transformation is complete, reliable, stable? Has the transformation genuinely captured and changed the essence of the pre-conversion person, text, or object? And if so, to what extent can such a transformation properly be said to have worked upon a person, text, or object whose irreducible identity has been preserved? Is the *fiction* of conversion the constructed and contrived nature of the transformation or the fictive assertion of a continuity of identity, or even of identity itself?

In this chapter, I want to bring these implicit questions into the foreground by focusing on mid- and late-seventeenth century English writings that raise the matter of an interior, irreducible self more explicitly and problematically than any of the material I have discussed thus far. If the early modern discourses of conversion betray an anxious uncertainty about the authenticity of religious transformation, the phenomenon of enthusiasm, which was a direct and extreme outgrowth of the reforming movements that serve as the framework for my analysis of conversion, makes these anxieties explicit. Even enthusiasts' most vehement critics found it difficult to dismiss claims of inspiration and calls to religious change in their entirety, for they understood that to do so would be to undermine the bedrock claims of Christianity as revealed truth. Yet such claims also threatened to disrupt emerging ideas about national coherence and identity because they pitted these fictions of individual conversion against the imagined communities that were taking shape. And yet once more, the tension generated by fictions of conversion between individual transformation and communal boundaries evoked the promises and perils of Jewish precedent.

As a final literary test case, I shall read the lively mid-seventeenth-century debates about enthusiasm in juxtaposition to John Milton's four-book epic, *Paradise Regained*. There has been substantial critical discussion about Milton's political, religious, and social connections to the religious radicalism of groups like the Quakers and Ranters.[1] Alongside these important studies of Milton's late poetry and the radical, extra-political religious movements of the second half of the seventeenth century, other readers have suggested links between the themes of *Paradise Regained* and *Samson Agonistes* on the one hand, and the concerns of more explicitly political religious radicals such as the Fifth Monarchists on the other.[2] These competing readings have raised a number of important questions: Is it possible to identify Milton in the late 1660s with the radical fringes of English politics and religion, when those fringes are so frayed and knotted? Are Milton's sympathies with the seemingly passive Quakers of the Restoration, or do they rest still with the earlier, more overtly political Friends and other groups like the Levellers, who caused such disruption in Cromwell's New Model Army? Does Milton reject out of hand the violent solutions of the Fifth Monarchy Men, or does he continue to support resistance in various forms to the restored—and very worldly—King of England? Is it possible to determine from *Paradise Regained*, a poem so deeply engaged in the matter of messianic salvation and its relation to history, Milton's attitudes toward these various enthusiastic movements? What is the relationship between the proto-Jewish messianism Milton's Jesus rejects in *Paradise Regained* and the eruption of Jewish messianic furor surrounding the figure of Sabbatai Sevi, whose conversion to Islam in 1666 exactly coincides with the period during which Milton was completing his four-book poem?

Of particular interest to me are the ways in which competing claims about the nature of religious enthusiasm had direct implications for language and its capacity to express—to exteriorize—the interiority of inspiration and transformation. The question of plain speech—of saying what one meant—was very much at the center of the disputes between religious radicals and their contemporary opponents during this period. George Fox, James Nayler, and other early Quaker writers and preachers insisted on a directness of speech, one that did not allow for the potential deceptiveness of irony. Their approach to rhetoric, especially biblical rhetoric, was notoriously complex, however, making claims for the plain meaning of Scripture while at the same time construing much of it as symbols or extended allegories. Language itself becomes, in this reading, a fiction of conversion with the capacity both to effect genuine transformation and catastrophically to mislead.

The poetics of *Paradise Regained*, its apparent coldness, its anti-imaginative stance, especially when compared to *Paradise Lost*, has long been the subject of critical discussion. There has been little effort, however, to address the literary qualities of the poem specifically in light of its highly ambivalent rendering of religious and political enthusiasm and its nervousness about millenarian calls for mass conversion. In what follows I offer a reading of portions of Milton's brief epic as literary embodiments of the poet's struggle with the nature of radical religion and messianism in Restoration England. I begin with an account of seventeenth-century discourses of enthusiasm, turn to specific elements of the Milton's writings (early and late) that gain meaning through comparisons to the diverse and often competing enthusiastic movements of early modernity (Quakers, Fifth Monarchists, Jewish Sabbatians, and others), and conclude with an analysis of how Milton's ambivalent engagements with these movements manifest themselves in the hermeneutics and poetics of *Paradise Regained*.

Enthusiasm: Possession, Performance, and Pathology

Claims of prophetic gifts and direct divine inspiration are as old as revealed religion itself, and, with predictable inevitability, periods noted for widespread outbreaks of such claims—periods of revivals, awakenings, and large-scale calls for conversion—are also periods that witness emerging critiques of these claims. The term "enthusiasm," from the Greek ενθουσια, the state of being ενθεοσ or possessed by a god, makes its first appearance in an English text in the second half of the sixteenth century.[3] As Michael Heyd has observed, however, the Protestant critique of enthusiasm began somewhat earlier, coinciding with the earliest stages of the Reformation, when Luther attacked the Zwickau prophets of Wittenburg in 1522.[4] The effect of Luther's repudiation of enthusiastic movements such as the Münster Anabaptists, whose theological views were far more consistent with his own reforming project than with the Catholic church, was manifold, but, most important for my purposes, it set the tone for ongoing hostilities between what had begun to emerge as a kind of normative Protestantism and its more radical extremes.[5]

For much of the century that followed Luther's attacks, enthusiasm was regarded by its opponents as a tactic of Satan to corrupt the faithful and produce false conversions. Always wary of the devil's ability to cite Scripture when it suited him, anti-enthusiasts portrayed their overzealous contemporaries as having been possessed, taken spiritual, mental, and often physical prisoner by diabolical forces. When Satan was not to blame, however, the phenomenon of specious divine possession was attributed to intentional affectation and deception. Just like false converts, men and women who claimed to be inspired by transcendent forces were regarded as charlatans and actors, playing the role to its fullest, for the purposes of personal and political gain and self-aggrandizement. In this sense, enthusiasm was rendered as inauthentic, insincere, and unreal. It is only in the beginning of the seventeenth century that a third kind of explanation for enthusiasm begins to emerge, that of mental illness. In his *Anatomy of Melancholy*, Robert Burton relies heavily on medieval medical treatises to put forth a forceful argument for the diagnosis of enthusiasm as a pathological symptom of melancholy. Having described at length the many actions and attitudes of enthusiasts in England and elsewhere, Burton offers the following summation: "Of those men I may conclude . . . they are certainly far gone with melancholy, if not quite mad, and have more need of physic than many a man that keeps his bed, more need of hellebore than those that are in Bedlam."[6] With this pharmacological prescription, Burton established a critical precedent for subsequent writings on religious enthusiasm by introducing a somatic component to the condition. While Burton's purpose was to cure the excesses of melancholic enthusiasm, the medical language had the further effect of giving this madness a reality and legitimacy—indeed, an authenticity—anchored in the body that it lacked when it was regarded primarily as deceptive play-acting. Burton's analysis, however, was not exclusively that of a physician interested in the mental health of individual patients. He remained very much aware of the tensions between private and public aspects of enthusiasm, remarking how "Brownists, Barrowists, Familists, and those Amsterdamian sects and sectaries are led all by so many private spirits. . . . We may say of these peculiar sects, their religion takes away not spirits only, but wit and judgment, and deprives them of their understanding; for some of them are so far gone with their private enthusiasms and revelations that they are quite mad, out of their wits."[7] These were, of course, the same Brownists, Separatists, and "Amsterdamian sects" targeted by Jonson in *The Alchemist* for their mendacious plots to enrich themselves; the same groups with which people like Henry Ainsworth and Hugh Broughton were identified, groups whose enthusiasm was coeval and identifiable with the push to convert and be converted. Burton's focus here is on the "private" and "peculiar" nature of these enthusiasms, suggesting a resistance to, or at least a wariness about, the collective, social nature of such movements. There remains some ambiguity in Burton's account as to what the first cause of enthusiasm really is. Do we trace its etiology back to the infection of private and discrete delusions? Or do those delusional fantasies find welcome reception and fertile ground in individuals who have already been corrupted by their associations with these "sects and sectaries"? The subsequent history of anti-enthusiastic writings shifts between these two competing etiologies, recording also the cultural anxieties arising from a discourse about a real, material pathology that has as one of its primary effects the unleashing of the imagination and the generation of unreal phantasms.

During the chaos of the Interregnum, a series of crucial texts on enthusiasm were published that sought to confirm the individual, pathological diagnosis (and its etiology in humoral imbalance) offered by Burton several decades earlier. Meric Casaubon, son of the great Huguenot scholar Isaac Casaubon and a protégé of Lancelot Andrewes and William Laud, published his *Treatise Concerning Enthusiasme* in 1654, hoping to combat a phenomenon he regarded as "the occasion of so many evils and mischiefs among men, as no other errour, or delusion of what kind soever."[8] Addressing the view of previous generations, that false claims to divine inspiration were made knowingly with the deliberate intent of deception, and not disputing such occurrences, Casaubon insists he writes about "a real, though but imaginary, apprehension of it in the parties, upon some ground of nature; a real, not barely pretended, counterfeit, and simulatory, for politick ends. . . . My business therefore shall be, as by examples of all professions in all ages, to shew how men have been very prone upon some grounds of nature, producing some extraordinary though not supernaturall effects; really not hypocritically, but yet falsely and erroneously, to deem themselves divinely inspired."[9] Casaubon's syntax, filled with qualifying subordinations, betrays the troubling conflation of body and mind: "real," that is, rooted in the body, "though but imaginary," that is, not authentically spiritual or divine in origin. The remaining treatise describes, diagnoses, categorizes, and offers several remedies to "natural *Enthusiasme*," by which Casaubon means "an extraordinary, transcendent, but natural fervency, or pregnancy of the soul, spirits, or brain, producing strange effects, apt to be mistaken for supernatural."[10] Casaubon's emphasis on the "real . . . but imaginary" nature of enthusiasm, and his bracketing of "counterfeit, simulatory" apprehensions as merely having political ends, reverse Richard Hooker's practical solution to the problem of the undetectability of church papistry. Hooker, it will be recalled, resolved the epistemological instability of conversion produced by the potential disjunction between inner and outer belief by fixing his attention on conforming church attendance. We cannot know the inner workings of a man's heart so we give him the benefit of the doubt. Casaubon appears to be responding to a similar concern about calling into question the *bona fides* of someone claiming divine inspiration—and enthusiast—recognizing that to do so is presumptuously to play God. We can recognize these apprehensions as mistakes, which still leaves open the important possibility—indeed, the necessity—of genuine, divine inspiration. But we dare not dismiss these apprehensions *in toto* as deliberately false, intentionally misleading.

Two years after the appearance of Casaubon's treatise, Henry More, who, as we saw in the previous chapter, was by no means hostile to esoteric study or the fictions of conversion they often entailed, published his *Enthusiasmus Triumphatus, or a Discourse of the Nature, Causes, Kinds, and Cure of Enthusiasme* (1656), an even more thoroughly medicalizing account of enthusiasm than that of Casaubon, one entirely committed to theories of internal causation. More asserts, "Enthusiasme is nothing else but a misconceit of being inspired. Now to be inspired, is to be moved in an extraordinary manner by the power or Spirit of God to act, speak, or think what is holy, just, and true. From hence it will be easily understood what Enthusiasme is, viz., A full, but false perswasion in a man the he is inspired."[11] In language that echoes Casaubon's "real, but though imaginary," More must wrestle with the paradox of an authentic misapprehension, a "full, but false perswasion." Since More does not wish to discount the possibility of true inspiration, which would, after all, undermine the very foundation of revealed religion itself, it is imperative that a method be developed to distinguish between the "misconceit of being inspired" and genuine divine influence, what with man's nature so "very prone to suspect some speciall preference of God in anything that is *great*, or *vehement*."[12]

As I noted above in my account of the incremental incursion of Paracelsian thought into England, the late sixteenth and early seventeenth centuries witnessed a shift from regarding illness as a function of humoral imbalance (the dominant model of medieval and Renaissance medicine, fully ascendant in Burton's *Anatomy of Melachol*y) to understanding illness as a reaction to the contamination of the body (or the mind) by an external organism or invasive influence.[13] In many respects, the seventeenth-century discourse of enthusiasm reflects this fitful transition. As the intellectual and political climate changed from the Interregnum and Protectorate to the Restoration, the mental pathology of enthusiasm became the means more generally to account for religious and political dissent. The connection worked in two directions: on the one hand, the pathologizing of such dissent had the effect of containing it within more manageable models of individual mental illness; on the other hand, the association of such ostensibly individualized matters as madness with revolt against king and bishop threatened to turn every madman into a danger to national stability. Enthusiasm could be contagious.

The published account of the case of William Franklin occupies a pivotal position in this history, clearly demonstrating the tensions between these conflicting etiological narratives. Transpiring at the same time as the New Model Army's defeat of Royalist forces, and imprisonment and execution of Charles I, the story of this false messiah, or "Pseudochristus," as his chronicler Humphry Ellis described him, is rife with all the anxieties and tensions created by the political and religious conflicts of the period.[14] Ellis begins his narrative by directly addressing the possible causes of Franklin's behavior:

> Besides sickness both in body and minde, [Franklin] hath been somewhat distracted in his brain. . . . This of his distemper I the rather write concerning him, that I may not be censured to conceal any thing that might in the least extenuate his offences. . . . While he hath been in prison in this City, I have several Times seen him, and had concerning his Opinions and Practises much conference with him, but could never see or hear, ought from him, which might argue him in the least to be so distempered; but rather in such a cautious wary manner expressing himself, that whatever he spake, was sufficient to shew him to be a man all this time in a sober minde, enjoying the right use of his *Intellectuals*, his understanding faculty, according to the strength of those parts he was endued withall, very free from any such natural distemper.[15]

In Ellis's opinion, though Franklin was reported to have suffered previously from "distracted fits" and other manifestations of mental illness, "yet I cannot admit any thing of such a natural distemper to be alledged to extenuate these great evils which he hath faln into."[16] Clearly aware of the growing tendency to attribute enthusiastic claims to humoral imbalances and other internally generated physiological explanations, Ellis seeks to set the record straight: this was no case of madness.

Ellis provides a detailed account of the process by which Franklin came to regard himself as Christ reincarnated, acquired followers, many of whom converted to become followers and assumed the identities of other biblical figures, thereby causing widespread disruption and disquiet. What is crucial for my analysis here is less the details of the behavior of Franklin and his followers than Ellis's repeated assertions that the cause of this blasphemy and the false conversions it produced was not mental illness but rather the sacrilegious environment of the period, in particular, the proliferation of Familists, "from whom I suppose he had sucked in all these wicked Principles,"[17] and the precedents of the Anabaptists, whom he blames for fostering a climate in which this kind of blasphemy could flourish. In these churches Ellis finds the roots of Antitrinitarianism, Arminianism, Socinianism, and the like: "Where have the *Scriptures* been so much slighted, and *Revelations* cryed up, as among them? and for *Revelations* how much have they pretended to them? especially when their deceitful pretence of shaking fits was so much in fashion of late amongst them? And so from this slighting of the Word of God have faln into all manner of Errors whatsoever."[18] If there is a disease in Franklin's story, it is social and communal, rather than private and individual, created by an imbalance of legislative and doctrinal humors and not physical, bodily ones. The real target of Ellis's narrative is not Franklin but the new freedom of religious expression and belief in a now kingless and bishopless England. In the absence of enforced church discipline, a religious free-for-all is inevitable, blasphemy will thrive, and with it the rampant and outrageous claims of enthusiasts everywhere. The problem is in the dissolution of boundaries, the ease with which individuals can lay claim to one religious identity, one inspired state or another. In a world without a single religious and political authority, conversion has become too easy.

The fuller political implications of claims of inspiration were taken up by Ellis's contemporary readership. A year after the publication of *Pseudochristus*, Thomas Hobbes addressed the relationship between political power and divine authority in the third part of his *Leviathan*. In "Of a Christian Common-Wealth," Hobbes warns of looming chaos:

> For when Christian men, take not their Christian Soveraign, for Gods Prophet; they must either take their owne Dreams, for the Prophecy

> they mean to bee goverened by, and the tumour of their own hearts for the Spirit of God; or they must suffer themselves to bee lead by some strange Prince; or by some of their fellow subjects, that can bewitch them, by slander of the government, into rebellion, without other miracle to confirm their calling, then sometimes an extraordinary successe, and Impunity; and by this means destroying all laws, both divine, and humane, reduce all Order, Government, and Society, to the first Chaos of Violence, and Civill Warre.[19]

If a lapse in discipline is the disease, Hobbes concludes, a reassertion of authority ought to be the cure. Hobbes's solution to the seemingly esoteric, immaterial challenge of unrestrained enthusiasm is eminently material and mundane. Civil war can only be avoided by the acknowledgment of the "Christian Soveraign" as the single divinely authorized power in the Commonwealth. This conclusion derives directly from Hobbes's earlier meditation on the impossibility of verifying the authenticity of claims of inspiration: "How God speaketh to a man immediately, may be understood by those well enough to whom he hath so spoken; but how the same should be understood by another, is hard, if not impossible to know. For if a man pretend to me, that God hath spoken to him supernaturally, and immediately, and I make doubt of it, I cannot easily perceive what argument he can produce, to oblige me to beleeve it."[20] In a manner that again recollects Richard Hooker's solution to the dilemma of church papistry and the potential for counterfeiting Catholics to participate in Anglican Church services,[21] Hobbes begins with a problem in epistemology and concludes with a political solution. Not unlike the Tempter in *Paradise Regained*, Hobbes correlates authentic, verifiable claims of divine inspiration with manifestly earthly power. In his late poem, Milton's Jesus resists precisely this connection, one that preoccupies much of the discourse on enthusiasm in the second half of the seventeenth century, especially after the Restoration of Charles II.

A particularly prolific Restoration critic of enthusiasm, Joseph Glanvill, offers an account of the revolt against King Charles and his execution that combines the language of religious enthusiasm, eschatological expectation, mental illness (with both internal and external cause), and political rebellion with a suspicion of fancy, *per se*, of the power the imagination has to be deceived and in turn to deceive. Insisting that "religion is of a calm and *pacifick* temper, like that of its Author,"[22] Glanvill writes that when the emotions and raptures that become part of religious practice and belief

> had *kindled* the *imagination*, and sent the *phansie* into the *Clouds* to flutter there in *mystical non-sense*: and when it was mounted on the *Wings* of the *Wind*, and got into the *Revelations* to *loosen* the *seals*, *pour* out the *vials*, and *phantastically* to interpret the *fates* of *Kingdoms*; when it flew into the *Tongue* in an *extravagant ramble*, and abused the Name and Word of God, mingling it with *canting*, *unintelligible* babble. I say, when the *diseasd* and *disturbed phansie* thus *variously displayed* it self, many made themselves believe that they were *acted* by the *Spirit*, and that those *wild agitations* of *sick Imagination*, were *divine motions*.[23]

Glanvill's description works to align the wide and conflicting array of enthusiasm's causes and effects. His purple prose runs the gamut, touching on such competing matters as internal and external influences, authentic and inauthentic agitations, and personal and political effects.

In her comprehensive analysis of culture of dissent in Milton's England, Sharon Achinstein has illustrated the many forms resistance took during the Restoration, underscoring, in particular, how the seemingly inward and esoteric discourse of inspiration and the workings of the Holy Spirit ought to be understood as "a strategic revaluation of the nature of human action" with significant political implications.[24] In their responses to the critics of enthusiasm, radicals and dissenters pursued modes of expression that celebrated inspiration, rapturous emotions, and the freedom to be acted upon and made use of by the will of God. If these dissenting poetics marked a surrender of human agency and a rejection of the role of reason, then so be it—though in some versions of radical Protestantism, reason became identified exclusively with the inner light of divine inspiration. Glanvill's anxieties about imagination and its relation to the forces of religious and political enthusiasm were not lost on the targets of his attacks. Rather than denying the extravagance of passion with which they were being negatively associated, Quakers like George Keith celebrated their inspiration in terms that cast their more conventional antagonists as torpid and emasculated, characterizations that would resonate powerfully for Milton in the two texts he paired for publication at the end of his poetic career, *Paradise Regained* and *Samson Agonistes*. Fully conversant in the somatic discourse of humors deployed by the likes of Casaubon and others, Keith describes the mockery of his opponents, who call their ecstatic reactions and transports from the indwelling spirit

> fancy, delusion, imagination, melancholy, some hypochondriack humor, a spirit of witcheries and delusion, and [who] persecute them who witness this blessed dispensation of life and glory, (though in a more steddy and fuller manner and measure) and [who] revile the servants and Ministers thereof, with the name of deceivers, and false Prophets, oh, oh, how have ye fallen from heaven to earth, how are ye sunk into the pit, wherein there is no water, how have ye lost your glory turned your glory into shame, and followed after lying vanities, how have ye suffered your selves to be lulled to sleep in the whores lap, with her bewitching voice who hath cut your Locks, wherein your strength lay, . . . it is departed from you, and the *Philistines* mock you, having put out your eyes, and you are become a hissing and reproach to day.[25]

Comparing his anti-Quaker antagonists to the decadent and weakened Samson, Keith urges the reader to resist the vain temptations of the world, its "lying vanities," asserting instead the power of Christ within the individual believer. As he insists several pages later, "ye who deny God his speaking immediately in man, ye deny all the work of God in man, and of his Son Jesus Christ, for by his Word, his immediate Word, he does all things, he speaks and it is done."[26] That a Quaker like Keith would contrast the strength of those who shared the inner illumination and indwelling of Christ celebrated by the Society of Friends with the worldly weakness of shorn and blinded Samson is especially significant for readers of Milton, for it is this very same tension that is arguably at stake in the joint appearance of *Paradise Regained* and *Samson Agonistes*.

"Something Like Prophetic Strain"

Milton's perception of the threat of sects, millenarian hopes, and political rebellion underwent its own evolution as he increasingly engaged in the controversies of his day. In some of his earliest prose tracts, written against the English prelacy, Milton seeks to minimize the threat posed by the progressively sectarian and fragmentary religious culture of the 1640s. He writes, "If God come to trie our constancy we ought not to shrink, or stand the lesse firmly for that, but passe on with more stedfast resolution to establish the truth though it were through a lane of sects and heresies on each side. Other things men do to the glory of God: but sects and errors it seems God suffers to be for the glory of good men, that the world may know and reverence their true fortitude and undaunted constancy in the truth."[27] Anticipating the more fully developed arguments of *Areopagitica*, where truth and goodness can only be found intermixed among the seeds of lies and evil, Milton regards the flourishing of sects and heresies as a necessary aspect of the trial of the faithful, a trial that should not be mitigated by the suppression of those led astray by a misplaced zeal. At the end of the day, or rather, at the end of time, the truth will out: "No wonder then in the reforming of a Church which is never brought to effect without the fierce encounter of truth and falsehood together, if, as it were the splinters and share of so violent a jousting, there fall from between the shock many fond errors and fanatick opinions."[28] Clearly critical of these "errors and fanatick opinions," Milton nevertheless gives them a role to play in the process of reformation. Indeed, Milton's advocacy of religious liberty (within certain well-known limits) that may produce errors and fanaticism is directly related to his support of marital liberty, i.e., the right to divorce. In one of his only explicit references to the same sectarian groups Ellis blamed for the flourishing of heresy and blasphemy, Milton offers a far more conciliatory opinion, suggesting that these religious zealots are channeling their frustrated and restrained impulses in ways that might not be necessary were they permitted other liberties:

> Seeing that sort of men who follow *Anabaptism*, *Famelism*, *Antinomianism*, and other *fanatick* dreams, (if we understand them not amisse) be such most commonly as are by nature addicted to a zeal of Religion, of life also not debausht, and that their opinions having full swinge, do end in satisfaction of the flesh, it may come with reason into the thoughts of a wise man, whether all this proceed not partly, if not cheefly, from the restraint of some lawfull liberty, which ought to be giv'n men, and is deny'd them. As by Physick we learn in menstruous bodies, where natures current hath been stopt, that the suffocation and upward forcing of some lower part, affects the head and inward sense with dotage and idle fancies.[29]

Drawing on somatic and humoral language not unlike the anti-enthusiastic writings of Casaubon and More, Milton offers a different remedy to these "fanatick dreams." Where the Anglicans Casaubon and More suggest tighter restraints to reign in the uncontrollable energies of an imagination charged with an imbalance of bodily humors, Milton proposes that these restraints be loosened so that the obstructions may be removed and "idle fancies" may be prevented. Enmeshed within the same evolving discourse of physical, individual, and social pathologies as his ideological antagonists, Milton's analysis of the "*fanatick* dreams" of Anabaptists and Familists is notably continuous with Casaubon's or More's explanation of the fancies of enthusiasts. Positioning Milton in relation to the disputatious discourse of enthusiasm thus becomes far more complex; one cannot simply identify parallels between his own religious and political thinking and that of the Quakers or other enthusiastic groups.

As a poet, as well as polemicist, Milton was especially concerned with the matter of fancy, having meditated on the role of the imagination in relation to melancholia in some of his earliest poetry, most notably the diptych of *L'Allegro* and *Il Penseroso*. The abstractions of these early poems already imply connections between melancholy (alternatively rejected and embraced) and the experience of possession, whether it is in *L'Allegro*'s consigning of melancholy's "horrid shapes, and shrieks, and sight unholy" to "some uncouth cell" (ll. 4–5), or in *Il Penseroso*'s preference for "something like Prophetic strain" (l. 174) having dissolved the poet into ecstasies (l. 165). Milton's later poetry builds upon these Burtonian associations, particularly in response to the increasingly problematic presence of religious enthusiasts who challenged so many central features of English Protestantism. As Karen Edwards has observed, the largely conservative project of pathologizing enthusiasm through its etiology in humoral imbalance means that a late poem like *Samson Agonistes* must make use of the religious, political, and imaginative power of melancholy without ever speaking its name. When the Son begins his first extended meditation on his own inspired calling in *Paradise Regained* he depicts his uncertainty about his role by way of an image that has its counterpart in *Samson*:

> O what a multitude of thoughts at once
> Awak'n'd in me swarm, while I consider
> What from within I feel myself, and hear
> What from without comes often to my ears,
> Ill sorting with my present state compar'd!
> (ll. 196–200)[30]

The thoughts that swarm inside the Son's head recollect the thoughts that swarm around Samson "like a deadly swarm / Of Hornets arm'd, no sooner found alone, / But rush upon me thronging" (*Samson Agonistes*, ll. 19–21). Samson and Jesus are (or believe themselves to be) prompted by divine influence, by the spirit of God. Their experiences are thus not all that dissimilar to those of the enthusiasts. There are important differences, however, between the menacing thoughts of self-recrimination that plague the blind and weakened Hebrew strong man and the multitude of thoughts that awaken the Son of God. In particular, the swarm in the Jesus' mind appears to be produced by the disjunction between what he feels within himself and what he hears from without. As my discussion of the developing account of enthusiasm's etiology has revealed, the distinction between internal and external influences serves as a key factor.

Concluding his recollection of his encounter with the Baptist, the Son offers another phrase that invites us to compare his situation with that of Samson:

> And now by some strong motion I am led
> Into this Wilderness; to what intent
> I learn not yet; perhaps I need not know;
> For what concerns my knowledge God reveals.
> (ll. 290–293)

In similar terms, Samson insists to the Chorus of Hebrews, "what I motion'd was of God" (l. 222) and later speaks of the "rouzing motions" (l. 1382) that lead him to the festival of Dagon at the close of the drama. The differences are important, too. Samson defends his actions by grammatically assuming agency over this divine motion ("what *I motion'd* was of God"). The "strong motion" in *Paradise Regained* renders the Son far more passive, responding to some external force. Milton contrasts the internal, and potentially inauthentic, motion experienced by Samson—which, by impelling him to take the woman of Timnah as a wife leads him to the mistaken belief that he should also marry Dalila—with the apparently external yet far more reliable motion that urges the Son into the wilderness.

If Edwards is correct to read Milton's rendering of Samson as an attempt at recovering the potential political value of melancholy (and its Burtonian associations with enthusiasm), what of the larger discourse of enthusiasm in *Paradise Regained*? To what extent does Milton defy contemporary critiques of enthusiasm and revalidate the language of religious fervor as effective, even necessary? In a later exchange with Satan, the Son offers the following observation:

But whence to thee this zeal? Where was it then
For *Israel*, or for *David*, or his Throne,
When thou stood'st up his Tempter to the pride
Of numb'ring *Israel*, which cost the lives
of threescore and ten thousand *Israelites*
By three days' Pestilence? Such was thy zeal
To *Israel* then, the same that now to me.
(3.407–413)

Zeal, a key term in debates over enthusiasm, is not in and of itself a sign either of authentic or inauthentic divine inspiration in Milton's poem. As this attack by the Son demonstrates, vehemence of expression, as a manifestation of zeal and ardor, is of neutral value and will take on the properties of the force that motivates it. The challenge thus becomes how to discern between true and false inspiration, how to know when the internal transformation is authentic or inauthentic. Hobbes anticipates this dilemma in his discussion of prophecy and inspiration: "Every man . . . now is bound to make use of his Naturall Reason, to apply to all Prophecy those Rules which God hath given us, to discern the true from the false."[31] By asserting his radical dependency on Natural Reason, Hobbes becomes highly skeptical of inspiration. "He is a true Prophet," Hobbes concludes, "which preacheth the Messiah already come . . . and he is a false one that denyeth him come, and looketh for him in some future Imposter."[32]

Hobbes is notoriously skeptical of all claims for inspiration but, as already seen, to doubt all inspired speech would be incompatible with the very basis of revealed religion. The faithful must have some confidence in the possibility of distinguishing God's true prophets from false. As Ellis, the chronicler of the false messiah, insisted, "Surely Christs sheep know the voyce of Christ, and can discern and distinguish it from the voyce of strangers."[33] Such assertions appear in many of the anti-enthusiast writings of the period. Casaubon assures his readers, "We would not be suspected by any, to question the truth and reality of supernatural: not only such, for which having the authority of the Holy Scriptures, no man can denie or question them, except he first deny or question the truth and reality of these as divine; but also of many others, which either good, though not infallible authority, or sound reason, upon due examination of circumstances, hath commended unto us for such."[34] More, who always regarded enthusiasm as having physiological causes, closes his own discussion with a variety of litmus tests for distinguishing true and false inspiration, but in the end he seems compelled to conclude that even those who are genuinely prompted by a religious spirit partake of melancholic tendencies.[35] Despite efforts to preserve some affirmative notion of supernatural inspiration and the transforming power of the divine, More's conclusions about the necessarily melancholic nature of those under the influence of religion betray the effect of the critique of enthusiasm on claims of religious conversion.

Anti-enthusiasts were not the only ones to wrestle with this difficulty. The writings of Quakers like George Fox and James Nayler offer similar pronouncements on how to distinguish divine truth from false claims: "If the seed speake, which is Christ, he hath no other Name, for the seed is Jesus Christ, and it is not blasphemy, but truth; but if the seed of the serpent speak, and say he is Christ, that is the Lyer and the Blasphemer, and the ground of all Blasphemy; and is not the seed which is Christ; but the head of the serpent is to be bruised, which is the cause of all enmity, strife and debate, with the seed of the Woman, which is Christ."[36] Fox's statement serves as a postscript to the published account of James Nayler's examination, trial, and suffering for the crime of heresy. As has been well documented by Leo Damrosch and others, Nayler's trial was a key moment in the history of the Quaker movement, forcing Fox and others publicly to distinguish their own doctrine of inner light and individual salvation from what others regarded as the blasphemous claims of Nayler and his followers that he was Jesus come again.[37] At stake in Nayler's trial, as Fox's own postscript suggests, was the claim, so central to Luther's original break with the Roman Church, that the individual's personal encounter with divine revelation (whether it be in the text of Scripture or in the heart of the believer) at that endlessly recursive moment of conversion is the central feature of Christian belief: *sola fide, sola gratia, sola scriptura*. The Quakers saw the Puritans as having betrayed the Reformation, while Puritans reviled Quakers and other enthusiasts because in them the Puritans saw their own iconoclastic, anti-ceremonialist, and antinomian tendencies exaggerated and distorted. Nayler, in turn, became the scapegoat for all who wished to delineate some limits to their calls for reform. As Knox observed, "[Nayler] suffered as the *reductio ad absurdam* of the Reformation experiment, with every man's hand against him."[38]

In her discussion of the literature of Dissent, Achinstein has shown how Milton's poetry served as a reference point for an oppositional literary mode that combined dissenting politics with inspired poetics.[39] If Milton's admirers and imitators looked to the rapturous and enthusiastic example of *Paradise*

Lost for precedent (while his detractors sought to recover the sacred truths he seemed to have ruined), it is less clear whether Milton was entirely comfortable following his own model. The poet of *Paradise Regained* does not completely embrace the dissenting approach expressed by many of his contemporaries, exhibiting instead an unease (and at times an outright hostility) toward the dissenting poetics of the literary enthusiasm he was regarded as having initiated. As devoted an opponent of monarchy as he was, Milton may have found himself in unlikely and uncomfortable company by being critical of Christian enthusiasts and millenarians in *Paradise Regained* since he would have been siding with Royalists and other supporters of the established church. The Son's refusal, throughout *Paradise Regained*, to prove himself to Satan, to authenticate his divine calling, is not unlike the conclusions drawn by Hobbes and others that proving inspiration is well-nigh impossible. "Of my Kingdom there shall be no end," the Son tells the Tempter, "Means there shall be to this, but what the means / Is not for thee to know, nor me to tell" (4.151–153). While it may be true that, as Achinstein argues, Milton battles against the "Restoration infatuation with pagan literary culture, its atheism, libertinism, courtliness, and decadence," I am less convinced by her characterization of the poetics of *Paradise Regained* as "authentic, inspired, and primary."[40] Milton's departure from Ramus in his *Artis Logicae* in the central matter of Right Reason reflects his rejection of prophetic insight as the self-sufficient basis for all knowledge.[41] His commitment to a process of deliberation that must always temper the experience of "some strong motion," and the conflict that can arise from such a confrontation, ought to be read in the context of a politics of inspiration that had such disastrous results in the years leading up to the completion of *Paradise Regained*.

Politicized Messianism and Ecclesiastical Conversion

While there may be good reasons to draw parallels between the late Milton and the Quakers, it is equally important to recognize the crucial differences, all of which, I suggest, stem from the status of Scripture. In this regard, it is especially noteworthy that Milton would have rejected the Quaker hermeneutics of Scripture for precisely the same reason his anti-enthusiast contemporaries did. The Quakers offered a radically spiritualizing reading of the Bible and Christ, resulting, by many accounts, in the utter de-historicizing of the gospel accounts of Jesus. Each believer is already a Christ, at least *in potentia*, as the Nayler episode so vividly demonstrated. In a later text by Henry More, appended to the published editions of *Enthusiasmus Triumphatus*, More renders the problem in these terms:

> For they intermingling so great severity and conspicuous signes of Mortification, the close keeping to the light within, and the not offending in the least manner the dictates of our consciences, but to walk evenly and sincerely before God and man, they intermingling, I say, these wholesome things with what is so abominable and dangerous, *viz.* the slighting of the history of Christ and making a meer Allegory of it, thereby voiding all that wisdome of God that is contained in the mysterie of Christianity, as it referres to the very person of Christ; this, I say, cannot proceed from any thing so likely as from the craft and watchfull malice of *Lucifer*, who undoubtedly envies Christ his Throne both in Heaven and in Earth, and therefore would bring one of these two mischiefes upon his Church, that is, either the slurring of the person of our Saviour, or else of that, without which he can take no complacency in his Chuirch, and that is, true and reall Sanctity or Holinesse.[42]

More takes particular issue with what he regards as a key feature of Quaker soteriology, the evacuation of meaningful significance from historical existence, not only in contemporary England but more radically in the lived experience of Jesus himself. The narrative of the gospels is far more than "meer Allegory," depicting as it does "the very person of Christ." Anticipating the very same accusation made by Milton's Jesus against Satan, More charges the Devil with tempting the faithful, by means of the Quakers, with a disruption of historical expectations. This accusation of de-historicization is repeated by other critics of the Quakers, as well. Henry Hallywell insists, "[The Quakers] account the Conception, Birth, Life, Death, Resurrection and Ascension of our Lord Jesus, as they were in the History and letter transacted in Judea to be a mere Fable. So that this may serve as a Caution once for all to every one that reads their Writings, that when they meet with any thing about our Saviour Jesus Christ, or Heaven or Hell or the day of Judgment, they may know the Quakers understand it in a Mystical sense."[43] It is at least one measure of the widespread nature of this view that a Quaker apologist like William Penn, writing in response to Hallywell's attacks, would feel obliged to clarify the position of his mentor and teacher,

George Fox, claiming that "by Christ crucified within, [Fox] does not deny that he was once crucified without."[44]

In his portrayal of the debate between the Son of God and Satan, Milton constructs a critique not unlike that of More's or Hallywell's. Though it would be folly to suggest that Milton's views did not evolve over the course of his literary career, in this one respect, at least, they remained remarkably constant: as early as the "Nativity Ode," when "wisest Fate says No / This must not yet be so," Milton insists upon the importance of achieving salvation within the processes of history. The Son of *Paradise Regained* arrives at the same conclusion in his conflict with Satan. While he may have defeated his nemesis by avenging the loss of paradise suffered by Adam, his victory must be achieved in history. Milton's notion of messianism is deeply historical, time-bound, material, even when it is figured in an inward-looking Jesus.[45] Milton charts an incremental process of time-bound transformation, not an instantaneous rupture.

In light of this historical view of redemption, we should contrast Milton's divergences from the radically ahistorical Quakers with his corresponding reactions to those other enthusiastic sectarians, the Fifth Monarchists. Unlike some of their millenarian contemporaries, the Fifth Monarchists were eager to elaborate the political, social, and economic structures of the kingdom of Christ. As B. S. Capp, the most important historian of the Fifth Monarchy movement, has observed, "The aim of the Fifth Monarchists was to use power to enforce godly discipline on the masses. Far from withering away in the millennium, the duties of the magistrate would expand into new spheres."[46] In 1661, when Thomas Venner and his small group of followers attempted their failed rebellion against the newly restored monarchy, Royalists had concrete evidence of the link between religious enthusiasm and political sedition. Indeed, in the wake of Venner's uprising, Quakers and other religious nonconformists went to great lengths to distance themselves from the political ambitions of these millenarians.

Milton's political pamphlets prior to the Restoration, even at the very beginning of the Interregnum, already contained within them the arguments he would need for distinguishing between political power and religious authority, a distinction that lay at the heart of his earlier anti-prelatical tracts. In *Eikonoklastes* Milton writes of Charles I, "He imagins *his own judicious zeal to be most concernd in his tuition of the Church.* So thought *Saul* when he presum'd to offer Sacrifice; for which he lost his Kingdom; So thought *Uzziah* when he went into the Temple; but was thrust out with a Leprosie for his opinion'd zeal, which he thought *judicious*. It is not the part of a King, because he ought to defend the Church, therfore to set himself supreme Head over the Church, or to meddle with Ecclesial Goverment, or to defend the Church otherwise then the Church would be defended; for such defence is bondage."[47] As we have already seen, zeal, for Milton, is a thing indifferent. It may serve as a powerful instrument for those genuine believers, inspired by God to bear witness to divine truth. It may also serve as an argument for the inappropriate exercise of political authority and physical force. In this case, Milton accuses Charles of improperly presuming authority in matters of "Ecclesial Government," where Kings should not meddle.

More than twenty years later, following the Restoration of Charles's son to the throne and the abortive attempt of Venner and his followers to replace England's monarchy with Christ's political authority, Milton returns to a similar division between earthly government and divine redemption, and the language of his poem recollects that of his earlier pamphlets. This time, his targets are on both sides of the political spectrum, Royalists and Fifth Monarchists. Satan prompts the Son to take up his royal crown—"But to a Kingdom thou art born, ordain'd / To sit upon thy Father *David's* Throne" (3.152–153)—so that he might save his people, who now suffer under "*Roman* yoke" and whose Temple has been repeatedly violated "with foul affronts / Abominations rather." The temptation continues,

And think'st thou to regain
Thy right by sitting still, or thus retiring?
So did not *Maccabaeus*. He indeed
Retired unto the Desert, but with arms;
And o'er a mighty King so oft prevail'd
That by strong hand his Family obtain'd,
Though Priests, the Crown, and *David's* throne usurp'd,
With *Modin* and her Suburbs once content.
If Kingdom move thee not, let move thee Zeal
And Duty; Zeal and Duty are not slow,
But on Occasion's forelock watchful wait:
They themselves rather are occasion best,
Zeal of thy Father's house, Duty to free
Thy Country from her Heathen servitude;
So shalt thou best fulfil, best verify,
The Prophets old, who sung thy endless reign,

The happier reign the sooner it begins.
Reign then; what canst thou better do the while?
(3.163–180)

Milton uses the Jewish notion of messiah as a foil here, standing in for all that the Christian messiah will not and must not be. The reference to *Maccabaeus* at line 165 is especially noteworthy, since the legacy of that particular episode in Jewish history is an ambivalent one, at best. While on the one hand, Judah Maccabee and his followers were responsible for liberating the Temple from its desecration at the hands of the Greeks, the line of Priest-Kings who descended from the Maccabean family quickly became known for corruption and displaced loyalties, offering, in Michael Fixler's words, the worst example "conceivable among the Jews of the degeneration of priestly zeal into ambition, cruelty, lust and sacrilege."[48] What is more, Satan yokes Zeal and Duty together, arguing that they should be sufficient motivation for the Son to begin his reign as a worldly messiah. Readers of *Eikonoklastes* need only think back to Milton's denunciation of Charles's zeal-driven assumption of improper ecclesial authority to recognize the implicit attack on all those who would lay claim to civil power to enforce religious goals, whether they be followers of Charles or Fifth Monarchists.[49] The kind of kingship Milton's Son advocates is, for the time being at least, an internal rule:

Yet he who reigns within himself, and rules
Passions, Desires, and Fears, is more a King;
Which every wise and virtuous man attains:
And who attains not, ill aspires to rule
Cities of men, or headstrong Multitudes,
Subject himself to Anarchy within,
Or lawless passions in him, which he serves.
But to guide Nations in the way of truth
By saving Doctrine, and from error lead
To know, and, knowing, worship God aright,
Is yet more Kingly;
(2.466–476)

David Loewenstein has suggested that in this utter rejection of temporal monarchy, *Paradise Regained* assumes a political stance even more radical than that of contemporary Quakers.[50] Yet the Son very clearly does not reject the eventual arrival of his kingdom on earth, however far in the unknown future that may be, and in this respect, if no other, Milton is closer to those who expected a temporal messianic reign than he is to the Quakers:

> Know therefore when my season comes to sit
> On *David's* Throne, it shall be like a tree
> Spreading and overshadowing all the Earth,
> Or as a stone that shall to pieces dash
> All Monarchies besides throughout the world,
> And of my Kingdom there shall be no end.
> (4.146–151)

The Son's final answer to Satan here echoes the spectacular millenarian prophecies—favorite texts of seventeenth-century enthusiasts of all varieties—in Daniel 2.34, 2.44, 4.11, and 7.12–14, and in Mark 4.30–32. By making use of the same texts that were offered as evidence of the imminent arrival of Christ's kingdom on earth by Venner, on the one hand, and as proof of the inner revelation and defeat of the enemies of Christ within by Nayler, Milton positions himself between these two radical forms of early modern messianism and also engages with another messianic movement—deeply embedded with English fictions of conversion—exactly contemporaneous with the period during which Milton was certainly planning and composing his brief epic, Jewish Sabbatianism.[51] As I have argued in the preceding chapters, this recourse to characteristically ambiguous Jewish precedent marks the text's struggle with both the promise and the peril of the transformative, conversionary energies embedded in the discourses of millenarianism, messianism, and enthusiasm.

The news of a Jewish enthusiast claiming the title of messiah and reports of his massive following throughout Europe, Asia, and North Africa found avid audience in an England that had been pondering the fate of the Jews in relation to its own status as chosen nation for more than half a century. When reports began to circulate in 1665 and 1666 of Sabbatai Sevi and the astonishing numbers of Jews who were greeting his identification as the messiah with excitement and anticipation, one might even say enthusiasm, many English men and women received the news with more than passing interest. Reports came in a variety of forms, from letters exchanged between mercantile trading partners to extended narratives such as that of Paul Rycaut, who became interested in the Jewish question upon hearing Cromwell raise the matter in 1655 and who initially published his account anonymously, as part of John Evelyn's *The History of the Three Late Imposters* (1669).[52] Rycaut marveled how "millions of People were possessed, when *Sabatai Sevi* first appear'd at *Smyrna*, and published himself to the *Jewes* for their *Messiah*, relating the greatness of their approaching Kingdome, the strong hand whereby God was about to deliver them from Bondage, and gather them from all partes of the World."[53] Throughout the 1660s we find extensive mention of the Sabbatian movement in English letters, sermons, and treatises; the interest was not limited to one political or religious group, either, and included Royalists, supporters of the Good Old Cause, members of the Royal Society, and Puritan divines. Michael McKeon has illustrated how widely the news of the Sabbatian movement circulated in late 1665 and 1666, finding its way into official English newspapers, private correspondences, and popular rumors.[54] The year 1666 was, of course, the *annus mirabilis* that witnessed so many apparently apocalyptic events, from the London Fire to the reappearance of the plague to the intensities of the second Anglo-Dutch War. In his poem commemorating this year of wonders, even the writer most directly associated with Restoration poetics, John Dryden, could not help making mention of the Jewish enthusiast: "The wily Dutch, who, like fallen angels, feared / This new Messiah's coming, there did wait, / And round the verge their braving vessels steered, / To tempt his courage with so fair a bait" ("Annus Mirabilis," stanza 114). Petrus Serrarius (1600–1669), an Anglo-Dutch theologian, was probably Sabbatai's most enthusiastic Christian follower, responsible for disseminating news about the Jewish messiah to Christian correspondents throughout Europe.[55]

While there is no explicit record of Milton having heard of (he was, after all, blind by 1665) or discussed the Sabbatian movement with any of contemporaries, it is difficult to imagine that he would not have encountered news about these extraordinary events that so fascinated his countrymen and women (of all political and religious stripes) at one time or another. We may even speculate about two specific connections. First, Milton's longtime friend and correspondent Henry Oldenberg, who had by this time become the secretary to the Royal Society, was so intrigued by the news of Sabbatai Sevi that he wrote several letters to Baruch Spinoza inquiring about the meaning of these events. Though there is no evidence of an ongoing relationship between Milton and Oldenberg beyond the late 1650s, it is entirely possible that they remained in communication with one another, either by letter or in person, well into the Restoration period. Second, Edward Phillips, Milton's nephew, pupil, and biographer, became John Evelyn's son's tutor some time after October 1663 and remained in that position until February 1665. What is more, Barbara Lewalski suggests that Milton had his own direct contacts with Evelyn.[56] Whether these contacts were before or after Evelyn's publication of his account of Sabbatai Sevi or before or after Milton began the planning and composition of *Paradise Regained* is a matter of speculation. It remains a tantalizing possibility, however, that the two spoke in some detail about this contemporary instance of a failed Jewish messianism.

I have argued elsewhere that Milton's writings should be viewed in the context of his perception of himself and of his fellow countrymen as occupying historical and religious positions parallel to those of the Jews in the wake of the destruction of the Temple, as rabbinic Judaism began to emerge.[57] Milton's work is not alone in suggesting these homologies; indeed, Serrarius offers an explicit comparison in his response to those Christians who doubt the validity of Sabbatai's claims. In his commentary on the first fourteen chapters of Isaiah, Serrarius accuses those contemporary Christians of being identical to the Jews who reacted so negatively to the advent of Christ![58] In the larger political and religious discourse of the period, the extremes of Jewish and English messianism become identified with one another around the time that Milton is planning and composing *Paradise Regained.* The Sabbatian movement became a cipher for different tensions characteristic of the Christian discourses of enthusiasm, messianism, and conversion. On the one hand, we find ongoing and explicit analogies between Sabbatai Sevi and the Quakers, not only in England but throughout Europe. The purpose of the comparison may have been in part to give the reader a better orientation concerning the phenomenon of the Jewish messiah by comparing the exotic to a phenomenon closer to home, namely, the Quakers. Nevertheless, the criticism of the Quakers themselves implied by such a comparison is unmistakable.[59] On the other hand, there are reports that stress the political and militaristic aspects of Sabbatai's followers, reports that strongly resonate with the memory of Venner's abortive Fifth Monarchy uprising only five years earlier. One letter describes how the Turkish Bashaw "resolved to march on with his Forces [against the Israelites], and coming within sight of the City, discovered an Innumerable multitude of people getting out of their Tent, whereupon the Turks gave Fire and shot against them, but after a little fighting, a pannick fear took them, and terror seized on them and made them cry out, *Who can fight these people, seeing our Arrows return back upon our selves!!*"[60] As seemingly incompatible as these two views are—the Sabbatians as Quakers and the Sabbatians as advocates of military action like Venner's Fifth Monarchists—they both manifest the anxieties felt by entrenched, normative Christianity in the face of various enthusiastic movements agitating for dramatic change, individually and collectively. These were movements of rapid, often violent, transformation over which they had little control. Evelyn draws the connection quite explicitly in his address to his reader, where he wishes that "our modern *Enthusiasts*, and other prodigious Sects amongst us, who Dreame of the like Carnal *Expectations*, and a *Temporal Monarchy*, might seriously weigh how nearly their *Characters* approach the *Style* and *Design* of these Deluded *Wretches*, least they fall into the *same Condemnation, and the Snare of the Devil*."[61]

Christian reactions to Sabbatai Sevi were part of a debate that was conducted between established intellectuals and clergymen, on the one hand, and those who challenged their status, on the other. Since many of the enthusiasts of the time, including Sabbatai Sevi, also challenged the secular authorities, this was a confrontation with obvious political as well as purely religious implications. The Jewish messiah from Smyrna thereby played a role in both the religious and political discourse in Europe of that period, offering a discursive site in which the fraught relationship between material/historical reality and religious authenticity could be interrogated. Rycaut positions himself in sympathy with the Jewish intelligentsia, the rabbis and elders in the community, who understand the extent of the threat the Sabbatians pose to the survival of the Jewish community.[62] Alongside the critique of popular beliefs among both Christians and Jews, there runs throughout Rycaut's text a sense of solidarity between the Christian elite (political, religious, and intellectual) and that part of the Jewish elite that opposed Sabbatai Sevi. The parallels between the Christian and Jewish enthusiastic movements were believed to be so strong that Rycaut even suggests that the Sabbatian movement was itself produced by Christian millenarian, proselytizing fervor.[63]

> According to the Predictions of several *Christian* Writers, especially of such who Comment on the *Apocalyps*, or Revelations, this Year of 1666 was to prove a Year of Wonders, of strange Revolutions in the World, and particularly of Blessing to the *Jewes*, either in respect of their Conversion to the *Christian* Faith, or of their Restoration to their Temporal Kingdome: This Opinion was so dilated, and fixt in the Countreys of the Reformed Religion, and in the Heads of Phanatical *Enthusiasts*, who Dreamed of a Fift Monarchy, the downfall of the *Pope*,

> and *Antichrist*, and the Greatness of the *Jewes*: In so much, that this subtile People judged this Year the time to stir, and to fit their Motion according to the season of the Modern Prophesies; whereupon strange Reports flew from place to place[64]

Rycaut's targets, though unnamed here, are clear; they include the likes of Serrarius, John Dury, Jan Comenius, and other radical millenarians, as well as sectarians like the Quakers.[65] The Sabbatian movement inevitably became enfolded within the extensive English discussions of Jewish restoration and conversion that were such defining elements of the discourse of Jews and Judaism in the seventeenth century. We may also observe how Rycaut's account anticipates Satan's temptation of the Son to "fit [his] Motion according to the season of the Modern Prophesies," or, as the Tempter puts it, "thy Kingdom, though foretold / By Prophet or by Angel, unless thou / Endeavor, as thy Father *David* did, / Thou never shalt obtain" (3.351–354). Satan speaks in the language of English millenary urgency and expectation.

Milton's project in his brief epic was to distinguish the true form of Christian messianic redemption from the false—and specifically Judaic—conception of the messiah that Jesus would have encountered among his contemporaries and which was now being revived both within the Jewish community (the Sabbatian movement) and in Christian Europe (the Fifth Monarchists and other politically motivated enthusiastic movements).[66] I think it is possible to extend Fixler's analysis further by reading *Paradise Regained* in its entirety as Milton's ambivalent response to the expectations of many of his contemporaries, whether they were advocates of a politicized messianism or promoters of an inner salvation that implied a retreat from material history and all its attendant struggles. Satan urges Jesus to acquire wealth in preparation for what he constructs as the Son's necessarily worldly mission of salvation.

> Great acts require great means of enterprise;
> Thou art unknown, unfriended, low of birth,
> A Carpenter thy Father known, thyself
> Bred up in poverty and straits at home;
> Lost in a Desert here and hunger-bit:
> Which way, or from what hope, dost thou aspire
> To greatness? whence Authority deriv'st?
> What Followers, what Retinue canst thou gain,

> Or at thy heels the dizzy Multitude,
> Longer than thou canst feed them on thy cost?
> Money brings Honor, Friends, Conquest, and Realms;
> What rais'd *Antipater* the *Edomite*,
> And his Son *Herod* placed on *Judah's* throne,
> (Thy throne) but gold, that got him puissant friends?
> Therefore, if at great things thou wouldst arrive,
> Get Riches first, get Wealth, and Treasure heap,
> Not difficult, if thou hearken to me,
> Riches are mine, Fortune is in my hand;
> They whom I favour thrive in wealth amain,
> While Virtue, Valor, Wisdom, sit in want.
>
> (2.412–431)

Roy Flannagan's note on "*Antipater* the *Edomite*, / And his Son *Herod* plac'd on *Judah's* Throne" (ll. 423–424) helpfully reminds the reader of the irony built into this reference to the family of Antipater who, as the Son must know, had sought to kill him as part of the massive slaughter of the innocents. Yet the reference to Herod is far more knowing and ironic even than Flannagan's note suggests, since Herod was considered by *Jews* to be the preeminent example of a false messiah, having laid claim to a specious lineage in order to become anointed in David's throne. The association of imposter messiahs, especially false Jewish messiahs, with the concept of enthusiasm, can be found in More's discussion of those melancholics who lead lives in public affairs:

> Wherefore those whose temper carries them most to Political affaires, who love rule and honour and have a strong sense of civil rights, Melancholy heating them makes them sometimes fancy themselves great Princes (at least by divine assignment) & deliverers of the people sent from God, such as were in likelyhood the false *Messiasses* that deceived the people of the Jews, as *Theudas* and that *Ægyptian Imposter*, also *Barcocab*, *Jonathas*, *Dositheus* and several others who it's likely, it being the common fame amongst the Jews that the *Messias* the deliverer was about that time to come, according to the heat and forwardness of their own Melancholy, conceited themselves to be him.[67]

The brief catalog of false messiahs had its much more extensive counterparts during the period and, following the conversion of Sabbatai to Islam, included this last imposter as the latest chapter. Satan's reference to Herod, in its association with the ongoing debate over messianic status, thus offers yet another reference to the recent Sabbatian fiasco.

Many of Milton's contemporaries, the Quakers and the Jews, as great as their differences were, seemed to round back in on each other (and George Fox recognized this—witness his extensive attempts at converting the Jews). The Jews—especially as they were portrayed through the enthusiastic excesses of the Sabbatian movement—embodied the most literalized messianism and eschatology discernable in the Scriptures, a literalization that was characteristic also of the Fifth Monarchy Men. Their apparent calls for a worldly deliverer who would be both a religious and political leader recapitulated the mistakes made by their ancestors during the life of Christ. Jews then and now misunderstood who and what the messiah really was supposed to be and to do. The Quakers, in their radically spiritualized account of Christian soteriology, seemed to present a complete break with any worldly notion of the deliverance to be offered by the messiah. For them, Christ's salvation was available and complete here and now to any who chose to acknowledge the inner light and the presence of Christ within them. There was no future deliverance, no temporally grounded eschaton to anticipate, no deferred or recursive conversion. It had arrived—irreversibly—for all.

Both these views represent the logical extremes of aspects of Milton's own messianic thinking. They are the extremes Satan presents to the Son as the only two possible interpretations of his prophesied kingdom: "A Kingdom [these prophecies] portend thee, but what Kingdom, / Real or Allegoric I discern not" (4.389–390). Milton writes his own account of how one discovers the meaning of Christ in *Paradise Regained*, thereby revealing how these satanic options are premised on a false binary. As has often been noted, Milton does not describe the Passion, Crucifixion, and Resurrection in his version of the recovery of paradise. Indeed, Milton is notoriously unwilling (or unable) to confront Christ's Passion is any of his poetry. Though that process is, ostensibly, the path by which all Christians are meant to believe paradise is regained, for Milton, the recovery of paradise occurs *before* that process. When the Son resists the wrong paths to salvation offered to him by Satan and correctly interprets his role despite the potential obscurity of the signs pointing the right way, he recovers the paradise that was lost. In much the same way that Satan tempts the Son with false hopes, I suggest that movements like the Quakers, the Fifth Monarchists, and the Sabbatians functioned as temptations, cautionary tales of false or inauthentic messiahs, fictions of conversion gone awry. In preparing his own poetic, necessarily imaginative representation of the true messiah, it was critical that Milton attended to these cautionary tales, since he was making himself vulnerable to the same accusations made against supporters of those other *pseudochristi*. The imaginative stakes of *Paradise Regained*, its poetics, thus take on further significance in relation to Milton's own ambivalent response to enthusiasm.

Enthusiasm, Figuration, and the Language of *Paradise Regained*

In his early prose, Milton offers several observations concerning the rhetorical qualities of religious writing. *Of Reformation* contrasts the occasional difficulties found within Scripture with the "more crabbed, more abstruse . . . knotty Africanisms, the pamper'd metafors; the intricat and involv'd sentences of the Father."[68] Intricacies are not identical to a rhetorical urgency, however, and Milton defends the vehemence of his own style by observing in a later anti-prelatical tract that "that feare and dull disposition, lukewarmenesse & sloth are not seldomer wont to cloak themselves under the affected name of moderation, then true lively zeale is customably dispareg'd with the terme of indiscretion, bitternesse, and choler."[69] This stylistic self-justification, replete with the Burtonian language of humoral balance and imbalance central to the discourses of enthusiasm, anticipates a veritable explosion of purple prose several pages later in *An Apology*:

> Some [of Christ's followers] also were indu'd with a staid moderation, and soundnesse of argument to teach and convince the rationall and sober-minded; yet not therefore that to be thought the only expedient course of teaching, for in times of opposition when either against new heresies arising, or old corruptions to be reform'd this coole unpassionate mildnesse of positive wisdome is not anough to damp and astonish the proud resistance of carnall and false Doctors, then (that I may have leave to soare a while as the Poets use) then Zeale whose substance is ethereal, arming in compleat diamond ascends his fiery Chariot drawn with two blazing Meteors figur'd like beasts, but of a higher breed then any the Zodiack yields, resembling two of those four which *Ezechiel* and S. *John* saw, the one visag'd like a Lion to expresse power, high autority and indignation, the other of cout'nance like a

> man to cast derision and scorne upon perverse and fraudulent seducers; with these the invincible warriour Zeale shaking lookely the slack reins drive over the heads of Scarlet Prelats, and such as are insolent to maintaine traditions, brusing their stiffe necks under his flaming wheels. Thus did the true Prophets of old combat with the false; thus Christ himselfe the fountaine of meeknesse found acrimony anough to be still galling and vexing the Prelaticall Pharisees.[70]

Striking for its embodiment of the very prophetic style it seeks to defend, this passage is also noteworthy for its recourse to the fraught binaries of authentic/inauthentic, material/immaterial, and carnal/spiritual we have identified as key features of the debates over enthusiasm more generally. Milton concludes with the example of Christ who, despite his characteristic meekness, was able to call upon the requisite rhetorical zeal to combat carnal Pharisees. Yet when, at the end of his career, the poet does produce his own imaginative rendition of the Savior in a pitched battle with the preeminent Adversary, the reader searches with some difficulty to discover those statements by the Son that partake of anything like this visionary, prophetic mode. If there is one character who finds occasion to express himself in the rhetoric of righteous indignation, it is Satan.

By way of a conclusion to my discussion, I now turn to the question of style in *Paradise Regained*, a question that has been raised frequently in discussions of the brief epic and most often prompted by a disappointment in the subdued tones of a poem that follows on the heels of the prophetic, visionary mode of *Paradise Lost*.[71] Sharon Achinstein has observed that Milton's Restoration legacy linked him with the dissenting tradition not simply on doctrinal grounds but also because "he represented what I shall call literary enthusiasm, a powerful force that embodied the most dangerous aspects of revolutionary energy: the conviction that one's ideas were divinely inspired and the belief that individual choice and experience could guide moral actions."[72] Annabel Patterson points out that Milton's addition of his note on "The Verse" to the 1674 edition of *Paradise Lost* "not only set Milton apart from the royalist poets of the Restoration . . . but by way of the phrase 'ancient liberty,' placed *Paradise Lost* and its refusal to rhyme firmly in the same political vocabulary that Milton had been developing from the moment he opened his commonplace book. Blank verse, open-ended, is enrolled in the service of the Good Old Cause."[73] The evidence of *Paradise Regained*, however, seems to suggest that Milton was not necessarily true to that legacy, shifting his poetics from a literary enthusiasm to one far more ambivalent about the ideological and religious implications of such a mode.

Just as Robert Burton locates the imagination within the same faculty that is vulnerable to melancholy, Casaubon, More, and other anti-enthusiastic writers forge an explicit link between enthusiasm and poetry. More writes, "A Poet is an *Enthusiast in jest*, and an Enthusiast is a *Poet in good Earnest*; Melancholy prevailing so much with him that he takes his no better than Poeticall fits and fragments for divine inspiration and *reall* truth."[74] Yet again, for More the matter hinges on the distinction between real and imaginary, authentic and inauthentic. What makes a poet different from an enthusiast is that a poet misleads (that is, he makes things up) knowingly, while an enthusiast misleads unwittingly. It is the difference between "make believe" and making others believe. In his writings, Casaubon not only associates poetry with enthusiasm but characterizes the very origins of the worship of false gods as a function of the poetic faculties, "so that as the beginning, growth and confirmation of Idolatry may be ascribed, as by many it is, unto Poets, and their authority; so to supposed Enthusiasms and Inspirations also, upon which that authority was chiefly grounded."[75] As N. H. Keeble has shown in his study of literary nonconformity, conformists like Casaubon, More, and other anti-enthusiasts resisted what they perceived to be the linguistic and literary abuses of religious dissenters, advocating a literature of clarity and common sense.[76] Indeed, Bishop Samuel Parker lamented how religious radicals

> have effectually turn'd all Religion into unaccountable Fansies and Enthusiasms, drest it up with pompous and empty Schemes of Speech, and so embrace a few gawdy Metaphors and Allegories, instead of the substance of true and real Righteousness. And herein lies the most material difference between the sober Christians of the Church of *England*, and out modern Sectaries, That we express the Precepts and Duties of the Gospel in plan and intelligible Terms, whilst they trifle them away by childish Metaphors and Allegories, and will not talk of Religion but in barbarous and uncouth Similitudes; and (what is more) the different Subdivisions among the Sects themselves are not so much distinguish'd by any real diversity of Opinions, as by variety of Phrases and forms of Speech, that are the peculiar *Shibboleths* of each Tribe.[77]

Advocating only half in jest an "Act of Parliament to abridge Preachers the use of fulsom and lushious Metaphors,"[78] Parker invokes the distinction between the "substance" of divine truths articulated plainly and the metaphors and allegories that, in their dependence on figuration, consist of nothing real or material.[79] Parker's call for a plain style reminds us of Herbert's Jordan poems, Cowley's hope for the baptism of poetry, and their implicit (Herbert) and explicit (Cowley) associations with the expected conversion of the Jews.

Quakers like Nayler and Fox, who were the primary targets of Parker's attacks, often turned the tables on such an accusation, claiming a plainness and directness to their own use of language that was not, they argued, a property of the detached moral instructions of conservative writers like Parker. As Keeble remarks, "for the nonconformist to be plain was not to appeal dispassionately to universals but to encourage others by being authentic, true to the experience of grace within oneself."[80] Fox and Nayler take their contemporaries to task, for example, for the practice of putting the Psalms to meter: "And the Singing of Psalmes, after their manner, we deny; for they sing *Davids* tremblings, quaking, and roarings, this they have turned into Meeter, as if we should see one of you lye roaring, crying, till your eyes should grow dim, and watering your Bed with your teares, and we should turne it into Meeter, and make a Rime of it, and take it, and goe among a company of ignorant People, and say, let us sing to the prayse and glory of God."[81] For language to be effective, whether it be the language of Scripture or the language of the preacher, it must be affective, i.e., evocative, personal, and transcendent. While not necessarily disputing the accusations of allegorizing and de-materializing leveled at them by their opponents, Quakers and other enthusiasts insisted that the material world of lived experience to which the presumably literal meaning of language referred was less real than the revelatory power of the divine immanence within each individual believer. As Nayler observes, in a text that is presented as a dialogue not unlike the exchanges between Satan and the Son in *Paradise Regained*,

> You are shut out of the scriptures, and they witnesse against you and your imagined wayes and worships, you that preach and pray, and not by the movings of the spirit of God, you are shut out of the scriptures, and your invented words and long prayers are condemned by them to be heathenish, and all your ordinances your singings and sacraments, which are not in the same spirit, is condemned by the scriptures, and

> whatever you do in your worships to God, and not in the power and guiding of the same eternall spirit, the scriptures witnesse against you and your worship and declares you to be led by a contrary spirit, which is not the same, and you are among the heathen who worship in vain; and receives no acceptance from God; for you receive for doctrines, the commandments of men & your fear towards God, is taught by the precepts of men, & not by the Spirit, & what you have is by tradition; and here you are shut out the scriptures.[82]

Nayler sees the liturgical and sacramental traditions that have accumulated around Scriptures as corrupting and inauthentic, heathenish and alienating. In his famous dismissal of books and learning, Milton's Son offers a parallel defense of the biblical plain style. The Scriptures contain all that one needs, both in the pleasures of artistic language and the depths of philosophical and political discourse. The Son derides the "Eloquence [of] Statists," preferring instead what is "plainest taught, and easiest learnt":

> But herein to our Prophets far beneath,
> As men divinely taught, and better teaching
> The solid rules of Civil Government
> In thir majestic unaffected style
> Than all the Oratory of *Greece* and *Rome.*
> (4.356–360)

In Milton's poem the stakes of the exchange parallel those in this argument by Nayler. Both texts stage the combat between a true understanding of Scripture and its pronouncements on salvation and messianic deliverance and false, satanic, antichristian readings of the same questions. The subdued tones of *Paradise Regained*, however, serve Milton to distance his Son from the critique of enthusiasm. In *Paradise Lost*, the poetic persona was a powerful presence, almost another character (regarded by some later readers as the true hero of the poem). *Paradise Regained* does not admit such a presence; were it to be a part of the poem, the problem of imaginative and poetical enthusiasm would be much more pronounced and difficult to defend against. The poem makes uneasy use of the prophetic registers—outrage, passion, fierceness, and even figuration—that arguably have a fully legitimate precedent in Scriptures and that Milton put to highly effective use in *Paradise Lost*.

The Son's celebration of unaffected style hearkens back to Milton's initial identification of the subject of the brief epic, which is, in turn, aligned with the nature of messianic identity:

With prosperous wing full summ'd, to tell of deeds
Above Heroic, though in secret done,
And unrecorded left through many an Age,
Worthy t'have not remained so long unsung.
(ll. 14–17)

The paradoxical yoking of deeds that are both "above Heroic" and "in secret done" reflects a resistance to the overwrought rhetoric of a fictive literary tradition that was wont to rely on the "invented words and long prayers" condemned by Fox and other Quakers as "heathenish." Milton is here recollecting his rejection of the classical heroic mode in the invocation to Book 9 of *Paradise Lost* as "Not that which justly gives Heroic name / To Person or to Poem" (*PL* 9.40–41). The narrator of *Paradise Regained* offers an account of Jesus' baptism that combines its transcendence—its inspirational enthusiasm—with noteworthy understatement:

to his great Baptism flock'd
With awe the Regions round, and with them came
From *Nazareth* the Son of *Joseph* deem'd
To the flood *Jordan*, came as then obscure,
Unmarkt, unknown. But him the Baptist soon
Descried, divinely warn'd, and witness bore
As to his worthier, and would have resign'd
To him his Heavenly Office, nor was long
His witness unconfirm'd; on him baptiz'd
Heaven open'd, and in likeness of a Dove
The Spirit descended, while the Father's voice
From Heav'n pronounc'd him his beloved Son.
(ll. 22–30)

The syntax and grammar of this description contrast with lines 33–105, which recount Satan's recognition of and reaction to the same event. The former offers a direct, paratactic account, standing in for an unmediated dissemination of the knowledge of the Son. The latter, involuted and hypotactic, obscures the central issue.

> Before him a great Prophet, to proclaim
> His coming, is sent harbinger, who all
> Invites, and in the consecrated stream
> Pretends to wash off sin, and fit them so
> Purified to receive him pure, or rather
> To do him honour as their King; all come,
> And he himself among them was baptiz'd,
> Not thence to be more pure, but to receive
> The testimony of Heaven, that who he is
> Thenceforth the Nations may not doubt; I saw
> The Prophet do him reverence; on him rising
> Out of the water, Heav'n above the Clouds
> Unfold her Crystal Doors, thence on his head
> A perfect Dove descend, whate'er it meant,
> And out of Heav'n the Sovran voice I heard,
> This is my Son belov'd, in him am pleas'd.
> (ll. 70–85)

As each phrase or clause in Satan's version modifies, even undermines, the previous one, style becomes linked with competing modes of knowledge. In the narrator's initial account, the son of Joseph approaches the Jordan "obscure / Unmarkt, unknown," yet his true identity is shortly confirmed by the Spirit's descent. Satan's parenthetical remark about the Dove's descent, "whate'er it meant," stunningly misses the point that should be obvious to all. Satan's ongoing efforts to compel the Son to confirm his identity notwithstanding, what remains uncertain is not the *status* of Jesus as the Son of God (or even as messiah), but rather the *meaning* of that identity. The question becomes a historical, political, and hermeneutical one, rather than an epistemological question of the authenticity of inspiration. As we have seen from the anti-enthusiastic discussions of Hobbes and others, such proof of validity is virtually unachievable. Milton's solution to the persistent, irresolvable dilemma of identity—a genuine self that is both the same and different as it experiences transformative revelation—posed by fictions of conversion is to dodge the question. The Son makes no effort to offer any proof of inspiration or identity. His uncertainty stems from a different set of interpretive dilemmas:

> Meanwhile the Son of God, who yet some days
> Lodg'd in *Bethabara*, where *John* baptiz'd,

Musing and much revolving in his breast
How best the mighty work he might begin
Of Savior to mankind, and which way first
Publish his Godlike office now mature,
One day forth walk'd alone, the Spirit leading
And his deep thoughts, the better to converse
With solitude, till, far from track of men,
Thought following thought, and step by step led on,
He enter'd now the bordering Desert wild,
And, with dark shades and rocks environ'd round,
His holy Meditations thus pursu'd.

(ll. 183–195)

In this, our first encounter with the Son's inner thoughts, we find him wondering how he should begin his work as Saviour and how he should make known his messianic status. He knows with utter confidence *who* he is. He is less certain, however, about *what* his identity means. The recognition of a divine calling is not identical with a complete understanding of how best to enact that divine calling.

A further striking example of the difference between the poetics of *Paradise Lost* and *Paradise Regained* appears several lines later in Book 1, when Satan first appears to the Son in disguise (itself a suggestion of the potential for certain kinds of language to be inauthentic and deceptive):

But now an aged man in Rural weeds,
Following, as seem'd, the quest of some stray Ewe,
Or wither'd sticks to gather, which might serve
Against a Winter's day when winds blow keen,
To warm him wet return'd from field at Eve,
He saw approach;

(ll. 314–319)

The poem introduces Satan in what at first looks a good deal like the georgic similes Milton used to such great effect in *Paradise Lost*. What seems to begin as a simile, however, becomes a narrative speculation about the identity of this still disguised figure. The poetic and rhetorical function of the epic simile is replaced by a more literalized resemblance, i.e., a disguise meant to give the impression of an old man in rustic clothes, that in turn is exposed for its deceptiveness, its unreality. Whereas in *Paradise Lost* figurative language is clearly relished even as it reveals the fallen nature of language, in *Paradise Regained* language, along with everything else, demands a conversion that eliminates its mediating and disfiguring qualities.

The apocalyptic prophecies central to the biblical tradition, and so often cited by Milton's contemporary enthusiasts (Quakers, Fifth Monarchists, Ranters, even Jewish Sabbatians), find their counterparts in Milton's poem more frequently within the temptations to power offered by the Adversary than in the responses of the Son.[83] The grand panoramic vista of all the great kingdoms and empires in the middle of Book 3 (ll. 266–309) falls firmly within the tradition of eschatological writings of Daniel and Revelation that predicted the destruction of all of Israel's historical enemies, biblical texts to which Naylor and Fox, Venner and Abiezer Coppe, turned time and again for support of their inspired claims. These satanic citations recollect the prophetic, apocalyptic mode—and their expectations for mass conversions—only to assert the poem's divergence from it. *Paradise Regained* largely avoids such discourse. Instead, Milton yokes these prophetic expectations to the ornate and flowery language of Romance (much to the displeasure of many of his critics):

> Such forces met not, nor so wide a camp,
> When *Agrican* with all his Northern powers
> Besieg'd *Albracca*, as Romances tell;
> The City of *Gallaphrone* , from thence to win
> The fairest of her Sex *Angelica*
> His daughter, sought by many Prowest Knights,
> Both *Paynim* , and the Peers of *Charlemane.*
> Such and so numerous was thir Chivalrie;
> (3.337–343)

The proximity (and implicit association) of the biblical with the classical mode parallels the very thrust of Satan's ensuing temptation, i.e., that without an alliance between Israel and one of the two pagan empires (Roman or Parthian) the messiah cannot hope to retain any political power and independence. By virtue of the Parthian "thou shalt regain," Satan insists, "without him not, / That which alone can truly reinstall thee / In *David's* royal seat, his true Successor" (ll. 371–373). The text proposes, then, that the impropriety (or rashness) of such apocalyptic ambitions is inextricably linked with a poetics of enthusiasm.

In *Paradise Lost* when the matter of perspective is at issue—either because what we are being asked to see is unimaginable to human vision or because our vision is being impaired or improved—our attention is called to the means of that perspective either not at all or only in the most artful ways, as in the famous references to Galileo's telescope or even when Michael must shift from vision to narration. In the longer epic the act of painting vivid pictures is itself of value; the images rendered are beautiful to contemplate and have the peculiar ability to transport us or to infuse us with a kind of second spirit, recollecting the very dynamics of enthusiasm so often attacked by its critics. Not so in *Paradise Regained*, where perspective is thematized in a very different manner:

> By what strange Parallax, or Optic skill
> Of vision, multiplied through air, or glass
> Of Telescope, were curious to inquire:
> And now the Tempter thus his silence broke.
> The city which thou seest no other deem
> Than great and glorious *Rome*, Queen of the Earth
> So far renown'd, and with the spoils enricht
> Of Nations; there the Capitol thou seest,
> Above the rest lifting his stately head
> On the *Tarpeian rock*, her Citadel
> Impregnable; and there Mount *Palatine*,
> Th'Imperial Palace, compass huge, and high
> The Structure, skill of noblest Architects,
> With gilded battlements, conspicuous far,
> Turrets, and Terraces, and glittering Spires.
> Many a fair Edifice besides, more like
> Houses of Gods (so well I have dispos'd
> My Airy Microscope) thou mayst behold,
> Outside and inside both, pillars and roofs
> Carv'd work, the hand of fam'd Artificers
> In Cedar, Marble, Ivory or Gold.
>
> (4.40–60)

Satan's seemingly innocent parenthetical remark, "so well I have dispos'd / My Airy Microscope," feels clumsy, out of place. When our vision, or the vision of the Son, is altered we are informed of that fact in the most direct way. The "Airy Microscope" is noteworthy as Satan's own technological innovation to improve the Son's vision; it stands in striking contrast to the "Optic Glass" (*PL*, 1.288) used by the Tuscan Artist to view the Moon. In the earlier poem, these technological aids to vision were introduced as part of the figurative landscape to which the events of the narrative were compared. A poem that recounts the Fall and loss of paradise through human agency, *Paradise Lost* is free to indulge in the power of the imagination "to descry new Lands" in the mind's eye. The brief epic stands in uneasy tension with those contemporaneous enthusiastic efforts imaginatively to find paradise without or within. This uneasiness may be recognized especially in the later poem's far more ambivalent recourse to the figurative language of comparison, a mode of language that depends for its effect on the tension between identity and difference, the same tension that occasions all the other fictions of conversion encountered in this book.

When the poem eventually does offer an extended simile of the sort with which we are familiar from the longer epic, it is occasioned by the final desperate attempts of Satan at the beginning of the last book of *Paradise Regained.* The epic simile, however, can no longer serve Milton in the way that it had in his earlier work. There, "the persuasive Rhetoric" wielded by Satan had successfully "won so much on *Eve.*" Eve's rashness and self-deception epitomize the impulsiveness, the self-blinding ambitions of those enthusiasts so eager to accelerate—or even ignore—historical process (and in the process, disobey the will of God). The Son does not make the same mistake and the poem's use of familiar literary conventions like the epic simile reflects this difference:

> But as a man who had been matchless held
> In cunning, overreach't where least he thought,
> To salve his credit, and for very spite,
> Still will be tempting him who foils him still,
> And never cease, though to his shame the more;
> Or as a swarm of flies in vintage time,
> About the wine-press where sweet must is pour'd,
> Beat off, returns as oft with humming sound;
> Or surging waves against a solid rock,
> Though all to shivers dash'd, th'assault renew,
> Vain batt'ry, and in froth or bubbles end;
> So Satan, whom repulse upon repulse
> Met ever, and to shameful silence brought,

Yet gives not o'er, though desperate of success,
And his vain importunity pursues.

(4.10–24)

The first of the three comparisons in the passage can hardly be said to offer a comparison at all, as it seems to describe Satan exactly as he now stands, "still . . . tempting him who foils him still." The second comparison, to the flies swarming about the winepress, places special emphasis on timeliness and how these processes bound up with time cannot be thwarted by interventions (by flies or by Satan). The final comparison suggests that Satan's previously persuasive rhetoric is really just so much "froth and bubbles." The epic narrator employs the epic simile precisely to depict the failure of Satan's rhetorical strategies, which are themselves allied with the deceptions of figurative language. The proliferation of images in this succession of comparisons is less a celebration of the power of poetic language (as it so often was in the longer epic) than an enactment of that language's futility. Indeed, the impassive Son manages to elude the grasp of this series of comparisons until the final one, where he emerges as the solid rock, the only fixed image in the entire passage.

What has changed between *Paradise Lost* and *Paradise Regained*? Both poems meditate in various ways on the fallenness of language and its tendency to deceive. In *Paradise Regained*, however, because Milton offers his imaginative version of the true messiah, the challenges raised in the discourse of enthusiasm become far more pressing. Though Milton may not sympathize politically or religiously with the opponents of enthusiasm, a poem that has as its main subjects the identification of the real Christian messiah and the correct understanding of authentic, divine inspiration, responds to the anxieties and tensions these clashes raised in ways Milton did not find necessary in his earlier epic. The memorable image of Satan's fall offers one of the only other epic similes in the poem.

But Satan, smitten with amazement fell
As when Earth's Son *Antaeus* (to compare
Small things with greatest) in *Irassa* strove
With *Jove's Alcides*, and oft foil'd still rose,
Receiving from his mother Earth new strength,
Fresh from his fall, and fiercer grapple join'd,
Throttl'd at length in th'Air, expir'd and fell;
So after many a foil the Tempter proud,

Renewing fresh assaults, amidst his pride
Fell whence he stood to see his Victor fall.
And as that *Theban* Monster that propos'd
Her riddle, and him who solv'd it not, devour'd,
That ounce found out and solv'd, for grief and spite
Cast herself headlong from th'*Ismenian* steep,
So struck with dread and anguish fell the Fiend . . .
(4.563–576)

The meta-fictional introduction of the comparison, "to compare / Small things with greatest," is both a knowing comment on the nature of metaphorical language and wonderfully ambiguous. Which is the small thing and which the greatest? Our assumption ought to be that Satan is the greater and Antaeus the smaller; yet the indulgence in the succession of classical mini-narratives (of Hercules and of Oedipus) diminishes Satan's stature. His denouement in the tenor of this simile is given three short, notably unenthusiastic words: "So Satan fell" (l. 581).

All three of Milton's late poems grapple with the role emotion must play in the "upright heart and pure." As he comments in the *Apology for Smectymnuus*, "each radicall humor and passion wrought upon and corrected as it ought, might be the proper mold and foundation of every mans peculiar gifts and virtues."[84] Michael Schoenfeldt has recently shown how Milton reads the Fall as "an internal revolt" among the appetites and passions and, citing *Paradise Lost* 12.83–95, that humanity's failure to reign in the passions is "the prime reason that God allowed the political affliction called monarchy to emerge."[85] The Son's definitive rejection of earthly kingship serves precisely to correct this human failing and gives special force to the angels' messianic hymn sung following the fall of Satan: "now thou has aveng'd / Supplanted *Adam*, and by vanquishing / Temptation, hast regain'd lost Paradise" (ll. 606–608). The angels praise the Son in noticeably direct, non-figurative language, saving their final words of imaginative comparison—"like an Autumnal Star / Or Lightning thou shalt fall from Heav'n trod down / Under his feet" (ll. 619–621)—for one last taunt of the defeated "Thief of Paradise." In one final gesture of quiet literalism, the Son "unobserv'd / Home to his Mother's house private" returns, eschewing any of the hue and cry identified with the discourses of enthusiasm and turning, instead, to the private sphere, a space in which the consolidation of alternative modes of identity and subjectivity will become increasingly compelling—though no less problematic.

Notes

INTRODUCTION

1. On the history of the English Puritans' relations with the Amsterdam Jewish community, see Keith L. Sprunger, *Dutch Puritanism: A History of English and Scottish Churches of the Netherlands in the Sixteenth and Seventeenth Centuries* (Leiden: E. J. Brill, 1982); Aaron Katchen, *Christian Hebraists and Dutch Rabbis: Seventeenth Century Apologetics and the Study of Maimonides* (Cambridge, MA: Harvard University Press, 1984); and Keith L. Sprunger, *Trumpets from the Tower: English Puritan Printing in the Netherlands, 1600–1640* (Leiden: E. J. Brill, 1994).

2. The ongoing and often intimate relationships between Jews and *conversos* throughout the fifteenth, sixteenth, and seventeenth centuries have been largely underestimated by most historians and are only now receiving the attention they deserve. There is still much to be learned about this fascinating feature of early modern Jewish history, but for my purposes, at least, it offers compelling evidence of the permeable and indistinct boundaries of identity and community that were thought to have been delineated far more starkly by conversion.

3. In his survey, Katchen recounts the ways in which Dutch Hebraists specifically made use of Maimonides' rulings concerning proselytes. He cites the particular examples of Johannes Coccejus, Dionysus Vossius, Guglielmus Vorstius, and George Gentius. See Katchen, 73, 218–219, and 332n119. Though Katchen provides these examples in unrelated contexts, it seems to me quite significant that one of the key areas in which these Christian readers consulted Maimonides was in questions of conversion, an area in which the contemporary Amsterdam Jewish community would have been even more enthusiastic in consulting the medieval Jewish legal authority.

4. During our time together at the University of Pennsylvania's Katz Center for Advanced Judaic Studies, working on different features of the theme of conversion, Theodor Dunkelgrün, Yosi Israeli, and Claude Stuczynski each made persuasive arguments concerning the role that *converso* pride in Jewish ancestry played in claims for a privileged place in Christian theology and history. I look forward to the publication of Dunkelgrün's work on Johannes Isaac Levita (1515–1577), Israeli's work on Pablo de Santa Maria (ca. 1352–1435), and Stuczynski's work on Alfonso de Santa Mariá de Cartagena (1384–1456). Stuczynski further suggests that Paul and his conversion figure prominently

in an emergent, self-consciously *converso* theology. Some *conversos* explicitly compared their experiences of transformation to Paul's conversion, rendering their religious changes as completions and fulfillments of the paradigm of Jewish conversion established by Paul.

5. John Donne, "Sermon Preached at S. Pauls . . . Upon the Day of S. Pauls Conversion. 1628/29," in *The Sermons of John Donne*, vol. 7, ed. Evelyn M. Simpson and George R. Potter (Berkeley: University of California Press, 1956), 324–325. For a perceptive analysis of Donne's sermons on Paul's conversion, see Gregory Kneidel, "John Donne's *Via Pauli*," *Journal of English and Germanic Philology* 100 (2001): 224–246.

6. John Donne, "Satire III," in *John Donne: The Complete English Poems*, ed. A. J. Smith (Harmondsworth: Penguin Books, 1986), 161–164, ll. 1, 5, 7. All subsequent quotations from Donne's English poetry are taken from this edition and followed by line number(s). Most scholars agree that Donne's satires were written between 1593 and 1597, with the third satire likely having been written in approximately 1596. Though Donne probably did not make the formal transition into the Church of England until well into the first decade of the seventeenth century, the satires give ample testimony to Donne's increasing disillusionment with the Catholic Church during this earlier period. For my purposes here, though, I am less interested in the specific timing of Donne's conversion or even, for that matter, that Donne was a convert than I am in his presentation of religion specifically in terms of conversion.

7. See Richard Strier's reading of Donne's satire in "Radical Donne: 'Satire III,'" *ELH* 60 (1993): 283–322.

8. Francis Petrarch, "Familiar Letters," in *Petrarch: The First Modern Scholar and Man of Letters*, ed. and trans. James Harvey Robinson (New York: G. P. Putnam, 1898), 311.

9. Petrarch, 313.

10. To be clear, I am not suggesting that this poem is about Donne's conversion to Anglicanism. Rather, I am reading it as an exploration of the liberating possibilities made available in the very idea of conversion itself, how choice and change are the means to achieve the Truth that all religions separately and exclusively promise. See also Molly Murray, *The Poetics of Conversion in Early Modern Literature: Verse and Change from Donne to Dryden* (Cambridge: Cambridge University Press, 2009), 82–92, which locates in Donne's "Satire III" a description of "a culture of confessional flux." Murray's reading is largely persuasive, though I am less convinced that the mockingly ironic tone she identifies in much of the poem also characterizes the idea of turning per se.

11. Petrarch, 316.

12. Scholarship on "turning Turk," i.e., conversion to Islam, has been especially rich in recent years, including Nabil I. Matar, *Islam in Britain, 1558–1685* (Cambridge: Cambridge University Press, 1998); Matar, *Turks, Moors, and Englishmen in the Age of Discovery* (New York: Columbia University Press, 1999); Daniel J. Vitkus, *Turning Turk: English Theater and the Multicultural Mediterranean, 1570–1630* (New York: Palgrave Macmillan, 2003); and Jonathan Burton, *Traffic and Turning: Islam and English Drama, 1579–1624* (Newark: University of Delaware Press, 2005). Michael Questier is among the foremost scholars on conversion to and from Catholicism in late sixteenth- and early seventeenth-century England. See his *Conversion, Politics, and Religion in England,*

1580–1625 (Cambridge: Cambridge University Press, 1996). Molly Murray's *The Poetics of Conversion* is one of several particularly recent and very insightful studies of conversion in relation to literature.

13. Janet Adelman, *Blood Relations: Christian and Jew in* The Merchant of Venice (Chicago: University of Chicago Press, 2008); David S. Katz, *Philo-Semitism and the Readmission of the Jews to England, 1603–1655* (Oxford: Clarendon Press, 1982); Michael Ragussis, *Figures of Conversion: "The Jewish Question" and English National Identity* (Durham, NC: Duke University Press, 1995); Jason Rosenblatt, *Renaissance England's Chief Rabbi: John Selden* (Oxford: Oxford University Press, 2006); and James Shapiro, *Shakespeare and the Jews* (New York: Columbia University Press, 1996).

CHAPTER 1

1. Joseph Mede, "The Mystery of *S. Paul's* Conversion: *or*, The Type of the Calling of the Jews," *Works*, ed. John Worthington, 4th ed. (London, 1677), 891–892. Mede died in 1639 and this table was probably composed in the 1620s at the same time that he was particularly engaged in his millenarian writings, the most influential of which, *Clavis Apocalytica*, was published in Latin in 1627. Mede took up the matter of the calling of Jews (and its relation to Paul's conversion) in Epistle XVII, 765–768 in Worthington's edition.

2. A. D. Nock, *Conversion: The Old and the New in Religion from Alexander the Great to Augustine of Hippo* (Oxford: Oxford University Press, 1933), 191.

3. Alan F. Segal, *Paul the Convert: The Apostolate and Apostasy of Saul the Pharisee* (New Haven, CT: Yale University Press, 1990), 19.

4. Paula Fredriksen, "Mandatory Retirement: Ideas in the Study of Christian Origins Whose Time Has Come to Go," *Studies in Religion/Sciences Religieuses* 35 (2006): 231–246. This essay revisits some of the arguments Frederiksen made in her earlier and influential essay, "Paul and Augustine: Conversion Narratives, Orthodox Traditions, and the Retrospective Self," *Journal of Theological Studies* 37 (1986): 3–34. See also Kirster Stendahl, "The Apostle Paul and the Introspective Conscience of the West," in *Paul among the Jews and Gentiles and Other Essasys* (Philadelphia: Fortress Press, 1976); and Larry Hurtado, "Convert, Apostate, or Apostle to the Nations: The 'Conversion' of Paul in Recent Scholarship," *Studies in Religion / Sciences Religieuses* 22 (1993): 273–284.

5. Nock, 191.

6. John Gaule, *Practique Theories: Or, Votiue Speculations Vpon Sauls Cruelty. Pauls Conuersion* (London, 1630), 342–343.

7. "Sermon Preached at S. Pauls, The Sunday of the Conversion of S. Paul [1624/5]," in *The Sermons of John Donne*, vol. 6, ed. Evelyn M. Simpson and George R. Potter (Berkeley: University of California Press, 1956), 209.

8. David Cressy, *Bonfires and Bells: National Memory and the Protestant Calendar in Elizabethan and Stuart England* (Berkeley: University of California Press, 1989), 39–40, cited in Kneidel, 226.

9. On creation and conversion in the writings of Augustine, see Marilyn J. Harran,

Luther on Conversion: The Early Years (Ithaca, NY: Cornell University Press, 1983), 28, and Frederick H. Russell, "Augustine: Conversion by the Book," in *Varieties of Religious Conversion in the Middle Ages*, ed. James Muldoon (Gainesville: University Press of Florida, 1997), 20–24. I have more to say about the function of reading and text in Augustine's conversion account at the beginning of Chapter 3.

10. Judith Pollman, "A Different Road to God: The Protestant Experience of Conversion in the Sixteenth Century," in *Conversion to Modernities: The Globalization of Christianity*, ed. Peter van der Veer (New York: Routledge, 1996), 54.

11. Benjamin Carier, *A Treatise . . . to forsake the Protestant Congregation and to Betake Himselfe to the Catholike Apostolike Roman Church* ([English Secret Press], 1614), 2–3.

12. Martin Luther, *Lectures on Romans*, Wilhelm Pauck, ed. and trans. (Philadelphia: Westminster Press, 1961), 322–323.

13. Harran, 87.

14. Plato, *The Republic*, trans. Robin Waterfield (Oxford: Oxford University Press, 1993), 521c.

15. See Bernard of Clairvaux, *Sermons on Conversion*, trans. Marie-Bernard Saïd (Kalamazoo, MI: Cistercian Publications, 1981). On the humanistic influence on Luther and his circle of early reformers, see Euan Cameron, *The European Reformation* (Oxford: Clarendon Press, 1991), 179.

16. See Murray, 47–51, which demonstrates a far more extensive influence of Augustine's *Confessions* in late sixteenth- and early seventeenth-century England than had been previously acknowledged. Murray writes specifically of the imprint of the *Confessions* on the writings of the Catholic convert William Alabaster. The appearance of Catholic and Protestant translations of the *Confessions* in 1620 and 1631, respectively, attests to its importance, not to mention the competing claims made for the text by the rival churches. A revealing example of the difference is in the eleventh chapter of Book VIII, the chapter in which Augustine recounts his conversion to Christianity. Describing his unsettled state prior to conversion, Augustine uses the term *aegrotabam*, which the Catholic translation renders as "sicke of Mind," while the Protestant translation uses "soule-sicke." The difference between a rational condition and a spiritual condition speaks directly to the different views Catholics and Protestants took regarding the process and possibilities for conversion, especially the role of reason.

17. John Calvin, *The Institution of Christian Religion*, trans. Thomas Norton (London, 1599), II.iii.5.

18. Heiko Oberman, "*Subito Conversio*: The Conversion of John Calvin," in *Reformiertes Erbe: Festschrift für Gottfried W. Locher zu seinem 80. Geburstag*, vol. 2, ed. Heiko Oberman, Ernst Saxer, Alfred Schindler, and Heinzpeter Stucki (Zurich: Theologischer Verlag Zürich, 1993), 291.

19. Calvin, III.iii.9.

20. The phrase "morphologies of conversion" is Edmund Morgan's, from *Visible Saints: The History of a Puritan Idea* (Ithaca, NY: Cornell University Press, 1965). Morgan summarizes the ten steps in this recursive process: attendance on the ministry of the word (perhaps accompanied by some outward misfortune); brought into the knowledge of the

law; awareness of one's own "peculiar and proper sins"; "legall feare" (conviction of sin); humiliation; God's elect find a serious consideration of the promise of salvation; sparking of a will and desire to believe; soul fights against doubt and despair; feeling of assurance and persuasion of mercy; "Evangelicall sorrow" (grief for sin because it is sin); God grants grace "to endeavor to obey his commandments by a new obedience" (pp. 68ff).

21. R. T. Kendall, *Calvin and English Calvinism to 1649* (Oxford: Oxford University Press, 1979). See also Charles L. Cohen, *God's Caress: The Psychology of Puritan Religious Experience* (Oxford: Oxford University Press, 1986), who points out the importance of Theodore Beza's theology as a modification of Calvin's stark predestinarian view in the linking of grace and works (11).

22. Cohen, 94.

23. Gaule, 351.

24. Michael C. Questier, *Conversion, Politics, and Religion in England, 1580–1625* (Cambridge: Cambridge University Press, 1996), 58.

25. Bruce Hindmarsh has taken the early Reformers' argument about the antiquity of their ways as an explanation for why there is really no genre of the conversion narrative in the sixteenth century. See *The Evangelical Conversion Narrative: Spiritual Autobiography in Early Modern England* (Oxford: Oxford University Press, 2005), 26.

26. Carier, 24. For more on Carier's notorious conversion, see Michael Questier, "Crypto-Catholicism, Anti-Calvinisim and Conversion at the Jacobean Court: The Enigma of Benjamin Carier," *Journal of Ecclesiastical History* 47 (1996): 45–64.

27. Questier, 8. See also 205–206.

28. See, for example, Alison Shell, "Multiple Conversion and the Menippean Self: The Case of Richard Carpenter," in *Catholicism and Anti-Catholicism in Early Modern English Texts*, ed. Arthur Marotti (New York: St. Martin's Press, 1999); Holly Crawford Pickett, "Dramatic Nostalgia and Spectacular Conversion in Dekker and Massinger's *The Virgin Martyr*," *SEL: Studies in English Literature, 1500–1800* 49 (2009): 437–462; and Murray, especially chapter 1.

29. See Alexandra Walsham, *Church Papists: Catholicism, Conformity, and Confessional Polemic in Early Modern England* (Rochester, NY: Boydell Press, 1993), for a seminal study of church-papistry and recusancy, revealing a complex and nuanced picture of the various alternatives English Catholics constructed for themselves. The picture that has emerged from recent work by Walsham, Questier, Peter Lake, and others is of a constantly changing response to enforced conformity.

30. See Christopher Haigh, *English Reformations: Religion, Politics, and Society under the Tudors* (Oxford: Clarendon Press, 1993), chapter 16, for a helpful summary of this stage of the English reformation. The recently published collection, *Recusancy and Conformity in Early Modern England: Manuscript and Printed Sources in Translation*, ed. Ginerva Crosignani, Thomas M. McCoog, S.J., and Michael Questier (Rome: Institutum Historicum Societatis Iesu, 2010), offers a rich source of newly available materials for the study of recusancy and church-papistry in the second half of the sixteenth century.

31. Questier, 124. See also Ramie Targoff, *Common Prayer: The Language of Public Devotion in Early Modern England* (Chicago: University of Chicago Press, 2001), who

has shown that modern dichotomies of inner and outer, private and public, ought not be presumed in understandings of the early modern approach to common worship and religious conformity.

32. J. E. Neale, *Elizabeth I and Her Parliaments*, vol. 2 (New York: W. W. Norton & Co., 1966), 296–297n48, cited in Strier, 295. See also Perez Zagorin, *Ways of Lying: Dissimulation, Persecution, and Conformity in Early Modern Europe* (Cambridge, MA: Harvard University Press, 1990), 229ff.

33. Daniel Featley, *Virtumnus romanus, or, A discovrse penned by a Romish priest . . . to prove that it is lawfull for a papist in England to goe to the Protestant church. . . : to whuch are adjoyned animadversions in the margin by way of antidote . . .* (London, 1642), 57.

34. Shell, 186.

35. Lionel Trilling, *Sincerity and Authenticity* (Cambridge, MA: Harvard University Press, 1971), 10. The "own self" in Trilling's phrase is, of course, the self to which Polonius advises Laertes to be true.

36. Richard Hooker, *Of the Laws of Ecclesiastical Polity*, vol. 5 (London, 1597), chapter 68, section 8.

37. Hooker, chapter 68, section 6.

38. See Zagorin and Lowell Gallagher, *Medusa's Gaze: Casuistry and Conscience in the Renaissance* (Stanford, CA: Stanford University Press, 1991), for rich discussions of these phenomena and their contributions to epistemological crises and ideological instabilities in Elizabethan and Jacobean England.

39. Featley, unpaginated preliminary advertisement.

40. Featley, 66 and 68.

41. Featley, 6.

42. I owe this wonderfully paradoxical formulation to David Nirenberg, who communicated it to me in personal correspondence.

43. Hooker, chapter 68, section 6.

44. II.xi of Calvin's *Institutes* discusses at length the relationship between the Old and New Testaments and offers a model of typological completion that can also be said to describe conversion from Judaism to Christianity as fulfillment. I shall discuss the relationship between typology and conversion below in Chapter 2.

45. Daniel Price, *Recusants Conuersion* (London, 1608), 12.

46. Thomas Cooper, *The Blessing of Japheth, Proving the Gathering of the Gentiles, and the Finall Couersion of the Jewes* (London, 1615), 21

47. John Foxe, *A Sermon Preached at the Christening of a Certaine Jew* (London, 1578), Mvi^{v}–Mvii^{r}. Adelman's analysis of Foxe's sermon appears in the first chapter of her book *Blood Relations*. My comments here draw extensively on her insights as I seek to draw attention specifically to the complex invocation and legacy of the Jewish convert in early modern English writing.

48. Foxe, Biii^{r}.

49. Foxe, [Bv^{r}].

50. David Graizbord, *Souls in Dispute: Converso Identities in Iberia and the Jewish Diaspora, 1580–1700* (Philadelphia: University of Pennsylvania Press, 2004), 117. See also

Yirmiyahu Yovel, *The Other Within: The Marranos: Split Identity and Emerging Modernity* (Princeton, NJ: Princeton University Press, 2009), who suggests, "The limpieza forced the Jewish designation upon the Marranos, while the Inquisition denied their right to adopt it. Thus, even if Marranos wished to accept the denomination of Jewish attached to them through limpieza, they were not permitted to do so. The Inquisition denied a person the right to be what the purity of blood rules said he could not escape. This left the Marrano suspended in the air. No identity could be supported by him as integral and coherent. . . . [The opposition between limpieza and the Inquisition] helped produce the typical Marrano situation as an inner exile, a person of unstable identity and, partly in a metaphorical sense, a new wandering Jew" (224).

51. Norman Roth, *Converso, Inquisition, and the Expulsion of the Jews from Spain* (Madison: University of Wisconsin Press, 1995), 3. Very recently, Javier Castaño has discovered evidence of large-scale forced conversions in certain regions of Spain nearly one hundred years earlier than the notorious period of the 1390s.

52. Arthur Hall, *A letter sent by F. A. touchyng the proceedings in a priuate quarrell and vnkindenesse* (London, 1576), Hiiir.

53. John Florio, *Qveen Annas New World of Words, or Dictionarie of the Italian and English tongues* (London, 1611), 300.

54. *Miscellaneous Works of Lancelot Andrewes*, ed. J. Bliss (Library of Anglo-Catholic Theology, xii, 1854), 94, cited in Katz, *Philo-Semitism*, 24. Cf. Katz, *Philo-Semitism*, 18–32, for a fuller discussion of Traske and the judaizing of the Traskites.

55. Frances, Lord Verulam, aka Francis Bacon, *Apophthegmes New and Old* (London, 1625), 196–198: no. 178.

56. Describing the Jew as the paradigmatic "Renaissance Man," Peter Berek has argued, "Though the Marrano Jew provides a convenient figure for cultural anxiety, the anxiety isn't about Marranism, or Jewishness, or even . . . about emerging ideas of race and nation, but about cultural change and a fluid sense of self that one could call 'modern.'" See "The Jew as Renaissance Man," *Renaissance Quarterly* 51 (1998): 128–162 (quotation from 158). While I agree with Berek that the anxieties for which the Jew figures as a cultural cypher are very much about change and flux, I do not accept his dismissal of Jewishness as irrelevant to these matters. What is more, as I argue below, it is important to link marranism with the fraught history of the English Reformation and the ongoing motility of English religious practices and identities. Furthermore, while the notion of Jewish flux registered cultural anxieties about change, it could also lend itself to more affirmative notions of change, notions that were gaining currency in late sixteenth- and seventeenth-century English self-definitions.

57. Roth, chapter 1.

58. David Gitlitz, *Secrecy and Deceit: The Religion of the Crypto-Jews* (Philadelphia: Jewish Publications Society, 1996), 81.

59. Sprunger, *Trumpets*, 70–71. Eliane Glaser has offered the provocative suggestion that Puritan philosemitism ought to be read as "triangulated opposition to Conformity." See her *Judaism without Jews: Philosemitism and Christian Polemic in Early Modern England* (New York: Palgrave Macmillan, 2007), 63.

60. David S. Katz, *The Jews in the History of England, 1485–1850* (Oxford: Clarendon Press, 1994), 65.

61. Graizbord, 50. See also Miriam Bodian, *Hebrew of the Portuguese Nation: Converso and Community in Early Modern Amsterdam* (Bloomington: Indiana University Press, 1997), 7–13.

62. Eric J. Griffin, *English Renaissance Drama and the Specter of Spain: Ethnopoetics and Empire* (Philadelphia: University of Pennsylvania Press, 2009), 119. Griffin also cites William of Orange's 1580 *Apologie*, in which he writes, "The greatest parte of the Spanyardes . . . are of the blood of the Moores and Jews" (47).

63. Foxe, Cii^{r}. Sharon Achinstein has shown that, in his *Book of Martyrs*, Foxe's attacks on and characterizations of the Jews function largely as polemics against Catholicism and in defense of English Protestantism's supersession. See "John Foxe and the Jews," *Renaissance Quarterly* 54 (2001): esp. 95ff.

64. See Jeffrey Shoulson, *Milton and the Rabbis: Hebraism, Hellenism, and Christianity* (New York: Columbia University Press, 2001), chapter 1.

65. Featley, unpaginated preliminary advertisement.

66. In his *Ways of Lying*, Perez Zagorin has also remarked on these parallels. See 61 and 134, especially. See also Shapiro, 26.

67. See Griffin for an account of the ambivalent representations of Spain and Spanishness in early modern English culture. Michael Ragussis has convincingly demonstrated that nineteenth-century British writings about Jews drew extensively on anti-Spanish, anti-Catholic sentiment. See his *Figures of Conversion*, chapter 4. My discussion here serves as a pre-history to Ragussis's seminal work on Jewish conversion in Victorian England.

68. Foxe, Mvii^{v}–Mviii^{r}.

69. Thomas Cooper, *The Converts First Love Discerned, Justified, Left, and Recovered, Resolving the Truth of and Effectual Conversion* (London, 1610), 17–18.

70. Thomas Cooper, *The Blessing of Japheth, Proving the Gathering of the Gentiles, and the Finall Conuersion of the Jewes* (London, 1615), 12.

71. Cooper, *The Blessing of Japheth*, 14.

72. Cooper, *The Blessing of Japheth*, 55.

73. Lancelot Andrewes, "Sermon Preached 10 February 1619, Before James at Whitehall."

74. The recent scholarship on early modern England's encounter with Islam is extensive. See for example, Matar, *Islam in Britain*; Matar, *Turks, Moors, and Englishmen*; Vitkus, *Turning Turk*; and Burton, *Traffic and Turning*.

75. Edward Kellet, *Retvrne from Argier. A Sermon Preached at . . . the re-admission of a relapsed Christian into our Church* (London, 1628), 35.

76. William Gouge, *A Recovery from Apostacy* (London, 1639), 19–20.

CHAPTER 2

1. I am, of course, fully aware of modern biblical criticism's identification of multiple sources for these patriarchal narratives, which explain the duplications, contradictions,

and name changes. My interest here, however, is in how early readers, Jewish and Christian, would have understood these passages. On the question of biblical names, their meanings, and their translations, see below, Chapter 3. The peculiar status of this particular name change will figure again in my consideration of an alchemical text attributed to "Abraham the Jew." See Chapter 4.

2. Janet Adelman, *Blood Relations: Christian and Jew in* The Merchant of Venice (Chicago: University of Chicago Press, 2008), 47–48.

3. Adelman quotes similar statements from the Bishops' Bible, Calvin's commentaries, and Henoch Clapham's *A Briefe of the Bible* (Edinburgh, 1596), locating the origins of such a reading in Augustine's *City of God*, 16.28.

4. Henry Ainsworth, *Annotations upon the First Book of Moses called Genesis* (London, 1616), N3r.

5. Ainsworth, K3r.

6. Thomas Haynes, *The Eqvall Wayes of God* (London, 1632), 22–23.

7. The apocryphal text *Joseph and Asenath* devotes much of its twenty-nine chapters to the details of Asenath's conversion and her decision to worship the God of Israel that preceded her marriage to Joseph. There remains some debate concerning the origin of this text—the earliest extant version is in Syriac and dates from the sixth century CE—but most scholars believe it to be a product of Hellenistic Judaism, composed in Greek between the first century BCE and the second century CE.

8. A noteworthy exception to this generalization about the traditional Jewish focus on Sinai in relation to the process of conversion is in the work of Maimonides, who looked to Abraham instead. Abraham's appeal to Maimonides appears to have been a function of the latter's insistence on the centrality of the intellectual process in one's coming to serve God. Abraham discovered God through his intellect, according to Maimonides, rather than through a supra-rational revelation. Maimonides is notoriously suspicious of these kinds of revelatory moments, as is evident in his definition of prophecy as an internal realization rather than an external imposition of God's presence. See, for example, his Letter to Obadiah the Proselyte.

9. The text calls attention to Moses' rootlessness. Pharaoh's daughter knows immediately upon seeing him that the infant Moses is a Hebrew. And when Moses does grow old enough to tour the Egyptian work sites, the narrator speaks of him going out "unto his brethren," the Hebrews (Ex. 2.11). Yet it is never made explicit that Moses is, himself, fully aware that he is of the Hebrew people and when Reuel's daughters describe him as an Egyptian we are left to wonder whether this characterization might have been acceptable to Moses until he learned otherwise. It takes God's call from the burning bush for Moses to accept his Hebrew origins. He refers to the children of Israel as his brethren for the first time only in Exodus 4.18. Freud would, of course, go on to make much of Moses' ambiguous origins in his *Moses and Monotheism*.

10. It is not without significance for my discussion that the word in Gershom's name that signals this sense of foreignness, *ger*, is precisely the term that comes to mean, in later rabbinic tradition, a proselyte. Adriane Leveen has taken useful note of the various forms of the stems *g'r'* and *g'r'sh'* (to exile or dismiss) that echo throughout Moses' story. See

his "Inside Out: Jethro, the Midianites, and a Biblical Constructions of the Outsider," *Journal for the Study of the Old Testament* 34 (2010): 395–417.

11. Rabbinic tradition took Jethro to task for his comparative formulation of God's greatness. In Devarim Rabbah 2.28, the rabbis say, "Jethro gave himself over to real idol worship, as it says, 'Now I know that God is greater than all the gods' (Ex. 18.11)." Naaman and Rahab, to whom I turn my attention later in this chapter, earn greater praise from the rabbis because their celebrations of God's power do not imply the existence of other gods.

12. Leveen has proposed a parallel reading to the one I am offering here, suggesting that the identification of Jethro as a priest of Midian specifically in moments when borders are crossed emphasizes his status as outsider and thereby enables his contribution to Moses and the Israelites. See Leveen, 405. Leveen further asserts that the alternative moniker the text uses to identify Jethro, "Moses' father-in-law," constructs him simultaneously as an insider. I am not entirely convinced by this reading. The very fact that Jethro's identity becomes derivative in this fashion—he is defined by whom his daughter has married—seems to me to diminish his individual standing and status. As we see below in my discussion of Ruth, this is often the paradox of biblical texts concerned with the integration and assimilation of the foreigner.

13. These are inconsistencies that can, of course, be explained by the theory of multiple sources for the Pentateuch, and I am largely persuaded by such explanations. The dissonance remains, however, in the redacted version and, more important for my purposes, ancient and early modern readers would not have had recourse to such theories.

14. See, e.g., *Tanhuma* Exodus 71, Exodus Rabbah 1.32, and Mishnat Rabbi Eliezer, among others.

15. See Louis H. Feldman, "Josephus' Portrait of Jethro," *The Quest for Context and Meaning: Studies in Biblical Intertextuality in Honor of James A. Sander*, ed. Craig A. Evans and Shemaryahu Talmon (Leiden: Brill, 1997), 573–594, reprinted in *Studies in Josephus' Rewritten Bible* (Leiden: Brill, 1998), 38–54. Feldman goes on to suggest that Josephus's omission of any suggestion of Jethro's conversion is a result of his sensitivity to the Roman world's hostility to and wariness of Jewish successes at proselytizing. It is a tantalizing hypothesis, but the evidence seems insufficient for such conclusions.

16. I have drawn on Judith Baskin's useful survey in this brief description of how Jethro was read by the early rabbis and church fathers. See her *Pharaoh's Counsellors: Job, Jethro, and Balaam in Rabbinic and Patristic Tradition* (Chico, CA: Scholars Press, 1983).

17. Richard Greenham, *The Workes of the Reverend and Faithfvll servant of Iesus Christ M. Richard Greenham* (London, 1612), 803. Greenham's works were first published posthumously by Henry Holland in 1599. I have made use of the fifth edition of the collected works.

18. Greenham, 803.

19. Andrew Willet, *Hexapla in Exodum* (London, 1608), 225. Willet's *Hexapla* are noteworthy for the diversity of sources they cite, ranging from Italian and Spanish Catholic clergy to German Protestants and French Huguenots. Willet's vehement anti-Catholicism does not seem to have necessarily prejudiced him against the value of

Catholic biblical scholarship. Alonso Tostado's case is particularly interesting since he had acquired a reputation, one with which Willet was likely familiar, as something of a Catholic maverick, having openly criticized both Pope Eugene IV and Juan de Torquemada (whose name was, of course, inextricably linked with the Inquisition and Catholic efforts to root out false converts).

20. John Lightfoot, *The Harmony of the Foure Evangelists* (London, 1644), 99.

21. See Alexander Ross, *Som Animadversions and Observations upon Sr. Walter Raleighs Historie of the World* (London, 1648), 27; and Henry Hammond, *A Letter of Resolution to Six Qæres, of Present Use in the Church of England* (London, 1652), 183.

22. Robert L. Cohen, "Form and Perspective in 2 Kings V," *Vetus Testamentum* 33 (1983): 177–178. In Chapter 3 I have a good deal more to say about the Hebrew term שוב and its complex relationship to Greek, Latin, and English terms for conversion.

23. Gerhard Von Rad, *Gottes Wirken in Israel* (1974), published in English as *God at Work in Israel*, trans. John H. Marks (Nashville: Abingdon Press, 1980), 51–54.

24. Cohen has also suggested that "Naaman is depicted as a marrano of sorts" (178), though he does not pick up on how such an identification is so fraught.

25. Thomas Fuller, "A Christening Sermon," *Ioseph's Partie-Colored Coat* (London, 1640), 165.

26. *The Holie Bible Faithfvlly Translated into English, Ovt of the Authentical Latine* (Douay, 1609), 771–772.

27. The recent collection by Crosignani et al., *Recusancy and Conformity in Early Modern England*, includes at least eight texts that cite Naaman's example, positively and negatively.

28. Featley, 47.

29. Featley, 50–52.

30. Featley, 50.

31. Ludwig Lavater, *The Book of Ruth Expounded in Twenty Eight Sermons, by Levves Lauaterus of Tyrgurine, and by hym published in Latine, and now translated in Englishe by Ephraim Pagitt, a childe of eleuen yeares of age* (London, 1586), 4.

32. Luke's parallel genealogy in 4.23ff. omits Rahab (and Tamar, Ruth, and Bathsheba, as well), an omission especially noteworthy given Luke's distinctive interest in female figures—Mary, Elizabeth, Mary Magdalene, Martha—in the life of Jesus. It may be that Matthew's Jewish emphasis makes the importance of Christ's female ancestors more central, whereas Luke's focus of women *during* Christ's life points to a different focus. Rabbinic tradition has Rahab marrying Joshua and producing a line of prophets. See Sifre Numbers, 78 and BT Megillah 14b, among others.

33. Bernard Robinson reads Rahab's story as a conversion story. See "Rahab of Canaan—and Israel," *Scandinavian Journal of the Old Testament* 23 (2009): 268. Mary Joan Winn Leith, on the other hand, detects an "ethnic slur reminiscent of the story of Lot's daughters," about whom I shall have more to say in my discussion of Ruth. See her "The Archaeology of Ruth," *Biblical Archaeology Review* 33 (2007): 22, 78.

34. A very late rabbinic midrash (probably from the fourteenth century) makes the tantalizing suggestion that the scarlet thread Rahab hung from her window was the very

same thread that had been tied around Zerah's wrist when he tried to emerge first from Tamar's womb in Genesis 38.28. How did Rahab come to have this thread? The midrash suggests that the spies were none other than Peretz and Zerah. See Midrash Hagadol Bereshit, Chaye Sara, 23:1. As I note below, Tamar's story is invoked by the stories of Rahab and Ruth in other more thematic ways, as well.

35. For this summary of Hellenistic Jewish and Patristic readings of Rahab, I have relied on the following studies: A. T. Hanson, "Rahab the Harlot in Early Christian Tradition," *Journal for the Study of the New Testament* 1 (1978): 53–60; Christopher Begg, "The Rahab Story in Josephus," *Liber Annuus* 55 (2005): 113–130; G. J. Swart, "Rahab and Esther in Josephus—An Intertextual Approach," *Acta Patristica et Byzantina* 17 (2006): 50–65; and Leith. Begg and Swart disagree over the explanation for Josephus's apparent deemphasizing of Rahab's "conversion." Begg (following Louis Feldman's extensive work on Josephus) suggests that this deemphasis reflects Josephus's sensitivity to contemporary Roman concerns about Jewish proselytism, whereas Swart is far less convinced that the evidence supports such a conclusion about Josephus's motivations.

36. Thomas Bentley, *The Sixt Lampe of Virginitie; Conteining a Mirrour for Maidens and Matrons* ([London?], 1582), 218.

37. William Gouge, *A learned and very useful commentary on the whole epistle to the Hebrews wherein every word and particle in the original is explained . . . : being the substance of thirty years Wednesdayes lectures at Black-fryers, London* (London, 1655), 154.

38. For an astute reading of the contradictory qualities of typology in Protestant reading practices, see Thomas H. Luxon, *Literal Figures: Puritan Allegory and the Reformation Crisis in Representation* (Chicago: University of Chicago Press, 1995), especially chapter 3.

39. As David Katz has shown, both Finch and Gouge served some time in prison for publishing this text and fomenting millenarian excitement. See Katz, *Philo-semitism*, 95–97.

40. William Gouge, *The Progresse of Divine Providence* (London, 1645).

41. Gouge, *A Learned and Very Useful Commentary*, 155–156.

42. Gouge, *A Learned and Very Useful Commentary*, 154.

43. Gouge, *A Learned and Very Useful Commentary*, 158.

44. Gouge, *A Learned and Very Useful Commentary*, 155–156. Several pages later, Gouge also uses Rahab's story to distinguish between what he regards as acceptable rhetorical equivocations—which rely on ambiguity rather than outright deception—and equivocations with which he associates the Jesuits, that is, "when a false speech is uttered, yet so as something is reserved in the mind, which if it were offered would make the speech true" (162). While Gouge is less bothered by Rahab's deception of the king's men, he is clearly struggling with the same dilemma that led to Augustine's concerns about Rahab in his *Contra Mendacio*. As I suggested in my comments on Daniel Featley's reading of Naaman's story, biblical fictions of conversion commonly elicited anxious discussions about equivocation, authenticity, and reliability.

45. See below, Chapter 3.

46. BT Yebamot 47a derives specific conversion laws from Ruth's story and Ruth

Rabbah 2.22 depicts an extensive pre-conversion dialogue meant to determine the potential proselyte's *bona fides*. Genesis Rabbah 59.9 and BT Sukkot 49b both compare Ruth to Abraham, identifying them as exemplary converts. For a helpful summary of rabbinic views concerning Ruth, see Leila Leah Bronner, "A Thematic Approach to Ruth in Rabbinic Literature," in *Reading Ruth: Contemporary Women Reclaim a Sacred Story*, ed. Judith A. Kates and Gail Twersky Reimer (New York: Ballantine Press, 1994), 146–169.

47. Bonnie Honig, "Ruth, the Model Emigree: Mourning and the Symbolic Politics of Immigration," *Political Theory* 25 (1997): 112–136. Honig's insightful analysis responds, in turn, to two earlier discussions of Ruth: Cynthia Ozick, "Ruth," in Kates and Reimer, *Reading Ruth*, and Julia Kristeva, *Nations without Nationalism*, trans. Leon S. Roudiez (New York: Columbia University Press, 1993). My discussion of Ruth draws on these and other recent readings of Ruth, especially feminist criticism, in the Kates and Twersky Reimer volume, as well as two volumes edited by Athalya Brenner, *A Feminist Companion to Ruth* (Sheffield: Sheffield Academic Press, 1993) and *Ruth and Esther: A Feminist Companion to the Bible*, Second Series (Sheffield: Sheffield Academic Press, 1999). Ozick's essay is reprinted in the former volume and Honig's essay is reprinted in the latter volume.

48. I am aware that later rabbinic rulings expanded the application of the levirate laws beyond the very specific parameters detailed in the biblical text. My point here is that the Ruth writer, who preceded these rabbinic innovations, had to open these laws up precisely in order to be able to make it possible for Ruth to become part of Israel. Ruth's story, which is exceptional in so many ways, ironically becomes precedent and therefore normalized in later rabbinic tradition.

49. The story of the daughters of Zelophechad, in Numbers 27.6–11, ensures inheritance to daughters when there are no brothers, but also specifies that in the absence of any living children, the inheritance goes to the male kinsman. Nowhere in this portion does it imply that the inheritance also requires the marriage to the childless man's widow.

50. BT Yebamot 76b. A parallel story appears in the midrashic collection *Sifri Devarim*, Ki Tetzeh, 249.

51. See, e.g., Ambrose's *Exposition on the Gospel of Luke*, quoted in *Ancient Christian Commentary on Scripture: Joshua, Judges, Ruth, 1–2 Samuel*, Old Testament IV, ed. John R. Fanke (Downers Grove, IL: InterVarsity Press, 2005), as well as commentary by Isidore of Seville, the *Glossa Ordinaria*, Hugh of St. Cher, and Nicholas of Lyra, all excerpted in *Medieval Exegesis in Translation: Commentaries on the Book of Ruth*, ed. and trans. Lesley Smith (Kalamazoo, MI: Medieval Institute Publications, 1996).

52. Nicholas of Lyra's *Postills* on Ruth are some of the most vivid examples of this deliberate distinction of interpretive approaches. Known for his historicizing of the Old Testament (and his extensive use of the medieval Jewish exegete, Rashi, in his commentary), Nicholas also included a separate series of comments on Ruth, with the title *Moraliter*. The *Glossa Ordinaria*, to which Nicholas's *Postills* were added in many printed editions, also graphically depicted this exegetical layering. See also Lesley Smith, "The Rewards of Faith: Nicholas of Lyra on Ruth," in *Nicholas of Lyra: The Senses of Scripture*, ed. Phillip D. W. Krey and Lesley Smith (Leiden: Brill, 2000), 45–58.

53. Kathleen Biddick, *The Typological Imaginary: Circumcision, Technology, History*

(Philadelphia: University of Pennsylvania Press, 2003), 23. I have found Biddick's rich discussion of the "Christian typological imaginary" to be especially evocative, even as I take issue with her underlying assertion that typology's form and function remain relatively unchanged from their first elaboration by Paul until the present. I do wish to suggest that a significant difference emerges in the deployment of typology in the early modern period, especially among English Protestant readers, and this difference is mutually constitutive with a shift in Christian representations of Jews and Judaism.

54. The bibliography on this shift is extensive. See, for example, James Samuel Preus, *From Shadow to Promise: Old Testament Interpretation from Augustine to the Young Luther* (Cambridge, MA: Harvard University Press, 1969); Henri de Lubac, *Medieval Exegesis*, vol. 1, *The Four Senses of Scripture*, trans. Mark Sebanc (Grand Rapids, MI: William B. Eerdmans Publishing, 1998); Debora Kuller Shuger, *The Renaissance Bible: Scholarship, Sacrifice, and Subjectivity* (Berkeley: University of California Press, 1994); Frances M. Young, *Biblical Exegesis and the Formation of English Culture* (Cambridge: Cambridge University Press, 1997); and Anthony Grafton and Joanna Weinberg, *"I have always loved the Holy Tongue": Isaac Casaubon, the Jews, and a Forgotten Chapter in Renaissance Scholarship* (Cambridge, MA: Harvard University Press, 2011).

55. Erich Auerbach's seminal essay "Figura" initiated a renewed interest in typology for literary studies, especially in its insistence on the difference between allegory and typology. See also Julia Reinhard Lupton, *Afterlives of Saints: Hagiography, Typology, and Renaissance Literature* (Stanford, CA: Stanford University Press, 1996), chapter 1, for a thoughtful reading our Auerbach's use of typology in relation to questions of genre and periodization.

56. Kim F. Hall, *Things of Darkness: Economies of Race and Gender in Early Modern England* (Ithaca, NY: Cornell University Press, 1995), 39.

57. Edward Topsell, *The Reward of Religion. Deliuered in sundrie Lectures vpon the Booke of Ruth, wherein the godly may see their daily and outwarde tryals, with the presence of God to assist them, and his mercies to recompence them* (London, 1596), 302.

58. Thomas Fuller, *A Comment on Ruth* (London, 1654), 2. The image of one shepherd and one sheepfold recollects the *Glossa Ordinaria*, which observes, "Vocabantur ergo duo populi per sanctos praedicatores ad consortiam fidei, & electorum Dei, ut ex diversis gregibus fieret unum ouile," "Therefore two peoples, of faith and of the chosen of God, will be called to marriage by holy preachers, so that one sheepfold may come from a diverse flock." Fuller's addition to the medieval commentary is noteworthy, for he uses the image to speak of Christ, the one shepherd who descends from Ruth, as well as the Church, i.e., the sheepfold.

59. Lavater, 44.

60. Topsell, 2.

61. Richard Bernard, *Ruths Recompense, or, a Commentarie on the booke of Ruth* (London, 1628), 88–91.

62. Recent work on Jessica's conversion has shed important light on the complex dynamics of gender, ethnicity, and Jewishness. See Adelman, *Blood Relations*, chapter 3; M. Lindsay Kaplan, "Jessica's Mother: Medieval Constructions of Jewish Race and

Gender in *The Merchant of Venice*," *Shakespeare Quarterly* 58 (2007): 1–30; Lisa Lampert, *Gender and Jewish Difference from Paul to Shakesepeare* (Philadelphia: University of Pennsylvania Press, 2004), chapter 5; and Mary Janell Metzger, " 'Now by My Hood, a Gentle and No Jew': Jessica, *The Merchant of Venice*, and the Discourse of Early Modern Identity," *PMLA* 113 (1998): 52–63. Metzger also remarks on the explicit analogy "between the transfer of [Portia's] person and property to Bassanio and the incorporation of Jessica's person and property into Lorenzo" (57). I return to Portia's "conversion" in Chapter 4.

63. Fuller, 108.

64. Metzger, 56.

65. On the laws of early modern coverture, see Amy Louise Erickson, *Women and Property in Early Modern England* (London: Routledge, 1993). The relationship of coverture laws to Ruth is especially complex since, as Erickson suggests, "the most effective means of restricting a woman's remarriage was the system of coverture and the threat of losing control of her property" (228).

66. Bernard, 123.

67. Lavater, 165.

68. This despite the fact that the Geneva gloss observes, in it comment on the Judah and Tamar story (Gen. 38.8), "This ordre was for y[e] preseruation of y[e] stocke, that y[e] childe begotten by the seconde brother shulde haue y[e] name and inheritance of y[e] first. Which is in the new Testament abolished." In its commentary on Deuteronomy 25.5, the gloss offers the more expansive interpretation of brother that was also found in rabbinic commentaries: "Because the Ebrewe worde signifieth not y[e] natural brother, & the worde, that signifieth a brother is takē also for a kinesman; it seemeth that it is not ment that the natural brothers wife, but some other of y[e] kindred, y[t] was in that degree w[c] might mary."

69. Topsell, 234.

70. Topsell, 52.

71. Topsell, 73.

72. Bernard, 46, 102.

73. Lavater, 32.

74. Fuller, 51. Fuller may have been splitting hairs, though, since a page before he wrote, "Yet not withstanding, if after long patience and forbearing with them, and long instructing them in the points of Religion; if still these *Pagans* continue retractary and obstinate, then sure the civill Magistrate who hath the lawfull dominion over them, may severely, though not cruelly, with *Josiah*, compell them to come to Church, and to perform the outward formalities of Gods worship" (50).

75. Lavater, 32.

76. Janet Adelman has shown how allusions to the Inquisition in *The Merchant of Venice* unsettle the play's different trial scenes and constitute the backdrop for Shylock's forced conversion at the end of Act IV. See *Blood Relations*, 124–128.

77. This inversion is structurally identical to the explosive inversion of Isaac and Ishmael in Paul's Letter to the Galatians (chapter 4), where Isaac, the fleshly ancestor to the Jews, becomes the spiritual ancestor to the children of the promise and Ishmael becomes the ancestor to the children of the law.

78. Lavater, 12.
79. Fuller, 39.
80. Bernard, 50.
81. Fuller, 27.
82. Fuller, 29.
83. Fuller, 210–211.

CHAPTER 3

1. On the Augustinian construction of reading as conversionary, see especially Brian Stock, *Augustine the Reader: Meditation, Self-Knowledge, and the Ethics of Interpretation* (Cambridge, MA: Harvard University Press, 1996). On the significant influence of this model of conversion through reading, see James Kearney, *The Incarnate Text: Imagining the Book in Reformation England* (Philadelphia: University of Pennsylvania Press, 2009), 145.

2. Kearney has addressed this feature of scriptural translation specifically with respect to Augustine's *Confessions*. He writes, "The epistemological problem of authenticity precedes the exegetical problem of meaning and understanding. And the authenticating voice is necessarily outside the body, outside language, outside history: the voice within speaks a truth which is neither Hebrew nor Greek nor Latin" (61–62).

3. David Lawton, *Faith, Text, and History: The Bible in English* (Charlottesville: University of Virginia Press, 1990), 66, among others, has discussed some implications of the homogenizing effect of Bible translations.

4. Hugh Broughton, *An Epistle to the Learned Nobilitie of England Touching Translating the Bible from the original* (London, 1597).

5. Hugh Broughton, "A Censure of the late Translation of our Churches" (London, 1611).

6. William Tyndale, "Preface to the Christian Reader," in *The New Testament of Our Saviour Iesus Christ* ([London?], 1536). The slippage between repentance and conversion was given even more influential expression vis-à-vis English Protestants by Calvin, who wrote several years after Tyndale, "The term repentance is derived in the Hebrew from conversion, or turning again; and in the Greek from a change of mind and purpose; nor is the thing meant inappropriate to both derivations, for it is substantially this, that withdrawing from ourselves we turn to God, and laying aside the old, put on a new mind. Wherefore, it seems to me, that repentance may be not inappropriately defined thus: A real conversion of our life unto God. . . . Accordingly, [the prophets] use indiscriminately in the same the sense, the expressions turning, returning to the Lord; repenting, doing repentance." Institutes III.iii.5, 21, cited in Peter Wilcox, "Conversion in the Thought of John Calvin," *Anvil* 14 (1997): 113–128.

7. For an exhaustive survey of the meanings attached to this Hebrew root, see William L. Holladay, *The Root SÛBH in the Old Testament, with Paricular Reference to Its Usages in Covenantal Contexts* (Leiden: Brill, 1958). Though the term denotes some kind of movement in its more literal sense (especially back to an initial point of departure), Holladay's analysis of the covenantal usages of the root shows convincingly that it connotes

a reversion to a God already known rather than a conversion to God as something new. Ambiguity and reversal in the meaning of the term nevertheless remain a possibility, as Jeremiah 8.4 demonstrates: "Moreover thou shalt say unto them, 'Thus saith the Lord, "Shall they fall, and not arise? Shall he turn away [ישוב], and not return [ישוב]?"'"

8. Pace William Barclay, who insists on the absolute identity of *shuv* and επιστρεψειν, I am suggesting an unavoidable connotative difference, however close the two words are in their immediate denotative meaning. See *Turning to God: A Study of Conversion in the Book of Acts and Today* (Philadelphia: Westminster Press, 1964), 24–25. As I argue in the pages that follow, this unavoidable difference is the gap that must be crossed by conversion.

9. Alloys H. Dirksen, *The New Testsament Concept of Metanoia* (Washington, DC: Catholic University Press, 1932); J. W. Heikkinen, "Notes on 'Epistrepho' and 'Metanoeo,'" *Ecumenical Review* 19 (1967): 313–316. Despite his tendentiously Catholic efforts to link the term μετανοια with formal methods of penance, Dirksen's overview is still useful for its careful comparison of the different terms used to translate Hebrew calls for return and repentance. Heikkinen's analysis is similarly compromised by its evangelical argument, though he, too, offers useful comparisons of the two Greek terms, *μετανοια* and επιστρεψωσιν. Alan Segal also remarks on Paul's consistent use of επιστρεψο and *μετανοια* to correspond with the Septuagint's translation of the Hebrew terms for repentance (Segal, *Paul the Convert*, 19). He is guilty of reasoning *post hoc ergo propter hoc*, however, when he takes this correspondence as a sign that Paul is self-consciously describing the conversion of the Gentiles to Christianity. That Paul's preaching is read in this way by later Christian interpreters is not grounds for assuming that Paul understood his use of the terms as signifying conversion in the medieval or early modern sense.

10. John Donne, "Sermon Preached at S. Pauls . . . Upon the Day of S. Pauls Conversion. 1628/29," [16?].

11. The misleading nature of the term "conversion" for the biblical period and the first decades after the death of Jesus has been argued most convincingly by Fredriksen in "Mandatory Retirement."

12. Hutter's polyglot bible, which included a complete Hebrew New Testament, was published in Nuremberg in 1599. Earlier versions of portions of the Gospels, especially Matthew (which was believed to have been written in Hebrew originally), appeared in Hebrew earlier in the sixteenth century (most notably by Sebastian Munster and Jean Mercier), though William Horbury has argued that these were produced to assist in anti-Jewish polemics and controversies, rather than to bring about Jewish conversions through persuasion and textual accessibility. See "The Hebrew Matthew and Hebrew Study," in *Hebrew Study from Ezra to Ben Yehuda*, ed. William Horbury (Edinburgh: T & T Clark, 1999), 122–131.

13. See Peter Burke, "Cultures of Translation in Early Modern Europe," in *Cultural Translation in Early Modern Europe*, ed. Peter Burke and R. Po-chia Hsia (Cambridge: Cambridge University Press, 2007), 7–38, for a rich overview of the history of translation activities during this period.

14. Michael Ryan, "Assembling New Worlds in the Sixteenth and Seventeenth Centuries," *Comparative Studies in Society and History* 23 (1981): 519–538.

15. For a particularly astute analysis of the convergence of discourses of antiquity with New World encounters, see David A. Lupher, *Romans in a New World: Classical Models in Sixteenth-Century Spanish America* (Ann Arbor: University of Michigan Press, 2003).

16. George Sandys, *OVIDS METAMORPHOSIS Englished by G[eorge] S[andys]* (London, 1626), A2[r-v].

17. Richard Marsden, "Cain's Face, and Other Problems: The Legacy of the Earliest English Bible Translations," *Reformation* 1 (1996): 29–51.

18. Joseph Addison, *The Spectator*, no. CDV, Saturday, June 14, 1712.

19. George Chapman, *Achilles Shield* (London, 1598), B2[r].

20. John Cheke, Letter in The courtier of Count Baldessar Castilio (London, 1561).

21. Recent scholarship on medieval and early modern Christian Hebraism has fleshed out many of the fraught relations that developed between Jews and Christians in this context and has complicated our understanding of, among other features of intellectual history, the process and progress of Renaissance humanism. See, inter alia, Allison P. Coudert and Jeffrey S. Shoulson, eds., *Hebraica Veritas? Christian Hebraists and the Study of Judaism in Early Modern Europe* (Philadelphia: University of Pennsylvania Press, 2004).

22. See Shoulson, *Milton and the Rabbis*, especially chapters 1 and 2; and introduction to Coudert and Shoulson, *Hebraica Veritas?*.

23. See Michael Lynn-George, *Epos: Word, Narrative, and the Iliad* (Basingstoke and London: Humanities Press International, 1988) for a summary of the classicists' case against Auerbach. There is, of late, something of an Auerbach revival, however, with a range of conferences and papers dedicated to the great twentieth-century comparativist. See, e.g., Egbert J. Bakker, "Mimesis as Performance: Rereading Auerbach's First Chapter," *Poetics Today* 20 (1999): 11–26; Robert S. Kawashima, "Verbal Medium and Narrative Art in Homer and the Bible," *Philosophy and Literature* 28 (2004): 103–117; and James I. Porter, "Erich Auerbach and the Judaizing of Philology," *Critical Inquiry* 35 (2008): 115–147.

24. John Ogle, *The Lamentation of Troy, for the death of Hector* (London, 1594), B3[r].

25. Thomas Playfere, "A SERMON PREACHED at the Court of Whitehall. March 10. 1598," *The VVhole Sermons* (London, 1623): 77–78.

26. This and all subsequent literal translations of Homer have been quoted from A. T. Murray's translation, *The Odyssey* (Cambridge, 1919), revised by George E. Dimock, 1995.

27. See, for example, 1.55–61, 5.339–350, 408–423, and 19.267–276.

28. For discussions of the meaning of names, especially Odysseus, in Homer's poetry, see W. B. Stanford, "The Homeric Etymology of the Name Odysseus," *Classical Philology* 47 (1952): 209–213; George E. Dimock, Jr., "The Name of Odysseus," *Hudson Review* 9 (1956): 52–70; Alice Mariani, "The Renaming of Odysseus," in *Critical Essays on Homer*, ed. Kenneth Atchity (Boston: G. K. Hall & Co., 1987), 211–233; Carolyn Higbie, *Heroes' Names, Homeric Identities* (New York: Garland Press, 1995); and Bruce Louden, "Categories of Homeric Wordplay," *Transactions of the American Philological Association* 125 (1999): 27–46.

29. The literature on naming in the Hebrew Bible is extensive. See Yair Zakovitch, "A Study of Precise and Partial Name Derivations in Biblical Etymology," *Journal for*

the Study of the Old Testament 15 (1980): 31–50; Yair Zakovitch, "Explicit and Implicit Name Derivations," *Harvard Archeological Review* 4 (1980): 167–181; Moshe Garsiel, *Biblical Names: A Literary Study of Midrashic Derivations and Puns*, trans. Phyllis Hackett (Ramat Gan: Bar Ilan University Press, 1991); Moshe Garsiel, "Puns and Names as a Literary Device in I Kings 1–2," *Biblia* 72 (1991): 379–386; and Moshe Garsiel, "Homiletic Name-Derivations as a Literary Device in the Gideon Narrative: Judges VI–VIII," *Vetus Testamentum* 43 (1993): 302–317. For a brilliant and provocative rejoinder to the standard reading of biblical names, see Herbert Marks, "Biblical Naming and Poetic Etymology," *Journal of Biblical Literature* 114 (1995): 21–42. My reading of Isaac's name is particularly indebted to Marks's insights into other biblical names.

30. As has been frequently noted, the 1611 Bible was never officially authorized, nor was it given the title "King James Bible" by the translators and editors. For brevity and clarity's sakes, however, I refer to this translation by its common names, the King James Bible or Version. It has, of course, appeared in numerous editions since its first publication. My references, unless otherwise noted, are to the first edition.

31. Philo Judaeus, *A Treatise on the Life of Moses*, 5–8.

32. See, for example, the Epistle Dedicatorie to *Odysses*, A4^{v}. In her *George Chapman* (New York: Twain Publishers, 1967), Charlotte Spivack attributes this approach to Chapman's Platonic idealism.

33. Claire McEachern has written suggestively about the paradoxical repercussions of the linguistic break from Rome: "In the fear of civil dissension arising from scriptural access we can read the official apprehension that the rebuke of authority enacted in the official break with Rome would be replicated indigenously, and with it, the revision of authority it enacted. . . . The conjoint fall into language and nation was thus elegiac in structure, in which the unity of one internally coherent tongue gives way to the atomized disparity of many. In this way Babel thus very much resembles the event of the Reformation at large in sixteenth-century Europe, as the Latin Vulgate was translated into the vernaculars of many countries, and national churches broke with papal control. Yet its resonances are specific to individual countries as well, for with the loss of the original tongue comes not only the distances among nations, but those semantic instabilities internal to a single nation—and indeed, within the person." See *The Poetics of English Nationhood, 1590–1612* (Cambridge: Cambridge University Press, 1996), 112–114.

34. For some of these earliest English instances, see Jean Delisle and Judith Woodsworth, eds., *Translators Through History* (Amsterdam: J. Benjamins, 1995).

35. Nicolas Udall, trans., *The first tome or volume of the Paraphrase of Erasmus vpon the newe testamente* (London, 1548), xi^{v}.

36. Martin Tyndale, "Obedience of a Christian Man," in *Doctrinal Treatises and Introductions to Different Portions of the Holy Scripture*, ed. Henry Walter (Cambridge: Parker Society, 1848), vol. 42, 148–149.

37. Martin Luther, *Weimarer Ausgabe*, Tischreden vol. 2, p. 648 #2771a (1532–1533). I would like to thank Stephen Burnett for helping me track down this comment in Luther's Table Talk. W. Schwarz distinguishes between the "inspiration principle" and the "philological principle" in the humanist and Reformation writings about Bible translation,

pitting Luther, who adopted the inspirational view, against Erasmus, whose philological efforts were at the heart of his humanist studies of the textual history of Scripture. See *Principles and Problems of Biblical Translation: Some Reformation Controversies and their Background* (Cambridge: Cambridge University Press, 1955). Kearney notes, "If Tyndale's skepticism about the ability of human 'wisdom' to comprehend scripture is Lutheran, his evident faith in the philological project to excavate and reclaim linguistic meaning is decidedly Erasmian" (78).

38. Cleland McAfee points out that, in contrast to Shakespeare or Milton, the vocabulary of the English Bible is strikingly sparse. Shakespeare used between fifteen and twenty thousand words in his plays and poetry. Milton's verse drew upon approximately thirteen thousand. The King James Bible makes use of only about six thousand different words, the vast majority of which are short, mostly monosyllabic, and of Anglo-Saxon origin. See Cleland McAfee, *The Greatest English Classic: A Study of the King James Version of the Bible and Its Influence on Life and Literature* (New York: Harper and Brothers, 1912), 105–109.

39. Richard Mulcaster, *The First Part of the Elementarie which Entreateth Chefelie of the Right Writing of our English Tung* (London, 1582), 167–168.

40. In her *Names in Renaissance English Culture* (Lewiston, ME: Mellen Press, 2001), Dorothy Litt has identified twenty-five prose works published between 1536 and 1631 concerned in one way or another with names. See, for example, "A Brief Table of the Interpretation of the Propre Names which are chiefly founde in the olde Testament," which was appended to the 1560 edition of the Geneva Bible; William Patten, *The Calendar of Scripture* (London, 1575); John Penkethman, *Onomatophylacium* (London, 1626); and Edward Lyford, *[Sefer M'Litzat Ha'Shemot], or, The True Interpretation and Etymologie of Christian Names* (London, 1655).

41. Michel de Montaigne, "Of Names," *Essays or Morall, Politike and Militarie Discourses of Michaell de Montaigne*, trans. John Florio (London, 1606), 149.

42. For the Chapman's source, see John Scapula, *Lexicon Graecolatinum novum* (Amsterdam, 1580), column 1033: "ΟΔΨΝΗ, dolor: proprie corporis."

43. Higbie, *Heroes' Names*, 163.

44. Kawashima, "Verbal Medium," 108–109.

45. The Latin Ulysses and its variant, Ulixes, appear to have evolved from earlier Greek variants on Οδυσσευς, including Ολυσσευς, Ουλιξευς, and Ουλιξης. By the time Chapman came to write his translations, the Latin Ulysses had virtually displaced the Greek Odysseus in western Europe.

46. Walter Benjamin's essential discussion of translation has revealed how this transformative "mode" epitomizes language's resistance to its own alienation in its efforts to assimilate the foreign. "The Task of the Translator," *Illuminations: Essays and Reflections*, trans. Harry Zohn (New York: Schocken Books, 1978).

47. Arnold, Lecture 3, 78, note.

48. *Odyssey*, 19.386–393.

49. Auerbach, "Odysseus' Scar," 6.

50. *Poetics* 1456A. 12. On the episodic, paratactical nature of Homer's poems, see

James Notopoulos, "Parataxis in Homer: A New Approach to Homeric Literary Criticism," *Transactions and Proceedings of the American Philological Association* 80 (1949): 1–23.

51. *Homeric Renaissance: The Odyssey of George Chapman* (London: Chatto and Windus, 1956), 138.

52. Robert Geroux, "Regarding Homer/Homer Regarding: Odysseus' Scar, Time, and the Origins of Subjectivity in Myth," *KronoScope* 5 (2005): 237–257, offers a compelling analysis of this scene and the effect of the temporal flattening in the original, which allows the narrator to uncover Odysseus, viewing him from all possible angles, even as Odysseus seeks to remain concealed and obscure. Chapman's remaking of the scene becomes all the more striking in light of Geroux's analysis, insofar as it seems to comply with Ulysses' will to resist full identification.

53. On the allegorical tradition of reading Homer see, *inter alia*, deForest Lord, *Homeric Renaissance*; Spivack, *George Chapman*; Richard Ide, "Exemplary Heroism in Chapman's *Odysses*," *SEL: Studies in English Literature, 1500–1900* 22 (1982): 121–136; Richard Lamberton, *Homer the Theologian: Neoplatonist Allegorical Reading and the Growth of the Epic Tradition* (Berkeley: University of California Press, 1986); and Anthony Grafton, "Renaissance Readers of Homer's Ancient Readers," *Homer's Ancient Readers: The Hermeneutics of Greek Epic's Earliest Exegetes* (Princeton, NJ: Princeton University Press, 1992), 149–172. See also Camille Bennett, "The Conversion of Vergil: The *Aeneid* in Augustine's *Confessions*," *Revue des Études Augustiniennes* 34 (1988): 47–69, for a helpfully contrasting view of Augustine's "conversion" of the *Aeneid* as explicitly non-allegorical, indeed, antithetical to Vergil's text.

54. Lyford, *The True Interpretation*. Italics are in the original.

55. Robert Miola, "On Death and Dying in Chapman's *Iliad*: Translation as Forgery," *International Journal of the Classical Tradition* 3 (1996): 48–64.

56. Aristotle, *Poetics*, 21. See Eric Cheyfitz, *The Poetics of Imperialism: Translation and Colonization from* The Tempest *to Tarzan* (Philadelphia: University of Pennsylvania Press, 1997), for a very suggestive discussion of how the figuration inherent in language produces its own self-alienation.

57. George Downame, *ABRAHAMS TRYALL, A Sermon preached at the Spittle, in Easter weeke Anno Domini 1602* (London, 1602).

58. Gerald Hammond makes a compelling case for the degree to which the King James translation succeeds far better than its predecessors in preserving the laconic, paratactic pacing of the original Hebrew. See *The Making of the English Bible* (New York: Philosophical Society, 1983). There are, however, difference and departures deserving of further consideration.

59. Shuger, *Renaissance Bible*, 48–49.

60. In his *Literal Figures: Puritan Allegory and the Reformation Crisis in Representation* (Chicago: University of Chicago Press, 1995), Thomas Luxon's discussion of this tension between the literal and the figurative in early modern typology constitutes an important counterbalance to Shuger's division between medieval and renaissance reading practices.

61. Gervaise Babington, *Certaine plaine, briefe, and comfortable notes vpon euerie chapter of Genesis* (London, 1592), 89^{v}.

62. Henoch Clapham, *AN ABSTRACT OF FAYTH, Grounded on Moses, and applied to the Common Creede* (London, 1606), 11.

63. Andrew Willett, *Hexapla in Genesis* (London, 1608), especially 234.

64. The Bible, HHh. iii.[r].

65. The Council of Trent's 1546 counter-Reformation polemic against vernacular translations of the Bible referred to the Vulgate's Latin as *authentica.*

66. *The NEVV TESTAMENT,* bi[v]–bii[r].

67. Babington, *Certaine plaine,* 80.

68. I owe this observation to Adam Nicolson, *God's Secretaries: The Making of the King James Bible* (New York: Harper Perennial, 2005), 74.

69. This is the one crucial exception to David Daiches's claim that in no case does the King James Version prefer either the Septuagint or the Vulgate to the Hebrew text. See *The King James Version of the Bible: An Account of the Development and Sources of the English Bible of 1611 with Special Reference to the Hebrew Tradition* (Chicago: University of Chicago Press, 1941), 206–207.

70. Francis Bacon, *Novum Organum* (London, 1620) 1.59.

71. Naomi Seidman, *Faithful Renderings: Jewish-Christian Difference and the Politics of Translation* (Chicago: University of Chicago Press, 2006).

CHAPTER 4

1. Marshall Hall, "Kabbalist 'Superstring' Physics," *The Non-Moving Earth and Anti-Evolution Web Page of the Fair Education Foundation, Inc.*, February 26, 2007, http://fixedearth.com/kabbalist%20Superstrings.htm, emphasis in the original.

2. Lawrence M. Principe and William R. Newman, "Some Problems with the Historiography of Alchemy," in *Secrets of Nature: Astrology and Alchemy in Early Modern Europe*, ed. William R. Newman and Anthony Grafton (Cambridge, MA: MIT Press, 2001). An article appearing in the *New York Times* several years ago, occasioned by a conference held by the Chemical Heritage Foundation in Philadelphia, brought this new trend in alchemy studies to the attention of the general public. See John Noble Wilford, "Transforming the Alchemists," *New York Times*, August 1, 2006.

3. Raphael Patai, *The Jewish Alchemists: A History and Source Book* (Princeton, NJ: Princeton University Press, 1994), 519.

4. Gershom Scholem, *Alchemy and Kabbalah*, trans. Klaus Ottman (Putnam, CT: Spring Publications, Inc., 2006), 85, originally published in German under the title *Alchemie und Kabbala* in *Eranos Yearbook* 46 (1977).

5. Brian P. Copenhaver, "Natural Magic, Hermetism, and Occultism in Early Modern Science," in *Reappraisals of the Scientific Revolution*, ed. David C. Lindberg and Robert S. Westman (Cambridge: Cambridge University Press, 1990), 280.

6. Joshua Trachtenberg takes this association for granted in the *The Devil and the Jews: The Medieval Conception of the Jew and Its Relation to Modern Anti-Semitism*, 2nd ed. (Philadelphia: Jewish Publication Society, 1983 [1943]), 72–74. See Scholem, *Alchemy*

and Kabbalah, part 1, which notes a core incompatibility between some of the basic symbology of Jewish Kabbalah and alchemical writings. Scholem does go on to cite some possible exceptions and he takes note of the relatively late emergence of something we might call Jewish Alchemy, though this phenomenon is largely responsive to, rather than an influence on, Christian esotericism. See also Moshe Idel, "The Origin of Alchemy According to Zosimos and a Hebrew Parallel," *Review des Études Juives* 145 (1986): 117–124, for a very early instance of parallels between Jewish and Hellenistic alchemical motifs. Additional late medieval Jewish alchemists have been discovered in Gerd Mentgen, "Jewish Alchemists in Central Europe in the Later Middle Ages: Some New Sources," *Aleph: Historical Studies in Science and Judaism* 9 (2009): 345–352.

7. Heinrich Cornelius Agrippa's *De occulta philsosophia* (1531 and 1533) rendered natural magic, alchemy, and Kabbalah as virtually identical to the Christian European reader. See Scholem, *Alchemy and Kabbalah*, 85–86.

8. Roger Bacon, *The mirror of alchimy, composed by the thrice-famous and learned fryer, Roger Bachon, sometimes fellow of Martin Colledge: and afterwards of Brasen-nose Colledge in Oxenforde. Also a most excellent and learned discourse of the admirable force and efficacie of art and nature, written by the same author. With certaine other treatises of the like argument* (London, 1597), 77.

9. The critical literature on this subject is extensive. On the question of developing medieval notions of ethnic and even racial purity, see Jonathan M. Elukin, "From Jew to Christian? Conversion and Immutability in Medieval Europe," in *Varieties of Religious Conversion in the Middle Ages*, ed. James Muldoon (Gainesville: University Press of Florida, 1997), 171–189. Within the early modern context, see, for example, Shapiro, *Shakespeare and the Jews*, and Shoulson, *Milton and the Rabbis*. Sharon Achinstein has suggested that at least within the writings of early modern England's foremost martyrologist, John Foxe, Jewish assimilability to a full Christian status was indeed possible. See Achinstein, "John Foxe and the Jews." As I have argued above in Chapter 1, I think Foxe's view of Jewish conversion is far more problematic than Achinstein allows.

10. Jonathan Gil Harris, *Foreign Bodies and the Body Politic: Discourses of Social Pathology in Early Modern England* (Cambridge: Cambridge University Press, 1998), 84.

11. Bacon, 77.

12. See Elisheva Carlebach, "Attributions of Secrecy and Perceptions of Jewry," *Jewish Social Studies* n.s., 2, no. 3 (1996): 115–136, for an important overview of the associations of secrecy with Jews in the late medieval and early modern periods. Perez Zagorin also draws the connection between esotericism and dissimulation in *Ways of Lying*, 11.

13. *De Alchimia* provides a characteristic example of what Patai called the posthumous conversion of non-Jewish alchemists to Judaism. It includes a text described as *Liber Secretorum Alchemiae Calidis filii Iazichi Judaei*, a well-known treatise on the *Secrets of Alchemy* by the important seventh-century Islamic scholar, Khalid ibn Yazid. There was nothing Jewish about ibn Yazid. The French version includes the text without characterizing ibn Yazid as Jewish; the English edition of the *Mirror of Alchimy* omits ibn Yazid's text entirely.

14. Harris, *Foreign Bodies*, 82–86.

15. On the connections between alchemy and commerce, see Pamela H. Smith, *The Business of Alchemy: Science and Culture in the Holy Roman Empire* (Princeton, NJ: Princeton University Press, 1994); Peggy Ann Knapp, "The Work of Alchemy," *Journal of Medieval and Early Modern Studies* 30 (2000): 575–599; Carl Wennerlind, "Credit-Money as the Philosopher's Stone: Alchemy and the Coinage Problem in Seventeenth-Century England," *History of Political Economy* 35 (2003): 234–261; and William Kerwin, *Beyond the Body: The Boundaries of Medicine and English Renaissance Drama* (Amherst: University of Massachusetts Press, 2005), 17–19.

16. Christopher Marlowe, *The Jew of Malta*, II.iii.177–179, 184–188, 190–192. Quotations from Marlowe are drawn from *Christopher Marlowe: The Complete Plays*, ed. Frank Romany and Robert Lindsey (London: Penguin Books, 2003). Jonathan Gil Harris has written brilliantly about the figure of the Jew in Marlowe's play in relation to discourses of physical, social, religious, and political corruption. See his *Foreign Bodies*, especially chapter 4, which connects Marlowe's Jewish caricatures with the Dutch Church Libel, a text wrongfully attributed to Marlowe, but which directly yokes an intense, sweeping xenophobia with specifically Jewish perfidy. For a reading that sees the Jewish features of these texts as ciphers for England's more substantial anxieties about the Spanish, see Griffin, *English Renaissance Drama*, chapter 4.

17. William Camden, *Annals, or the History of the Most Renowned and Victorious Princess Elizabeth, Late Queen of England*, trans. Robert Norton (1630), cited in *The Merchant of Venice*, Longman Cultural Edition, ed. Lawrence Danson (New York: Longman, 2005), 120.

18. Having undertaken a thorough review of the documentary evidence concerning Lopez's life and trial, David Katz has concluded that Lopez may very well have been caught up in some of the many plots to assassinate Elizabeth I, though he somewhat inexplicably insists that "Lopez's Jewish origin was not a key element in his prosecution." See *The Jews in the History of England*, 108. Whether or not the trial made much of Lopez's suspected Jewishness, it is clear that his Jewish-*marrano* identity was central to the way the events were reported and remembered. It can hardly be a coincidence that Marlowe's play was revived immediately after Lopez's execution or that Shakespeare turned his own dramatic attention to the figure of the Jew some three years later. See Stephen Greenblatt, *Will in the World: How Shakespeare Became Shakespeare* (New York: Norton, 2004), chapter 9, and Adelman, *Blood Relations*, 7. Adelman writes, "The near-legendary status of these (perhaps legendary) last words suggest the extent to which the conviction that he was a crypto-Jew went hand-in-hand with the conviction that he was a treacherous would-be killer of Christians."

19. François Secret, "Littérature et Alchimie: A la Fin du XVIe et au Début du XVIIe Siècle," *Bibliothèque d'Humanisme et Renaissance* 35 (1973): 104–105; and Ku-Ming (Kevin) Chang, "Toleration of Alchemists as a Political Question: Transmutation, Disputation, and Early Modern Scholarship on Alchemy," *Ambix* 54 (2007): 245–273.

20. Nicolas Flamel, *His Exposition of the Hieroglyphicall Figures Faithfully, and religiously done into English out of the French and Latine copies. By Eirenæus Orandus* (London, 1624), 8–9.

21. Jeremy Cohen, *Living Letters of the Law: Ideas of the Jew in Medieval Christianity* (Berkeley: University of California Press, 1999), chap. 1.

22. Augustine of Hippo, *Sermo* 5.5 and *Ennarationes in Psalmos* 56.9.

23. Augustine develops this argument about the dispersion of the Jews in particular detail in his *Tractatus adversus Iudaeos*, though it can be found in many other portions of his writings, including his commentary on Psalm 56 where he speaks of the Jews as *librarii nostri*. There he writes, in language quite parallel to Abraham the Jew's title page, of how the Jews *dispersi sunt per omnes gentes*, "were dispersed throughout all the nations."

24. Stanton Linden suggests that the text Flamel claims to have found was the *Esh Metsaref*, a Jewish alchemical treatise the original of which has been lost and which has only been preserved in translation in the *Kabbalah Denudata*. See Stanton J. Linden, *Darke Hierogliphicks: Alchemy in English Literature from Chaucer to the Restoration* (Lexington: University Press of Kentucky, 1996), 207. I see no reliable basis for this assertion.

25. Flamel, 126–127. Robert Jütte has very helpfully suggested to me that Canches is likely a variant spelling of the name Sanchez, a fairly common name in the Iberian *converso* community. There may, in fact, be the kernel of genuine encounter between Flamel (or a later ghostwriter) and a converted Jew within this story, though one would have to proceed very carefully in its reconstruction.

26. Flamel, 128.

27. James Shapiro offers a more extended account of Broughton's dealings with Reuven and his notoriety in England in his *Shakespeare and the Jews*, 146–151.

28. My brief summary of this exchange owes a great deal to the important research of Joseph Hacker. Professor Hacker's work on the relationship between Broughton and Reuven, which has yet to be published, was presented at a seminar in the fall of 1999 on Christian Hebraism at the University of Pennsylvania's Katz Center for Advanced Judaic Studies.

29. Quotations from Jonson's play are drawn from *Ben Jonson's Plays and Masques*, ed. Richard Harp (New York: W. W. Norton & Company, 2001).

30. See, for example, Walter Cohen, *Drama of a Nation: Public Theater in Renaissance England and Spain* (Ithaca, NY: Cornell University Press, 1985); Jonathan Haynes, "Representing the Underworld: *The Alchemist*," *Studies in Philology* 86 (1989): 18–41; and Catherine Gimelli Martin, "Angels, Alchemists, and Exchange: Commercial Ideology in Court and City Comedy, 1596–1610," in *The Witness of Times: Manifestations of Ideology in Seventeenth Century England*, ed. Katherine Z. Keller and Gerald J. Schiffhorst (Pittsburgh: Duquesne University Press, 1993).

31. Jonson returned to the topic of alchemy six years after the first performance of *The Alchemist* in his *Mercury Vindicated from the Alchemists at Court*, a court masque that thematizes the conflict between artifice and nature, pitting Mercury as a natural force against, and eventually eluding the mastery of, Vulcan and his alchemical minions.

32. Francis Bacon reviews these attacks in his essay "On Usury," ultimately with an eye toward speaking of usury "usefully." See Cohen, *Drama of a Nation*, 295–300. As I write this in late 2010, I read daily of serious discussions among economists and policy analysts over whether or not to return to the "gold standard" as a remedy for

an ailing economy poisoned by "toxic assets" and "esoteric financial instruments" that dumbfounded even those who invented and sold them. It seems we have come full circle.

33. As far as I can tell, Catherine Gimelli Martin is the only modern critic to have offered a reading of these two plays alongside one another. See "Angels, Alchemists, and Exchange." In an oft-cited discussion of the Jew as cipher in early modern England, Peter Berek suggests that negative representations of Jews in English culture coincide exclusively with anxieties about the rapid transformations occurring within English society. See Berek, "The Jew as Renaissance Man." While I find Berek's analysis helpful, it seems to me too much to downplay the matter of religious difference and transformation, especially insofar as early modern England had undergone—and continued to grapple with—rapid shifts and reversals in religious identity. John Klause draws connections between Jewish Marranism and Catholic recusancy in *The Merchant of Venice*, though in the end his specific identification of Robert Southwell's writings as sources of Shakespeare's Jew remains circumstantial and unconvincing. See John Klause, "Catholic and Protestant, Jesuit and Jew: Historical Religion in The Merchant of Venice," *Religion and the Arts* 7 (2003): 65–102.

34. Quotations from Shakespeare's play are drawn from Lawrence Danson's Longman Cultural Edition.

35. See above, Chapter 2. On coverture in Shakespeare, see B. J. Sokol and Mary Sokol, *Shakespeare, Law, and Marriage* (Cambridge: Cambridge University Press, 2003), esp. 127. The function of coverture in *The Merchant of Venice*, and especially as a means for understanding Portia's marriage to Bassanio, has recently come under productive examination. See, in particular, Natasha Korda, "Dame Usury: Gender, Credit, and (Ac)counting in the Sonnets and *The Merchant of Venice*," *Shakespeare Quarterly* 60 (2009): 129–153.

36. On the necessarily impossible conversion of Shylock, see Heather Hirschfeld, " 'We All Expect a Gentle Answer, Jew': *The Merchant of Venice* and the Psychotheology of Conversion," *ELH: English Literary History* 73 (2006): 61–81; and Brett D. Hirsch, "Counterfeit Possessions: Jewish Daughters and the Drama of Failed Conversion in Marlowe's *The Jew of Malta* and Shakespeare's *The Merchant of Venice*," *Early Modern Literary Studies* 19 (2009): 4.1–37.

37. Jason P. Rosenblatt and Winfried Schleiner, "John Selden's Letter to Ben Jonson on Cross-Dressing and Bisexual Gods [With Text]," *English Literary Renaissance* 29 (1999): 44–74.

38. The *locus classicus* for discussions of *prisca sapientia* and *prisca theologia* is Frances A. Yates, *Giordano Bruno and the Hermetic Tradition* (London, 1964). See Charles B. Schmidt, "Perennial Philosophy: From Agostino to Steuco to Leibniz," *Journal of the History of Ideas* 27 (1966): 505–532, and Schmidt, "Prisca Theologia e Philosophia Perennis: due temi del Rinascimento italtiano e la loro fortuna," in *Il Pensiero del Rinascimento e il tempo nostro,* ed. Giovannagiola Tarugi (Florence: L. S. Olschki, 1970), 211–236; D. P. Walker, *The Ancient Theology: Studies in Christian Platonism from the Fifteenth to the Eighteenth Century* (Ithaca, NY: Cornell University Press, 1972), and Stephen A. McKnight, *The Modern Age and the Recovery of Ancient Wisdom: A Reconsideration of Historical Consciousness, 1450–1650* (Columbia: University of Missouri Press, 1991).

39. See Geoffrey Chaucer, "The Canon's Yeoman's Tale," ll. 331–336, for an early description of the alchemical stink, and compare to Chaucer's notorious retelling of the blood libel in his "Prioress's Tale," where the Jews seek to cover up their murder of the young Christian child by throwing the body into a pit, "Where as this Jewes purgen hire entraille" (l. 121), drawing upon the association of Jews with excretory functions.

40. Cheryl Lynn Ross, "The Plague of *The Alchemist,*" *Renaissance Quarterly* 41 (1988): 442–443.

41. On the conflation of the Calvinist *electus* and the alchemical *adeptus,* see Robert M. Schuler, "Jonson's Alchemists, Epicures, and Puritans," in *Medieval and Renaissance Drama in England,* vol. 2, ed. J. Leeds Barroll (New York: AMS Press, 1985), 172–191.

42. See Cecil Roth, *A History of the Jews in England,* 2nd ed. (Oxford: Clarendon Press, 1949), 144 and 280; and E. R. Samuel, "Portuguese Jews in Jacobean London," *Transactions of the Jewish Historical Society of England* 18 (1958): 171–230. Miriam Bodian notes that 1609–1610 were years in which there was a dramatic increase in the number of Portuguese *conversos* who emigrated from Portugal, many of them to Amsterdam, where Jonson's Anabatist brethren had also fled.

43. Deborah E. Harkness, "'Strange' Ideas and 'English' Knowledge: Natural Science Exchange in Elizabethan London," in *Merchants and Marvels: Commerce, Science, and Art in Early Modern Europe,* ed. Pamela H. Smith and Paula Findlen (New York: Routledge, 2002), 139.

44. On Jonson's conversion see James P. Crowley, "'He took his religion by trust': The Matter of Ben Jonson's Conversion," *Renaissance and Reformation/Renaissance et Réforme* 22, no. 1 (1998): 53–70.

45. Peter Stallybrass and Allon White, *The Politics and Poetics of Transgression* (Ithaca, NY: Cornell University Press, 1986), 77.

46. Lynn Meskill has written suggestively of Jonson's use of "choral interventions" in his plays, including *The Alchemist,* to buffer himself from the dangerous implications of embracing and deploying something as volatile and scatological as alchemy. See Lynn S. Meskill, *Ben Jonson and Envy* (Cambridge: Cambridge University Press, 2009), 124–125.

47. See, for example, Gerard Cox, "Apocalyptic Projection and the Comic Plot of The Alchemist," *ELR* 13 (1983): 70–87; and Richard Harp, "Ben Jonson's Comic Apocalypse," *Cithara* 34 (1994): 34–41.

48. Though I have not found any earlier critic who has addressed Ananias's name in Jonson's play, Maurice Hussey has written provocatively, if not fully convincingly, on what he regards as Jonson's covert sympathies for the Puritans as embodied in the figure of Ananias. See "Ananias the Deacon: A Study of Religion in Jonson's *The Alchemist,*" *English: The Journal of the English Association* 9 (54): 207–212.

49. See Katherine Eggert, "*The Alchemist* and Science," in *Early Modern English Drama: A Critical Companion,* ed. Garrett A. Sullivan, Jr., Patrick Cheney, and Andrew Hadfield (Oxford: Oxford University Press, 2006), 200–212.

50. Gaule, 348.

51. J. T. Young, *Faith, Medical Alchemy, and Natural Philosophy: Johan Moariaen, Reformed Intelligencer, and the Hartlib Circle* (Aldershot: Ashgate, 1998), 173.

52. [Thomas Vaughan], *Magia adamica or the antiquitie of magic, and the descent thereof from Adam downwards, proved. Whereunto is added a perfect, and full discoverie of the true coelum terrae, or the magician's heavenly chaos, and first matter of all things. By Eugenius Philalethes* (London, 1650), 10–11.

53. See Charles Webster, *Paracelsus: Medicine, Magic, and Mission at the End of Time* (New Haven, CT: Yale University Press, 2008), for an excellent recent account of Paracelsus's life, thought, and times.

54. See Allen Debus, *The English Paracelsians* (New York: Franklin Watts, 1965).

55. Robert Bostocke, *The difference betwene the auncient phisicke* (London, 1585), Hvii^{v}–Hviii^{r}, cited in Debus, 57–59.

56. Though I am using these terms somewhat interchangeably here, there are, in fact, shades of difference amongst them.

57. The Hebraic *locus classicus* for vitalism is Genesis 2:7, when Yahweh creates the first man as a "living soul" (נפש חיה). See Daniel Boyarin, *Carnal Israel: Reading Sex in Talmudic Culture* (Berkeley: University of California Press, 1993); Jason P. Rosenblatt, *Torah and Law in* Paradise Lost (Princeton, NJ: Princeton University Press, 1994), chap. 2; and Shoulson, *Milton and the Rabbis*, chap. 4.

58. John Rogers, *The Matter of Revolution: Science, Poetry, and Politics in the Age of Milton* (Ithaca, NY: Cornell University Press, 1996), 8ff.

59. Debus, *The English Paracelsians*. Despite its continuing importance, Debus's analysis has been modified more recently, to distinguish different strains of Paracelsian thought in England. See, for example, Rogers, *The Matter of Revolution*, especially chap. 1.

60. Elias Ashmole, *Theatrum Chemicum Britannicum* (London, 1652), a reprint of the London edition with a new introduction by Allen G. Debus (New York: Johnson Reprint Corporation, 1967), 446–447.

61. Paracelsus, *Of the Chymical Transmutation of Metals and Minerals & the Geneaology and Generation of Metals and Minerals. Also Of the Urim and Thummim of the Jews*, trans. Robert Turner (London, 1657), 52, emphasis added.

62. Copenhaver, "Natural Magic," 280. As Anthony Grafton has shown, Isaac Casaubon's exposure of the fraudulent provenance of the *corpus hermeticum* was rooted in his recognition of the biblical and Hebraic origins of many of the corpus's claims and idioms. See "Protestant vs. Prophet: Isaac Casaubon on Hermes Trismegistus," *Journal of the Warburg and Courtauld Institutes* 46 (1983): 78–93.

63. Robert Fludd, *Mosaicall Philosophy* (London, 1659), 40.

64. Vaughan, *Magia Adamica*, 42–43.

65. Vaughan, *Magia Adamica*, 76.

66. Ashmole, A4^{v}.

67. Vaughan, *Magia Adamica*, 53–54.

68. Ashmole, 453.

69. Antoine Faivre, *Access to Western Esotericism* (Albany: State University of New York Press, 1994).

70. Paracelsus, *Labyrinthus medicorum errantium* (1553), cited in H. Friedenwald, *The*

Jews and Medicine (Baltimore: Johns Hopkins University Press, 1955), 1:55, in turn cited by David Ruderman, *Jewish Thought and Scientific Discovery in Early Modern Europe* (New Haven, CT: Yale University Press, 1995), 221 and 245.

71. *Paracelsus his Aurora, & treasure of the philosophers. As also the water-stone of the wise men; describing the matter of, and manner how to attain the universal tincture. Faithfully Englished and published by J. H.* (Oxford, 1659), 178–180.

72. Ashmole, A2ʳ.

73. *Paracelsus His Aurora*, 221–222.

74. Menasseh ben Israel, *The Hope of Israel, the English Translation by Moses Wall, 1652*, ed. Henry Méchoulan and Gérard Nahon, trans. Richenda George (Oxford: Oxford University Press, 1987), 154–155.

75. I first learned about Abramo Colorni from Daniel Jütte, who completed his dissertation on Jewish alchemists in 2011. I am grateful to Dr. Jütte for the very helpful references with which he provided me in our extended conversations. Jütte published some of his preliminary findings in "Abramo Colorni, jüdischer Hofalchemist Herzog Friedrichs I., und die Hebraische Handelskompanie des Magino Gabrielli in Würtemberg am Ende des 16. Jahrhundert. Ein biographishcer und methodologishcer Beitrag zur jüdischen Wissenschaftsgeschichte," *Aschkenas* 15 (2005): 435–498. See also Ariel Toaff, *Il Prestigiatore di Dio: Avventure e Miracoli di un Alchimista Ebreo nelle Corti del Rinascimento* (Milan: Rizzoli, 2010).

76. The literature on the 1655 Whitehall Conference and the readmission controversy is substantial. A useful reading of the most detailed and notorious tract written against the readmission of Jews to England, William Prynne's *Short Demurrer*, can be found in Avrom Saltman, *The Jewish Question in 1655: Studies in Prynne's Demurrer* (Ramat Gan: Bar Ilan University Press, 1995). My discussion in this chapter relies heavily on the crucial work by David Katz and James Shapiro, especially regarding the readmission controversy and its role in the formation of English identity. See Katz, *Philo-Semitism*, and Shapiro, *Shakespeare and the Jews*. I have elsewhere offered my own understanding of this complex dynamic, in Shoulson, *Milton and the Rabbis*, especially chapter 1.

77. Ashmole, A2ᵛ.

78. *An Apology against a Pamphlet Called a Modest Confutation of the Animadversions upon the Remonstrant against Smectymnvvs* in *Complete Prose Works of John Milton*, ed. Don M. Wolfe (New Haven: Yale University Press, 1953–1982), 1:704. In his first anti-prelatical tract, *Of Reformation*, Milton wrote of the "*Precedencie* which God gave this *Iland*, to be the first *Restorer* of *buried Truth*" (1:526). Atypical and idiosyncratic as he was, in this respect at least, Milton was giving voice to a view held by many of his contemporaries.

79. See above, Chapter 1.

80. I do not mean to suggest that all alchemists were political and religious radicals or that all religious and political radicals admired alchemy, rather that the convergence of conservative religious and political arguments with opposition to esotericism was often accompanied by an overt hostility to Judaism and Jewish readmission. See J. Andrew

Mendelsohn's very important corrective to earlier tendencies to align alchemy exclusively with radical politics and religion, "Alchemy and Politics in England, 1649–1665," *Past and Present* 135 (1992): 30–78.

81. The critical literature on Vaughan's poetry and its alchemical background includes Elizabeth Holmes, *Henry Vaughan and the Hermetic Philosophy* (Oxford: Basil Blackwell, 1932); Wilson O. Clough, "Henry Vaughan and the Hermetic Philosophy," *PMLA* 48 (1933): 1108–1130; Richard Walters, "Henry Vaughan and the Alchemists," *Review of English Studies* 23 (1947): 107–122; Harold Fisch, *Jerusalem and Albion: The Hebraic Factor in Seventeenth-Century Literature* (New York: Schocken Books, 1964); Alan Rudrum, "The Influence of Alchemy in the Poems of Henry Vaughan," *Philological Quarterly* 49 (1970): 469–490; Thomas O. Calhoun, *Henry Vaughan: The Achievement of the* Silex Scintillans (Newark: University of Delaware Press, 1981); Linden, *Darke Hierogliphickes*; and Alan Rudrum, "'These fragments I have shored against my ruin': Henry Vaughan, Alchemical Philosophy, and the Great Rebellion," in *Mystical Metal of Gold: Essays on Alchemy and Renaissance Culture*, ed. Stanton Linden (New York: AMS Press, 2007), 325–338.

82. Linden, *Darke Hierogliphicks*, 103.

83. Linden, *Darke Hierogliphicks*, chap. 6.

84. On the differences between Donne's and Herbert's "generic" use of alchemical imagery and Vaughan's more detailed deployment, see Rudrum, "The Influence of Alchemy." Another contemporary of Vaughan, Andrew Marvell, has also been identified as having made far more extensive use of alchemical language and thought; see Lyndy Abraham, *Marvell and Alchemy* (Aldershot: Scolar Press, 1990). As Christopher Hill has noted, Marvell's poetry includes its own rather knowing reference to the conversion of the Jews; see "'Till the Conversion of the Jews,'" in *The Collected Essays of Christopher Hill*, vol. 2, *Religion and Politics in 17th Century England* (Amherst: University of Massachusetts Press, 1986), 269–300.

85. This and all subsequent quotations from Henry Vaughan are taken from *The Complete Poems*, ed. Alan Rudrum (New Haven, CT: Yale University Press, 1981).

86. Abraham Cowley, *Poems* (London, 1656), (b)2v.

87. As Jonathan Gil Harris has recently suggested, Herbert's poetics, informed by a Calvinist typology, depicts the misapprehension of the spiritual meaning in material signs as a "Jewish choice." Harris's provocative analysis argues further, however, that even as the typological structure of such readings seems to posit a temporal displacement of the material sign with its spiritual meaning, and thus Jew with Christian, there is also a palimpsestic persistence of this ostensibly transcended untimely matter: "Untranscended 'Jewish' matter is less the stuff of superseded history than the condition of the Protestant age, at least for now." See *Untimely Matter in the Time of Shakespeare* (Philadelphia: University of Pennsylvania Press, 2009), 44–54.

88. Nabil I. Matar, "George Herbert, Henry Vaughan, and the Conversion of the Jews," *SEL: Studies in English Literature* 30 (1990): 83–84.

89. Edward Spencer, *A Briefe Epistle to the Learned Menasseh Ben Israel* (London, 1650). See John Sparrow, "*The Hope of Israel, A Briefe Epistle*, and *Silex Scintillans*,"

Transactions of the Jewish Historical Society of England 20 (1956–61): 233–238, for a reconstruction of the authorship and dating of this *Epistle*.

90. The final stanza of Donne's "The Broken Heart," a poem that speaks of love's vulnerability, reads,

Yet nothing can to nothing fall,
Nor any place be empty quite,
Therefore I think my breast hath all
Those pieces still, though they be not unite;
And now as broken glasses show
A hundred lesser faces, so
My rags of heart can like, wish, and adore,
But after one such love, can love not more.

91. Linden, *Darke Hierogliphikes*, 227–232. Linden describes the poem as "Hermetic" and "Neo-Platonic" but in the end seeks to minimize its heterodoxies, asserting that Vaughan saw "no fundamental incompatibility or contraditions between his borrowings [from these esoteric traditions] and the more traditional Christian ideas that he espouses." My reading seeks to preserve the more unsettling qualities of these apparent contraditions.

92. See Arthur H. Williamson, "Latter Day Judah, Latter Day Israel: The Millennium, the Jews, and the British Future," in *Chiliasmus in Deutschland und England im 17. Jahrhundert*, ed. Martin Brecht et al. (Göttingen: Vanderhoeck and Ruprech, 1988), and especially Hill, "'Till the Conversion of the Jews,'" for persuasive accounts of the associations readers of the 1650s would have made between conversionary expectations and references to Daniel and other apocalyptic literature.

93. Principe and Newman, "Some Problems with the Historiography of Alchemy," 398 and 400.

94. William R. Newman, *Gehennical Fire: The Lives of George Starkey, an American Alchemist in the Scientific Revolution* (Cambridge, MA: Harvard University Press, 1994), 98–99. See also Lawrence M. Principe, *The Aspiring Adept: Robert Boyle and His Alchemical Quest* (Princeton, NJ: Princeton University Press, 1998), 189, and William R. Newman and Anthony Grafton, "Introduction: The Problematic Status of Astrology and Alchemy in Premodern Europe," in *Secrets of Nature: Astrology and Alchemy in Early Modern Europe*, ed. William R. Newman and Anthony Grafton (Cambridge, MA: MIT Press, 2001), 24.

CHAPTER 5

1. Insisting on a Milton historically engaged to the last, Christopher Hill has read *Paradise Regained* as the poet's final effort to distance himself from the increasingly apolitical stance of groups like the Quakers or Ranters. Hill remarks, "By 1660 Milton would

have criticized most proponents of the third culture, whether Ranters or Quakers, on these grounds: they ignored the world as it really is, in all its brutality: they were fundamentally unserious, as self-regarding as a modern hippie." See Christopher Hill, *Milton and the English Revolution* (New York: Viking Press, 1977), chap. 30. While still seeking to preserve the political content of the poem, subsequent readers have argued for a more sympathetic connection between the late Milton and the Quakers. See Steven Marx, "The Prophet Disarmed: Milton and the Quakers," *SEL: Studies in English Literature* 32 (1992): 111–128, and David Loewenstein, "The Kingdom Within: Radical Religious Culture and the Politics of *Paradise Regained*," *Literature and History*, 3rd Series, 3 (1994). This essay has been revised and expanded in Loewenstein's *Representing Revolution in Milton and his Contemporaries: Religion, Politics, and Polemics in Radical Puritanism* (Cambridge: Cambridge University Press, 2001).

2. Gary Hamilton, "*Paradise Regained* and the Private Houses," in *Of Poetry and Politics: New Essays on Milton and his World*, ed. P. G. Stanwood (Binghamton: Medieval and Renaissance Texts and Studies, 1995), 239–248, David Quint, *Epic and Empire: Politics and Generic Form from Virgil to Milton* (Princeton, NJ: Princeton University Press, 1993), and Ashraf Rushdy, *The Empty Garden: The Subject of Late Milton* (Pittsburgh: University of Pittsburgh Press, 1992), have all underscored the anti-monarchist, dissenting stance of Milton's brief epic. Laura Lunger Knoppers has written suggestively about Thomas Venner's abortive uprising in 1661 and its role in what looks to be a retreat from political engagement in *Paradise Regained*. See Laura Lunger Knoppers, *Historicizing Milton: Spectacle, Power, and Poetry in Restoration England* (Athens: University of Georgia Press, 1994). In a crucial earlier study of Milton's evolving political stance, Michael Fixler has argued compellingly for reading Milton's brief epic in relation to the spectacular rise and fall of the Jewish messiah, Sabbatai Sevi, in 1666–1667 and the shattered expectations of contemporary Jews for political as well as religious salvation. See Michael Fixler, *Milton and the Kingdoms of God* (Evanston, IL: Northwestern University Press, 1964).

3. The *OED* cites E. K.'s 1579 gloss to Spenser's *Shepheardes Calender* as the earliest appearance of the term: "a certaine *enthousiasmos* and celestiall inspiration."

4. Michael Heyd, *"Be Sober and Reasonable": The Critique of Enthusiasm in the Seventeenth and Early Eighteenth Centuries* (Leiden: Brill, 1995), 11. The capsule history of responses to enthusiasm that follows owes a great deal to Heyd's important work. It is not my intention here to rehash Heyd's conclusions, but rather to highlight several recurring and evolving themes in the literature of enthusiasm, pro and contra, so as to establish specific connections with Milton's poetry and prose.

5. For some especially perceptive comments on this matter, see R. A. Knox's important early analysis of enthusiasm since the earliest stages of Christianity, *Enthusiasm: A Chapter in the History of Religion* (Oxford: Oxford University Press, 1950), chap. 7.

6. Robert Burton, *The Anatomy of Melancholy* (London, 1628), third partition, section IV, member i, subsection 4.

7. Burton, 3.IV.i.4.

8. Meric Casaubon, *A Treatise Concerning Enthusiasme, As it is an Effect of Nature* (London, 1654), 3. See Grafton and Weinberg, *'I have always loved the Holy Tongue'*, for a

fascinating analysis of the elder Casaubon's peripatetic journeys that eventually led him to England and, in particular, his involvement in several very public cases of "false" or disrupted Jewish conversion.

9. Casaubon, *A Treatise*, 4.

10. Casaubon, *A Treatise*, 17.

11. Henry More, *Enthusiasmus Triumphatus* (London, 1656), 2.

12. More, *Enthusiasmus Triumphatus*, 16.

13. Harris, *Foreign Bodies*, 22.

14. The story is told at length in Humphry Ellis, *Pseudochristus: Or, a True and Faithful Relation of the Grand Impostures, Abominable Practises, Horrid Blasphemies, and Gross Deceits; Lately spread abroad and acted in the County of Southampton, by William Frankelin and Mary Gadbury, and their Companions* (London, 1650). The author claims to have met and talked with most of the implicated parties in the course of composing his account.

15. Ellis, *Pseudochristus*, 6.

16. Ellis, *Pseudochristus*, 7.

17. Ellis, *Pseudochristus*, 48.

18. Ellis, *Pseudochristus*, 58.

19. Thomas Hobbes, *Leviathan*, ed. C. B. Macpherson (New York: Penguin Press, 1983), part III, chap. 36.

20. Hobbes, *Leviathan*, part III, chap. 32.

21. See above, Chapter 1.

22. Joseph Glanvill, *A Loyal Tear Dropt on the Vault of Our Late Martyred Sovereign* (London, 1667), 7. I first encountered Glanvill's tract in Karen Edwards's fascinating essay, "Inspiration and Melancholy in *Samson Agonistes*," in *Milton and the Ends of Time: Essays on the Apocalypse and the Millennium*, ed. Juliet Lucy Cummins (Cambridge: Cambridge University Press, 2003).

23. Glanvill, *A Loyal Tear*, 27–28.

24. Sharon Achinstein, *Literature and Dissent in Milton's England* (Cambridge: Cambridge University Press, 2003), 9.

25. George Keith, *Immediate Revelation . . . Not Ceased* (n.p., 1668), 29–30.

26. Keith, *Immediate Revelation*, 55–56.

27. *The Reason of Church-Government, Complete Prose Works of John Milton*, ed. Don M. Wolfe (New Haven, CT: Yale University Press, 1953–1982), 1.794–795.

28. *The Reason of Church-Government*, *YP* 1.796.

29. *Doctrine and Discipline of Divorce*, *YP* 2.278–79.

30. This and all other quotations from Milton's poetry are taken from *John Milton: Complete Poems and Major Prose*, ed. Merritt Y. Hughes (New York: Macmillan Press, 1957).

31. Hobbes, *Leviathan*, part III, chap. 36.

32. Hobbes, *Leviathan*, part III, chap. 36.

33. Ellis, *Pseudochristus*, 62.

34. Casaubon, *A Treatise*, 60–61.

35. More, *Enthusiasmus Triumphatus*, 58ff.

36. George Fox, "Postscript," *A True Narrative of the Examination, Tryall, and Sufferings of James Nayler* (London, 1656), 49.

37. Leo Damrosch, *The Sorrows of the Quaker Jesus: James Nayler and the Puritan Crackdown on the Free Spirit* (Cambridge, MA: Harvard University Press, 1996).

38. Knox, *Enthusiasm*, 164.

39. Achinstein, *Literature and Dissent*, 154–157.

40. Achinstein, *Literature and Dissent*, 235.

41. For a more detailed account of Milton's understanding of Right Reason and how it differs from followers of Ramus and the inner light of antinomian enthusiasts, see P. Albert Duhamel, "Milton's Alleged Ramism," *PMLA* 67 (1952), 1035–1053, and Joan S. Bennett, *Reviving Liberty: Radical Christian Humanism in Milton's Great Poems* (Cambridge, MA: Harvard University Press, 1989), 11 and 111–112.

42. Henry More, "Mastix his Letter," 307.

43. Henry Hallywell, *An Account of Familism as it is Revived and Propagated by the Quakers* (London, 1673), 103.

44. William Penn, *Wisdom Justified of her Children, from the Ignorance & Calumny of H. Hallywell* (n.p., 1673), 106.

45. See David Loewenstein, *Milton and the Drama of History: Historical Vision, Iconoclasm, and the Literary Imagination* (Cambridge: Cambridge University Press, 1990).

46. B. S. Capp, *The Fifth Monarchy Men: A Study in Seventeenth-century English Millenarianism* (London: Faber and Faber, 1972), 136–140.

47. *Eikonoklastes*, *YP* 3.491.

48. Fixler, *Milton and the Kingdoms of Heaven*, 263.

49. For more extensive discussions of *Paradise Regained* in relation to the radical militancy of Venner's uprising, see Knoppers, *Historicizing Milton*; and Loewenstein, "The Kingdom Within"; see also Ken Simpson, "The Apocalypse," and Barbara Lewalski, "Milton and the Millennium," both in *Milton and the Ends of Time*.

50. Loewenstein, *Representing Revolution*, 250

51. John Coffey has offered a similar argument, positioning Milton among the likes of John Goodwin, Henry Vane, Algernon Sidney, and Edmund Ludlow, all of whom "were absorbed by questions concerning the timing and meaning of their deliverance. . . . Each would . . . have distanced himself from both the rashness of Thomas Venner, and the new 'peace principle' of George Fox. As defenders of the Good Old Cause, they stood between Fifth Monarchist belligerence and Quaker pacifism." See "Pacifist, Quietist, or Patient Militant? John Milton and the Restoration," *Milton Studies* 42, ed. Albert C. Labriola (Pittsburgh: Duquesne University Press, 2002), 155.

52. See Sonia P. Anderson, *An English Consul in Turkey: Paul Rycaut at Smyrna, 1667–1678* (Oxford: Oxford University Press, 1989), for a detailed account of Rycaut's travels and writings.

53. John Evelyn, *The History of the Three Late Famous Imposters, viz. Padre Ottomano, Mahomed Bei, and Sabatai Sevi. The One, pretended Son and Heir to the Late Grand Signio, The Other, a Prince of the Ottoman Family, but in truth, a Valachian Counterfeit. And the*

Last, the Suppos'd MESSIAH of the Jews, in the Year of the true Messiah, 1666 (London, 1669), 42–43. Rycaut would republish his account in 1680 under his own name as part of his *History of the Turkish Empire.*

54. Michael McKeon, "Sabbatai Sevi in England," *AJS Review* 2 (1977).

55. Ernestine G. E. van der Wall has compiled a remarkable list of Serrarius's correspondents, who included a striking cross-section of English political and religious society: Nathaniel Homes (Menasseh ben Israel's correspondent), Henry Oldenburg (secretary of the Royal Society), Joshua Sprigge (Congregationalist minister), Anthony Grey (friend of Baptist Henry Jessey), the millenarians John Dury and Jan Comenius, and many others. These correspondents, in turn, passed the news of Sabbatai Sevi on to a veritable "who's who" list of English writers and intellectuals, including the Fifth Monarchist Thomas Chappell, James Fitton (Henry Jessey's successor in his London Baptist congregation), Robert Boyle, Lord Brereton, Secretary of State Joseph Williamson, Oxford Hebraist Edward Pococke, and astrologer Samuel Jeake. See her "A Precursor of Christ or a Jewish Imposter? Petrus Serrarius and Jean de Labadie on the Jewish Messianic Movement around Sabbatai Sevi," *Pietismus und Neuzeit* 14 (1988): 112–113.

56. Barbara Lewalski, *The Life of John Milton*, rev. ed. (Oxford: Basil Blackwell, 2003), 458.

57. See my *Milton and the Rabbis*, chaps. 1 and 2.

58. This Dutch commentary was published under the title of *Verklaringe over des propheten Jesaia veertien eerste capittelen* (Amsterdam, 1666). I am relying on van der Wall's summary, 116–118.

59. For an extended discussion of this aspect of the reports of Sabbatai Sevi in Christian Europe, see Michael Heyd, "The 'Jewish Quaker': Christian Perceptions of Sabbatai Zevi as an Enthusiast," in *Hebraica Veritas? Christian Hebraists and the Study of Judaism in Early Modern Europe* (Philadelphia: University of Pennsylvania Press, 2004).

60. "The Restauration of the Jews: Or, A true Relation of Their Progress and Proceedings in order to the regaining of their Ancient Kingdom Being of the Substance of several LETTTERS Viz. from ANTWERP, LEGORN, FLORENCE, etc. (London, 1665). This and three other English pamphlets have been reprinted with annotations in Mordechai Wilinsky, "Four English Pamphlets on the Sabbatian Movement" [Hebrew], *Zion* 17 (1952): 156–172.

61. Evelyn, *The History.*

62. See, for example, Evelyn, *The History*, 78–79.

63. Gershom Scholem's magisterial account of the Sabbatian movement, *Sabbatai Sevi: The Mystical Messiah*, trans. R. J. Zwi Werblowsky (Princeton, NJ: Princeton University Press, 1973), especially chap. 5, takes strong issue with this claim.

64. Evelyn, *The History*, 41–42.

65. Among the most avid promoters of Jewish conversion in the 1650s, 1660s, and 1670s was George Fox, who wrote numerous appeals to members of the Jewish community and engaged in far more detailed exchanges about the proper understanding of those prophetic texts that anticipated the ends of time and the final redemption of God's faithful.

66. Fixler, 237–271.

67. More, *Enthusiasmus Triumphatus*, 30.

68. *Of Reformation*, *YP* 1.568.

69. *An Apology Against a Pamphlet*, *YP* 1.868–869.

70. *An Apology Against a Pamphlet*, *YP* 1.900.

71. See, for example, Christopher Ricks, "Over-Emphasis in *Paradise Regained*," *Modern Language Notes* 76 (1961): 701–704; Stanley Fish, "Inaction and Silence: The Reader in *Paradise Regained*," *Calm of Mind: Tercentenary Essays on* Paradise Regained *and* Samson Agonistes *in Honor of John S. Diekhoff*, ed. Joseph A. Wittreich, Jr., James G. Taaffe, and Jane Cerny (Cleveland: Press of Case Western Reserve University, 1971), 24–47; Fish, "Things and Actions Indifferent: The Temptation of Plot in *Paradise Regained*," in *Milton Studies* XVII, ed. James D. Simmonds (Pittsburgh: University of Pittsburgh Press, 1983), 163–185; Emory Elliott, "Milton's Biblical Style in *Paradise Regained*," in *Milton Studies* 6, ed. James D. Simmonds (Pittsburgh: University of Pittsburgh Press, 1974), 227–241; Alan Fisher, "Why Is *Paradise Regained* So Cold?" in *Milton Studies* 14, ed. James D. Simmonds (Pittsburgh: University of Pittsburgh Press, 1980), 195–217; Wayne C. Anderson, "Is *Paradise Regained* Really Cold?" *Christianity and Literature* 34 (1983): 15–23; Alastair Fowler, "*Paradise Regained*: Some Problems of Style," in *Medieval and Pseudo-Medieval Literature*, ed. Piero Boitani and Anna Torti (Tübingen: G. Narr, 1984), 181–189; and Louis L. Martz, "*Paradise Regained*: Georgic Form, Georgic Style," in *Milton Studies* 42, ed. Albert C. Labriola and David Loewenstein (Pittsburgh: Duquesne University Press, 2003), 7–25.

72. Sharon Achinstein, "Milton's Spectre in the Restoration: Marvell, Dryden, and Literary Enthusiasm," *Huntington Library Quarterly* 59 (1997): 8. This article has been expanded in Achinstein's book, *Literature and Dissent*, chap. 6. See also an important early essay, George Williamson, "The Restoration Revolt against Enthusiasm," *Studies in Philology* 30 (1930): 571–603, which draws links between Restoration philosophical and religious sensibilities and the idea of a true and correct language, all of which are realized in an opposition to Enthusiasm. These connections explain why the poets with whom we most often associate the Restoration—Dryden, Pope, and others—would have promoted a decorous, anti-metaphorical style.

73. Annabel Patterson, *Reading between the Lines* (Madison: University of Wisconsin Press, 1993), 257.

74. More, *Enthusiasmus Triumphatus*, 20.

75. Casaubon, *A Treatise*, 8–9.

76. N. H. Keeble, *The Literary Culture of Nonconformity in Later Seventeenth-Century England* (Athens: University of Georgia Press, 1987), 245.

77. Samuel Parker, *A Discourse of Ecclesiastical Politie Wherein the Authority of the Civil Magistrate over the Consciences of Subjects in Matters of Religion is Asserted, the Mischiefs and Inconveniences of Toleration Represented, and all Pretenses Pleaded in behalf of Liberty of Conscience are Fully Answered* (London, 1670), 4–75.

78. Parker, *Discourse of Ecclesiastical Politie*, 75–76.

79. For a discussion of the rhetoric of enthusiasm and its relation to evolving

figurations of, and cultural anxieties regarding, the body, see Clement Hawes, *Mania and Literary Style: The Rhetoric of Enthusiasm from the Ranters to Christopher Smart* (Cambridge: Cambridge University Press, 1996). On the specific phenomenon of Quaker Shibboleths and their relationships to early modern rhetoric, see Hugh Ormsby-Lennon, "From Shibboleth to Apocalypse: Quaker Speechways During the Puritan Revolution," *Language, Self, and Society: A Social History of Language*, ed. Peter Burke and Roy Porter (Cambridge: Cambridge University Press, 1991), 72–112.

80. Keeble, 249.

81. George Fox and James Nayler, *Severall Papers: Some of them given forth by George Fox; other by James Nayle, Ministers of the Eternall Word of God, raysed up after the long night of Apostacy to direct the world, to waite for the Revelation of Jesus Christ, and to turne their minds to the true light, that they may be reconciled to God* (London, 1653), 5. The title page includes the following description: "Wherein the plaine, honest, and sober conversation of the Saints in feare and trembling, is justified, against the idle babblings of formall Professors, (the wicked fashions and Heathenish Customs of this Nation) and of all sorts of Persons, under pretence of civility."

82. James Nayler, *All Vain Janglers, Imitatours and Licentious Persons, Shut out of the Scriptures, who are not guided by the same spirit that gave them forth* (London, 1654), 2. The dialogic form was a favorite mode of early Quaker writings, one used frequently by Fox, especially in his writings to the Jews.

83. There are some exceptions to this general tendency. See, for example, my discussion above of the Son's citation of Daniel's prophecy.

84. *An Apology against a Pamphlet*, 1.900.

85. Michael Schoenfeldt, "'Commotion Strange': Passion in *Paradise Lost*," in *Reading the Early Modern Passions: Essays in the Cultural History of Emotion*, ed. Gail Kern Paster, Katherine Rowe, and Mary Floyd-Wilson (Philadelphia: University of Pennsylvania Press, 2004), 63–64.

Bibliography

PRIMARY SOURCES

Addison, Joseph. *The Spectator*, June 14, 1712.

Ainsworth, Henry. *Annotations upon the First Book of Moses called Genesis.* London, 1616.

Ambrose. "Exposition on the Gospel of Luke." In *Ancient Christian Commentary on Scripture: Joshua, Judges, Ruth, 1–2 Samuel*, edited by John R. Franke. Downers Grove, IL: InterVarsity Press, 2005.

Andrewes, Lancelot. *Miscellaneous Works of Lancelot Andrewes.* Volume 12. Edited by J. Bliss. London: Library of Anglo-Catholic Theology, 1854.

———. "Sermon Preached 10 February 1619, Before James at Whitehall."

Ashmole, Elias. *Theatrum Chemicum Britannicum.* London, 1652.

Babington, Gervaise. *Certaine plane, briefe, and comfortable notes vpon euerie chapter of Genesis.* London, 1592.

Bacon, Francis. *Novum Organum.* London, 1620.

Bacon, Roger. *The mirror of alchimy, composed by the thrice-famous and learned fryer, Roger Bachon, sometimes fellow of Martin Colledge: and afterwards of Brasen-nose Colledge in Oxenforde. Also a most excellent and learned discourse of the admirable force and efficacie of art and nature, written by the same author. With certaine other treatises of the like argument.* London, 1597.

Bentley, Thomas. *The Sixt Lampe of Virginitie; Conteining a Mirrour for Maidens and Matrons.* [London?], 1582.

Bernard, Richard. *Ruths Recompense, or, a Commentarie on the booke of* Ruth. London, 1628.

The Bible and Holy Scriptures. Geneva, 1560.

Bostocke, Robert. *The difference betwene the auncient phisicke, first taught by the godly forefathers, consisting in vnitie peace and concord.* London, 1585.

Broughton, Hugh. *A Censure of the Late Translation of our Churches.* London, 1611.

———. *An Epistle to the Learned Nobilitie of England Touching Translating the Bible from the original.* London, 1597.

Burton, Robert. *The Anatomy of Melancholy.* London, 1628.

Calvin, John. *The Institution of Christian Religion.* Translated by Thomas Norton. London, 1599.

Camden, William. *Annals, or the History of the Most Renowned and Victorious Princess Elizabeth, Late Queen of England.* Translated by Robert Norton. London, 1630.

Carier, Benjamin. *A Treatise . . . to forsake the Protestant Congregation and the Betake Himselfe to the Catholike Apostolike Roman Church.* N.p., 1614.

Casaubon, Meric. *A Treatise Concerning Enthusiasme.* London, 1654.

Chapman, George. *Achilles Shield.* London, 1598.

———. *Homers Odysees.* London, 1614.

———. *The Iliads of Homer.* London, 1611.

Cheke, John. "Letter." In *The courtyer of Count Baldessar Castillo.* Translated by Thomas Hoby. London, 1561.

Clairvaux, Bernard of. *Sermons on Conversion.* Translated by Marie-Bernard Saïd. Kalamazoo, MI: Cistercian Publications, 1981.

Clapham, Henoch. AN ABSTRACT OF FAYTH, *Grounded on Moses, and applied to the Common Creede.* London, 1606.

Cooper, Thomas. *The Blessing of Japheth, Proving the Gathering of the Gentiles, and the Finall Conuersion of the Jewes.* London, 1615.

———. *The Converts First Love Discerned, Justified, Left, and Recovered, Resolving the Truth of and Effectual Conversion.* London, 1610.

Cowley, Abraham. *Poems.* London, 1656.

Donne, John. *The Complete English Poems.* Edited by A. J. Smith. Harmondsworth: Penguin Books, 1986.

———. *The Sermons of John Donne.* Edited by Evelyn M. Simpson and George R. Potter. Volumes 6–7. Berkeley: University of California Press, 1956.

Downame, George. ABRAHAMS TRYALL: *A Sermon preaced at the Spittle, in Easter weeke Anno Domini 1602.* London, 1602.

Eliis, Humphry. *Pseudochristus.* London, 1650.

Elwood, Thomas. *The History of the Life of Thomas Elwood.* London, 1714.

Evelyn, John. *The History of the Three Late Famous Imposters.* London, 1669.

Featley, Daniel. *Virtumnus romanus, or, A discovrse penned by a Romish priest wherein he endevours to prove that it is lawfull for a papist in England to goe to the Protestant church, to receive the communion, and to take the oathes, both of allegiance and supremacie : to which are adjoyned animadversions in the in the [sic] margin by way of antidote against those places where the rankest poyson is couched.* London, 1642.

Flamel, Nicolas. *His Exposition of the Hieroglyphicall Figures . . . Faithfully, and . . . religiously done into English out of the French and Latine copies. By Eirenæus Orandus.* London, 1624.

Florio, John. *Qveen Anna's New World of Words, or Dictionarie of the Italian and English tongues.* London, 1611.

Fludd, Robert. *Mosaicall Philosophy: Grounded upon the Essentiall Truth or Eternal Sapience. Written first in Latin, and afterwards thus rendred into English.* London, 1659.

Fox, George. "Postscript." In *A True Narrative of the Examination, Tryall, and Sufferings of James Nayler.* London, 1656.

Fox, George, and James Nayler. *Severall Papers.* London, 1653.

Foxe, John. *A Sermon Preached at the Christening of a Certaine Jew.* London, 1578.

Frances, Lord Verulam [Francis Bacon]. *Apophthegmes New and Old.* London, 1625.

Fuller, Thomas. *A Comment on Ruth.* London, 1654.

———. *Ioseph's Partie-Colored Coat.* London, 1640.

Gaule, John. *Practique Theories: Or, Votiue Speculations Vpon Sauls Cruelty. Pauls Conuersion.* London, 1630.

Glanvill, Joseph. *A Loyal Tear Dropt on the Vault of Our Late Martyred Sovereign.* London, 1667.

Gouge, William. *A Learned and Very Useful Commentary on the Whole Epistle to the Hebrews.* London, 1655.

———. *The Progresse of Divine Providence.* London, 1645.

———. *A Recovery from Apostacy. Set out in a Sermon Preached in Stepny . . . at the receiving of a Penitent Renegado.* London, 1639.

Greenham, Richard. *The Workes of the Reverend and Faithfvll servant of Iesus Christ M. Richard Greenham.* London, 1612.

Hall, Arthur. *A letter sent by F.A. touchyng the proceedings in a priuate quarell and vnkindnesse betweene Arthur Hall, and Melchisedech Mallerie gentleman.* London, 1576.

Hallywell, Henry. *An Account of Familism as it is Revived and Propagated by the Quakers.* London, 1673.

Hammond, Henry. *A Letter of Resolution to Six Qæres, of Present Use in the Church of England.* London, 1652.

Hayne, Thomas. *The Eqvall Wayes of God.* London, 1632.

Hobbes, Thomas. *Leviathan.* Edited by C. B. Macpherson. New York: Penguin Press, 1983.

The Holie Bible Faithfvlly Translated into English, Ovt of the Authentical Latine. Douay, 1609.

The Holy Bible, Conteyning the Old Testament and the New, Newly Translated out of the Originall tongues: & with the former Translations diligently compared and reuised by his Maiesties Speciall Commandement. Appointed to be read in Churches. London, 1611.

Homer. *The Odyssey.* Translated by A. T. Murray. Cambridge, MA: Harvard University Press, 1919.

Hooker, Richard. *Of the Laws of Ecclesiastical Polity.* Volume 5. London, 1597.

Israel, Menasseh ben. *The Hope of Israel, The English Translation by Moses Wall, 1652.* Edited by Henry Méchoulan and Gérard Nahon. Translated by Richenda George. Oxford: Oxford University Press, 1987.

Jonson, Ben. *Ben Jonson's Plays and Masques.* Edited by Richard Harp. New York: W. W. Norton & Company, 2001.

Keith, George. *Immediate Revelation . . . Not Ceased.* 1668.

Kellet, Edward. *Retvrne from Argier. A Sermon Preached at Minhead in the County of Somerset the 16. Of March, 1627 at the re-admission of a relapsed Christian into our Church.* London, 1628.

Lavater, Ludwig. *The Book of Ruth Expounded in Twenty Eight Sermons, by Levves*

Lauaterus of Tyrgurine, and by hym published in Latine, and now translated in Englishe by Ephraim Pagitt, a childe of eleuen yeares of age. London, 1586.
Lightfoot, John. *The Harmony of the Foure Evangelists.* London, 1644.
Luther, Martin. *Lectures on Romans.* Edited by Wilhelm Pauck. Translated by Wilhelm Pauck. Philadelphia: Westminster Press, 1961.
———. *Tischreden [Table Talk].*
Lyford, Edward. *[Sefer M'litzat Ha'Shemot], or, The True Interpretation and Etymologie of Christian Names.* London, 1655.
Marlowe, Christopher. *The Complete Plays.* Edited by Frank Romany and Robert Lindsey. London: Penguin Books, 2003.
Mede, Joseph. "The Mystery of S. Paul's Conversion: or, The Type of the Calling of the Jews." In *The Works of the Pious and Profoundly-Learned Joseph Mede*, by Joseph Mede, edited by John Worthington, 891–892. London, 1677.
Milton, John. *Complete Poetry and Major Prose.* Edited by Merritt Y. Hughes. New York: Macmillan Press, 1957.
———. *Complete Prose Works of John Milton.* Edited by Don M. Wolfe. 8 volumes. New Haven, CT: Yale University Press, 1953–1982.
Montaigne, Michel de. "On Names." In *The Essayes or Morall, Politike and Militarie Discourses of Michaell de Montaigne*, by Michel de Montaigne. Translated by John Florio. London, 1606.
More, Henry. *Enthusiasmus Triumphatus.* London, 1656.
———. *Observations Upon Anthroposophia Theomagica, and Anima Magica Abscondita. By Alazonomastix Philalethes.* London, 1650.
Mulcaster, Richard. *The First Part of the Elementarie which Entreateth Chefelie of the Right Writing of our English Tung.* London, 1582.
Nayler, James. *All Vain Janglers, Imitatours, and Licentious Persons, Shut out of the Scriptures.* London, 1654.
The NEVV TESTAMENT of Iesus Christ, Translated Faithfvlly into English. Rheims, 1582.
Ogle, John. *The Lamentation of Troy, for the death of Hector.* London, 1594.
Paracelsus. *Of the Chymical Transmutation of Metals and Minerals & the Geneaology and Generation of Metals and Minerals. Also Of the Urim and Thummim of the Jews.* Translated by Robert Turner. London, 1657.
———. *Paracelsus his Aurora, & treasure of the philosophers. As also the water-stone of the wise men; describing the matter of, and manner how to attain the universal tincture. Faithfully Englished and published by J. H.* Oxford, 1659.
Parker, Samuel. *A Discourse of Ecclesiastical Politie.* London, 1670.
Patten, William. *The Calendar of Scripture.* London, 1575.
Penkethman, John. *Onomatophylacium.* London, 1626.
Penn, William. *Wisdom Justified of Her Children.* 1673.
Petrarch, Francis. *Petrarch: The First Modern Scholar and Man of Letters.* Edited by James Harvey Robinson. Translated by James Harvey Robinson. New York: G. P. Putnam, 1898.
Plato. *The Republic.* Translated by Robin Waterfield. Oxford: Oxford Univeristy Press, 1993.

Playfere, Thomas. "a sermon preached at the Court of Whitehall. March 10. 1598." In *The VVhole Sermons*, by Thomas Playfere. London, 1623.

Price, Daniel. *Recusants Couersion.* London, 1608.

The Restauration of the Jews, Or, A True Relation of Their Progress and Proceedings in order to the regaining of their Ancient Kingdom. London, 1665.

Ross, Alexander. *Som Animadversions and Observations upon Sr. Walter Raleighs Historie of the World.* London, 1648.

Sandys, George. OVIDS METAMORPHOSIS *Englished by G[eorge] S[andys].* London, 1626.

Scapula, John. *Lexicon Graecolatinum novum.* Amsterdam, 1580.

Shakespeare, William. *The Merchant of Venice: Longman Cultural Edition.* Edited by Lawrence Danson. New York: Longman, 2005.

Spencer, Edward. *A Briefe Epistle to the Learned Menasseh Ben Israel. In Answer to his, Dedicated to the Parliament.* London, 1650.

Topsell, Edward. *The Reward of Religion. Deliuered in sundrie Lectures vpon the Booke of Ruth, wherein the godly may see their daily and outwarde tryals, with the presence of God to assist them, and his mercies to recompence them.* London, 1596

Tyndale, William. *Obedience of a Christian Man.* Volume 42. In *Doctrinal Treatises and Introductions to Different Portions of the Holy Scripture*, edited by Henry Walter. Cambridge: Parker Society, 1848.

———. "Preface to the Christian Reader." In *The New Testament of Our Saviour Iesus Christ.* [London?], 1536.

Vaughan, Henry. *The Complete Poems.* Edited by Alan Rudrum. New Haven, CT: Yale University Press, 1981.

Vaughan, Thomas. *Magia Adamica or the antiquitie of magic, and the descent thereof from Adam downwards, proved . . . By Eugenius Philalethes.* London, 1650.

Willet, Andrew. *Hexapla in Exodum.* London, 1608.

———. *Hexapla in Genesin.* London, 1608.

SECONDARY SOURCES

Abraham, Lyndy. "The Alchemical Code in Marvell's 'To His Coy Mistress.'" *Sydney Studies* 16 (1990): 54–77.

———. *Marvell and Alchemy.* Aldershot: Scolar Press, 1990.

Achinstein, Sharon. "John Foxe and the Jews." *Renaissance Quarterly* 54 (2001): 86–120.

———. *Literature and Dissent in Milton's England.* Cambridge: Cambridge University Press, 2003.

———. "Milton's Spectre in the Restoration: Marvell, Dryden, and Literary Enthusiasm." *Huntington Library Quarterly* 59 (1997): 1–30.

Adams, John Charles. "Ramist Concepts of Testimony, Judicial Analogies, and the Puritan Conversion Narrative." *Rhetorica* 9 (1991): 251–268.

Adelman, Janet. *Blood Relations: Christian and Jew in* The Merchant of Venice. Chicago: University of Chicago Press, 2008.

Albrecht, Roberta. *The Virgin Mary as Alchemical and Lullian Reference in Donne.* Selinsgrove, PA: Susquehanna University Press, 2005.

Anderson, Sonia P. *An English Consul in Turkey: Paul Rycaut at Smyrna, 1667–1678.* Oxford: Oxford University Press, 1989.

Anderson, Wayne C. "Is *Paradise Regained* Really Cold?" *Christianity and Literature* 34 (1983): 15–23.

Aschkenasy, Nehama. "'I Went Away Full, and the Lord Has Brought Me Back Empty': Language as Female Empowerment in Ruth." In *Reading Ruth: Contemporary Women Reclaim a Sacred Story,* edited by Judith A. Kates and Gail Twersky Reimer, 111–124. New York: Ballantine Books, 1994.

Auerbach, Erich. "'Figura.'" In *Scenes from the Drama of European History,* 11–78. Translated by Ralph Manheim. Minneapolis: University of Minnesota Press, 1994.

———. "Odysseus' Scar." In *Mimesis: The Representation of Reality in Western Literature.* 3–23. Translated by William R. Trask. Princeton, NJ: Princeton University Press, 1953.

Baker, Herschel. *The Wars of Truth: Studies in the Decay of Christian Humanism in the Earlier Seventheenth Century.* Cambridge, MA: Harvard University Press, 1952.

Bakker, Egbert J. "Mimesis as Performance: Rereading Auerbach's First Chapter." *Poetics Today* 20 (1999): 11–26.

Barclay, William. *Turning to God: A Study of Conversion in the Book of Acts and Today.* Philadelphia: Westminster Press, 1964.

Barth, Christoph. "Notes on 'Return' in the Old Testament." *Ecumenical Review* 19 (1967): 310–312.

Baskin, Judith R. *Pharaoh's Counsellors: Job, Jethro, and Balaam in Rabbinic and Patristic Tradition.* Chico, CA: Scholars Press, 1983.

Begg, Christopher. "The Rahab Story in Josephus." *Liber Annuus* 55 (2005): 113–130.

Beichtman, Philip. *Alchemy of the Word: Cabala of the Renaissance.* Albany: State University of New York Press, 1998.

Benjamin, Walter. "The Task of the Translator." In *Illuminations: Essays and Reflections,* 69–82. Translated by Harry Zohn. New York: Schocken Books, 1978.

Bennett, Camille. "The Conversion of Vergil: *The Aeneid* in Augustine's Confessions." *Revue des Études Augustiniennes* 34 (1988): 47–69.

Bennett, Joan S. *Reviving Liberty: Radical Christian Humanism in Milton's Great Poems.* Cambridge, MA: Harvard University Press, 1989.

Berek, Peter. "The Jew as Renaissance Man." *Renaissance Quarterly* 51 (1998): 128–162.

Biddick, Kathleen. *The Typological Imaginary: Circumcision, Technology, and History.* Philadelphia: University of Pennsylvania Press, 2003.

Bodian, Miriam. *Hebrew of the Portuguese Nation: Converso and Community in Early Modern Amsterdam.* Bloomington: Indiana University Press, 1997.

Boyarin, Daniel. *Carnal Israel: Reading Sex in Talmudic Culture.* Berkeley: University of California Press, 1993.

Brachlow, Stephen. *The Communion of the Saints: Radical Puritan and Separatist Ecclesiology, 1570–1625.* Oxford: Oxford University Press, 1988.

Brenner, Athalya, ed. *A Feminist Companion to Ruth*. Sheffield: Sheffield Academic Press, 1994.

———, ed. *Ruth and Esther: A Feminist Companion to the Bible*. Sheffield: Sheffield Academic Press, 1999.

Brinton, Alan. "St. Augustine and the Problem of Deception in Religious Persuasion." *Religious Studies* 19 (1983): 437–450.

Burke, Peter. "Cultures of Translation in Early Modern Europe." In *Cultural Translation in Early Modern Europe*, edited by Peter Burke and R. Po-chia Hsia, 7–38. Cambridge: Cambridge University Press, 2007.

Burton, Jonathan. *Traffic and Turning: Islam and English Drama, 1579–1624*. Newark: University of Delaware Press, 2005.

Caldwell, Patricia. *The Puritan Conversion Narrative: The Beginnings of American Expression*. Cambridge: Cambridge University Press, 1983.

Calhoun, Thomas O. *Henry Vaughan: The Achievement of the* Silex Scintillans. Newark: University of Delaware Press, 1981.

Cameron, Euan. *The European Reformation*. Oxford: Clarendon Press, 1991.

Cancik, Hubert. "Lucian on Conversion: Remarks on Lucian's Dialogue Nigrinos." In *Ancient and Modern Perspectives on the Bible and Culture: Essays in Honor of Hans Dieter Betz*, edited by Adela Yarbro Collins, 26–48. Atlanta: Scholars Press, 1998.

Capp, B. S. *The Fifth Monarchy Men: A Study in Seventeenth-Century English Millenarianism*. London: Faber and Faber, 1972.

Carey, George. "A Biblical Perspective." In *Entering the Kingdom: A Fresh Look at Conversion*, edited by Monica Hill, 9–21. Harrow: Hodder and Stoughton, 1986.

Carlebach, Elisheva. "Attributions of Secrecy and Perceptions of Jewry." *Jewish Social Studies* n.s., 2, no. 3 (1996): 115–136.

———. *Divided Souls: Converts from Judaism to Germany, 1500–1750*. New Haven, CT: Yale University Press, 2001.

Chang, Ku-Ming (Kevin). "Toleration of Alchemists as a Political Question: Transmutation, Disputation, and Early Modern Scholarship on Alchemy." *Ambix* 54 (2007): 245–273.

Cheyfitz, Eric. *The Poetics of Imperialism: Translation and Colonization from The Tempest to Tarzan*. Philadelphia: University of Pennsylvania Press, 1997.

Clough, Wilson O. "Henry Vaughan and the Hermetic Philosophy." *PMLA* 48 (1933): 1108–1130.

Coffey, John. "Pacifist, Quietist, or Patient Militant? John Milton and the Restoration." In *Milton Studies Volume 17*, edited by Albert C. Labriola. Pittsburgh: Duquesne University Press, 2002.

Cohen, Charles L. *God's Caress: The Psychology of Puritan Religious Experience*. Oxford: Oxford University Press, 1986.

———. "Two Biblical Models of Conversion: An Example of Puritan Hermeneutics." *Church History* 58 (1989): 182–196.

Cohen, Jeremy. *Living Letters of the Law: Ideas of the Jew in Medieval Christianity*. Berkeley: University of California Press, 1999.

Cohen, Robert L. "Form and Perspective in 2 Kings V." *Vetus Testamentum* 33 (1983): 171–184.

Cohen, Walter. *Drama of a Nation: Public Theater in Renaissance England and Spain.* Ithaca, NY: Cornell University Press, 1985.

Conn, Walter. *Christian Conversion: A Developmental Interpretation of Autonomy and Surrender.* New York: Paulist Press, 1986.

Copenhaver, Brian P. "Natural Magic, Hermeticism, and Occultism in Early Modern Science." In *Reappraisals of the Scientific Revolution*, edited by David C. Lindberg and Robert S. Westman. Cambridge: Cambridge University Press, 1990.

Coudert, Allison P., and Jeffrey S. Shoulson, eds. *Hebraica Veritas? Christian Hebraists and the Study of Judaism in Early Modern Europe.* Philadelphia: University of Pennsylvania Press, 2004.

Cox, Gerard. "Apocalyptic Projection and the Comic Plot of *The Alchemist.*" *English Literary Renaissance* 13 (1983): 70–87.

Crane, David. "The Poetry of Alchemy and the Alchemy of Poetry in the Work of Thomas and Henry Vaughan." *Scintilla* 1 (1997): 115–122.

Cressy, David. *Bonfires and Bells: National Memory and the Protestant Calendar in Elizabethan and Stuart England.* Berkeley: University of California Press, 1989.

Crosignani, Ginevra, Thomas M. McCoog, S.J., and Michael Questier, eds. *Recusancy and Conformity in Early Modern England: Manuscript and Printed Sources in Translation.* Rome: Institutum Historicum Societatis Iesu, 2010.

Crowley, James P. "'He took his religion by trust': The Matter of Ben Jonson's Conversion." *Renaissance and Reformation/Renaissance et Réforme* 22 (1998): 53–70.

Cummins, Juliet, ed. *Milton and the Ends of Time.* Cambridge: Cambridge University Press, 2003.

Daiches, David. *The King James Version of the Bible: An Account of the Development and Sources of the English Bible of 1611 with Special Reference to the Hebrew Tradition.* Chicago: University of Chicago Press.

Daly, Lawrence J. "Psychohistory and St. Augustine's Conversion Process." *Augustiniana* 28 (1978): 231–254.

Damrosch, Leo. *The Sorrows of the Quaker Jesus: James Nayler and the Puritan Crackdown on the Free Spirit.* Cambridge, MA: Harvard University Press, 1996.

de Lubac, Henri. *Medieval Exegesis: The Four Senses of Scripture.* Translated by Mark Sebanc. Grand Rapids, MI: William B. Eerdmans, 1998.

Debus, Allen. *The English Paracelsians.* New York: Franklin Watts, 1965.

Delisle, Jean, and Judith Woodsworth. *Translators through History.* Amsterdam: J. Benjamins, 1995.

Dimock, George E., Jr. "The Name Odysseus." *Hudson Review* 9 (1956): 52–70.

Dirksen, Aloys H. *The New Testament Concept of Metanoia.* Washington, DC: Catholic University of America, 1932.

Dobbs, Betty Jo Teeter. *The Janus Face of Genius: The Role of Alchemy in Newton's Thought.* Cambridge: Cambridge University Press, 1991.

Duhamel, P. Albert. "Milton's Alleged Ramism." *PMLA* 67 (1952): 1035–1053.

Edwards, Karen. "Inspiration and Melancholy in *Samson Agonistes*." In *Milton and the Ends of Time: Essays on the Apocalypse and the Millennium*. Cambridge: Cambridge University Press, 2003.

Eggert, Katherine. "*The Alchemist* and Science." In *Early Modern English Drama: A Critical Companion*, edited by Garrett A. Sullivan, Jr., Patrick Cheney, and Andrew Hadfield, 200–212. Oxford: Oxford University Press, 2006.

Elliott, Emory. "Milton's Biblical Style in *Paradise Regained*." In *Milton Studies 6*, edited by James D. Simmonds, 227–241. Pittsburgh: University of Pittsburgh Press, 1974.

Elukin, Jonathan M. "From Jew to Christian? Conversion and Immutability in Medieval Europe." In *Varieties of Religious Conversion in the Middle Ages*, edited by James Muldoon, 171–189. Gainesville: University Press of Florida, 1997.

Erickson, Amy Louise. *Women and Property in Early Modern England*. London: Routledge, 1993.

Faivre, Antoine. *Access to Western Esotericism*. Albany: State University of New York Press, 1994.

Faur, José. *In the Shadow of History: Jews and Conversos at the Dawn of Modernity*. Albany: State University of New York Press, 1992.

Feldman, Louis H. "Josephus' Portrait of Jethro." In *The Quest for Context and Meaning: Studies in Biblical Intertextuality in Honor of James A. Sander*, edited by Craig A. Evans and Shemaryahu Talmon, 573–594. Leiden: Brill, 1997. Reprinted in *Studies in Josephus' Rewritten Bible*, 38–54. Leiden: Brill, 1998.

Feola, Vittoria. "Elias Ashmole's *Theatrum Chemicum Britannicum* (1652): The Relation between Antiquarianism and Science in Seventeenth-Century England." In *Renaissance Medievalisms*, edited by Konrad Eisenbichler, 321–343. Toronto: Centre for Reformation and Renaissance Studies, 2009.

Fernández-Armesto, Felipe. "Conceptualizing Conversion in Global Perspective: From Late Antiquity to Early Modern." In *Conversion to Christianity from Late Antiquity to the Modern Age: Considering the Process in Europe, Asia, and the Americas*, edited by Calvin B. Kendall, Oliver Nicholson, William D. Phillips, Jr., and Marguerite Ragnow, 13–44. Minneapolis: Center for Early Modern History, 2009.

Fisch, Harold. *Jerusalem and Albion: The Hebraic Factor in Seventeenth-Century Literature*. New York: Schocken Books, 1964.

Fish, Stanley. "Inaction and Silence: The Reader in *Paradise Regained*." In *Calm of Mind: Tercentenary Essays on Paradise Regained and Samson Agonistes in Honor of John S. Diekhoff*, edited by Joseph A. Wittreich, Jr., James G. Taaffe, and Jane Cerny, 24–47. Cleveland: The Press of Case Western Reserve, 1971.

———. "Things and Actions Indifference: The Temptation Plot in *Paradise Regained*." In *Milton Studies 17*, edited by James D. Simmonds, 163–185. Pittsburgh: University of Pittsburgh Press, 1983.

Fisher, Alan. "Why Is *Paradise Regained* So Cold?" In *Milton Studies 14*, edited by James D. Simmonds, 195–217. Pittsburgh: University of Pittsburgh Press, 1980.

Fixler, Michael. *Milton and the Kingdoms of God*. Evanston, IL: Northwestern University Press, 1964.

Fleck, Jade C. "A Grammar of Eschatology in Seventeenth-Century Theological Prose and Poetry." In *Reform and Counterreform: Dialectics of the Word in Western Christianity since Luther*, edited by John C. Hawley, 59–76. Berlin: Mouton de Gruyter, 1994.

Fleming, James Dougal. *Milton's Secrecy and Philosophical Hermeneutics.* Hampshire: Ashgate, 2008.

Fowler, Alastair. "*Paradise Regained*: Some Problems of Style." In *Medieval and Pseudo-Medieval Literature*, edited by Piero Boitani and Anna Torti, 181–189. Tübingen: G. Narr, 1984.

Fredrikson, Paula. "Mandatory Retirement: Ideas in the Study of Christian Origins Whose Time Has Come to Go." *Studies in Religion/ Sciences Religieuses* 35 (2006): 231–246.

———. "Paul and Augustine: Conversion Narratives, Orthodox Traditions, and the Retrospective Self." *Journal of Theological Studies* 37 (1986): 3–34.

Gallagher, Eugene V. *Expectation and Experience: Explaining Religious Conversion.* Atlanta: Scholars Press, 1990.

Gallagher, Lowell. *Medusa's Gaze: Casuistry and Conscience in the Renaissance.* Stanford, CA: Stanford University Press, 1991.

García-Arenal, Mercedes, and Gerard Wiegers. *A Man of Three Worlds: Samuel Pallache, a Moroccan Jew in Catholic and Protestant Europe.* Translated by Martin Beagles. Baltimore: Johns Hopkins University Press, 2003.

Garsiel, Moshe. *Biblical Names: A Literary Study of Midrashic Name Derivations and Puns.* Translated by Phyllis Hackett. Ramat Gan: Bar Ilan University Press, 1991.

———. "Homiletic Name-Derivations as a Literary Device in the Gideon Narrative: Judges VI–VIII." *Vetus Testamentum* 43 (1993): 302–317.

———. "Puns and Names as a Literary Device in I Kings 1–2." *Biblia* 72 (1991): 379–386.

Geroux, Robert. "Regarding Homer/Homer Regarding: Odysseus' Scar, Time, and the Origins of Subjectivity in Myth." *KronoScope* 5 (2005): 237–257.

Gitlitz, David M. *Secrecy and Deceit: The Religion of the Crypto-Jews.* Philadelphia: Jewish Publication Society, 1996.

Glaser, Eliane. *Judaism without Jews: Philosemitism and Christian Polemic in Early Modern England.* New York: Palgrave Macmillan, 2007.

Grafton, Anthony. "Protestant vs. Prophet: Isaac Casaubon on Hermes Trismegistus." *Journal of the Warburg and Courtauld Institutes* 46 (1983): 78–93.

———. "Renaissance Readers of Homer's Ancient Readers." In *Homer's Ancient Readers: The Hermeneutics of Greek Epic's Earliest Exegetes*, edited by Anthony Grafton, 149–172. Princeton, NJ: Princeton University Press, 1992.

Grafton, Anthony, and Joanna Weinberg. *"I have always loved the Holy Tongue": Isaac Casaubon, the Jews, and a Forgotten Chapter in Renaissance Scholarship.* Cambridge, MA: Harvard University Press, 2011.

Graizbord, David. *Souls in Dispute: Converso Identities in Iberia and the Jewish Diaspora, 1580–1700.* Philadelphia: University of Pennsylvania Press, 2004.

Grassl, Gary C. "Joachim Gans of Prague: The First Jew in English America." *American Jewish History* 86 (1998): 195–217.

Greenblatt, Stephen. *Will in the World: How Shakespeare became Shakespeare.* New York: W. W. Norton, 2004.

Gregory, Brad S. "'To the Point of Shedding Your Blood': The Bible, Communities of Faith, and Martyrs' Resistance to Conversion in the Reformation Era." In *Conversion: Old Worlds and New,* edited by Kenneth Mills and Anthony Grafton, 66–86. Rochester: University of Rochester Press, 2003.

Griffin, Eric J. *English Renaissance Drama and the Specter of Spain: Ethnopoetics and Empire.* Philadelphia: University of Pennsylvania Press, 2009.

Haigh, Christopher. *English Reformations: Religion, Politics, and Society under the Tudors.* Oxford: Clarendon Press, 1993.

Hall, Kim F. *Things of Darkness: Economies of Race and Gender in Early Modern England.* Ithaca, NY: Cornell University Press, 1995.

Hames, Harvey. *The Art of Conversion: Christianity and Kabbalah in the Thirteenth Century.* Leiden: Brill, 2000.

———. "Jewish Magic with a Christian Text: A Hebrew Translation of Ramon Llull's Ars Brevis." *Traditio* 54 (1999): 283–300.

Hamilton, Gary. "*Paradise Regained* and the Private Houses." In *Of Poetry and Politics: New Essays on Milton and his World,* edited by P. G. Stanwood, 239–248. Binghamton: Medieval and Renaissance Texts and Studies, 1995.

Hammond, Gerald. *The Making of the English Bible.* New York: Philosophical Library, 1983.

Hanson, A. T. "Rahab the Harlot in Early Christian Tradition." *Journal for the Study of the New Testament* 1 (1978): 53–60.

Harkness, Deborah E. "'Strange' Ideas and 'English' Knowledge: Natural Science Exchange in Elizabethan London." In *Merchants and Marvels: Commerce, Science, and Art in Early Modern Europe,* edited by Pamela H. Smith and Paula Findlen. New York: Routledge, 2002.

Harp, Richard. "Ben Jonson's Comic Apocalypse." *Cithara* 34 (1994): 34–41.

Harran, Marilyn J. *Luther on Conversion: The Early Years.* Ithaca, NY: Cornell University Press, 1983.

Harris, Jonathan Gil. *Foreign Bodies and the Body Politic: Discourses of Social Pathology in Early Modern England.* Cambridge: Cambridge University Press, 1998.

———. *Sick Economies: Drama, Mercantilism, and Disease in Shakespeare's England.* Philadelphia: University of Pennsylvania Press, 2004.

———. *Untimely Matter in the Time of Shakespeare.* Philadelphia: University of Pennsylvania Press, 2009.

Harrison, Peter. "Curiosity, Forbidden Knowledge, and the Reformation of Natural Philosophy in Early Modern England." *Isis* 92 (2001): 265–290.

Hawes, Clement. *Mania and Literary Style: The Rhetoric of Enthusiasm from the Ranters to Christopher Smart.* Cambridge: Cambridge University Press, 1996.

Hawkins, Anne Hunsaker. *Archetypes of Conversion: The Autobiographies of Augustine, Bunyan, and Merton.* Lewisberg, PA: Bucknell University Press, 1985.

Haynes, Jonathan. "Representing the Underworld: *The Alchemist.*" *Studies in Philology* 86 (1989): 18–41.

Healy, Margaret. *Fictions of Disease in Early Modern England: Bodies, Plagues, and Politics.* New York: Palgrave, 2001.

Hefner, Robert W. "World Building and the Rationality of Conversion." In *Conversion to Christianity: Historical and Anthropological Perspectives on a Great Transformation,* edited by Robert W. Hefner, 3–44. Berkeley: University of California Press, 1993.

Heikkinen, J. W. "Notes on 'Epistrepho' and 'Metanoeo.'" *Ecumenical Review* 19 (1967): 313–316.

Heyd, Michael. *"Be Sober and Reasonable": The Critique of Enthusiasm in the Seventeenth and Early Eighteenth Centuries.* Leiden: Brill, 1995.

———. "The 'Jewish Quaker': Christian Perceptions of Sabbatai Zevi as an Enthusiast." In *Hebraica Veritas? Christian Hebraists and the Study of Judaism in Early Modern Europe,* edited by Allison P. Coudert and Jeffrey S. Shoulson. Philadelphia: University of Pennsylvania Press, 2004.

Higbie, Carolyn. *Heroes' Names, Homeric Identities.* New York: Garland Press, 1995.

Hill, Christopher. *Milton and the English Revolution.* New York: Viking Press, 1977.

———. *"Till the conversion of the Jews."* In *The Collected Essays of Christopher Hill: Religion and Politics in 17th Century England,* volume 2, 269–300. Amherst: University of Massachusetts Press, 1986.

Hindmarsh, D. Bruce. *The Evangelical Conversion Narrative: Spiritual Autobiography in Early Modern England.* Oxford: Oxford University Press, 2005.

Hirsch, Brett D. "Counterfeit Possessions: Jewish Daughters and the Drama of Failed Conversion in Marlowe's *The Jew of Malta* and Shakespeare's *The Merchant of Venice.*" *Early Modern Literary Studies* 19 (2009): 4.1–37.

Hirschfeld, Heather. "'We All Expect a Gentle Answer, Jew': *The Merchant of Venice* and the Psychotheology of Conversion." *ELH: English Literary History* 73 (2006): 61–81.

Hodder, Alan D. "In the Glasse of God's Word: Hooker's Pulpit Rhetoric and the Theater of Conversion." *New England Quarterly* 66 (1993): 67–109.

Holladay, William L. *The Root SÛBH in the Old Testament, with Particular Reference to Its Usages in Covenental Contexts.* Leiden: Brill, 1958.

Holmes, Elizabeth. *Henry Vaughan and the Hermetic Philosophy.* Oxford: Basil Blackwell, 1932.

Honig, Bonnie. "Ruth, the Model Emigreé: Mourning and the Symbolic Politics of Immigration." *Political Theory* 25 (1997): 112–136.

Horbury, William. "The Hebrew Matthew and Hebrew Study." In *Hebrew Study from Ezra to Ben-Yehuda,* edited by William Horbury, 122–131. Edinburgh: T & T Clark, 1999.

Hurtado, Larry. "Convert, Apostate, or Apostle to the Nations: The 'Conversion' of Paul in Recent Scholarship." *Studies in Religion/Sciences Religieuses* 22 (1993): 273–284.

Hussey, Maurice. "Ananias the Deacon: A Study of Religion in Jonson's *The Alchemist.*" *English: The Journal of the English Association* 9, no. 54 (1953): 207–212.

Ide, Richard S. "Exemplary Heroism in Chapman's *Odysses.*" *SEL: Studies in English Literature, 1500–1900* 22 (1982): 121–136.

Idel, Moshe. "The Origin of Alchemy according to Zosimus and a Hebrew Parallel." *Revue des Études Juives* 145 (1986): 117–124.

Janacek, Bruce. "Thomas Tymme and Natural Philosophy: Prophecy, Alchemical Theology, and the Book of Nature." *Sixteenth Century Journal* 30 (1999): 987–1007.

Jütte, Daniel. "Abramo Colorni, jüdischer Hofalchemist Herzog Friedrichs I., und die Hebraische Handelskompanie des Magino Gabrielli in Würtemberg am Ende des 16. Jahrhundert. Ein biographischer und methodologischer Beitrag zur jüdischen Wissenschaftsgeschichte." *Aschkenas* 15 (2005): 435–498.

Kaplan, M. Lindsay. "Jessica's Mother: Medieval Constructions of Jewish Race and Gender in *The Merchant of Venice.*" *Shakespeare Quarterly* 58 (2007): 1–30.

Kassell, Lauren. "'All was this land full fill'd of faerie,' or Magic and the Past in Early Modern England." *Journal of the History of Ideas* 67 (2006): 107–122.

Katchen, Aaron. *Christian Hebraists and Dutch Rabbis: Seventeenth Century Apologetics and the Study of Maimonides' Mishneh Torah.* Cambridge, MA: Harvard University Press, 1984.

Kates, Judith A., and Gail Twersky Reimer, eds. *Reading Ruth: Contemporary Women Reclaim a Sacred Story.* New York: Ballantine Books, 1994.

Katz, David S. *The Jews in the History of England, 1485–1850.* Oxford: Clarendon Press, 1994.

———. *Philo-Semitism and the Readmission of the Jews to England, 1603–1655.* Oxford: Clarendon Press, 1982.

Kaufmann, Michael W. *Institutional Individualism: Conversion, Exile, and Nostalgia in Puritan New England.* Hanover, MA: University Press of New England, 1998.

Kawashima, Robert S. "Verbal Medium and Narrative Art in Homer and the Bible." *Philosopher and Literature* 28 (2004): 103–117.

Kearney, James. *The Incarnate Text: Imagining the Book in Reformation England.* Philadelphia: University of Pennsylvania Press, 2009.

Keeble, N. H. *The Literary Culture of Nonconformity in Later Seventeenth-Century England.* Athens: University of Georgia Press, 1987.

Kendall, R. T. *Calvin and English Calvinism to 1649.* Oxford: Oxford University Press, 1979.

Kerwin, William. *Beyond the Body: The Boundaries of Medicine and English Renaissance Drama.* Amherst: University of Massachusetts Press, 2005.

Kilcher, Andreas. "Scientia cabalistica as Scientia universalis: Encyclopedism and Kabbalism in the 16th and 17th Centuries." *Kabbalah: Journal for the Study of Jewish Mystical Texts* 5 (2000): 129–154.

Klause, John. "Catholic and Protestant, Jesuit and Jew: Historical Religion in *The Merchant of Venice.*" *Religion and the Arts* 7 (2003): 65–102.

Knapp, Peggy Ann. "The Work of Alchemy." *Journal of Medieval and Early Modern Studies* 30 (2000): 575–599.

Kneidel, Gregory. "John Donne's Via Pauli." *Journal of English and Germanic Philology* 100 (2001): 224–246.

Knight, Sarah. "'He is indeed a kind of Scholler-Mountebank': Academic Liars in Jacobean Satire." In *Shell Games: Studies in Scams, Frauds, and Deceits (1300–1650)*, edited by Mark Crane, Richard Raiswell, and Margaret Reeves, 59–80. Toronto: Centre for Reformation and Renaissance Studies, 2004.

Knoppers, Laura Lunger. *Historicizing Milton: Spectacle, Power, and Poetry in Restoration England.* Athens: University of Georgia Press, 1994.

Knox, R. A. *Enthusiasm: A Chapter in the History of Religion.* Oxford: Oxford University Press, 1950.

Korda, Natasha. "Dame Usury: Gender, Credit, and (Ac)counting in the Sonnets and *The Merchant of Venice.*" *Shakespeare Quaterly* 60 (2009): 129–153.

Krentz, Edgar. "Conversion in Early Christianity." In *Ancient and Modern Perspectives on the Bible and Culture*, edited by Adela Yarbro Collins, 49–58. Atlanta: Scholars Press, 1998.

Kristeva, Julia. *Nations without Nationalism.* Translated by Leon S. Roudiez. New York: Columbia University Press, 1993.

Kruger, Steven F. *The Spectral Jew: Conversion and Embodiment in Medieval Europe.* Minneapolis: University of Minnesota Press, 2006.

Lamberton, Richard. *Homer the Theologian: Neoplatonist Allegorical Reading and the Growth of the Epic Tradition.* Berkeley: University of California Press, 1986.

Lampert, Lisa. *Gender and Jewish Difference from Paul to Shakespeare.* Philadelphia: University of Pennsylvania Press, 2004.

Lawton, David. *Faith, Text, and History: The Bible in English.* Charlottesville: University of Virginia Press, 1990.

Leimberg, Inge. "The Letter Lost in George Herbert's 'The Jews.'" *Studies in Philology* 90 (1993): 298–321.

Leith, Mary Joan Winn. "The Archaeology of Rahab." *Biblical Archaeological Review* 33 (2007): 22, 78.

Leveen, Adriane. "Inside Out: Jethro, the Midianites, and a Biblical Construction of the Outsider." *Journal for the Study of the Old Testament* 34 (2010): 395–417.

Lewalski, Barbara K. *The Life of John Milton.* Revised. Oxford: Basil Blackwell, 2003.

———. "Milton and the Millennium." In *Milton and the Ends of Time*, edited by Juliet Cummins. Cambridge: Cambridge University Press, 2003.

Linden, Stanton J., ed. *The Alchemy Reader: From Hermes Trismegistus to Isaac Newton.* Cambridge: Cambridge University Press, 2003.

———. *Darke Hierogliphicks: Alchemy in English Literature from Chaucer to the Restoration.* Lexington: University Press of Kentucky, 1996.

———. "Smatterings of the Philosopher's Stone: Sir Thomas Browne and Alchemy." In *Mystical Metal of Gold: Essays on Alchemy and Renaissance Culture*, edited by Stanton J. Linden, 339–364. New York: AMS Press, 2007.

Litt, Dorothy. *Names in Renaissance English Culture.* Lewiston, ME: Mellen Press, 2001.

Loewenstein, David. "The Kingdom Within: Radical Religious Culture and the Politics of Paradise Regained." *Literature and History* 3rd ser., 3 (1994).

———. *Milton and the Drama of History: Historical Vision, Iconoclasm, and the Literary Imagination.* Cambridge: Cambridge University Press, 1990.

———. *Representing Revolution in Milton and His Contemporaries: Religion, Politics, and Polemics in Radical Puritanism.* Cambridge: Cambridge University Press, 2001.

Lord, George deForest. *Homeric Renaissance: The Odyssey of George Chapman.* London: Chatto and Windus, 1956.

Louden, Bruce. "Categories of Homeric Wordplay." *Transactions of the American Philological Association* 125 (1995): 27–46.

Lupher, David A. *Romans in a New World: Classical Models in Sixteenth-Century Spanish America.* Ann Arbor: University of Michigan Press, 2003.

Lupton, Julia Reinhard. *Afterlives of Saints: Hagiography, Typology, and Renaissance Literature.* Stanford, CA: Stanford University Press, 1996.

Luxon, Thomas H. *Literal Figures: Puritan Allegory and the Reformation Crisis in Representation.* Chicago: University of Chicago Press, 1995.

Lynn-George, Michael. *Epos: Word, Narrative, and the* Iliad. Basingstoke and London: Humanities Press International, 1988.

Maciejko, Pawel. "Sabbatian Charlatans: The First Jewish Cosmopolitans." *European Review of History—Revue européenne d'histoire* 17, no. 3 (2010): 361–378.

Mariani, Alice. "The Renaming of Odysseus." In *Critical Essays on Homer*, 211–223. Boston: G. K. Hall, 1987.

Marks, Herbert. "Biblical Naming and Poetic Etymology." *Journal of Biblical Literature* 114 (1995): 21–42.

Marsden, Richard. "Cain's Face, and Other Problems: The Legacy of the Earliest English Bible Translations." *Reformation* 1 (1996): 29–51.

Martin, Catherine Gimelli. "Angels, Alchemists, and Exchange: Commercial Ideology in Court and City Comedy, 1596–1610." In *The Witness of Times: Manifestations of Ideology in Seventeenth Century England*, edited by Katherine Z. Keller and Gerald J. Schiffhorst. Pittsburgh: Duquesne University Press, 1993.

Martz, Louis L. Paradise Regained*: Georgic Form, Georgic Style.* In *Milton Studies 42*, edited by Albert C. Labriola and David Loewenstein, 7–25. Pittsburgh: Duquesne University Press, 2003.

Marx, Steven. "The Prophet Disarmed: Milton and the Quakers." *SEL: Studies in English Literature, 1500–1900* 32 (1992): 111–128.

Mascetti, Yaakov. "'This is the famous stone': George Herbert's Poetic Alchemy in 'The Elixir.'" In *Mystical Metal of Gold: Essays on Alchemy and Renaissance Culture*, edited by Stanton J. Linden, 301–324. New York: AMS Press, 2007.

Matar, Nabil I. "George Herbert, Henry Vaughan, and the Conversion of the Jews." *SEL: Studies in English Literature* 30 (1990): 79–92.

———. *Islam in Britain, 1558–1685.* Cambridge: Cambridge University Press, 1998.

———. "Milton and the Idea of the Restoration of the Jews." *SEL: Studies in English Literature* 27 (1987): 109–124.

———. *Turks, Moors, and Englishmen in the Age of Discovery.* New York: Columbia University Press, 1998.

McAfee, Cleland. *The Greatest English Classic: A Study of the King James Version of the Bible and Its Influence on Life and Literature.* New York: Harper and Brothers, 1912.

McEachern, Claire. *The Poetics of English Nationhood, 1590–1612.* Cambridge: Cambridge University Press, 1996.

McGee, J. Sears. "Conversion and the Imitation of Christ in Anglican and Puritan Writing." *Journal of British Studies* 15 (1976): 21–39.

———. *The Godly Man in Stuart England: Anglicans, Puritans, and the Two Tables, 1620–1670.* New Haven, CT: Yale University Press, 1976.

McKeon, Michael. "Sabbatai Sevi in England." *AJS Review* 2 (1977): 131–169.

McKnight, Stephen A. *The Modern Age and the Recovery of Ancient Wisdom.* Columbia: University of Missouri Press, 1991.

Mebane, John S. "Renaissance Magic and the Return of the Golden Age: Utopianism and Religious Enthusiasm in *The Alchemist.*" In *Renaissance Drama* n.s. 10 (1979): 117–139, edited by Leonard Barkan.

Mendelsohn, J. Andrew. "Alchemy and Politics in England, 1649–1665." *Past and Present* 135 (1992): 30–78.

Mentgen, Gerd. "Jewish Alchemists in Central Europe in the Later Middle Ages: Some New Sources." *Aleph: Historical Studies in Science and Judaism* 9 (2009): 345–352.

Meskill, Lynn S. *Ben Jonson and Envy.* Cambridge: Cambridge University Press, 2009.

Metzger, Mary Janell. "'Now by My Hood, a Gentle and No Jew': Jessica, *The Merchant of Venice*, and the Discourse of Early Modern Identity." *PMLA* 113 (1998): 52–63.

Milton, Anthony. "A Qualified Intolerance: The Limits and Ambiguities of Early Stuart Anti-Catholicism." In *Catholicism and Anti-Catholicism in Early Modern English Texts*, edited by Arthur F. Marotti, 85–115. New York: St. Martin's Press, 1999.

Miola, Robert S. "On Death and Dying in Chapman's *Iliad*: Translation as Forgery." *International Journal of the Classical Tradition* 3 (1996): 48–64.

Moran, Bruce T. *Distilling Knowledge: Alchemy, Chemistry, and the Scientific Revolution.* Cambridge, MA: Harvard University Press, 2005.

Morgan, Edmund S. *Visible Saints: The History of a Puritan Idea.* Ithaca, NY: Cornell University Press, 1965.

Murray, Molly. *The Poetics of Conversion in Early Modern English Literature: Verse and Change from Donne to Dryden.* Cambridge: Cambridge University Press, 2009.

Myers, Benjamin. "Prevenient Grace and Conversion in *Paradise Lost.*" *Milton Quarterly* 40 (2006): 20–36.

Neale, J. E. *Elizabeth I and Her Parliaments.* 2nd ed. Volume 2. New York: W. W. Norton, 1966.

Newman, William R. *Gehennical Fire: The Lives of George Starkey, an American Alchemist in the Scientific Revolution.* Cambridge, MA: Harvard University Press, 1994.

———. *Promethean Ambitions: Alchemy and the Quest to Perfect Nature.* Chicago: University of Chicago Press, 2004.

Newman, William R., and Anthony Grafton. "Introduction: The Problematic Status of Astrology and Alchemy in Premodern Europe." In *Secrets of Nature: Astrology and Alchemy in Early Modern Europe*, edited by William R. Newman and Anthony Grafton. Cambridge, MA: MIT Press, 2001.

Newman, William R., and Anthony Grafton. *Secrets of Nature: Astrology and Alchemy in Early Modern Europe.* Cambridge, MA: MIT Press, 2001.

Newman, William R., and Lawrence M. Principe. *Alchemy Tried in Fire: Starkey, Boyle, and the Fate of Helmotian Chymistry.* Chicago: University of Chicago Press, 2002.

Nicholl, Charles. *The Chemical Theatre.* London: Routledge & Kegan Paul, 1980.

Nicolson, Adam. *God's Secretaries: The Making of the King James Bible.* New York: Harper Perennial, 2005.

Nock, A. D. *Conversion: The Old and the New in Religion from Alexander the Great to Augustine of Hippo.* Oxford: Oxford University Press, 1933.

Notopoulos, James A. "Parataxis in Homer: A New Approach to Homeric Literary Criticism." *Transactions and Proceedings of the American Philological Association* 80 (1949): 1–23.

Nummedal, Tara E. "The Problem of Fraud in Early Modern Alchemy." In *Shell Games: Studies in Scams, Frauds, and Deceits (1300–1650)*, edited by Mark Crane, Richard Raiswell, and Margaret Reeves, 37–58. Toronto: Centre for Reformation and Renaissance Studies, 2004.

Nuttall, Geoffrey F. *The Holy Spirit in Puritan Faith and Experience.* Oxford: Basil Blackwell, 1946.

Oberman, Heiko A. *"Subita Conversio": The Conversion of John Calvin.* In *Reformiertes Erbe: Festschrift für Gottfried W. Locher zu seinem 80. Geburtstag*, volume 2, edited by Heiko A. Oberman, Ernst Saxer, Alfred Schindler, and Heinzpeter Stucki, 279–296. Zurich: Theologischer Verlag Zürich, 1993.

Ormsby-Lennon, Hugh. "From Shibboleth to Apocalypse: Quaker Speechways During the Puritan Revolution." In *Language, Self, and Society: A Social History of Language*, edited by Peter Burke and Roy Porter, 72–112. Cambridge: Cambridge University Press, 1991.

Patai, Raphael. *The Jewish Alchemists: A History and Source Book.* Princeton, NJ: Princeton University Press, 1994.

Patterson, Annabel. *Reading between the Lines.* Madison: University of Wisconsin Press, 1993.

Peters, Gerald. *The Mutilating God: Authorship and Authority in the Narrative of Conversion.* Amherst: University of Massachusetts Press, 1993.

Pettit, Norman. *The Heart Prepared: Grace and Conversion in Puritan Spiritual Life.* New Haven, CT: Yale University Press, 1966.

Pickett, Holly Crawford. "Dramatic Nostalgia and Spectacular Conversion in Dekker and Massinger's *The Virgin Martyr.*" *SEL: Studies in English Literature, 1500–1900* 49 (2009): 437–462.

Pinkus, Karen. *Alchemical Mercury: A Theory of Ambivalence.* Stanford, CA: Stanford University Press, 2010.

Pollmann, Judith. "A Different Road to God: The Protestant Experience of Conversion in the Sixteenth Century." In *Conversion to Modernities: The Globalization of Christianity,* edited by Peter van der Veer, 47–64. New York: Routledge, 1996.

Popkin, Richard H. "Can One Be a True Christian and a Faithful Follower of the Law of Moses? The Answer of John Dury." In *Secret Conversions to Judaism in Early Modern Europe,* edited by Martin Muslow and Richard H. Popkin, 33–50. Leiden: Brill, 2004.

Porter, James I. "Erich Auerbach and the Judaizing of Philology." *Critical Inquiry* 35 (2008): 115–147.

Preus, James Samuel. *From Shadow to Promise: Old Testament Interpretation from Augustine to the Young Luther.* Cambridge, MA: Harvard University Press, 1969.

Principe, Lawrence M. *The Aspiring Adept: Robert Boyle and his Alchemical Quest.* Princeton, NJ: Princeton University Press, 1998.

Principe, Lawrence M., and William R. Newman. "Some Problems with the Historiography of Alchemy." In *Secrets of Nature: Astrology and Alchemy in Early Modern Europe,* edited by William R. Newman and Anthony Grafton. Cambridge, MA: MIT Press, 2001.

Questier, Michael. *Conversion, Politics, and Religion in England, 1580–1625.* Cambridge: Cambridge University Press, 1996.

———. "Crypto-Catholicism, Anti-Calvinism and Conversion at the Jacobean Court: The Enigma of Benjamin Carier." *Journal of Ecclesiastical History* 47 (1996): 45–64.

Questier, Michael, and Healy Simon. "'What's in a Name?': A Papist's Perception of Puritanism and Conformity in the Early Seventeenth Century." In *Catholicism and Anti-Catholicism in Early Modern English Texts,* edited by Arthur F. Marotti. New York: St. Martin's Press, 1999.

Quint, David. *Epic and Empire: Politics and Generic Form from Virgil to Milton.* Princeton, NJ: Princeton University Press, 1993.

Rad, Gerhard Von. *God at Work in Israel.* Translated by John H. Marks. Nashville: Abingdon Press, 1980.

Ragussis, Michael. *Figures of Conversion: "The Jewish Question" & English National Identity.* Durham, NC: Duke University Press, 1995.

Rattansi, Piyo, and Antonio Clericuzio. *Alchemy and Chemistry in the 16th and 17th Centuries.* Dordrecht: Kluwer, 1994.

Rees, B. R. "The Conversion of Saint Augustine." *Trivium* 14 (1979): 1–17.

Ricks, Christopher. "Over-Emphasis in *Paradise Regained.*" *Modern Language Notes* 76 (1961): 701–704.

Robinson, Bernard P. "Rahab of Canaan—and Israël." *Scandinavian Journal of the Old Testament* 23 (2009): 257–273.

Rogers, John. *The Matter of Revolution: Science, Poetry, and Politics in the Age of Milton.* Ithaca, NY: Cornell University Press, 1996.

Rosenblatt, Jason P. *Renaissance England's Chief Rabbi: John Selden.* Oxford: Oxford University Press, 2006.

———. *Torah and Law in Paradise Lost.* Princeton, NJ: Princeton University Press, 1994.

Rosenblatt, Jason P., and Wilfred Schleiner. "John Selden's Letter to Ben Jonson on Cross-Dressing and Bisexual Gods [With Texts]." *English Literary Renaissance* 29 (1999): 44–74.

Ross, Cheryl Lynn. "The Plague of *The Alchemist.*" *Renaissance Quarterly* 41 (1988).

Roth, Cecil. *A History of the Jews in England.* 2nd ed. Oxford: Clarendon Press, 1949.

Roth, Norman. *Converso, Inquisition, and the Explusion of the Jews from Spain.* Madison: University of Wisconsin Press, 1995.

Ruderman, David. *Jewish Thought and Scientific Discovery in Early Modern Europe.* New Haven, CT: Yale University Press, 1995.

Rudrum, Alan. "The Influence of Alchemy in the Poems of Henry Vaughan." *Philological Quarterly* 49 (1970): 469–490.

———. "'These fragments I have shored against my ruin': Henry Vaughan, Alchemical Philosophy, and the Great Rebellion." In *Mystical Metal of Gold: Essays on Alchemy and Renaissance Culture,* edited by Stanton J. Linden, 325–338. New York: AMS Press, 2007.

Rushdy, Ashraf. *The Empty Garden: The Subject of Late Milton.* Pittsburgh: University of Pittsburgh Press, 1992.

Russell, Frederick H. "Augustine: Conversion by the Book." In *Varieties of Relgious Conversion in the Middle Ages,* edited by James Muldoon, 13–30. Gainesville: University Press of Florida, 1997.

Russell, G. A., ed. *The 'Arabick' Interest of the Natural Philosophers in Seventeenth-Century England.* Leiden: Brill, 1994.

Ryan, Michael T. "Assembling New Worlds in the Sixteenth and Seventeenth Centuries." *Comparative Studies in Society and History* 23 (1981): 519–538.

Saltman, Avrom. *The Jewish Question in 1655: Studies in Prynne's* Demurrer. Ramat Gan: Bar-Ilan University Press, 1995.

Samuel, E. R. "Portuguese Jews in Jacobean London." *Transactions of the Jewish Historical Society of England* 18 (1958): 171–230.

Schmidt, Charles B. "Perennial Philosophy: From Agostino to Steuco to Leibniz." *Journal of the History of Ideas* 27 (1966): 505–532.

———. "Prisca Theologia e Philosophia Perennis: due temi del Rinascimento italiano e la loro fortuna." In *Il Pensiero del Rinascimento e il tempo nostro,* edited by Giovannagiola Tarugi, 211–236. Florence: L. S. Olschki, 1970.

Schoenfeldt, Michael. "'Commotion Strange': Passion in *Paradise Lost.*" In *Reading the Early Modern Passions: Essays in the Cultural History of Emotions,* edited by Gail Kern Paster, Katherine Rowe, and Mary Floyd-Wilson. Philadelphia: University of Pennsylvania Press, 2004.

Scholem, Gershom. *Alchemy and Kabbalah.* Translated by Klaus Ottman. Putnam, CT: Spring Publications, 2006.

———. *Sabbatai Sevi: The Mystical Messiah.* Translated by R. J. Zwi Werblowsky. Princeton, NJ: Princeton University Press, 1973.

Schuler, Robert M., ed. *Alchemical Poetry, 1575–1700.* New York: Garland Publishing, 1995.

———. "Jonson's Alchemists, Epicures, and Puritans." In *Medieval and Renaissance Drama in England*, volume 2, edited by J. Leeds Barroll, 172–191. New York: AMS Press, 1985.

———. "Some Spiritual Alchemies of Seventeenth-Century England." *Journal of the History of Ideas* 41 (1980): 293–318.

Schwarz, W. *Principles and Problems of Biblical Translation: Some Reformation Contoversies and Their Background.* Cambridge: Cambridge University Press, 1955.

Scult, Mel. *Millennial Expectations and Jewish Liberaties: A Study of the Efforts to Convert the Jews in Britain, up to the Mid-Nineteenth Century.* Leiden: Brill, 1978.

Secret, François. "Littérature et Alchimie: A la Fin du XVIe et au Début du XVIIe Siècle." *Bibliothèque d'Humanisme et Renaissance* 35 (1973).

Segal, Alan F. *Paul the Convert: The Apostolate and Apostasy of Saul the Pharisee.* New Haven, CT: Yale University Press, 1990.

Seidman, Naomi. *Faithful Renderings: Jewish-Christian Difference and the Politics of Translation.* Chicago: University of Chicago Press, 2006.

Shapiro, James. *Shakespeare and the Jews.* New York: Columbia University Press, 1996.

Shell, Alison. "Multiple Conversion and the Menippean Self: The Case of Richard Carpenter." In *Catholicism and Anti-Catholicism in Early Modern English Texts*, edited by Arthur F. Marotti. New York: St. Martin's Press, 1999.

Shoulson, Jeffrey S. *Milton and the Rabbis: Hebraism, Hellenism, and Christianity.* New York: Columbia University Press, 2001.

Shuger, Debora Kuller. *The Renaissance Bible: Scholarship, Sacrifice, and Subjectivity.* Berkleley: University of California Press, 1994.

Simpson, Ken. "The Apocalypse." In *Milton and the Ends of Time*, edited by Juliet Cummins. Cambridge: Cambridge University Press, 2003.

Sloan, Grietje. "The Transformation of Religious Conversion from the Renaissance to the Counter-Reformation: Petrarch and Caravaggio." *Historical Reflections/Reflexions Historiques* 15 (1988): 131–149.

Smalley, Beryl. *The Study of the Bible in the Middle Ages.* 2nd ed. Notre Dame: University of Notre Dame Press, 1964.

Smith, Lesley, ed. *Medieval Exegesis in Translation: Commentaries on the Book of Ruth.* Translated by Lesley Smith. Kalamazoo, MI: Medieval Institute Publications, 1996.

———. "The Rewards of Faith: Nicholas of Lyra on Ruth." In *Nicholas of Lyra: The Senses of Scripture*, edited by Philip D. W. Krey and Lesley Smith, 45–58. Leiden: Brill, 2000.

Smith, Pamela H. *The Business of Alchemy: Science and Culture in the Holy Roman Empire.* Princeton, NJ: Princeton University Press, 1994.

Sokol, B. J, and Mary Sokol. *Shakespeare, Law, and Marriage.* Cambridge: Cambridge University Press, 2003.

Sparrow, John. "The Hope of Israel, A Briefe Epistle, and Silex Scintillans." *Transactions of the Jewish Historical Society of England* 20 (1956–61): 233–238.

Spivack, Charlotte. *George Chapman*. New York: Twayne Publishers, 1967.

Sprunger, Keith L. *Dutch Puritanism: A History of English and Scottish Churches of the Netherlands in the Sixteenth and Seventeenth Centuries*. Leiden: Brill, 1982.

———. *Trumpets from the Tower: English Puritan Printing in the Netherlands, 1600–1640*. Leiden: Brill, 1994.

Stallybrass, Peter, and Allon White. *The Politics and Poetics of Transgression*. Ithaca, NY: Cornell University Press, 1986.

Stanford, W. B. "The Homeric Etymology of the Name Odysseus." *Classical Philology* 47 (1952): 209–213.

Stendahl, Krister. "The Apostle Paul and the Introspective Conscience of the West." In *Paul among the Jews and Gentiles and Other Essays*. 199–215. Philadelphia: Fortress Press, 1976.

Stock, Brian. *After Augustine: The Meditative Reader and the Text*. Philadelphia: University of Pennsylvania Press, 2001.

———. *Augustine the Reader: Meditation, Self-Knowledge, and the Ethics of Interpretation*. Cambridge, MA: Harvard University Press, 1996.

Strier, Richard. "Radical Donne: Satire III." *ELH* 60 (1993): 283–322.

Stromberg, Peter G. *Language and Self-Transformation: A Study of the Christian Conversion Narrative*. Cambridge: Cambridge University Press, 1993.

Suarez, Michael F. "Against Satan, Sin, and Death: Thomas Traherne and the 'Inward Work' of Conversion." In *Reform and Counterreform: Dialectics of the Word in Western Christianity since Luther*, edited by John C. Hawley, 77–103. Berlin: Mouton de Gruyter, 1994.

Swart, G. J. "Rahab and Esther in Josephus—An Intertextual Approach." *Acta Patristica et Byzantina* 17 (2006): 50–65.

Targoff, Ramie. *Common Prayer: The Language of Public Devotion in Early Modern England*. Chicago: University of Chicago Press, 2001.

Tilton, Hereward. *The Quest for the Phoenix: Spiritual Alchemy and Rosicrucianism in the Work of Count Michael Maier*. Berlin: Walter de Gruyter, 2003.

Toaff, Ariel. *Il Prestigiatore di Dio: Avventure e Miracoli di un Alchimista Ebreo nelle Corti del Rinascimento*. Milan: Rizzoli, 2010.

Trachtenberg, Joshua. *The Devil and the Jews: The Medieval Conception of the Jew and Its Relation to Modern Anti-Semitism*. 1943. 2nd ed. Philadelphia: Jewish Publication Society, 1983.

Trilling, Lionel. *Sincerity and Authenticity*. Cambridge, MA: Harvard University Press, 1971.

van der Veer, Peter. "Introduction." In *Conversion to Modernities: The Globalization of Christianity*, edited by Peter van der Veer, 1–21. New York: Routledge, 1996.

van der Wall, Ernestine G. E. "A Precursor of Christ or a Jewish Imposter? Petrus Serrarius and Jean de Labadie on the Jewish Messianic Movement around Sabbatai Sevi." *Pietismus und Neuzeit* 14 (1988).

Vitkus, Daniel J. *Turning Turk: English Theater and the Multicultural Mediterranean, 1570–1630*. New York: Palgrave Macmillan, 2003.

Walker, D. P. *The Ancient Theology: Studies in Christian Platonism from the Fifteenth to the Eighteenth Century*. Ithaca, NY: Cornell University Press, 1972.

Wallace, Dewey D., Jr. *Puritans and Predestination: Grace and English Protestant Theology, 1525–1695*. Chapel Hill: University of North Carolina Press, 1982.

Walsham, Alexandra. *Church Papists: Catholicism, Conformity, and Confessional Polemic in Early Modern England*. Rochester, NY: Boydell Press, 1993.

Walters, Richard H. "Henry Vaughan and the Alchemists." *Review of English Studies* 23 (1947): 107–122.

Watkins, Owen. *The Puritan Experience: Studies in Spiritual Autobiography*. New York: Schocken Books, 1972.

Webster, Charles. *Paracelsus: Medicine, Magic, and Mission at the End of Time*. New Haven, CT: Yale University Press, 2008.

Wells, David F. *Turning to God: Biblical Conversion in the Modern World*. Carlisle, Cumbria: Paternoster Press, 1989.

Wennerlind, Carl. "Credit-Money as the Philosopher's Stone: Alchemy and the Coinage Problem in Seventeenth-Century England." *History of Political Economy* 35 (2003): 234–261.

Wilcox, Peter. "Conversion in the Thought and Experience of John Calvin." *Anvil* 14, no. 2 (1997): 113–128.

Williamson, Arthur H. "George Buchanan, Crypto-Judaism, and the Critique of European Empire." In *Secret Conversions to Judaism in Early Modern Europe*, edited by Martin Muslow and Richard H. Popkin, 19–32. Leiden: Brill, 2004.

———. "Latter Day Judah, Latter Day Israel: The Millennium, the Jews, and the British Future." In *Chiliasmus in Deutschland und England im 17. Jahrhundert*, edited by Martin Brecht, Frederich de Boor, Klaus Deppermann, and Ulrich Gäbler. Göttingen: Vanderhoeck and Ruprecht, 1988.

Williamson, George. "The Restoration Revolt Against Enthusiasm." *Studies in Philology* 30 (1930): 571–603.

Willinsky, Mordechai. "Four English Pamphlets on the Sabbatian Movement." *Zion* 17 (1952): 156–172.

Woodbridge, Linda. *Vagrancy, Homelessness, and English Renaissance Literature*. Urbana: University of Illinois Press, 2001.

Yates, Frances A. *Giordano Bruno and the Hermetic Tradition*. London, 1964.

Yates, Julian. "Parasitic Geographies: Manifesting Catholic Identity in Early Modern England." In *Catholicism and Anti-Catholicism in Early Modern England*, edited by Arthur F. Marotti, 63–84. New York: St. Martin's Press, 1999.

Young, Frances M. *Biblical Exegesis and the Formation of Christian Culture*. Cambridge: Cambridge University Press, 1997.

Young, J. T. *Faith, Medical Alchemy, and Natural Philosophy: Johan Moariaen, Reformed Intelligencer, and the Hartlib Circle*. Aldershot: Ashgate, 1998.

Yovel, Yirmiyahu. *The Other Within: The Marranos: Split Identity and Emerging Modernity.* Princeton, NJ: Princeton University Press, 2009.

Zagorin, Perez. *Ways of Lying: Dissimulation, Persecution, and Conformity in Early Modern Europe.* Cambridge, MA: Harvard University Press, 1990.

Zakovitch, Yair. "Explicit and Implicit Name Derivations." *Harvard Archeological Review* 4 (1980): 167–181.

———. "A Study of Precise and Partial Name Derivations in Biblical Etymology." *Journal for the Study of the Old Testament* 15 (1980): 31–50.

Index

Acknowledgments

The list of friends and colleagues who have contributed to this project in ways large and small is long and varied. It's a real pleasure to thank so many wise and generous people as it also occasions the additional delight of looking back on the evolution of this book.

I began thinking about conversion very soon after I had completed my first book under the wonderful auspices of the University of Pennsylvania's Katz Center for Advanced Judaic Studies. While enjoying a final few months in that rich and stimulating environment during my first term as a fellow, I had the opportunity to develop some of my initial hypotheses in conversation with Guy Stroumsa, Matt Goldish, Michael Heyd, and Allison Coudert, not to mention the irrepressible and inimitable David Ruderman, who has created a true scholar's paradise at the Katz Center. During that early stay at Penn, I also had the privilege of participating in an early modern works-in-progress group convened by Katherine Rowe, which included Julian Yates, Lauren Shohet, Kristen Poole, and others. It was in their company that I presented the first version of the proposal that ultimately became this book and, as I look back on those early conversations, I am amazed and impressed at how prescient these scholars were in anticipating what some of my major themes and challenges would be. Though the book's completion came, perhaps, a little later than I would have liked, I am truly delighted that I was able to finish a full draft during my second full-year stint at the Katz Center. The second time was as richly invigorating and stimulating as the first; the cohort of fellows provided essential feedback and helped me to discover features of my analysis that had remained latent or underexplored. Here I want to acknowledge all the fruitful exchanges, formal and informal, that I had with the 2010–2011 Katz Center cohort and other scholars who were in its orbit: Anne Orovetz Albert, Kathleen Biddick, Javier Castaño, Theodor Dunkelgrün, Ayala Eliyahu, Netanel Fisher, Rela Geffen, Sarah Gracombe, Elliot Horowitz, Yosi Israeli, Sarah Japhet, Robert Jütte, Ephraim Kanarfogel,

Yoseph Kaplan, Birgit Klein, Fabrizio Lelli, Pawel Maciejko, Barbara Meyer, David Nirenberg, David Satran, Ellie Schainker, Sabine Schmidtke, Katja Smid, Claude Stuczynski, and Paola Tartakoff. In addition to David Ruderman, who once again deserves thanks for creating such a special place for scholarship, I want to mention, with gratitude for her enthusiastic support, Natalie Dohrmann, who ran the center during the year David was on leave.

Between these two years at the Katz Center, I had many opportunities to share parts of this project with a wide range of intellectually generous and demanding readers, among them Ellie Bagley, Leslie Brisman, Jonathan Decter, Jonathan Elukin, Todd Endelman, David Feldman, Jamie Ferguson, Stanley Fish, Noam Flinker, Eliane Glaser, David Glimp, the late Marshall Grossman, Liora Halperin, Richard Halpern, Peter Herman, Susannah Heschel, Sujata Iyengar, Eric Jacobson, Heather James, David Katz, Michael Lieb, David Loewenstein, Catherine Gimelli Martin, Robert Miola, Feisal Mohamed, Meredith Neuman, David Norton, Beth Quitslund, Jason Rosenblatt, Elizabeth Sauer, Regina Schwartz, and Richard Strier. My colleagues at the University of Miami were supportive every step of the way, and I feel very fortunate to have been part of such a stimulating intellectual community. I especially wish to thank Anne Cruz, John Fitzgerald, Richard Godbeer, Tom Goodmann, Henry Green, William Scott Green, Karl Gunther, Pamela Hammons, Mary Lindemann, Patrick McCarthy, Brenna Munro, Ranen Omer-Sherman, Frank Palmeri, John Paul Russo, Patricia Saunders, Mihoko Suzuki, and Tim Watson. In recent years I have also enjoyed a second academic home at the Bread Loaf School of English, and, though the teaching demands during the summers may have delayed the completion of this project a little, the time spent learning from my extraordinary colleagues there has more than compensated. Thanks especially to Isobel Armstrong, Michael Armstrong, Emily Bartels, Sara Blair, Dare Clubb, Jonathan Freedman, John Fyler, Jennifer Green-Lewis, Jacques Lezra, Victor Luftig, Jim Maddox, Will Nash, Margery Sabin, Robert Stepto, Jennifer Wicke, Susanne Wofford, and Michael Wood.

Jerry Singerman has been as supportive an editor as I could have hoped for, shepherding this project expertly through the approval process and quickly into production. Indeed, the entire editorial and production staff at the University of Pennsylvania Press has been extremely helpful and attentive. Two reader's reports, one from an anonymous reader and the other by Katherine Eggert, offered extremely helpful suggestions for clarifying and sharpening the arguments of individual chapters and the book as a whole.

Words fail me when I consider the unflagging support of my parents, Robyn and Bruce Shoulson. They have provided me with so much over the years; my work would be unimaginable without their generosity and love. My gratitude to Margery Sokoloff, my partner, friend, and love of my life, knows no bounds. This book is as much hers as it is mine. Finally, a word of thanks to Sophia, Oliver, and Emily, whose patience as their father worked on this book was admirable. But it was (and is) their inquisitiveness that kept (and keeps) me going. My soul is truly bound up with theirs.

This project was generously supported by a Max Orovitz Summer Research Fellowship from the University of Miami, as well as two year-long fellowships at the University of Pennsylvania's Katz Center for Advanced Judaic Studies. A portion of Chapter 5 first appeared in *Milton Studies*. I wish to thank the University of Pittsburgh Press for permission to reprint the material here.

www.ingramcontent.com/pod-product-compliance
Lightning Source LLC
Chambersburg PA
CBHW030825310726
48980CB00006B/641/J
* 9 7 8 0 8 1 2 2 4 4 8 2 3 *